# LEGAL WRITING FOR PARALEGALS

STEVE BARBER, J.D.
ADJUNCT PROFESSOR
UNIVERSITY OF EVANSVILLE

*PARTNER IN THE LAW FIRM OF:*
BARBER AND HAMILTON

SOUTH - WESTERN PUBLISHING CO.

2 3 4 5 6 7 8 9 0 D 1 0 9 8 7 6 5 4 3 2

Printed in the United States of America

Acquisitions Editor: Betty B. Schechter
Editorial Production Manager: Linda R. Allen
Production Editor: Sally E. Reinders
Designer: James DeSoller
Production Artist: Sophia Renieris
Associate Photo Editor/Stylist: Linda Ellis

PHOTO CREDITS

p. 1 Computer Consoles, Inc. (''CCI''), Rochester, NY
p. 107 Comstock

Library of Congress Cataloging-in-Publication Data

Barber, Steve
Legal writing for paralegals / Steve Barber.
p. cm.
Includes index.
ISBN 0-538-70632-5
1. Legal composition. 2. Legal assistants—United States.
I. Title.
KF250.B37 1992
808'.06634—dc20 91-27003
CIP

# PREFACE

Although writing skills are a core component of a paralegal education, most legal-writing texts are directed toward graduate students of law and fail to provide the background information that paralegal students need. As a result, the writing course often becomes a struggle. As its title suggests, *Legal Writing for Paralegals* addresses this problem and fills this void by approaching the subject from the paralegal's perspective.

This text demonstrates the relationship of legal writing to the entire legal process, introduces the basics of technical writing, and guides the student through both theoretical and practical applications of the craft. With a focus on straightforward language devoid of "legalese," it repeatedly prompts the student to be aware of who will eventually read the writing.

*Legal Writing for Paralegals* is adaptable to a wide range of paralegal programs and offers a solid foundation to paralegals bound for all types of law practices.

## ABOUT THE TEXTBOOK

*Legal Writing for Paralegals* presents its material in three basic segments—introductory, document-specific, and methodological. Chapters 1 and 2 introduce the components of legal writing as a communication form and examine the existing body of written law and the legal thought process. Crucial to the text is Chapter 3, Research Strategies for Legal Writing, a comprehensive, well-illustrated chapter that identifies and describes how to use virtually every major source of legal information a paralegal is likely to need.

Chapters 4 through 8 examine each of the five most common forms of legal writing: memoranda, briefs, correspondence, pleadings, and transaction documents. Their similarities, differences, requisite formats, and individual characteristics are addressed in detail.

The final chapters of *Legal Writing for Paralegals* explore methodology. Structure—design, parallelism, division, classification, and sequencing—is treated in Chapter 9, while writing "diseases" and how to avoid them are presented in Chapter 10. Chapter 11 takes a thoughtful look at style and offers numerous suggestions for polishing the final document. The book concludes with a study of editing procedures and techniques in Chapter 12.

Supplementing and illustrating the text is an extensive Appendix, to which the student is referred frequently. Sample documents drawn from actual cases are designed to enliven the material and help students relate to situations they are likely to encounter in their paralegal careers.

## ABOUT THE STUDENT RESOURCE MANUAL

For each chapter of the text, the student Resource Manual presents a Summary of the important points and concepts covered. These summaries not only prepare students for the exercises and activities that follow, but also serve as convenient aids for test review.

Objective Study Exercises at the conclusion of each Summary help students evaluate how much they have learned. (Answers to Study Exercises are found at the end of the chapter.) Next, a series of Writing Exercises provides an opportunity to practice the newly acquired skills. Finally, students are encouraged to expand their writing proficiency by completing one or more Enrichment Activities.

Like the *Legal Writing for Paralegals* text, the student Resource Manual contains a substantial Appendix of cases and briefs that relate to the material discussed in both volumes.

## ABOUT THE INSTRUCTOR'S MANUAL

To help the instructor derive maximum benefit from *Legal Writing for Paralegals*, each chapter of the Instructor's Manual opens with a list of specific Learning Objectives. These objectives are followed by several pages of Lecture Material designed to serve as a guide for opening a classroom discussion on the chapter topics. A number of Teaching Suggestions are offered, and answers are given for the Writing Exercises that appear in the student Resource Manual.

Each chapter of the Instructor's Manual contains a Chapter Test and provides answers for these questions.

## ABOUT THE AUTHOR

Steve Barber earned his Juris Doctor degree from Indiana University School of Law, where he was inducted into the Order of the Coif. It was also at Indiana University that Mr. Barber earned his B.A. degree and membership in Phi Beta Kappa. He is an adjunct instructor in the Paralegal Program at the University of Evansville (Indiana), where he has taught legal research and legal writing since 1976. An attorney in private practice in Evansville, Mr. Barber has published various law-related articles.

## ACKNOWLEDGMENTS

No text is written alone. Elizabeth Richardson was my talented consulting editor. She made this text readable. If mistakes remain, it is because I was too stubborn to accept her suggestions.

Many of my colleagues read early versions of the manuscript and freely offered criticisms, a few of which I heeded. In this regard I thank Ross Rudolph, Clark Robinson, Frank Hahn, Debbie Howard, Joseph Vreeland, Stan Levco, and the Honorable Scott Bowers.

Ted Lockyear, Daniel McGinn, David Shaw, Clark Robinson, and Jack Schroeder all provided materials that I used in this text, and they have my gratitude. So do my paralegal students, who acted as experimental subjects with early versions of the manuscript. So many of them provided help on this project that space does not permit thanking them separately here, but they know who they are. However, I must thank Evelyn Hansen-Davis and Shannon Barnes for help in finding examples and in checking citations. Also, particularly helpful was law librarian Helen Reed, one of my former students.

Finally, I thank my law partner, John Hamilton, for his patience, and I thank my secretaries, Jo Jackson and Janet Williams, for their loyalty and perseverance.

## DEDICATION

This text is dedicated to my wife, Mary Ann Hughes, and my children, Kathryn and Michael. Their presence and encouragement made this project enjoyable. Without their support, it would not have been completed.

Steve Barber

# SUMMARY OF CONTENTS

# CONTENTS

# 1 INTRODUCTION TO LEGAL WRITING

Once upon a time there was a small corporation whose president retained two law firms. One was a large firm that drafted all the corporation's contracts, handled its tax matters, and represented it in negotiations and in court. The other law firm was a small one, and its job was to explain to the president of the corporation in plain English exactly what the contracts, forms, and other documents drafted by the large firm meant. (ALI-ABA Committee on CPE, *The Practical Lawyer* 35, no. 1, January 1989.)

When they are not talking, legal professionals spend most of their time writing. Although the general public tends to believe a lawyer's day is spent in court, the truth is that most of the lawyer's day is spent in an office. In any given day, a lawyer might prepare a court pleading, a demand letter, a will, and a brief. Often the lawyer will request a paralegal to prepare the initial draft of these documents for the lawyer's review. Hence a paralegal must have a working familiarity with the variety of legal documents.

## VARIETY OF LEGAL DOCUMENTS

On the first day at work, a paralegal should be able to write an intraoffice memorandum (an expository form of writing), a brief (an argumentative form of writing), a contract or lease (a descriptive form of writing), or a motion to file with a court. So it is helpful to know what these documents are. Because the function is different for each form of writing, this text will group documents into the following categories: litigation documents, briefs, memoranda, transaction documents, and correspondence.

## Litigation Documents

Let's begin with court pleadings and motions. A civil action is usually commenced when one party (the **plaintiff**) files a **complaint** against another party (the **defendant**) in a lawsuit, or files a petition such as that required in an adoption or an estate proceeding. A complaint states the basis of the lawsuit and identifies the relief sought. The complaint is usually accompanied by a **summons**, the document advising the defendant that some action must be taken within a specified period. When a complaint is filed, the statute of limitations is tolled or stopped.

The defendant must file a response to the complaint. One response is an **answer**, which admits or denies the allegations made in the complaint. Instead of answering the complaint, a defendant may ask the court to dismiss the complaint or petition. More typically, the defending party may ask the court for more time to prepare an answer or a motion to dismiss. Paralegals must know how to draft and file these documents and others. If a defendant decides to assert a claim against the plaintiff, a pleading known as a **counterclaim** will be used. In some lawsuits defendants make claims against codefendants; this is accomplished by filing a **cross-claim**.

As a lawsuit progresses, each party will want to learn more about the facts of the adversary's case. Such information is obtained through what lawyers refer to as the **discovery process**. Most courts permit liberal discovery of information from the adverse party. One party may file **interrogatories** (written questions) to the other party for this purpose. In addressing these questions, often it is the paralegal who consults with the client and prepares answers for the attorney's review. If your client wants the opposing party to be examined by an impartial physician, a **request for examination** must be filed; if your client wishes to inspect documents held by the opposition, a **request for production of documents** will be necessary. To admit that certain facts are true requires filing a **request for admissions**. Lawyers often delegate the preparation of discovery requests and answers to the paralegal staff. Of course, the attorneys must review all discovery documents.

Throughout a lawsuit, parties will file various motions with the court. A **motion** is simply a request to the court to take some sort of action. Some motions are accompanied by **affidavits**, written statements of facts made under oath. The **affiant** (person making an affidavit) signs the document before a notary public. Paralegals typically interview witnesses and prepare affidavits based on the information learned through the interview.

When a court rules on a motion or on the merits of a case, it may ask the attorney who prevailed to provide an entry or a decree for the court to sign. This document is sometimes called a **court order**. The **decree** or order is another document often drafted by a paralegal.

If a case proceeds to a trial, you will prepare subpoenas for witnesses. A **subpoena** is an order by the court for a witness to appear at a particular place at a designated time. (See Figure 1-1.) A subpoena may direct the witness to bring certain documents or items to court. This is a **subpoena *duces tecum***. As trial

**FIGURE 1-1 SUBPOENA**

**State of Indiana**
**Vanderburgh County** ss.

VANDERBURGH SUPERIOR COURT

______________________________

______________________________
Plaintiff

vs.

______________________________

______________________________
Defendant

No.______________

# SUBPOENA

**The State of Indiana to the Sheriff of Vanderburgh County, Greeting:**

We command you to Summon______________________________
______________________________
______________________________
______________________________
______________________________

If__________may be found in your bailiwick, to be and appear before Division__________ in the Vanderburgh Superior Court, on the__________day of______________________A. D., 19____ at ______o'clock____M. at the City-County Courts Building in the City of Evansville, then and there in said Court to give evidence and the truth to say in behalf of______________________________ in a certain cause now pending in said court wherein______________________________ is plaintiff and wherein______________________________ is defendant, and not depart the Court without leave thereof.

Herein Fail Not, and of this Writ make due service and return.

WITNESS, the Clerk of said Court, at Evansville, this__________day of______________________19____

______________________________Clerk

By______________________________Deputy

______________________________
Attorney

approaches, the attorney/paralegal team will prepare witness lists and exhibit lists to advise the opposition as to witnesses and exhibits that will be used. Jury instructions will be required for a jury trial.

After the case is decided, certain motions may be needed to initiate an appeal. These pleadings vary from jurisdiction to jurisdiction. One jurisdiction may require the filing of a simple notice of appeal while another jurisdiction may require an elaborate assignment of errors.

The paralegal must have a working knowledge of how to prepare court pleadings for filing. Although some pleadings may be found in formbooks, many of the necessary documents must be written from scratch. Even if you begin your drafting by using forms, be sure to tailor each one carefully to the particular facts of your client's case.

The litigation paralegal will spend much of the day doing just this type of writing, which will be discussed in depth in Chapter 6.

### Briefs

At times during litigation, the court may expect the parties to prepare a **brief** in support of or in opposition to a motion. If a judge is unsure whether a motion should be granted, he or she will ask the parties to provide a written argument.

A brief is an argument of factual and legal reasons as to why your client's position should prevail. To write a brief, you will need to research the applicable law. The brief may be on a topic as simple as the speed limit in a school zone, or it may focus on more complicated issues. The opposition will also file a brief to argue its side of the question. Because it is an argumentative form of writing, a brief is functionally different from the other court documents we have discussed. (However, as your paralegal skills become more sophisticated, you will learn to use court pleadings for an argumentative advantage.)

When a party files a motion to dismiss or a motion for **summary judgment** (a motion asking the court to dispose of the case without trial), the court almost certainly will require a brief to support the motion. If the parties argue over whether they should be required to answer certain discovery requests, again the court may require supporting briefs. The parties will research the applicable rules and court cases to see if precedent supports their arguments. The resulting documents are called trial briefs.

A trial brief is filed with a trial court or court of original jurisdiction. A trial court is where the parties usually present evidence through witnesses and exhibits. A judge or jury hears the testimony and decides which party should prevail.

Sometimes after a case is lost, a party may decide to appeal the case to a higher court—a court with appellate jurisdiction over the trial court. In such a proceeding, the parties will file appellate briefs. Usually the **appellant** (the appealing party) will file the first brief, and the **appellee** (the party who defends an appeal) will file a response brief. The appellant will then file a reply brief. Many appellate courts set forth rigid rules for the form of trial briefs. They may require that you provide certain information in your brief and adhere to specific page limitations, margin requirements, and color standards for the covers. A party that fails to comply with these rules may lose the appeal.

Brief writers attempt to persuade courts that points of law should be applied to benefit their clients. Parties may ask the court either to establish a precedent or to apply an existing precedent to decide the case. The parties may have a dispute over a court rule or over a constitutional provision. Writing briefs is one of the best ways for a paralegal to learn how lawyers think. Chapter 5 deals with writing briefs.

### Memoranda

Often a senior partner will ask a younger associate or a paralegal to investigate the law on a particular subject. Such a request might be a simple matter of looking up a few cases on a topic, or it might involve researching and reporting on a rather complicated issue. In another situation a client may ask for a legal opinion on a topic. Of course, paralegals cannot give legal advice to clients, but they can prepare answers to such inquiries so that lawyers can provide the advice. This is the function of the intraoffice **memorandum**. In a brief you argue a position; in a memorandum you describe what you believe to be the existing law. Although some may refer to a brief as a memorandum, in this text a memorandum is strictly an intraoffice document.

A legal memorandum is the vehicle for a legal journalist to tell the reader what the law is on a given subject. It is descriptive and objective. A memorandum is intended to inform a reader of the law as it relates to a particular situation. Chapter 4 examines the techniques of writing legal memoranda.

### Transaction Documents

A law professor once quipped that lawyers are involved only when there is tragedy or something of value exchanges hands, adding that the only exception is adoptions, which actually stem from tragic situations. There is more truth in that statement than most legal professionals care to admit. Lawyers are routinely asked to document large transactions. In fact, as transactions become more complicated, the work of lawyers becomes more complicated as well. Although we frequently hear clients say that they yearn for the day when a handshake was sufficient, the reality is that yesterday's handshake has been replaced by legal documents.

A real estate exchange wherein the seller conveys property to the purchaser by passing a ceremonial handful of sticks is neither practical nor possible when the transaction involves, for example, a New York condominium. Centuries ago such ceremonies occurred so rarely that witnesses would remember details of an event if ownership disputes later developed. Land in transactions of that period usually included many miles of unfenced boundary. Who owned the five feet at the edge was not a real concern, whereas in the exchange of a small city lot it is. The function of the early real estate ceremony is met today by a deed. Lawyers typically prepare **transaction documents** to memorialize events. Wills, trusts, corporate minutes, and bills of sale are other transaction documents.

Other documents must be prepared to record a **bilateral agreement** (an agreement containing mutual promises of performance). Common examples include the lease and the contract. In a bilateral agreement the drafter is not only recording an event or transaction, but also planning a future relationship for the parties. Unlike the parties to pleadings, the parties to transaction documents do not want their documents read by a court. In fact, they prepare these documents in an effort to stay out of court. As a paralegal you should be able to prepare simple contracts and leases with minimal supervision from a lawyer. We will discuss the drafting of these documents in Chapters 8, 9, and 10.

### Correspondence

Most texts on legal writing omit instruction on the most common task of lawyers and paralegals: writing correspondence. Preparing quality correspondence may be the most neglected activity of a law office, yet often the clients' only impression of the law firm derives from the correspondence they receive. Demand letters (letters demanding payment of debt), settlement proposals, client reports, and letters between counsel are just a few of the letters you may prepare in the course of a week. Some correspondence may be as uncomplicated as confirming a telephone call or telling the client of a date for a hearing, but other correspondence may be expository or even argumentative, such as in a settlement demand letter. Because this activity is so common, it deserves special treatment in the paralegal curriculum. Chapter 7 discusses legal correspondence, including examples of several commonly written letters.

## THE IMPORTANCE OF LEGAL WRITING SKILLS

Clients pay substantial fees to have lawyers prepare legal documents. Paralegals often are assigned the task of drafting those documents for an attorney's review and approval. Paralegals probably spend more of their time writing than doing any other single activity. As a result, good writing skills are a prerequisite to success as a paralegal. Based on the documents that paralegals prepare, cases may be won or lost and deals may close or go sour. Thus a measure of the firm's success depends on your performance.

Paralegals who are intimidated by the legal writing process may be surprised to learn that many lawyers have little formal writing training. Perhaps this lack of training is why many lawyers lack the expertise to draft simple legal documents. In fact, the public has become tired of reading ineptly drafted documents, especially documents written in archaic legalese. Recently, laws have been passed requiring lawyers to write simply so that documents can be read and understood by the people who will be using them.

Remember the last time you read a signature card to open a bank account? How about an insurance contract? Your apartment lease? Your mortgage? Even lawyers have trouble understanding the meaning of some of these documents, but gradual improvement has occurred over the past two decades. Under the federal pension reform legislation (ERISA), for example, the plan description that is distributed to employees must be written in language the average participant can understand. Leases in New York must now be written in simple language. When Jimmy Carter was president, he ordered the simplification of federal regulations. The 1975 Magnuson-Moss Warranty Act required that warranties for consumer products be written in "simple and readily understandable language." Numerous other laws have been passed or proposed calling for consumer documents to be written in understandable language. These laws are part of what is known as the **Plain English movement**—a movement away from so-called legalese. As you read this text, notice how court rules mandate "simple" pleadings, how consumer documents must be readable, and how briefs should be written so the court can easily follow the gist of the argument.

Paralegals should not be at any disadvantage in writing understandably. If you write a document clearly, if it is logical and understandable to you, the document should pass muster with any audience. Changes are evolving quickly in this area, so paralegals should not be intimidated by legal jargon. No law says that legal documents must be written in archaic legalese! But before you are paid to prepare that first legal document, you should understand how legal writing compares to other forms of writing.

## CHARACTERISTICS OF LEGAL WRITING

A legal document is a form of communication. All written communication has four components: an author, an audience, a writing, and a speech community. It is helpful to consider your role as a legal professional in relation to these components.

### The Author

Lawyers and paralegals are professional writers, although they seldom look at themselves that way. The legal profession claims the exclusive right to prepare legal documents. Laws in most states boost this claim by prohibiting nonlawyers from engaging in the unauthorized practice of law. In fact, it is a crime in most states to perform the work of a lawyer for a client unless you are admitted to the bar. Even filling in forms may violate these statutes. As a result, lawyers enjoy a virtual monopoly in this area. Lawyers as authors of legal documents enjoy a unique privilege. Paralegals can prepare legal documents and not violate these laws only if their work is properly supervised by an attorney.

**The Legal Author's Goals.** Most authors write with a goal to entertain, to sell books or articles, to teach, to sell products, or to create. In contrast, legal professionals use language as a tool to help clients. Lawyers use **nonemotive language** (language without emotional content) to make a contract or to file a motion with a court. The lawyer uses language to help parties set up a relationship. That relationship might be the relationship of a landlord and tenant, of a bank and borrower, or of a buyer and seller.

At other times the legal writer uses **emotive language** (language meant to provide an emotional response such as in a sales pitch) in a brief to persuade a court to take a particular course of action. Always the legal writer composes these documents without providing a clue as to what he or she personally feels about the transaction, the motion, or the argument.

The legal writer owes a duty to the client but owes no duty to the other side of a suit or transaction except to act within the bounds of ethics and the law. Lawyers exercise the duty to a client by coloring a motion or a contract to favor that client. Another author (the opposing lawyer) may rewrite the document to recolor it for another client's advantage. Still another lawyer may research the same document years later and try to interpret it differently from the intended meaning of the original authors.

**The Legal Author's Responsibilities.** With these privileges associated with the practice of law come responsibilities. In filing court pleadings we will see how court rules protect against abuses. A court may impose fines on a party for filing frivolous or sham pleadings. In filing briefs we will see how practical restraints help ensure that arguments are presented fairly. In drafting contracts and leases we will see how the ***contra proferentem rule*** may protect against a drafter sneaking questionable provisions into a transaction document. This *contra proferentem* rule says that ambiguity in a document is construed against the document's author. So if the author of a legal document creates doubt as to how the document should be interpreted, the doubt will be resolved against the author.

Paralegals provide services, and their time is charged to the client. When paralegals prepare legal documents for a client, they need to start the writing process knowing they too are professional writers, they too represent the interests of the client, and they too have constraints as to how that role is satisfied.

## The Audience

Most writers want a wide audience. Usually the wider the audience, the better the compensation. This rule does not apply to legal professionals. You might conclude the audience for a legal document is the client, but it is not that simple. Certainly the client is part of the audience; however, the audience is more varied than the immediate parties to the transaction. Publishers target their audience. Although lawyers are professional writers, they seldom consider that they are writing for an audience. The ultimate reviewer of legal documents is a court; the immediate audience is the parties to the event or transaction. A secondary audience is the possible assignees, beneficiaries, heirs, and successors to the transaction. A peripheral audience includes attorneys and other persons who may review the document years later in connection with future transactions.

**Courts.** Obviously, the ultimate audience for most legal documents is a court, yet the good drafter of a contract or lease will try to avoid this audience. The legal professional normally does not want a contract or lease to end in a court dispute. However, a drafter cannot ignore the possibility that the document could end in a dispute no matter how well it is drafted. The drafter must anticipate that the document might end in litigation.

Trial lawyers who dream of writing the script for their next trial often fail to realize that whenever they draft a document they are preparing the "testimony" relating to a transaction. These lawyers are forgetting their audience. An agreement you prepare may be the only material testimony introduced at trial regarding the transaction.

Each time you draft a document, remember this: even if you fail to meet your primary goal of avoiding litigation, you can still succeed in drafting the script so a court can understand it and interpret it to your client's benefit. Every document should be prepared as if it will ultimately be read in court.

**Clients.** Clients are the immediate audience for most legal documents. If you write an agreement that can be understood by your client and disputes do arise during its term, attorneys may not have to become involved in the interpretation process. Clearly written transaction documents enable clients to solve problems without legal assistance.

A good drafter writes so that clients (the first audience) understand the documents. After all, the client pays the legal professional for the legal work. It is the client who will consult the document in the future. Draft the document anticipating any problems that later may arise between the parties to the transaction.

When amicable parties first appear at a lawyer's office, sometimes it's difficult to believe there will ever be a problem between them. But while parties may be eager for an agreement at the time a document is prepared, it does not follow that they will be on the same friendly footing throughout the term of the agreement. Moreover, an attorney who has handled estates also realizes that even close-knit families cannot always agree on the disposition of a deceased's property. That is why any loose ends should be taken care of at the time of the consummation of the agreement, if possible, while parties are eager to do business.

**Successors to the Transaction.** The immediate parties to the legal document do not make up the total universe of its users. If the document is assignable (i.e., if its rights or duties can be transferred to a person not a party to the document) or if one of the parties dies, other persons may claim rights under the document. When a document is initially executed, the parties may have little anticipation of ever litigating any disputes. Yet as any practicing attorney should know, their in-laws and spouses may eventually spark a controversy that can be solved only by litigation. A drafter may believe that a contract between two siblings will never be litigated; yet if one of the siblings dies, the in-laws may not be quite as friendly. The party eager to start a new business and the party eager to retire may both change their minds as time goes on. During negotiations, the typical layperson tends to doubt that the other party would ever breach the agreement, yet contracts are broken every day.

Suppose that a legal professional haphazardly drafts an agreement between two friends or relatives and later finds that the agreement ends in litigation after both have assigned their interests to third parties. The drafter can mutter about unforeseeability, but this problem was not unforeseeable; the drafter merely failed to consider the wider audience.

Thus the audience for a legal document will encompass third parties (friends, relatives, or others with whom the original party has legal relationships) and parties who might step into the shoes of the original parties (such as a receiver or a trustee in bankruptcy). Your wider audience may be quite expansive. Shareholders may change, a corporation may merge or expand, partners may die. The Internal Revenue Service may audit the transaction, and the accountant may take a deduction or credit based on its tax ramifications. Third parties, such as a trustee or a creditor in a bankruptcy proceeding, will not read a document with the view of the friend or relative with whom your client originally negotiated the transaction. These events are not unforeseeable or even unexpected. They represent daily possibilities. Paralegals must be aware of the audience beyond the immediate parties, including all possible assignees, beneficiaries, heirs, and successors to the transaction.

**Subsequent Reviewers of the Transaction.** The audience includes attorneys who may review an instrument of title in an abstract decades later, or an attorney consulted to find a loophole in the agreement. It might include a bank that is asked to lend monies on the basis of the agreement. This peripheral audience cannot be ignored. Remember, it is difficult to know every person who might read the document you prepare. Some will read it with a friendly view and others may read it with disgust. Try to look far beyond your client when you envision your audience.

## The Writing

The writing has an important function in law. In fact, some transactions must be in writing to be enforceable. The written document will be used to memorialize the transaction. If a transaction later ends in litigation, the document you prepared may be used as evidence in the case.

**The Necessity of the Writing.** The laws that require certain transactions to be documented in writing are called **statutes of frauds**, and they vary from state to state. Most state statutes of frauds require written documents for contracts that will not be performed within one year, real estate contracts, and contracts involving certain minimum values. Although there are exceptions, an oral contract is unenforceable if it does not comply with the statute of fraud requirements. As Sam Goldwyn purportedly put it, "a verbal agreement isn't worth the paper it's printed on."

In addition to statutes of frauds we have **parol evidence rules**, which provide that a party cannot by means of oral testimony contradict or vary the terms of a written document. If a written contract specifies payment of ten dollars, for example, parties are not usually permitted at trial to testify that they meant five dollars. Although there are various exceptions to parol evidence rules, the law favors the written word over sworn testimony. (One such exception is the partial integration doctrine, which permits the use of oral evidence to prove provisions not inconsistent with the written terms.)

Written agreements serve as evidence of the parties' agreement. The writing cautions and reminds parties of their obligations. In our society written documents to record information replace the ritual ceremonies of earlier ages. A legal document defines relationships between parties, provides for sanctions, and grants privileges or rights to a party. A deed, a power of attorney, or a will memorializes an event or an intent. When times were less litigious, oral agreements or handshakes may have been sufficient. But as the complexity of transactions increased, it became unrealistic to rely solely on the memory of individuals who witnessed an agreement between parties.

The complexity of our legal system is a direct response to the complexities of everyday society. Paralegals must be aware of these complexities as they prepare documents for clients, remembering that the function of any legal document is to anticipate and avoid litigation as much as is foreseeably possible.

**Functions of the Writing.** The drafter of a transaction document such as a contract creates a relationship. The relationship may have been partially negotiated before the parties appeared at the law office, but usually it is still forming at that time. Typically, when a paralegal first meets a client, the parties announce they have reached an agreement and need only the "paperwork." Seldom is this the case.

In the situation where an individual has just sold his or her house on contract, for example, it would not be unusual for the client to inform the attorney that all "terms and conditions" of the agreement have been established, when in fact all that has been established is the price and perhaps the term of the payments. Legal professionals preparing their first contract consult a formbook and suddenly realize (usually after the client has left the office) that such concerns as taxes and insurance have not even been discussed. Most parties do not anticipate future problems in their relationships. They fail to anticipate what would happen if the house were to burn before the purchaser took possession or if the purchaser could not secure financing. Just as frequently, the parties overlook such obvious concerns as who must pay the taxes or the insurance premiums.

A legal document may be consulted at various times by the parties—and the expectation is that the parties will find ready answers to future problems when they look at that document. The law permits parties to fix the rules that will be used by them to solve difficulties that occur during the life of the transaction. This concept of freedom of contract is fundamental to understanding the role of a drafter in preparing bilateral agreements for parties.

Paralegals must also approach the drafting process with Murphy's law in mind—what *can* go wrong probably *will* go wrong. Drafting is a litigation-avoidance process; but if a document does end in litigation, the drafter wants sufficient evidence to record the transaction favorably for the client. Even though this aim should be evident, many lawyers tend to overlook it.

In summary, important observations of the function of a written record should be made: First, in every type of legal document the drafter attempts to reflect either past, present, or future intentions of the parties. Second, the document may create rights, duties, privileges, or responsibilities. An important function of legal writing is to encapsulate agreements; but more often, the function is to *finish* the agreement for the parties. Finally, the drafter must ensure that the writing is in compliance with the applicable statute of frauds and any other legal requirements.

## The Speech Community

A written communication can be understood only if one knows the rules of the speech community. Lawyers and paralegals are, of course, part of a wider speech community.

Language experts call the study of the rules of our speech community **semiotics**. Semiotics consists of the study of **semantics** (the meaning of words), **syntactics** (the relationship of words to one another), and **pragmatics** (the effect of words on us). In Chapter 10, we will look at how semantics and syntactics can help you write more clearly.

If a dispute arises as to the meaning of words, the courts are ultimately responsible for resolving the controversy. Courts have developed their own speech rules to resolve such disputes. Many of these rules have Latin names, such as *ejusdem generis*, *noscitur a sociis*, and *expressio unius est exclusio alterius*. These terms are not as difficult to understand when we explain them in English. Other rules such as consistency principles and the precedent antecedent doctrine are somewhat self-explanatory. Because as a paralegal you will be drafting legal documents for clients, it is helpful to understand the speech rules used by courts. At the end of this chapter, you will see that although these rules have been used for centuries, they are not always effective at providing a means to resolve language disputes. Nevertheless, you should acquire familiarity with the concepts.

**Consistency Principles**. A court attempts to read a disputed document to ascertain the intent of the parties according to the common meaning of the terms, unless technical terms are used. All words in an agreement must be considered in determining the meaning of the contract without rendering any word, phrase, or paragraph ineffective or meaningless, if possible. Each word, phrase, or term is presumed to have the same meaning throughout the document. Each time a different word, phrase, or term is used, a different meaning is presumed. The consistency requirement provides the underpinning for many of the basic rules used by the courts in construing documents. Throughout this text you will see examples of errors that resulted from inconsistency. The first drafting principle is that every term must be consistent with every other term. This principle flows, of course, from logic. But it also flows from the court decisions that hold that the intention of the parties must be determined by reading the instrument as a whole.

**Specific Limits General**. Specific words limit the meaning of more general words. Lawyers refer to this rule by its Latin name, ***ejusdem generis***, defined in *Black's Law Dictionary* as follows:

> where general words follow an enumeration of persons or things, by words of a particular and specific meaning, such general words are not construed in their widest extent, but are to be held as applying only to persons or things of the same general kind or class as that specifically mentioned.[1]

Now let's explain what the rule actually means. Suppose a teacher says, "Peter, Paul, and the other students will be permitted to go to recess." Does this include all the rest of the students? Use of the *ejusdem generis* rule might lead to the conclusion the boys can go but not the girls. When you list people or things, you do not give them their widest meaning. You limit the meaning to those in the same class as those specifically listed. Since you enumerated only boys, girls may not be included under "other students."

For another example, in a pornography statute, the words, "book, pamphlet, picture, motion picture film, paper, letter, writing, print," was held not to include phonograph records since the statute listed only objects that you could see or view.[2]

Similarly, where a person promised to pay "all unpaid taxes and mortgages shown of record and all other liens. . .," the phrase "all other liens" was construed to only include *recorded* documents and not an unrecorded mortgage.[3]

The *ejusdem generis* doctrine is applied frequently when words of enumeration are followed by words such as "other," "any other," or "otherwise." This doctrine applies when the enumerated terms can be classified with similar characteristics.

**Context Clues**. Often the meaning of a word or phrase is interpreted by surrounding words. According to *Black's*, ***noscitur a sociis*** means that "general and specific words are associated with and take color from each other,"[4] restricting a general word to a less general meaning in relationship with other words in the sentence. This rule simply says when there is a word of doubtful meaning, the meaning for the doubtful word can be ascertained by looking at other words associated with it. This is the same rule you learned in grade school to use context clues to discover the meaning of other words in the paragraph. The courts simply use a Latin word to tell you how to find the meaning of a doubtful word by looking at other words associated with the doubtful word in the document.

**Intended Omissions**. ***Expressio unius est exclusio alterius*** (expression of one thing is the exclusion of another) provides that if a writing specifies an exception or condition, then other exceptions or conditions not mentioned were intended to be excluded. Let us look at a simple example. A man leaves his estate "to my children except for my oldest son." An illegitimate son attempts to claim his share of the estate. The *exclusio alteris* doctrine holds that if you specifically identify one thing or category, you mean to exclude the others. Since the man specified an exception there would be no other exception intended so the illegitimate son would be able to share in the estate.

In *Akey v. Murphy*, 229 So. 2d 276, 279 (Fla. App. 1969), a physician withdrew from a partnership. The partnership agreement limited a physician who quit the partnership from practicing for two years in a defined area. The partners sued to enforce this agreement. The applicable statute voided contracts that restrained a person from "exercising a lawful profession, trade or business of any kind." However, another section made an exception permitting those in "business" to contract not to compete. Is a professional partnership a business? Using the *expressio unius* doctrine, the court held that the exception did not apply to a professional partnership.

Simply put, this doctrine presumes that omissions are intended.

**Rules of Construction.** The rules of drafting must anticipate rules of construction used by the courts. However, the rules or canons of construction are not nearly as important as you might think at first blush because for each of these rules or canons there is a counterrule. As Karl Llewellyn noted,

> When it comes to presenting a proposed construction in court, there is an accepted conventional vocabulary. As in argument over points of caselaw, the accepted convention still, unhappily requires discussion as if only one single correct meaning could exist. Hence there are two opposing canons on almost every point. . . .
>
> Plainly, to make any canon take hold in a particular instance, the construction contended for must be sold, essentially, by means other than the use of the canon: The good sense of the situation and a simple construction of the available language to achieve that sense, by tenable means, out of the statutory language.[5]

What this means is that a court can reach a result, and then select the canon of construction to validate that result, since there is an opposing canon on each point. Christopher and Jill Wren have charted the rules and counterrules, and we include them here as Figure 1-2. As you can see, for every rule there is a counterrule to permit the court to reach a result opposite the rule if necessary.

A student of the drafting process will gain little insight by studying the court decisions, except perhaps in identifying problem situations. Judges are not linguistics experts. Decisions are made and then rationalized.

What is important for the paralegal to understand is that each document is a communication. When the law requires a deed to use precise words such as "convey and warrant" or requires that an option to purchase real estate use "binding or irrevocable," then these legal rules for this speech community must be followed. A brief might have precise format requirements; again these rules must be followed. In most situations, however, language rules simply direct precision of expression. Learn the language rules, but do not be intimidated by them.

## APPLYING WRITING SKILLS TO THE LEGAL WRITING PROCESS

Legal writing skills are not always commensurate with general writing or grammar skills. Examples better illustrate this point. Each of us can remember an English teacher telling us not to repeat the same word over and over in our writing, and as young students we took this rule to heart. Yet this rule is contrary to a fundamental rule of drafting that holds consistency is of paramount concern. The consistency principle states that every time the same meaning or concept is expressed, the same word or phrase or clause should be used. Every time a different meaning or concept is intended, a different word or phrase or clause should be used. If the foremost principle of drafting is to write as simply as possible for the transaction, the second most important rule is to follow this consistency principle. Most inexperienced drafters find it difficult to use the same word over and over again in the same document, yet consistency demands this approach.

When we became more sophisticated, our English teachers taught us to write "impersonally." This maxim led us to use passive voice constructions, inversions such as "there are. . ." and windups such as "it is evident. . . ." Scholarly writers tend to prefer passive voice. From a legal drafting standpoint, however,

**FIGURE 1-2 CONSTRUCTION RULES AND COUNTERRULES**

| Rule | Counterrule |
|---|---|
| • A statute cannot go beyond its text. | • To effect its purpose a statute may be implemented beyond its text. |
| • If language is plain and unambiguous it must be given effect. | • Not when literal interpretation would lead to absurd or mischievous consequences or thwart manifest purpose. |
| • Words and phrases which have received judicial construction before enactment are to be understood according to that construction. | • Not if the statute clearly requires them to have a different meaning. |
| • Every word and clause must be given effect. | • If inadvertently inserted or if repugnant to the rest of the statute, they may be rejected as surplusage. |
| • The same language used repeatedly in the same connection is presumed to bear the same meaning throughout the statute. | • This presumption will be disregarded where it is necessary to assign different meanings to make the statute consistent. |
| • Words are to be interpreted according to the proper grammatical effect of their arrangement within the statute. | • Rules of grammar will be disregarded where strict adherence would defeat purpose. |
| • Punctuation will govern when a statute is open to two considerations. | • Punctuation marks will not control the plain and evident meaning of language. |
| • Expression of one thing excludes another. | • The language may fairly comprehend many different cases where some only are expressly mentioned by way of example. |

Source: Christopher G. Wren and Jill Robinson Wren, *The Legal Research Manual* (A-R Editions, Inc., 1983), p. 88.

the conscious use of active voice ensures that the actor who is delegated a duty or responsibility has been properly identified. After all, legal documents involve people. Use of active voice in legal drafting ensures that we identify who does what to whom.

Many legal professionals are not taught how to transfer other general writing rules to the drafting process. Consider the problem of *ejusdem generis*, the doctrine that if a general word follows a series of specific words, the general word becomes limited by the special words. In the example ''cars, trucks, and other motor vehicles,'' the drafter may have intended to expand the words to include more than cars and trucks. However, the *ejusdem generis* doctrine tells us that ''other motor vehicles'' must be in the same class as a car or a truck. Certainly you may argue, as many scholars do, that the drafter did not intend to limit the words ''other motor vehicles'' to vehicles precisely like cars and trucks. Whether the drafter also intended to encompass a motorcycle, a jeep, or moped by the term ''other vehicles'' may have been frustrated by the *ejusdem generis* rule. The legal scholars bicker as to whether this rule should be used.

Doubtless these same scholars were once chastised by their writing teachers for using the word ''etc.'' Such usage, they were told, left what was being included open to question. The drafter who uses the general words ''other vehicles'' commits the same offense as the elementary student who uses the abbreviation ''etc.'' Neither usage is acceptable. Just as any competent writer will avoid ''etc.,'' so must any competent drafter avoid situations that lead to the application of the *ejusdem generis* doctrine.

Another universal grammar lesson is that of the vague referent. Most first-year college students are required to take an English composition course. How many of you encountered an instructor who pretended not to understand what the word ''it'' or ''this'' referred to at the beginning of a sentence? Teachers of English comp seem to enjoy circling the word ''it'' and asking in the margin, ''What does 'it' refer to?'' Unfortunately, the same students who learn this lesson may later become lawyers and turn to such legal abominations as ''such,'' ''said,'' ''hereinabove,'' and ''hereinafter.'' These are the legal counterparts of the vague referents that we were taught to avoid.

## Beyond Technical Writing

Legal writing involves different branches of technical writing, requiring specialized emphasis and knowledge of particular grammatical principles. The legal writer must become familiar with rules of technical writing, but rules alone are not enough. Legal writers must also master the unique features of the legal writing process. For example, the rule of consistency discussed earlier—the premise that each time the same meaning or concept is intended, the same word or phrase is used—is uniquely important to the legal drafting process.

By integrating theories from technical writing, editing, and legal drafting, you will acquire the requisite skills for legal writing. You must develop a propensity to spot problem words as well as problem grammatical constructions. You will learn that successive prepositional phrases, the participle, and certain conjunctives are symptoms of equivocation. And as you apply this knowledge, you should develop a readable style compatible with the aims of the Plain English movement.

Although it is helpful to categorize and understand the problems of legal writing, it is more helpful to find solutions for these problems. Consider again the *ejusdem generis* situation of ''cars, trucks, and other motor vehicles.'' Students will typically opine no paralegal could be expected to enumerate all possible situations: it would take pages of words to solve this problem. Unfortunately, that is how most drafters think, but the answer is just the opposite. If you reconceptualize the problem, a simple phrase—"any motor vehicle"—may solve the problem. *Ejusdem generis* situations are avoided through reconceptualization, not further enumeration. When strings of words are used, reduce the words to the "lowest common denominator." Faced with the temptation to write "give, devise and convey," for example, the drafter need only use "give." Reduction to the lowest common denominator is accomplished by deleting the extra words.

Like a baseball player attempting to learn golf, sometimes the worst student of legal writing is one who has already been exposed to the language of law and has accepted lawyers' use of centuries-old jargon without asking why this archaic language survives in the 1990s. In one lamentably true-to-life cartoon, a client hands a document to a lawyer with an instruction to "add some legalese." Sadly, some paralegals perceive this as their role and are amazed to be told that it is not only acceptable, but preferable to draft documents in simple English. This may be the foremost principle of legal writing: *Write so that you and the client can understand the transaction*. Remember that a crude agreement drafted by a lay person can be just as valid a contract as the most sophisticated document drafted by a Wall Street law firm. There is no one correct method for approaching legal writing. The purpose of writing is to communicate, and communication is the goal of every legal professional.

Transaction documents and pleadings are among the forms of legal writing that require great precision and accuracy. In these areas, this text stresses principles to achieve such precision and accuracy. We have attempted to explore rationales for rules and principles set forth in this text. If you discard a writing principle, you will do so with full awareness of the risks of such a decision. Every time a principle of drafting is ignored, the risk of ambiguity lurks.

As paralegals begin to understand the techniques for drafting agreements, they read even the newspaper differently. They notice how a reporter uses ambiguity in writing a news article; they notice how a cartoonist uses equivocation for humor; they see how deliberate ambiguity calls attention to a sales pitch. Learning writing skills helps develop reading skills as well.

## Learning About Your Subject Matter

In some respects a good legal writer is like any other good writer. A good writer, like a good actor, learns as much about the subject matter as possible before beginning to write. The skilled paralegal writer will try to learn as much as possible from the client. If the client is a retailer, the paralegal must learn about retailing. If the client is in the fishing business, the paralegal must know the problems of the fishing business. The hardest lesson for a paralegal to learn is that law is fact-intensive: A complaint is a story about a wrong; the paralegal must learn about the story. A contract is a map of a relationship; the paralegal must learn the details of the relationship. A real estate agreement is likely to concern the sale of a house; the paralegal should know what can go wrong in a house. A skilled paralegal learns the facts.

This book will set forth the rules for competent writing techniques. After reading it, you should be able to draft a document that can be understood by a reasonably intelligent client. Throughout your professional life you will continue to practice and polish these legal writing techniques.

## ENDNOTES

1 *Black's Law Dictionary* 608 (5th ed. 1979).

2 *State v. Alpen*, 338 U.S. 680 (1950).

3 *Whicker v. Hushaw*, 64 N.E. 460, 159 Ind. 1 (1902).

4 *Black's Law Dictionary* 1209 (5th ed. 1979).

5 Karl Llewellyn, *Remarks on the Theory of Appellate Decision and the Rules or Canons About How Statutes Are to Be Construed,* 3 Vand. L. Rev. 395, 401 (1950).

# 2 THE LAW AND LEGAL THOUGHT PROCESS

> Now if I have made one point in this discussion it should be this: that a case read by itself is meaningless, is nil, is blank, is blah. (K. Llewellyn, *Bramble Bush* [New York: Ocean Publications, 1960], 54.)

The concept of written law is a rather recent phenomenon. Prior to the adoption of the Magna Charta in 1215, law was what the king decided; law vacillated with the whims of the ruler. Similarly, the method of resolving disputes by court cases has evolved only recently. Several hundred years ago disputes were resolved by dueling. It was believed the winner survived because of the grace of God. Now the rule of law, not a fight to the death, determines the outcome of disputes. Paralegals must be able to find the rules of law relating to their client's disputes. Therefore we will examine the sources of the law and how to analyze these sources.

## SOURCE LAW

Rules of law are contained in constitutions, cases, statutes, court rules, and ordinances. This law is **primary authority**. Primary authority is the source law.

In contrast, **secondary authority** is something written about the law. It might be an encyclopedia, an article, or a book. Although most paralegals will have had legal research training before they start legal writing, many do not fully appreciate the relationship among the different sources of law in our legal system.

When a paralegal writes a brief or memorandum on an issue of law, the paralegal must cite the primary authority or source law that controls the issue. As we describe the various sources of law, we will discuss how lawyers and paralegals cite each of these legal authorities. A citation is the form used to tell the reader how to look up the material. Learning to use correct citation form is essential.

## Constitutions

Law in the United States stems from the U.S. Constitution, the highest law in the nation. In addition to the federal Constitution, each state follows its own constitution. Thus we have a federal system and various state systems of government. *No* law can conflict with the federal Constitution, but other than that a state's constitution is the highest authority for that state.

**United States Constitution.** Under the U.S. Constitution, three branches of government enact, interpret, and enforce laws: The legislative branch (Congress) has the power to pass statutes; the judiciary branch (the courts) resolves disputes as to the interpretation of these laws; the executive branch administers and enforces the laws.

Constitutional amendments grant certain rights to the people. For example, the First Amendment to the U.S. Constitution is the basis of the right to freedom of the press. An example of the proper form for citing Constitutional provisions is: U. S. Const. Amend. I, Section 1. Figure 2-1 contains the text of the First Amendment.

**FIGURE 2-1 THE FIRST AMENDMENT**

**AMENDMENT I**

Congress shall make no law respecting an establishment of religion, or prohibiting the free exercise thereof; or abridging the freedom of speech, or of the press; or the right of the people peaceably to assemble, and to petition the Government for a redress of grievances.

**State Constitutions.** State constitutions are typically modeled after the federal Constitution. State constitutions provide for state legislatures to pass laws; they also establish state court systems and grant rights to citizens.

## Statutes

Most people understand that laws are contained in statutes. In fact, much law in the United States is made by statute. Statutes are primary authority.

Federal statutes are passed by Congress. State statutes are passed by state legislatures. Examples of federal statutes include the Social Security Administration program, the Internal Revenue Act, the Occupational Safety and Health Act (OSHA), and the Securities laws. Examples of state statutes are divorce, insurance, and property laws.

**Publication of Federal Statutes.** Congress has provided that its statutes be published in the official federal sessions record, ***Statutes at Large***. Comprising many volumes, *Statutes at Large* presents laws in chronological order as they are passed by Congress. To look for a particular statute, a researcher must examine every volume because many statutes have been modified or changed by later statutes. The laws are not arranged topically, and there is no index. Therefore it is practically impossible to use *Statutes at Large* to research statutory authority.

Most attorneys and paralegals turn to the ***United States Code*** (U.S.C.) for statutory research. In the *U.S. Code*, Congress has compiled all related statutes together. For example, all Social Security laws are grouped together under one title and all labor laws under another. If a conflict arises in interpreting the law as set out in *Statutes at Large* and the U.S. Code, then *Statutes at Large* controls. Material from the *Statutes at Large* is considered to be positive law, which means it can be used as proof of the law. Actually, the *U.S. Code* is also used as positive law unless someone points out a conflict between it and the *Statutes at Large.*

Almost always, the paralegal who researches a federal statute will use an annotated edition of the *U.S. Code.* Considered to be the most useful source for statutory research, an **annotated code** is published by a private publishing company (e.g., West or Lawyer's Co-operative). It follows the *U.S. Code* format, but contains additional information after each statute as well as a summary of cases that have interpreted it. A typical citation looks like this:

42 U.S.C. Section 1983 (1970).

The number 42 references the title and 1983 the section of the *U.S. Code;* the symbol § is often used to indicate the word ''Section.'' Figure 2-2 is a copy of that statute.

**FIGURE 2-2 42 U.S.C. SECTION 1983**

**42 U.S.C. Section 1983**

Every person who, under color of any statute, ordinance, regulation, custom, or usage, of any State or Territory or the District of Columbia, subjects, or causes to be subjected, any citizen of the United States or other person within the jurisdiction thereof to the deprivation of any rights, privileges, or immunities secured by the Constitution and laws, shall be liable to the party injured in an action at law, suit in equity, or other proper proceeding for redress. For the purposes of this section, any Act of Congress applicable exclusively to the District of Columbia shall be considered to be a statute of the District of Columbia.

**State Statutes.** State legislatures pass laws that are first published as session laws. These session laws are usually then codified like the federal statutes. In other words, these session laws are made into a code. Paralegals use annotated codes to research issues concerning state law.

## Regulations

Prior to the Great Depression of 1929, the U.S. government supported few administrative agencies. During the depression era, however, Congress attempted to deal with the disturbing economic situation by passing statutes that established a number of them. A federal **administrative agency** is an entity established by law to administer a congressional grant of power. The federal agencies established during the depression were given considerable discretion to administer relief programs. As they gained expertise, these agencies passed **regulations** clarifying and defining the scope of their discretion.

**Federal Regulations: an Example.** Let's see how this works today in practice. The Social Security Administration statute holds that a claimant is entitled to benefits if he or she is unable to engage in "substantial, gainful employment." The language is broad. The Social Security Administration has passed regulations telling how to determine whether a claimant meets this standard. For example, if the claimant has a heart impairment, the regulations say the claimant must have a medical problem that meets the particular criteria shown in Figure 2-3.

**FIGURE 2-3 EXCERPT FROM THE SOCIAL SECURITY REGULATIONS—CARDIAC**

**Part 404, Subpt. P, App. 1** **20 CFR Ch. III (4-1-90 Edition)**

4.01 Category of Impairments, Cardiovascular System

4.02 *Congestive heart failure (manifested by evidence of vascular congestion such as hepatomegaly, peripheral or pulmonary edema).* With:

A. Persistent congestive heart failure on clinical examination despite prescribed therapy; or

B. Persistent left ventricular enlargement and hypertrophy documented by both:

1. Extension of the cardiac shadow (left ventricle) to the vertebral column on a left lateral chest roentgenogram; and

2. ECG showing QRS duration less than 0.12 second with $S_{v1}$ plus $R_{v5}$ (or $R_{v6}$) of 35 mm. or greater *and* ST segment depressed more than 0.5 mm. *and* low, diphasic or inverted T waves in leads with tall R waves: or

C. Persistent "mitral" type heart involvement documented by left atrial enlargement shown by double shadow on PA chest roentgenogram (or characteristic distortion of barium-filled esophagus) and either:

1. ECG showing QRS duration less than 0.12 second with $S_{v1}$ plus $R_{v5}$ (or $R_{v6}$) of 35 mm. or greater *and* ST segment depressed more than 0.5 mm. *and* low, diphasic or inverted T wavers in leads with tall R waves, or

2. ECG evidence of right ventricular hypertrophy with R wave of 5.0 mm. or greater in lead $V_1$ *and* progressive decrease in R/S amplitude from lead $V_1$ to $V_5$ or $V_6$; or

D. Cor pulmonale (non-acute) documented by both:

1. Right ventricular enlargement (or prominence of the right out-flow tract) on chest roentgenogram or fluoroscopy; and

2. ECG evidence of right ventricular hypertrophy with R wave of 5.0 mm. or greater in lead $V_1$ *and* progressive decrease in R/S amplitude from lead $V_1$ to $V_5$ or $V_6$

4.03 *Hypertensive vascular disease.* Evaluate under 4.02 04 4.04 or under the criteria for the affected body system.

4.04 *Ischemic heart disease with chest pain or cardiac origin as described in 4.00E* With:

A. Treadmill exercise test (see 4.00 F and G) demonstrating one of the following at an exercise level of 5 METs or less:

1. Horizontal or downsloping depression (from the standing control) of the ST segment to 1.0 mm. or greater, lasting for at least 0.08 second after the J junction, and clearly discernible in at least two consecutive complexes which are on a level baseline in any lead; or

2. Junctional depression occurring during exercise, remaining depressed (from the standing control) to 2.0 mm. or greater for at least 0.08 second after the J junction (the so-called slow upsloping ST segment), and clearly discernible in at least two consecutive complexes which are on a level baseline in any lead; or

3. Premature ventricular systoles which are multiform or bidirectional or are sequentially inscribed (3 or more); or

4. ST segment elevation (from the standing control) to 1 mm. or greater; or

5. Development of second or third degree heart block; or

B. In the absence of a report of an acceptable treadmill exercise test (see 4.00G), one of the following:

1. Transmural myocardial infarction exhibiting a QS pattern or a Q wave with amplitude at least 1/3rd of R wave and with a duration of 0.04 second or more. (If these are present in leads III and

**FIGURE 2-3 EXCERPT FROM THE SOCIAL SECURITY REGULATIONS—CARDIAC (Cont.)**

**Social Security Administration, HHS** **Part 404, Subpt. P, App. 1**

a VF only, the requisite Q wave findings must be shown, by labelled tracing, to persist on deep inspiration; or

2. Resting ECG findings showing ischemic-type (see § 4.00F1) depression of ST segment to more than 0.5 mm. in either (a) leads I and a VL and $V_6$ or (b) leads II and III and a VF or (c) leads $V_3$ through $V_6$; or

3. Resting ECG findings showing an ischemic configuration or current of injury (see 4.00F1) with ST segment elevation to 2 mm. or more in either (a) leads I and a VL and $V_6$ or (b) leads II and III and a VF or (c) leads $V_3$ through $V_6$; or

4. Resting ECG findings showing symmetrical inversion of T waves to 5.0 mm. or more in any two leads except leads III or aVR or $V_1$ or $V_3$; or

5. Inversion of T wave to 1.0 mm. or more in any of leads I, II, aVL, $V_2$ to $V_6$ *and* R wave of 5.0 mm. or more in lead aVL *and* R wave greater than S wave in lead aVF; or

6. "Double" Master Two-Step test demonstrating one of the following:

a. Ischemic depression of ST segment to more than 0.5 mm. lasting for at least 0.08 second beyond the J junction and clearly discernible in at least two consecutive complexes which are on a level baseline in any lead; or

b. Development of a second or third degree heart block; or

7. Angiographic evidence (see 4.00H) (obtained independent of Social Security disability evaluation) showing one of the following:

a. 50 percent or more narrowing of the left main coronary artery; or

b. 70 percent or more narrowing of a *proximal* coronary artery (see 4.00H3) (excluding the left main coronary artery); or

c. 50 percent or more narrowing involving a long (greater than 1 cm.) segment of a proximal coronary artery or multiple proximal coronary arteries; or

8. Akinetic or hypokinetic myocardial wall or septal motion with left ventricular ejection fraction of 30 percent or less measured by contrast or radio-isotopic ventriculographic methods; or

C. Resting ECG findings showing left bundle branch block as evidenced by QRS duration of 0.12 second or more in leads I, II, or III *and* R peak duration of 0.06 second or more in leads I, aVL, $V_5$, or $V_6$, unless there is a coronary angiogram of record which is negative (see criteria in 4.04B7).

4.05 *Recurrent arrhythmias* (not due to digitalis toxicity) resulting in uncontrolled repeated episodes of cardiac syncope and documented by resting or ambulatory (Holter) electrocardiography.

4.09 *Myocardiopathies, rheumatic or syphilitic heart disease*. Evaluate under the criteria in 4.02, 4.04, 4.05, or 11.04.

4.11 *Aneurysm of aorta or major branches* (demonstrated by roentgenographic evidence). With:

A. Acute or chronic dissection not controlled by prescribed medical or surgical treatment; or

B. Congestive heart failure as described under the criteria in 4.02; or

C. Renal failure as described under the criteria in 6.02; or

D. Repeated syncopal episodes.

4.12 *Chronic venous insufficiency* of the lower extremity with incompetency or obstruction of the deep venous return, associated with superficial varicosities, extensive brawny edema, stasis dermatitis, and recurrent or persistent ulceration which has not healed followng at least 3 months of prescribed medical or surgical therapy.

4.13 *Peripheral arterial disease*. With:

A. Intermittent claudication with failure to visualize (on arteriogram obtained independent of Social Security disability evaluation) the common femoral or deep femoral artery in one extremity; or

B. Intermittent claudication with marked impairment of peripheral arterial circulation as determined by Doppler studies showing:

1. Resting ankle/brachial systolic blood pressure ratio of less than 0.50; or

2. Decrease in systolic blood pressure at ankle or exercise (see 4.00K) to 50 percent or more of preexercise level *and* requiring 10 minutes or more to return to preexercise level; or

C. Amputation at or above the tarsal region due to peripheral arterial disease.

The regulations provide for similar standards for other medical problems. The Social Security regulations also have several charts detailing how to factor age, education and work experience into the disability equation. For instance, if you can lift only ten pounds and cannot stand and walk for prolonged periods, the Social Security regulations say you can do only sedentary work. If a claimant is restricted to sedentary employment, Social Security will determine whether the claimant qualifies for disability benefits by looking at the chart in Figure 2-4.

**FIGURE 2-4 SOCIAL SECURITY REGULATIONS SEDENTARY GRID**

| Rule | Age | Education | Previous Work Experience | Decision |
|---|---|---|---|---|
| 201.01 . . . . . | Advanced age | Limited or less . . . . . . . . . | Unskilled or none . . . . . . . | Disabled. |
| 201.02 . . . . | . . do . . . . | . . . . . . do . . . . . . . . . . . . | Skilled or semiskilled—skills not transferable[1]. | Do. |
| 201.03 . . . . | . . do . . . . | . . . . . . do . . . . . . . . . . . . | Skilled or semiskilled—skills transferable[1]. | Not disabled. |
| 201.04 . . . . | . . do . . . . | High school graduate or more—does not provide for direct entry into skilled work[2]. | Unskilled or none . . . . . . . | Disabled. |
| 201.05 . . . . | . . do . . . . | High school graduate or more—provides for direct entry into skilled work[2]. | . . . . . . do . . . . . . . . . . . . | Not disabled. |
| 201.06 . . . . | . . do . . . . | High school graduate or more—does not provide for direct entry into skilled work[2]. | Skilled or semiskilled—skills not transferable[1]. | Disabled. |
| 201.07 . . . . | . . do . . . . | . . . . . . do . . . . . . . . . . . . | Skilled or semiskilled—skills transferable[1]. | Not disabled. |
| 201.08 . . . . | . . do . . . . | High school graduate or more—provides for direct entry into skilled work[2]. | Skilled or semiskilled—skills not transferable[1]. | Do. |
| 201.09 . . . . | Closely approaching advanced age. | Limited or less . . . . . . . . . | Unskilled or none . . . . . . . | Disabled. |
| 201.10 . . . . . | . . do . . . . | . . . . . . do . . . . . . . . . . . . | Skilled or semiskilled—skills not transferable. | Do. |
| 201.11 . . . . . | . . do . . . . | . . . . . . do . . . . . . . . . . . . | Skilled or semiskilled—skills transferable. | Not disabled. |
| 201.12 . . . . . | . . do . . . . | High school graduate or more—does not provide for direct entry into skilled work[3]. | Unskilled or none . . . . . . . | Disabled. |
| 201.13 . . . . . | . . do . . . . | High school graduate or more—provides for direct entry into skilled work.[3] | . . . . . . do . . . . . . . . . . . . | Not disabled. |
| 201.14 . . . . . | . . do . . . . | High school graduate or more—does not provide for direct entry into skilled work[3]. | Skilled or semiskilled—skills not transferable. | Disabled. |
| 201.15 . . . . . | . . do . . . . | . . . . . . do . . . . . . . . . . . . | Skilled or semiskilled—skills transferable. | Not disabled. |

**FIGURE 2-4 SOCIAL SECURITY REGULATIONS SEDENTARY GRID (Cont.)**

| Rule | Age | Education | Previous Work Experience | Decision |
|---|---|---|---|---|
| 201.16 . . . . . | . . do . . . . | High school graduate or more—provides for direct entry into skilled work[3]. | Skilled or semiskilled—skills not transferable. | Do. |
| 201.17 . . . . . | Younger individual age 45–49. | Illiterate or unable to communicate in English. | Unskilled or none . . . . . . . | Disabled. |
| 201.18 . . . . . | . . do . . . . | Limited or less—at least literate and able to communicate in English. | . . . . . . . . . do . . . . . . . . . | Not disabled. |
| 201.19 . . . . . | . . do . . . . | Limited or less . . . . . . . . . | Skilled or semiskilled—skills not transferable. | Do. |
| 201.20 . . . . | . . do . . . . | . . . . . . do . . . . . . . . . . . . | Skilled or semiskilled—skills transferable. | Do. |
| 201.21 . . . . | . . do . . . . | High school graduate or more | Skilled or semiskilled—skills not transferable. | Do. |
| 201.22 . . . . | . . do . . . . | . . . . . . do . . . . . . . . . . . . | Skilled or semiskilled—skills transferable. | Do. |
| 201.23 . . . . | Younger individual age 18–44. | Illiterate or unable to communicate in English. | Unskilled or none . . . . . . . | Do.[4] |
| 201.24 . . . . | . . do . . . . | Limited or less—at least literate and able to communicate in English. | . . . . . . do . . . . . . . . . . . . | Do.[4] |
| 201.25 . . . . | . . do . . . . | Limited or less . . . . . . . . . | Skilled or semiskilled—skills not transferable. | Do.[4] |
| 201.26 . . . . | . . do . . . . | . . . . . . do . . . . . . . . . . . . | Skilled or semiskilled—skills transferable. | Do.[4] |
| 201.27 . . . . | . . do . . . . | High school graduate or more | Unskilled or none . . . . . . . | Do.[4] |
| 201.28 . . . . | . . do . . . . | . . . . . . do . . . . . . . . . . . . | Skilled or semiskilled—skills not transferable. | Do.[4] |
| 201.29 . do . . | . . . . . . . . . | . . . . . . do . . . . . . . . . . . . | Skilled or semiskilled—skills transferable. | Do.[4] |

1. See 201.00 (f)
2. See 201.00 (d)
3. See 201.00 (g)
4. See 201.00 (h)

The Social Security statute merely says disability benefits are payable if a person cannot perform "substantial, gainful employment." The regulations published by the Social Security Administration define what the term "substantial, gainful employment" means. This is just one example of how an administrative agency will fill in and give meaning to its statutory mission.

**Publication of Regulations.** All federal regulations are published in the *Federal Register.* The *Federal Register* contains proposed regulations for the different federal agencies. This process affords affected parties the opportunity to protest or otherwise address the merits of a regulation before it is enacted. When a regulation is enacted by an agency, the regulation must appear in the *Federal Register.* This process notifies the public of the action of the agency. The function of the *Federal Register* is to provide information about regulations. Because its listings appear in chronological order, it is not generally used as a primary research tool. The *Code of Federal Regulations* (C.F.R.) is used for that purpose. Like the *U.S. Code*, the *Code of Federal Regulations* is organized according to subject matter. The *Code of Federal Regulations* is published in pamphlets; each year a new set is released. *Code of Federal Regulations* citations look like this:

47 C.F.R. Section 73.609 (1980)

## Ordinances

Counties and cities also pass laws. These laws are called ordinances. A city ordinance might deal with zoning, building permits, sewer tap-in fees, or sidewalks. Local ordinances are usually published at the local level and can be located by contacting a county clerk or city clerk. An ordinance is cited like this:

FORT WORTH, TEX., REV. ORDINANCES ch. 34, art. I, Section 15 (1950)

Figure 2-5 contains an Evansville, Indiana, ordinance dealing with animals.

## Cases

Although most people know that law is made by statutes, their notion of how law comes from cases is relatively vague. It is important for paralegals to understand the history of case law.

**The Common Law.** In England, much law was initially decreed by judges through their court decisions. This was referred to as the **common law**. Much of the English common law was adopted by state courts in the United States and continues to grow and change as judges make new decisions in court cases today. This is what we call our common law.

In a sense, this is an odd way to make law. Two parties have a dispute. The dispute ends in court. One party prevails. The loser appeals the case to an appellate court. Both sides file briefs with the appellate court, which consists of a panel of judges. An appellate judge renders a written decision. The decision gives a written explanation of the rationale used for deciding the case the way it was decided. The case becomes a precedent to be followed in later cases; in other words, it becomes law. A case is a primary authority just like a statute. A case is sometimes referred to as a decision or judicial opinion.

This is how *stare decisis* works. ***Stare decisis*** is the doctrine that says legal precedents must be followed. This is the basis for the development of the common law. A precedent is an earlier decided case and can be either binding or persuasive. A **binding precedent** is a case decided by a higher court in the same jurisdiction. A **persuasive precedent** is a case decided by a court in another jurisdiction or by a lower court in the same jurisdiction.

**FIGURE 2-5 EVANSVILLE ORDINANCE ON ANIMALS**



**§ 90.04 Prohibited Acts.**

(A) No person shall do the following prohibited acts.

(1) Be a custodian of a prohibited animal as identified in § 90.05.

(2) Be a custodian of, or permit, an animal nuisance.

(3) Be a custodian of a dangerous animal; however, the exemptions provided under § 90.03(C) shall also be applicable to this provision.

(4) Be a custodian of a dog that is not under restraint, or of a nuisance animal.

(5) Confine an animal in an area which is unclean, overcrowded, or inadequately ventilated.

(6) Deprive an animal from the opportunity for adequate exercise or access to fresh air, or maintain a large animal in a lot of less than 10,000 square feet per animal.

(7) Be a custodian of an animal that has not been properly licensed pursuant to this chapter, nor be a custodian of any animal that has not been vaccinated with a rabies vaccine approved by the State Board of Health if the animal is capable of carrying or transmitting rabies.

(8) Abandon an animal.

(9) Sell chickens or ducklings younger than eight weeks of age in quantities of less than 25 to a single purchaser.

(10) Give away any live reptile, bird, or mammal as a prize for, or as an inducement to enter, any contest, game, or other competition, or as an inducement to enter a place of amusement, or offer such a vertebrate as an incentive to enter into any business agreement whereby the offer was for the purpose of attracting trade.

(11) Be the custodian of an animal and fail to provide the animal with sufficient, good, and wholesome food and water, proper shelter, protection from the weather, veterinary care when needed to prevent suffering, and with humane care and treatment.

(12) Expose any known poisonous substance, whether or not mixed with food, so that such poisonous substance shall be liable to be eaten by any domestic animal.

(13) Leave an animal unattended in a vehicle when conditions in that vehicle would constitute a health hazard to the animal.

(14) Fail to confine in a secure building or enclosure a female dog or cat in heat so as to prevent conception except during instances of planned breeding.

(15) Be a custodian of a vicious animal. A finding that an animal is a vicious animal shall supersede a finding of an animal being an animal nuisance or a dangerous animal.

(B) No person shall fail to obey the provisions of this chapter or any restrictions, regulations, or orders issued by the Commission pursuant to the terms of this chapter.

(C) No person shall fail to maintain in a sanitary manner the premises occupied by an animal, whether the animal is kept in a structure, fence, pen, or fastened, hitched, or leashed. Custodians of an animal shall regularly, and as often as necessary, maintain all animal areas or areas of animal contact to prevent unsanitary conditions on the property and to prevent odor from escaping from the property of the custodian.

('62 Code, Art. 2, Ch. 20, 57) (Ord. G-80-49, passed 4-13-81; Am. Ord. G-87-4, passed 4-6-87; Am. Ord. G-87-37, passed 12-14-87) Penalty, see § 90.99

Courts can change precedents if they were wrongly decided or if changes in society require a different look at the dispute. Use of *stare decisis* ensures uniformity of results. It also ensures predictability. The attorney/paralegal team can review the law to advise a client on a course of action. *Stare decisis* ensures equality of treatment and fairness in decision making.

Courts make law through the common law. Yet as we have seen, legislatures also make law through statutes. If parties do not agree as to how a statute should be interpreted, the courts will resolve the dispute for them. These cases are also law and will be used as precedents in resolving future statutory disputes. In this regard, federal and state courts operate the same way.

**The Court System.** In order to understand when court decisions are binding on their clients, paralegals must understand the structure of federal and state courts.

***Federal Courts.*** A federal court system includes trial courts called district courts. Some decisions by the federal district courts are published by West Publishing Company in a set of books called the *Federal Supplement* (abbreviated as F. Supp.). A citation from this set of books would look like this:

*Jones v. Smith*, 444 F. Supp. 66 (S.D. Ind. 1960).

The 444 is the volume number, and 66 is the page number in that volume on which *Jones v. Smith* begins. A party dissatisfied with a decision of a district court can appeal the case to a circuit court of appeals with jurisdiction over the state in which the case was tried. Figure 2-6 shows a map of the thirteen circuit courts of appeal in the United States. The case will not be retried in the circuit court of appeals; instead, the parties prepare briefs to be read by a three-judge panel of that court. The panel will render a written decision. Often the court allows the attorneys to present oral arguments addressing their most important grounds for appeal. In Chapter 5, you will learn how to draft briefs for the appeals court.

Circuit Court decisions are released in another publication by West Publishing Company. That set of books is called the *Federal Reporter* and is cited like this:

*Smith v. Jones*, 456 F.2d 66 (7th Cir. 1961)

Decisions of a circuit court of appeals are binding on the district courts located within its circuit.

If a party does not like a circuit court of appeals decision, the case can be appealed to the U. S. Supreme Court. A decision by the U.S. Supreme Court is a binding precedent. Supreme Court decisions appear in an official set of reporters called the *United States Reports* (U.S.). One unofficial set, the *Supreme Court Reporter* (S. Ct.), is published by West; another unofficial set, *United States Supreme Court Reports, Lawyers Edition* (L. Ed. or L. Ed. 2d) is published by Lawyer's Co-operative. A citation to a Supreme Court case looks like this:

*Jones v. Smith*, 66 U.S. 55 (1962)

POINTER: Some courts prefer that you use a full citation to both the official and unofficial reporters. Then the citation to *Jones v. Smith* **would look like this:**

*Jones v. Smith*, 66 U.S. 55, 35 S. Ct. 60, 20 L. Ed 550 (1962)

***State Courts.*** The typical state system is structured like the federal system:

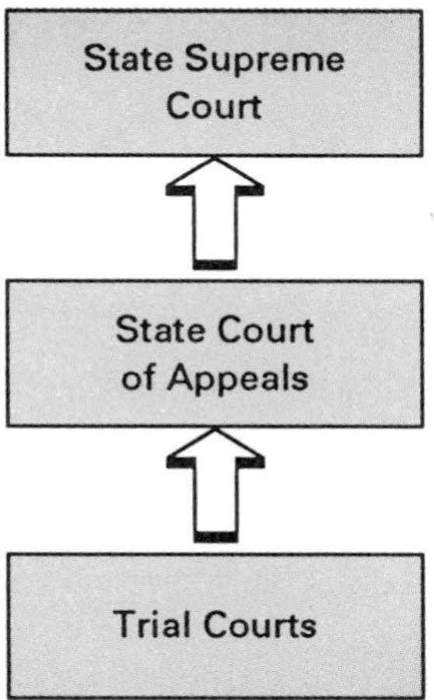


As in the federal system, a state case begins in the trial court. A judge presiding at a bench trial or a jury seated at a jury trial will decide the issues of fact and credibility. If a party does not agree with a trial court decision, the case can be appealed to an appellate court. The decisions of the appellate courts are binding on the trial courts. State courts of appeal may be divided into districts or regions covering different portions of the state, similar to how the circuit courts of appeal are divided at the federal level.

A party still unsatisfied with a decision of an appeals court can appeal to the highest court in the state, usually called the state supreme court. A decision by the highest court in the state is binding on that state's lower courts of appeal and trial courts. Its decision constitutes the only persuasive precedent for courts in other states or in the federal system.

A party still unsatisfied with a decision by the state supreme court may be able to appeal to the U.S. Supreme Court.

**Publication of a Case.** When a case is decided, the opinion is typewritten and sent to the parties. This opinion is called a **slip opinion.** In some states the slip opinion must be published in an **official reporter**—a set of books designated by the court as the place where its cases are required to be published. This slip opinion is also sent to private publishing companies such as West and Lawyers Co-operative. Some states have now designated West Publishing Company as their official publisher and thus do not publish their own sets of reporters. A citation to both an official and an **unofficial reporter** is sometimes called a **parallel citation** because both sources reference the same case.

When West or Lawyers Co-operative reviews a case, an editor reads the case and summarizes all its legal points. The summary appears as a series of **headnotes** before the decision (see Figure 2-7). These summaries also appear in digests, as we will see in Chapter 3.

**FIGURE 2-6 THE FEDERAL COURTS OF APPEAL**

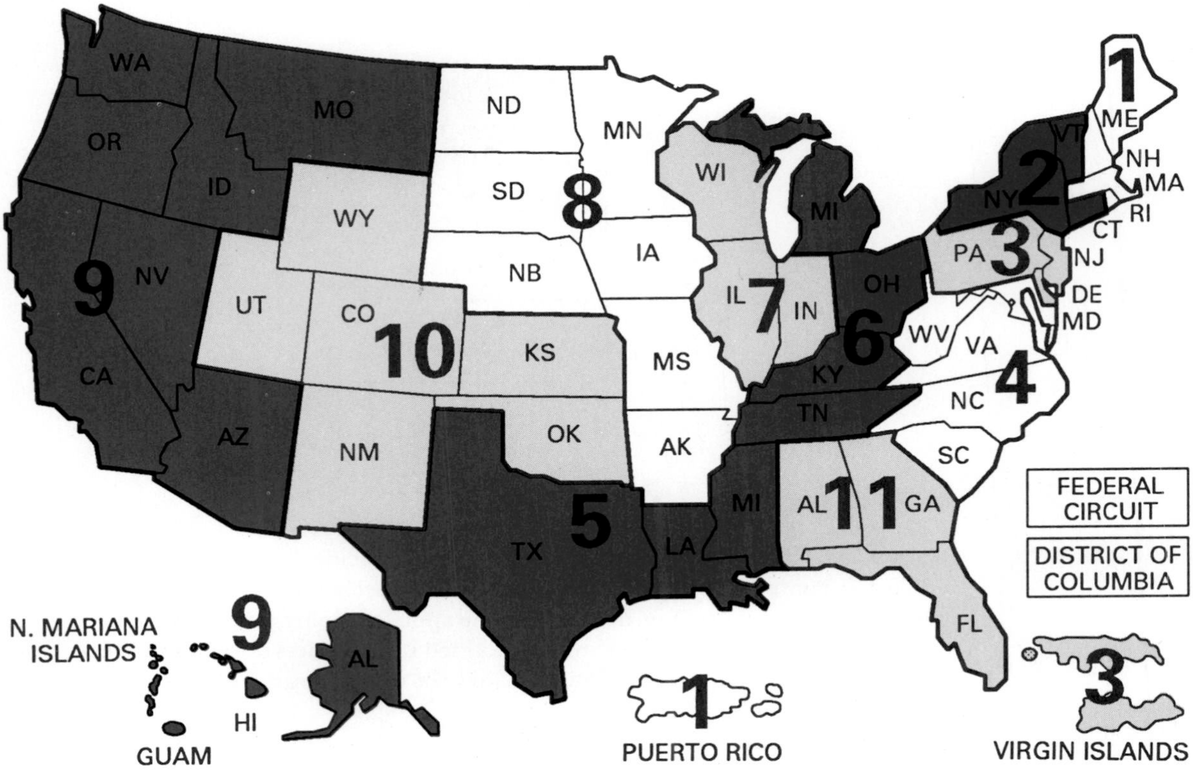

West Publishing Company has established a National Reporter System and prints state appellate court decisions in its regional reporters. West has divided the states by an economic classification (although some economists would disagree with West's rationale). For example, cases from New York, Massachusetts, Indiana, Illinois, and Ohio appear in the *North Eastern Reporter.* (Figure 2-8 shows the breakdown of the various regions.) California cases are put into two separate reporters by West: the *Pacific Reporter* and the *California Reporter.* New York cases appear in West's *New York Supplement* as well as in the *North Eastern Reporter.*

Figure 2-9 is a diagram of the court system in the United States with sample citations.

## Court Rules

Courts adopt rules to direct the course of litigation. These rules tell how to initiate a case by filing a complaint, how to gather information about the case from other parties through the discovery process, and how a case is brought to trial. The Federal Rules of Civil Procedure (FRCivP) govern practice before the district courts. The Federal Rules of Appellate Procedure (FRAP) govern practice before the U.S. circuit courts of appeal. The Supreme Court Rules tell how to take a case before the Supreme Court.

**FIGURE 2-7 HEADNOTES APPEAR BEFORE DECISIONS IN CASE REVIEWS PUBLISHED BY WEST AND LAWYERS CO-OPERATIVE**

**784 FEDERAL REPORTER, 2d SERIES**

UNITED STATES of America

v.

Erin M. NOLAN, Appellant.

No. 85-3459.

United States Court of Appeals, Third Circuit.

Submitted Under Third Circuit Rule 12(6) Feb. 19, 1986.

Decided Feb. 28, 1986.

Defendant was convicted in the United States District Court for the Western District of Pennsylvania, Maurice B. Cohill, Jr., Chief Judge, of possessing checks stolen from the mail, and she appealed. The Court of Appeals, Sloviter, Circuit Judge, held that mail placed through a mail slot in the outer door of a two-family residence and which fell to the floor in a common area was in an authorized depository for mail matter and, therefore, the defendant could be convicted of stealing checks addressed to the occupant of the other unit in the residence.

Affirmed.

**1. Post Office ⚷ 44** ← *headnote*

Mail which had been placed through mail slot in outer door of two-family residence and which fell to floor in common area was in authorized depository for mail matter, and, thus, defendant who removed mail from common area which was not addressed to her could be convicted of possessing checks stolen from the mail. 18 U.S.C.A. § 1708.

**2. Post Office ⚷ 44** ← *headnote*

Defendant did not obtain lawful possession of mail addressed to other occupant of two-family residence when she removed it from floor in common area after it had been dropped through mail slot where she was not authorized to receive other occupant's mail. 18 U.S.C.A. § 1708.

**FIGURE 2-8 WEST'S NATIONAL REPORTER SYSTEM**

| Regional Reporter | States Included |
|---|---|
| Atlantic | Connecticut, Delaware, Maine, Maryland, New Hampshire, New Jersey, Pennsylvania, Rhode Island, Vermont |
| North Eastern | Illinois, Indiana, Massachusetts, New York, Ohio |
| North Western | Iowa, Michigan, Minnesota, Nebraska, North Dakota, South Dakota, Wisconsin |
| Pacific | Alaska, Arizona, California, Colorado, Hawaii, Idaho, Kansas, Montana, Nevada, New Mexico, Oklahoma, Oregon, Utah, Washington, Wyoming |
| South Eastern | Georgia, North Carolina, South Carolina, Virginia, West Virginia |
| South Western | Arkansas, Kentucky, Missouri, Tennessee, Texas |
| Southern | Alabama, Florida, Louisiana, Mississippi |

**FIGURE 2-9 U.S. COURT SYSTEM WITH SAMPLE CITATIONS**

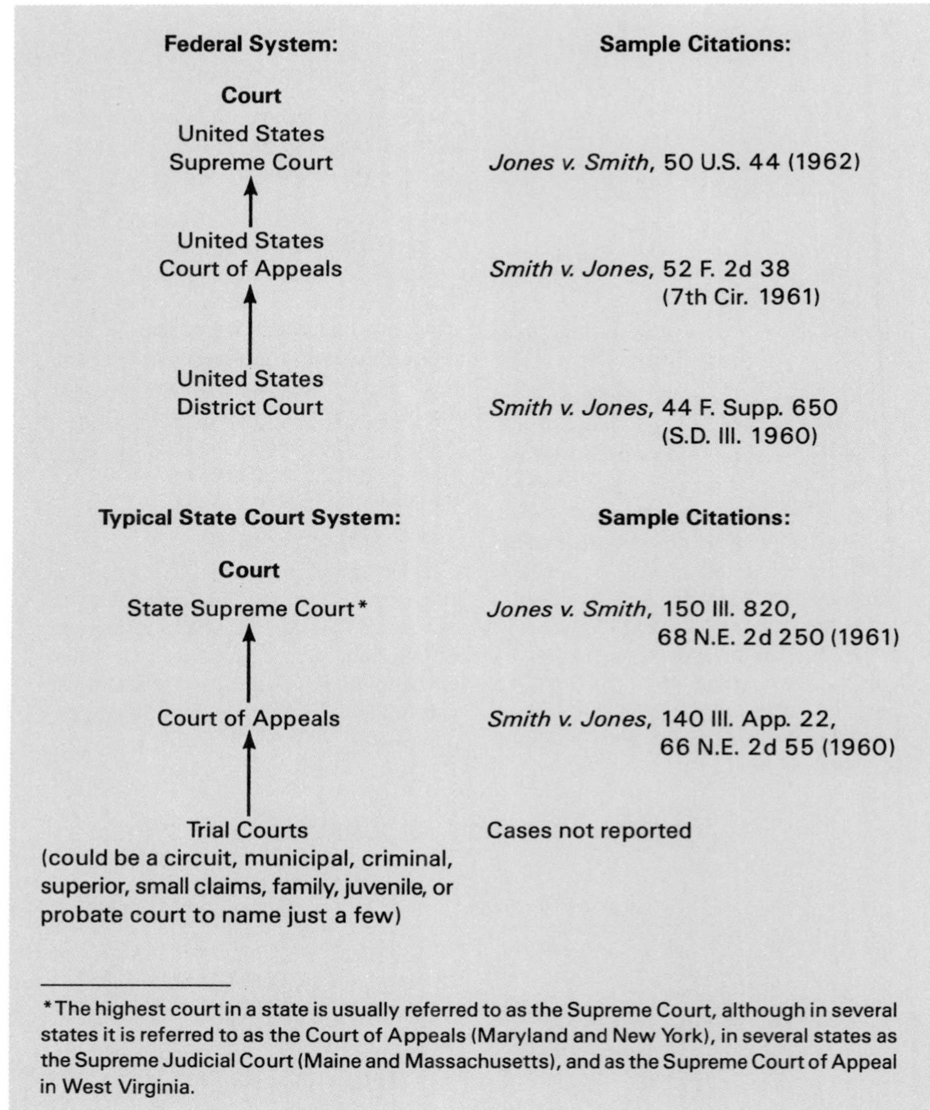

Federal System:
Sample Citations:
Court
United States Supreme Court
*Jones v. Smith*, 50 U.S. 44 (1962)
United States Court of Appeals
*Smith v. Jones*, 52 F. 2d 38 (7th Cir. 1961)
United States District Court
*Smith v. Jones*, 44 F. Supp. 650 (S.D. Ill. 1960)
Typical State Court System:
Sample Citations:
Court
State Supreme Court*
*Jones v. Smith*, 150 Ill. 820, 68 N.E. 2d 250 (1961)
Court of Appeals
*Smith v. Jones*, 140 Ill. App. 22, 66 N.E. 2d 55 (1960)
Trial Courts (could be a circuit, municipal, criminal, superior, small claims, family, juvenile, or probate court to name just a few)
Cases not reported
*The highest court in a state is usually referred to as the Supreme Court, although in several states it is referred to as the Court of Appeals (Maryland and New York), in several states as the Supreme Judicial Court (Maine and Massachusetts), and as the Supreme Court of Appeal in West Virginia.


The Federal Rules of Civil Procedure apply to all district courts. However, most individual district courts issue specific rules dealing with the practice before that court. These are referred to as local rules. Local rules govern more ministerial matters, such as how many copies of a brief to file.

The federal circuit courts of appeal operate according to the Federal Rules of Appellate Procedure and the U.S. Supreme Court has its own Rules. Before deciding to seek a writ of certiorari or of appeal, for example, a practitioner must thoroughly review the pertinent rules to see if all requirements for the writ or the appeal have been satisfied.

State court rules are usually modeled after federal rules, but these rules will vary from jurisdiction to jurisdiction. Like the Federal Rules of Civil Procedure, state court rules describe how to initiate a case, how to learn information about the case through discovery, and how to make motions. Rule 12 of the Federal Rules of Civil Procedure would be cited like this:

Fed. R. Civ. P. 12

## ANALYSIS OF CASE LAW

Cases are law. Before a paralegal can write a memorandum or a brief about how these cases determine the outcome of a legal problem, the paralegal must understand how to analyze the case or series of cases. The ability to analyze a case is not a skill that lawyers and paralegals acquire naturally; it is a learned skill. The ability to analyze a case comes from mastering a process. Let's look at how this process works.

### The Case Analysis Process

Consider first a rather straightforward case: *Mauller v. City of Columbus*, 552 N.E. 2d 500 (Ind. App. 1 Dist. 1990). Read *Mauller* on Appendix page 234.

The case contains only a single issue. The holding of this case (what the case decided) is plainly stated. This holding or principle of law decided by a court is called the ***ratio decidendi***. (When a judge makes an extraneous comment in a case, it is termed an ***obiter dictum*** (something said "by the way"). *Dicta* are not binding on other lower courts, although lower courts may decide to follow the language. *Mauller* is not difficult to read.

Now read *Griswold v. Connecticut* in the Resource Manual Appendix. This case is more typical. The party appealing this case has a number of complaints or issues. The holding may be more difficult to derive. Now remember that this case is law. Reread the case and describe what law this court just made. The holding or *ratio decidendi* of this case (even though it is not explicitly stated) is primary authority, just as a statute would be. A paralegal must be able to deduce the holding from a case.

Now consider a situation where there might be ten such cases affecting the analysis of your client's case. It is possible that the holding in each of the ten cases is only deducible by a careful reading of each case. Each of the cases may contain *obiter dicta* that are not really necessary to the determination of that particular case. You need to be able to separate this extraneous information from the holding or *ratio decidendi* of these cases.

**Background on the Case Analysis Process.** To tackle the analysis of cases and statutes, paralegals must understand the legal thought process.

***Law School Training.*** Law school courses in case analysis are taught in a most peculiar fashion. Students read a textbook that contains only cases. The texts contain minimal commentary or explanations—just case after case. When the law student attends class, the professor only asks questions. The professor *never* gives an answer. So the law student only has cases to read with no explanation and a professor who conducts class by asking questions and never giving any answers. How does the student learn?

As the professor asks questions about the case, he or she hopes the student takes a position. After the student commits to a position, the professor directs a series of hypotheticals that cause the student to hedge and then fudge on the position. Usually the student will be forced to modify or change the original position; at times students will be forced to take positions completely contrary to their original ones. A student might even be led back to his or her original position by another series of hypothetical questions. This question-and-answer process is the so-called Socratic method.

College students usually acquire information from lectures. When college students become law students, they expect to be given definitions, rules, and explanations. These things never come. Why do law students (and some paralegals) go through this training process? What is the purpose of the Socratic method?

Before we answer that question, let's go through the first day of law school. Before you go to class you are expected to read the first case in the textbook. In most instances the case is nearly impossible to read because it is written in legalese, yet the professor expects you to be able to read and understand the case. You begin with a legal dictionary, which usually serves as the pillow for the young lawyer or paralegal. But you still have trouble keeping track of who is the appellant and who is the appellee and whether the appellee was the plaintiff or the defendant in the trial court.

## The Case Brief

To grasp the meaning of a case, the student learns how to ''brief a case.'' Briefing a case is different from writing a brief, which we discussed in Chapter 1. Briefing a case is a technique for sifting out the important information. The student takes an outline and then reads a case, putting information found in the case under the appropriate headings in the outline.

The outline for briefing a case varies from text to text. The technique varies from student to student. Some teachers swear there are five steps to briefing a case, and some are convinced there are eleven steps. Others insist there are sixteen. We will use five steps: The facts, the issue, the procedural posture, the holding, and the legal reasoning.

**Majority, Dissenting, and Concurring Opinions.** Before we begin to brief a case, it is important to understand which part of the case we are briefing. Refer to *Griswold* and look at the justices who decided the case. There are nine justices on the U.S. Supreme Court. A vote is taken on how the justices feel the case should be decided, usually after the parties have filed briefs on the case and presented oral arguments. If in the majority, the chief justice assigns the job of writing the majority opinion. If the chief justice is in the minority, the senior justice in the majority makes this assignment. The justices then write drafts of their opinions. One justice may disagree with the reasoning used by another justice, yet agree with the justice's result. In such a case, he or she may decide to write a separate concurring opinion. A **concurring opinion** is a decision by one or more justices who agree with the majority result but disagree with the logic used to reach the result. A justice who does not agree with the majority may decide to write a **dissenting opinion**. Note that in *Griswold* there are examples of each. We will brief only the majority opinion written by Justice Douglas. As you read it through, see if Justice Douglas's reasoning was adopted by a majority of the court.

Not every published decision has a majority, dissenting, and concurring opinion. In federal district court only one judge hears a case and issues a decision, thus there is only one judicial opinion. Only in courts where there is more than one judge to agree or disagree, do you find dissenting and concurring opinions.

## The Five-Step Brief: an Example

Let's use our five-step technique on *Griswold v. Connecticut*, the case you read in the Resource Manual Appendix. As you will see later, this decision has important consequences on current cases in the U. S. Supreme Court.

Many paralegals contend that constitutional law cases are difficult to understand. We believe that the step-by-step briefing process will help you begin to understand what is happening in this case.

**Step 1—The Facts.** First, identify the parties. This step helps you keep a scorecard as to who was the prevailing party in the lower court, whether that party was the plaintiff or defendant in the lower court, and which of the parties is the appellant and which the appellee in the current case.

POINTER: The party taking an appeal is termed the appellant. The party defending on an appeal is termed the appellee.

When students brief their first case, they usually include too many facts. Include only **relevant facts** (facts that relate to the issue decided) and **material facts** (facts that have an impact on the outcome) of that issue. Include only the facts that gave rise to the dispute. Do not include what happened in the lower courts. Your facts might read:

> The Griswolds counseled couples about available contraceptive devices for the Planned Parenthood League of Connecticut. They were charged with a criminal offense of aiding and abetting a person who used a "drug, medicinal article, or instrument for the purpose of preventing conception."

Note that these facts are written so you can understand what the parties are fighting about.

POINTER: When you start writing a memorandum or a brief, remember how you learned to separate relevant and material facts from court opinions. This is a skill that you need to practice again and again.

**Step 2—The Issue.** The party who loses a case is usually unhappy about more than one ruling that occurred. When losing parties begin to list what a judge did wrong, they commonly do it by framing issues. In this case, an issue might be stated as follows:

> Whether Sections 53-32 and 54-196 of the General Statutes of Connecticut constitute an unconstitutional invasion of privacy in contravention of the Third, Fourth, Fifth, Ninth, and Fourteenth Amendments to the U.S. Constitution.

An issue is a legal question that the court is considering. Usually there are many issues raised on appeal. Notice how the issue helps to frame the legal dispute so the court knows what questions it must decide. The issue in a case serves the same function as the question asked in a formal debate. A well-written issue focuses the debate.

**Step 3—The Procedural Posture.** The procedural posture is the present status of the case. Cases end in many different ways. Sometimes a complaint is dismissed. Sometimes a motion for summary judgment is granted. Some cases are decided by jury. In each of these situations, the judge must look at the case in a different way. If a party files a motion to dismiss a complaint, for example, the court must assume all the facts in the complaint, as well as any reasonable inferences from these facts, are true, before ruling on the motion. If the court grants a motion for summary judgment, the parties cannot have any genuine issues of material fact in dispute.

The procedural posture might be a pretrial motion, a motion to compel discovery, or a motion for summary judgment. If the issues are before an appellate court, the status might be "an appeal from a judgment" or "an appeal from the granting of a motion for summary judgment."

Preparing the procedural posture of the case helps focus these questions for you. In the judicial opinion the court will usually tell what standard has been used to look at the case.

The procedural posture of *Griswold* is as follows:

> The Griswolds were convicted after trial to the court and were sentenced to pay a fine of one hundred dollars each. After appeals to the state Appellate and Supreme Court, the convictions were affirmed. This case is on appeal to the Supreme Court of the United States.

**Step 4—The Holding.** The **holding** is the decision of the court. When a paralegal writes the holding for the first time, usually it will read something like this:

> The Connecticut statutes are unconstitutional as violating the marital right of privacy, a fundamental right guaranteed by the First, Fourth, Fifth, Ninth and Fourteenth Amendments of the U. S. Constitution.

Justice Douglas said there was a right of privacy. He said that the right of privacy prevented the state of Connecticut from regulating the sale of contraceptives.

Two people who read this decision may disagree as to how narrowly or how broadly this holding should be stated. One person might agree that the court was announcing a broad right of marital privacy. One scholar might conclude this right of privacy applies to the right to have an abortion; another might conclude *Griswold* should not be so broadly interpreted. That person might read the right of privacy as applying only to situations where the state is preventing the sale of contraceptives. A holding will be interpreted differently by different lawyers.

**Step 5—The Legal Reasoning.** The last step in briefing a case is describing how the court reasoned to the holding. In this case, Justice Douglas said there was a right of privacy. Where did this right come from? Notice Justice Goldberg agreed there was a right of privacy. But how did Justice Goldberg disagree with Justice Douglas as to where this right came from? Legal reasoning answers these questions. Understanding the legal reasoning often is the key to answering how broadly or narrowly a case should be applied.

A court may reason to a decision in different ways. It might use a settled principle from a case or statute and apply it to the facts of the case, or it might narrow or expand the principle from a precedent or statute. In briefing the case you should consider how the principle was derived from other cases. Perhaps it was taken directly from another case or perhaps it was derived from a pattern in other cases. A paralegal should be able to trace how the legal principles used in a case were derived and applied.

Now that you have completed the process of briefing *Griswold*, go back and reread the case. Now you should have a better grasp of what this case is saying and what everyone is arguing about.

Whenever you read a case that has bearing on a project, you should prepare a brief of that case. This will provide you with insight into the meaning and ramifications of the case. As you read and brief more and more cases, the process will become faster and more uniform. After years of practice, your case briefs will become shorter and shorter until you can do them mentally, without actually writing out the five steps. It takes practice. Because most paralegals are not taught according to the case method, they should hone their skills by preparing a case brief any time they read a case that has an impact on their research project.

Briefing a case breaks down the case so it can be understood no matter how complex the issue or issues. The more you do it, the more it works.

## SYNTHESIS OF CASE LAW

Once the law student begins to understand the first case in the textbook, he or she goes on to read the second. The second case in the textbook is very much like the first. There may be some differences in facts, but the result will be the same or only slightly different. The law student briefs the case and prepares to discuss it in detail the next day in class. At this point, however, the astute student questions why the author would include two cases so much alike in the textbook. When the student goes to class on the second day, the professor again questions the students about the assigned case, but this time the questions touch on the principles from the first case as well.

The third case turns out to be similar to the first and second cases. This process is repeated for weeks at a time. What is happening?

### Case Synthesis: an Example

A case read by itself is seldom meaningful. Related cases must be read together. Let's examine this approach from the right-of-privacy perspective. In *Griswold*, the court said there was a marital right of privacy. In *Roe v. Wade*, 410 U.S. 113 (1973), the court said this right of privacy extended to the right to an abortion (prior to viability). The court held that a state had no justifiable interest prior to viability. After *Roe*, Ohio wrote a statute that required all abortions after the first trimester be performed in a hospital. In *Akron v. Akron Center for Reproductive Health*, 462 U.S. 416 (1983), the court held that this law unduly burdened abortions. In another case, the court held that a state could not determine viability because this was the function of a physician. *Coluotti v. Franklin*, 439 U.S. 379 (1979). After all, only a physician could consider gestational age, weight, and lung maturity.

A legal professional reading these cases would conclude that the state cannot place undue restrictions on abortions, and that physicians—not the state—must determine viability. Now the state of Missouri wanted to challenge these principles. So Missouri wrote a statute that read as follows:

> Before a physician performs an abortion on a woman he has reason to believe is carrying an unborn child of twenty or more weeks gestational age, the physician shall first determine if the unborn child is viable by using and exercising that degree of care, skill, and proficiency commonly exercised by the ordinary skillful, careful, and prudent physician engaged in similar practice under the same or similar conditions. In making this determination of viability, the physician shall perform or cause to be performed such medical examinations and tests as are necessary to make a finding of gestational age, weight, and lung maturity of the unborn child and shall enter such findings and determinations of viability in the medical record of the mother. Mo. Ann. Stat. 188.029 (Vernon 1989).

This statute said every physician intending to perform an abortion in Missouri *must* determine viability. Notice how this statute challenged the prior logic of the cases. Missouri was placing a burden before viability on the right of a woman to have an abortion. Yet this statute required a physician to do only what was a physician function according to *Akron*—test for viability. But this testing was obviously a burden on abortion. The state of Missouri was using the Socratic method on the Supreme Court in testing the principles it had previously set. This case was resolved in *Webster v. Reproductive Health Services*, 109 S. Ct. 3040 (1989). The result is not important to the point. The point is that cases seemingly consistent can conflict when facts are changed. The state of Missouri found an inconsistency and tested it with a statute.

## The Necessity of Case Synthesis

Earlier in the chapter we asked two questions: Why do law students (and some paralegals) go through a training process in which they get only questions, no answers, from professors? What is the purpose of the Socratic method? The answer is that the process forces students to synthesize cases. Students are required to find a pattern or generalize why cases are consistent, and be able to identify why some cases are decided inconsistently.

Synthesizing is a thought process beyond merely describing a case. For example, the *Dictionary of Occupational Titles* (published by the U.S. Department of Labor, 1977) tells us what a paralegal typically does:

> Researches law, investigates facts, and prepares documents to assist LAWYER (profess. & kin): Researches and analyzes law sources such as statutes, recorded

> judicial decisions, legal articles, treaties, constitutions, and legal codes to prepare legal documents such as briefs, pleadings, appeals, wills, contracts, deeds, and trust instruments for review, approval, and use by attorneys. Appraises and inventories real and personal property for estate planning. Investigates facts and law of case to determine causes of action and to prepare case accordingly. Files pleadings with court clerk. Prepares affidavits of documents and maintains document file. Delivers or directs delivery of subpoena to witnesses and parties to action. May direct and coordinate activities of law office employees. May prepare office accounts and tax returns. May specialize in litigation, probate, real estate, or corporation law. May search patent files to ascertain originality of patent application and be designated PATENT CLERK (gov. ser).

To perform this work, the paralegal should be able to synthesize case law. Synthesizing law is a process of generalizing principles from a series of cases or from a case to a factual pattern. This generalizing process is taught in law school through the Socratic method. The professor continually asks questions until students are forced to generalize answers from the cases they have read.

On the last day of the semester a final case analysis exam is given. In many instances it is the only grade the student will receive. After reading cases for an entire semester, the student expects the exam to consist of general questions about these cases. Wrong.

If the cases you studied all semester were in the area of the right of privacy, the exam might be a hypothetical fact situation like this:

> A scientist has been studying how to create artificial life by regeneration of cell tissue. However, the experiment goes sour when an assistant decides to make clones of the scientist. He takes cells from the scientist's hair and there are now 1,000 artificial scientists incubating in the laboratory. The assistant intends to make even more of these clones. The scientist wants to turn off the incubator, which would result in the death of the clones. The assistant seeks an injunction.

Your entire semester grade will now hinge on the answer to this ridiculous question. What is the point? The law professor does not really care about the result as much as about the principled manner in which the students handle the factual and legal synthesizing process. Put simply, how does the student handle the change in the factual position to precedent legal principles? The student must become aware that changing facts may or may not affect what legal principle is used in deciding a case. When a client comes to your office and tells of a problem, you learn to assess whether these facts are similar to or different from cases already decided. We term this **fact synthesizing**.

To write about a case, the paralegal must first understand the case and then be able to relate that case to all other cases relevant to the research. Then the paralegal must apply the case principles to a fact pattern. Now try to answer the test hypothetically.

## ANALYSIS AND SYNTHESIS OF CONSTITUTIONS, STATUTES, REGULATIONS, RULES, AND ORDINANCES

In case analysis, the student learns to derive principles from cases. However, constitutions, statutes, regulations, rules, and ordinances themselves state the general rule. The analytical process is the same for all of these written authorities, and we will examine it by looking at several statutory problems.

Statutory analysis is a process. The first step is to read the statute to see if it clearly answers the inquiry. Step two is to research other statutes that might also have an impact on the answer. If other statutes are found, read them together to see if the original interpretation is affected. Sometimes you'll find that a statute has a purpose section explaining why it was passed; such a provision will also lend insight into how the statute should be interpreted. Step three is to look for cases that interpret the statute. This step is necessary only if the first and second steps do not answer the question, which is the situation whenever there is any ambiguity or any vagueness in the statute, given the factual pattern you are researching. The fourth step is to synthesize the statutory provisions with the case law.

Finally, in rare situations you may also consider any legislative history of the statute. Such history will include the debates over the passage of the statute, the legislative committee reports, and any committee hearings. A researcher will cite legislative history if the statute literally produces an absurd result or if it is ambiguous.

### Statutory Analysis: an Example

When a statute deals with your client's problem, sometimes a quick glance will give the answer you need. If you want to know what blood alcohol level constitutes a driving-while-intoxicated offense, simply look at the applicable statute.

At other times the answer will not be so easy to find. Consider a federal criminal statute that prohibits theft from the U. S. Mail. In part, the statute reads as follows:

> Whoever steals, takes, or abstracts, or by fraud or deception obtains, or attempts to obtain, from or out of any mail, post office, or station thereof, letter box, mail receptacle, or any mail route or other authorized depository for mail matter, or from a letter or mail carrier, any letter, postal card, package, bag, or mail, or abstracts or removes from any such letter, package, bag, or mail, any article or thing contained therein, or secretes, embezzles, or destroys any such letter, postal card, package, bag, or mail, or any article or thing contained therein . . . . 18 U.S.C.A. Section 1708.

The statute seems straightforward enough. But the question is, how broadly should "authorized depository for mail matter" be interpreted? Fortunately, there are several cases that provide some guidance in answering this question. So to begin the analysis of your answer, read the cases just as you would in a common-law matter. One case reads in part as follows:

> It is not unusual for multifamily dwellings to have only a single mail slot for all mail addressed to the building's inhabitants rather than a mail box for each unit. Were mail delivered through such a slot to drop into a box, it is clear that the

> box would be an "authorized depository for mail matter." See *Rosen v. United States*, 245 U.S. 467, 38 S. Ct. 148, 62 L. Ed. 406 (198) (unlocked boxes in common hallway of a building are authorized mail depositories of the tenant businesses). See also *United States v. Lopez*, 457 F. 2d at 398-99 (Section 1708 covered the taking of mail left in front of addressee's door because "mail route" includes an addressee's doorstep). Where, as in this case, there are no such boxes and the floor in the common hallway rather than an enclosed box is the resting spot, that area must be considered a "mail receptacle" for purposes of Section 1708. Under the earlier authority in this court, the district court did not err as a matter of law in its construction of 18 U.S.C. Section 1708. *U.S. v. Nolan*, 784 F. 2d 496, 498 (3d Cir. 1986).

Another case defines "depository for mail matter" in another context:

> Once an item is delivered to the address indicated by the sender and lawfully received at that address, the item ceases to be in the mail and the protection which Section 1708 provides terminates. On the other hand, when the postal authorities misdelivered postal matter, the postal matter does not cease to be "mail" at the instant of its lawful removal from an authorized depository.
>
> To categorize misdelivered mail with improperly addressed mail would effectively foreclose the application of Section 1708 to the former. The situations in which one would have the requisite intent to steal at the moment he withdraws his mail from its receptacle are few. In the normal case, which this case typifies, only after the removal does the intent arise and the theft occur. *U.S. v. Anton*, 547 F. 2d 493, 495 (1976).

The analysis from this point should not be too difficult.

## ORGANIZING THE SOURCE AUTHORITY

Paralegals learn research skills in legal research courses. Paralegals learn writing skills in a legal writing course. In actual practice, the paralegal often completes the research and then has difficulty shifting to the writing process. The paralegal suffers from the same writer's block experienced by other writers. At times the paralegal will tear up page after page before even completing the second sentence. Writer's block usually happens because the thought process is not complete. Writing and rewriting that first sentence sometimes helps one think, but this is an arduous process. Most of the time, writer's block can be prevented simply by writing and organizing during the research phase.

When preparing term papers, students often learn to organize subjects on index cards. When a new subject appears, a new card is used. Then students organize the index cards before starting the writing process. Lawyers use legal pads rather than index cards.

### Defining the Scope of the Subject

When beginning any legal research, the first problem is usually defining the scope of the subject. As the research progresses, subtopics or subissues emerge. Start a new page for each new category of issues or line of cases. These subissues will often splinter into even narrower issues.

## Separating the Issues

By keeping issues separate, the materials organize almost automatically as part of the process. If a case is particularly pertinent to the issue or if there is a particular quote that answers the query, either copy it or write down the page for the quote. Paralegals may find it helpful to copy the title page of the case (for the citation later) and any pages dealing with the researched issue, if the case is too lengthy. Then keep the cases dealing with particular issues separate from one another. As the research process progresses, review the facts from the researched cases to see if more factual information is necessary or if your facts differ from the researched materials.

To help separate the issues, compare cases to see why results change. If there is a lead case (a case cited frequently as precedent) see how the facts of later decided cases change the legal rule used in the later decisions. Look back at the lead case in the privacy area, *Griswold v. Connecticut*, which you read in the Resource Manual Appendix. As you researched that case, you saw how this led to the abortion cases and how the results of these cases changed when the facts changed.

*Griswold* has led to other lines of cases beyond those of abortion. For example, *Griswold* was the case used by the Alaska Supreme Court to hold that Alaskans have a right to possess small amounts of marijuana in the privacy of their homes. (However, the Alaskan courts have held this right did not extend to cocaine.)

Sometimes this splintering process can become arduous. Nonetheless, the more the researcher goes through an organization process during the research stage and pays attention to factual differences in the cases, the easier the writing process will be. Of course, this is not to imply the research and writing stages are mutually exclusive. They are not. Actually a writer may go back to the research stage many times before the writing project is complete. However, by starting the writing thought process in the research stage, the actual writing will flow much easier than it will if the thought process begins at the computer or typewriter.

Most paralegal students have difficulty with this prewriting stage. In fact, I see the typical paralegal student often in the law library during the early sessions of a writing course. He or she has copied a stack of cases, unorganized and inches thick. These cases are read and researched but never categorized. These students come to me in despair. I must show them how to organize that first issue. Once they understand how to categorize in issues and subissues, they are ready to start writing. Try to categorize early in the research project. It helps.

# 3 RESEARCH STRATEGIES FOR LEGAL WRITING

> . . . [The Law Library] is to us all that the laboratories of the university are to the chemists and physicists, the museum of natural history to the zoologists, the botanical garden to the botanists. (C.C. Langdell, "The Harvard Law School," 3 *Law Q. Rev.* 123, 124, 1887.)

Paralegals come to the writing process with legal research capabilities that range from in-depth legal research coursework to no training whatsoever. In Chapter 2, we saw that a paralegal's job as generally performed in the United States requires the ability to "[r]esearch and analyze law sources such as statutes, recorded judicial decisions, legal articles, treaties, constitutions, and legal codes to prepare legal documents such as briefs, pleadings, appeals, wills, contracts, deeds and trust instruments. . . ." (*Dictionary of Occupational Titles*, U.S. Department of Labor, 1977.) In fact, almost every paralegal job requires some ability to look up law. A paralegal cannot write a simple court pleading without knowing the court rules and cannot write a simple letter demanding a tenant to surrender possession of an apartment without knowing property law. Paralegals must have the training to answer simple legal research questions.

**POINTER: The paralegal may not directly give clients legal advice. Giving such advice could be construed as the illegal practice of law. All work of the paralegal must be reviewed by an attorney. The attorney is the person ultimately responsible for your work.**

All competent paralegals are comfortable in a law library. A law library has a wide variety of books including form books with sample pleadings. There are also forms for leases, contracts, and trusts. If a paralegal is preparing to interview a witness, Am. Jur. *Proof of Facts* (now in its third series by Lawyers Co-op) suggests questions for the paralegal to ask in almost any type of case. If a paralegal is preparing interrogatories, sample questions can be found in form books such as Bender's *Forms of Discovery* (published by Matthew Bender). Paralegals familiar with the resources of a law library can direct their own job growth opportunities.

## THE GAP BETWEEN CASE LOCATION AND CASE SYNTHESIS

No matter how in-depth the paralegal's experience has been in a law library, there is a gap between knowing how to look up a case or statute and knowing how to find legal authority for a memorandum or brief. Even when a paralegal has completed a course in legal research, usually that experience consisted of looking up specific cases or specific statutes, typical assignments in such courses. Some assignment instructions even identify the book in which the answer can be found. However, most legal writing in actual practice involves locating and synthesizing a number of cases or statutes. The answer to an issue may involve reading and analyzing several statutes and several cases interpreting each of the statutes.

## HOW TO GATHER INFORMATION TO BEGIN WRITING

Although there are many fine points to legal research, most legal authority can be located by following the methods set out in this chapter, which will show the paralegal how to gather the necessary information for beginning the writing process.

### Identifying the Controlling Rule of Law

If a paralegal is asked to prepare a memorandum or a brief on an issue of law, the initial task is to identify the rule of law controlling the answer to the query. In Chapter 2, we identified the sources for these rules of law. The source law for a particular problem may be a constitution, a statute, a regulation, an ordinance, or a case. In many research situations, the researcher merely has to look up these source materials to find the answer to the problem.

**Strategies When There Is No Controlling Rule of Law.** In some instances there may be no rule of law that addresses the given problem. For example, in Chapter 2 we examined *Griswold v. Connecticut*. Before *Griswold* was decided, no right to marital privacy was recognized in any recorded case. Before *Griswold*, no matter how hard researchers looked, they would have found no rule of law establishing a right to marital privacy. Eventually they would have realized the problem was not answered within the existing body of law as then interpreted.

When a researcher discovers that no existing cases or statutes apply, the research process does not stop. Instead, it is simply refocused or expanded, and the paralegal must look at the existing law from a different perspective. One approach is to extrapolate or analogize a principle from the existing case principles. Another approach is to either expand or narrow an existing principle to cover the problem. The researcher can merge several principles to make a new principle or identify a new principle from the pattern of other cases. The courts will use both inductive and deductive reasoning in these situations.

Paralegals must rid themselves of any notion that rules of law are totally fixed or predictable. Most legal research does not result in exact answers. That is why lawsuits involve more than one party; the parties can argue both sides of the question. In many educational experiences, students are taught there are correct and incorrect answers. In legal research, however, there is not always a correct or incorrect answer. Nor is there necessarily a correct or incorrect way to analyze a legal problem. This lack of definitive answers frustrates paralegals and young lawyers.

### When to Stop Researching and Start Writing

A paralegal must be able to locate *all* relevant primary authority and have the ability to apply the rules from these authorities to particular factual situations. The paralegal must know when the answer has been located and know when no answer can be found. The paralegal also needs the ability to recognize the fuzziness of some answers. The paralegal decides what books to use or what books to ignore. The paralegal must be able to determine the scope of the research project. Legal research calls for the use of good judgment. Finally, legal research requires the ability to know when to stop the research process and when to start the writing process.

The thought process for most legal writing begins during the research stage. Some good legal work is completely thought out before the first draft of the memorandum or brief is finished. At other times the thought process continues through the copy-editing stage. To the extent possible, begin developing your theory of the case as you locate and synthesize the source law. Although you may have been acquainted with legal research through other courses, try to look at legal research as a process or strategy rather than simply a technique for finding specific cases and statutes.

## BACKGROUND ON THE RESEARCH PROCESS

There are two threshold questions every researcher should answer before proceeding with any legal research. First, what is the source authority? Is it a constitutional provision, a statute, a regulation, a court rule, a case, or some other authority? Second, what jurisdiction's law will determine the outcome of the case? Answering these questions will frame the research project and save many hours of research time. For example, it does not make sense to look for Kansas cases when researching an Ohio law problem. Nor does it make sense to look through regulatory authority when the answer to the query is in the case law.

Identifying jurisdiction is usually very simple, although there are situations where federal courts in **diversity cases** (federal lawsuits involving parties who live in different states) will use the law of the forum state rather than federal law. Occasionally conflicts arise as to which law will apply, but usually these are not the sorts of problems a paralegal will research without considerable experience or significant direction.

After answering the two threshold questions, the paralegal will select a finding tool to locate the primary authority. Before using any legal research tool, however, the paralegal should remember that every legal research system is designed either to help find primary authority or to explain the primary authority. Every legal research system needs a means to index or look up the information and a means to update or make the information current.

## The Index: Access to Research Tools

After you answer the two threshold questions, the next step is to try to select words for providing access to the indexes to the various research tools. Although paralegals have been exposed to legal research by many different methods, they seldom recognize how similar legal research is to other forms of research. Virtually every text, including the one you are reading, contains a table of contents (a topical index) at its front and a subject-matter or descriptive-word index at its rear. Although the indexing elements may bear different names or may not appear in the traditional front-back locations, all law books contain at least one index. Most have both the topical (table of contents) and the descriptive-word (subject) index. Once paralegals understand this basic fact, they feel more comfortable with the indexing used by most legal resources.

**How to Use an Index.** To research any legal problem, the paralegal must look under the right words in the indexes. Usually a good way to penetrate a legal index is to use the so-called **TAPP rule**. TAPP is an acronym for Things, Actions, Persons, and Places. Use of the TAPP rule enables the researcher to categorize the facts into ways the publisher might have indexed the legal problem. Let's consider a hypothetical to see how the TAPP rule might work.

> Your client's child, age 15, is bitten by a neighbor's dog while crossing the neighbor's backyard in Evansville, Indiana. The dog has never bitten anyone before, but it has snarled and snapped at others. The lawyer for whom you work is concerned because in some states an owner is not liable unless the dog has bitten someone before. (The dog gets one free bite.) She wants you to research Indiana law on this subject: Is Indiana a one-bite or a two-bite state?

Using the TAPP rule, you begin by identifying what Thing is involved. In this case, it is a dog. (In another situation the Thing might be a product, drugs, or contraband, for example.) The second fact to identify in using the TAPP rule is the Action involved. In this case it would be a negligence or tort action. (The Action in other situations could range from a criminal or a maritime action to an antitrust case or an adoption.) When thinking of the Action, consider also what relief is sought (money damages in this case) or what defense to the action is involved. In some cases, the relief sought might be an injunction or a writ. A defense might be waiver, contributory negligence, or incurred risk.

Persons refers to the legal relationship of the parties such as landlord-tenant, assignor-assignee, lawyer-client, bailor-bailee. In our hypothetical, one Person is the dog owner or landlord. The Person bitten might be a trespasser, a licensee, or an invitee.

Places refers to the places where the wrong or offense took place. Did it occur in a supermarket, on a sidewalk, in an alley, or in a home? In our hypothetical, the Place appears to have been a backyard.

Use the TAPP rule to rethink any factual problem. It really works as a means to penetrate most legal indexes because legal indexes are prepared with the TAPP rule in mind.

Before beginning your research, it is important to remember that all legal systems have some indexing means to access the legal information from the system. Every time you use a new legal finding tool, determine what indexing method accesses the information from the system. Then you will understand how that research tool works.

### The Importance of Updating Research

Law sometimes involves finding very old statutes and cases, but often it involves finding what cases were decided today that might change the law relating to the issue you are researching. Law-book publishers use several different methods to keep the researcher abreast of changes in the law. Some issue **pocket parts** or supplements. A pocket part is simply a pamphlet designed to fit in a pocket holder in the back of a book. Periodically (usually annually) the publisher sends a new set of pocket supplements to the subscribers to update the pocket supplements from the previous period. Some use replacement pamphlets instead of pocket supplements or use the pamphlets along with pocket supplements.

Other publishers use a loose-leaf system. In these sets of books, pages with new information replace pages with the outdated information. Publishers also use volume replacement. The publisher sends new volumes to the subscribers, and the old volumes are discarded. As you use sets of law books and other legal research tools, look to see what updating techniques their publishers employ. Failure to use the available updating materials is a common mistake of paralegals. Don't fall into that trap. Law research is continually updated.

## THE RESEARCH PROCESS

Remember that you are seeking the source or primary law. This means that you are looking for a constitutional provision, a statute, an ordinance, a case, or a court rule. The paralegal cites this primary authority to answer legal problems in memoranda or to argue a legal problem in a brief. Recall the critical threshold question: What is the source authority? Is it a case or some other authority? The answer to this question will dictate how you proceed. Case law and statutory law require different paths of research.

### Secondary Sources

Lawyers are given in-depth course training in certain basic areas such as torts, civil procedure, contracts, property, and constitutional law. Many paralegals lack this in-depth course training necessary for researching some legal problems. To overcome this deficiency, paralegals must preliminarily acquaint themselves with the general legal principles relating to their research projects. Remember that most legal research is a process of locating general principles and then gradually narrowing the search for more specific principles. Remember also that the search is for primary authority.

However, to acquaint yourself with the necessary background principles, often you will start with a secondary source such as an encyclopedia. Of course, if a paralegal understands the legal issue and is fairly certain the source authority is a case, then he can go directly to a digest. Similarly, if a paralegal understands the legal issue and is fairly certain the source authority is a statute, then she can go directly to an annotated code. Although most competent paralegals can address many problems this way, there will be times when they lack even a basic understanding of the problem. In such situations there are secondary sources designed to provide this elementary knowledge. We will discuss these secondary sources in detail in this section.

Sometimes one secondary source is more accurate than another. Do not hesitate to use several techniques to aid in the search or to verify your conclusion. No single tool works best in every situation. Knowing which tool to start with is something learned through experience. Because a particular tool seems to answer your question, do not assume that it is correct or that there is no room for additional thought. Read the primary authority yourself to see if there is room for additional thought.

During the preliminary research stage, find out what jurisdiction's law is at issue and determine whether a constitution, statute, case, or other law will answer the question presented. Read for background. Use secondary sources for this background. Use a state or national encyclopedia, an A.L.R. article, or a treatise. Sometimes that will be all you need to read. Do not start with a preconceived notion that the law will be answered by one statute or by one case or even answered at all by the research project. Do not expect exact answers to your problems. Most important, question what you read. But always read the cases and statutes that are the primary authority. Relying on summaries from a secondary source inhibits the legal thought process; sometimes these summaries are incomplete or even wrong. Nonetheless, secondary sources are an invaluable research aid.

Finally, as you become more involved in the issues, there is no reason not to return to the preliminary stages to recheck your understanding of the background principles. Legal research is a continuing process.

**Encyclopedias.** When grade school students write their first reports, they explore their topics in an encyclopedia. An encyclopedia is designed to give background information on a subject. Legal encyclopedias are designed for the same purpose: to give background explanations and an overview of legal principles.

Most states have an encyclopedia dealing with the law of that state only. For example, the *Indiana Legal Encyclopedia* deals only with Indiana law. So if a paralegal needs background information on an issue of Indiana law, the *Indiana Legal Encyclopedia* will serve this purpose very adequately.

Legal encyclopedias are simple to use. The topics are broken down under alphabetical headings just as in general encyclopedias. There are entries on

Abandonment, on Contracts, on Torts, and on Trials, for instance. Each of these topics is further broken down into subtopics. Separate volumes contain an alphabetical subject-matter index, and this index is usually the best place to begin.

Let's go back to the dog-bite situation. A client's child has been bitten by a dog, and the lawyer has asked you to determine whether Indiana is a one-bite or two-bite state. You are not quite sure what your boss meant about "one-bite or two-bite," but no one is there to give any further explanation.

So you look first in the volume index of the *Indiana Legal Encyclopedia*. You look under Dogs (see Figure 3-1). This directs you to "Viciousness, notice, **Anim § 17**." The actual entry in Section 17 under Animals explains the law to you (Figure 3-2).

According to the law in Indiana, an owner is liable for a dog bite even if the dog has not bitten anyone before, *if* the dog has previously demonstrated "dangerous propensities." The footnotes in the text of the encyclopedia refer to cases supporting the statements. It is important to read the footnotes because they give the citations to the applicable cases or statutes.

By starting your research with an encyclopedia, you found not only the necessary background information, but also the source authority to answer the query. Now, to finish the research, turn to the pocket part under Animals Section 17 (Figure 3-3). Each cited case provides a further explanation of the dog-bite issue.

In addition to state encyclopedias, there are two national encyclopedias: *Corpus Juris Secundum* (C.J.S.) and *American Jurisprudence* (Am. Jur. 2d). Using these encyclopedias is identical to using the *Indiana Legal Encyclopedia*. In either C.J.S. or Am. Jur. 2d, turn first to the subject index. If you started with Am. Jur. 2d in the one-bite/two-bite hypothetical, you would look under Dogs (see Figure 3-4). This index entry directs you to various sections under the Ani(mal) listing. Figure 3-5 shows the explanation given in Section 95, followed by footnotes to cases supporting this position.

Encyclopedias provide basic information on legal principles. Most encyclopedias feature more case law than statutory law. Encyclopedias can lead directly to the source law in many common legal problems. Read the footnotes to find the source authority for the principle referenced by the text materials.

Always follow up by using the pocket parts to update the search. Both *Corpus Juris Secundum* and *American Jurisprudence* are updated by pocket parts. Am. Jur. also has a separate loose-leaf volume for new topics; appropriately enough, it is called the *New Topic Service*. Am. Jur. 2d also replaces its income tax volume annually. Old volumes are then discarded. Paralegals should have little difficulty using encyclopedias.

**American Law Reports.** New law is made in different subject areas every year as new problems filter through the court system. Lawyers Co-operative Publishing Company publishes a series of articles on these new areas in its *American Law Reports* (A.L.R.). However, what was new when the first series was launched in 1919 is old law today. A.L.R. is now in a fourth series, and a separate series (A.L.R. Fed.) deals exclusively with federal problems. These different series are updated in several ways.

**FIGURE 3-1 EXCERPT FROM INDEX VOLUME OF THE *INDIANA LEGAL ENCYCLOPEDIA***

767 **DOMICILE**

**FIGURE 3-2 SUMMARY OF A POINT OF LAW IN THE *INDIANA LEGAL ENCYCLOPEDIA***

## § 17. — Notice of Viciousness

*Black Letter Summary*

**Liability for injuries by an animal generally depends on notice of its dangerous propensities.**

While the owner of an animal which is, by nature, wild and ferocious is negligent in permitting it to roam at large,[9] the owner of a domestic animal is not liable for injuries to a third person in absence of proof of previous knowledge of its vicious character,[10] or proof that by exercise of reasonable care such knowledge could have been obtained,[11] except for consequences which may be anticipated because of its well known disposition and habits.[12] However, an owner has been held liable where domestic animals escaped and committed a trespass on the land of another though the owner had in fact no notice of such propensity.[13]

The keeper of a vicious animal, known to be such, is responsible for its safe keeping as much as if he were the owner, and he is liable for injuries to other animals[14] and is liable to any person without fault who is injured by the animal, irrespective of negligence of fault in taking care of the animal.[15]

9. Indianapolis Abattoir Co. v. Bailey, 1913, 102 N.E. 970, 54 Ind.App. 370.
10. Klenberg v. Russell, 1890, 25 N.E. 596, 125 Ind. 531.
Indianapolis Abattoir Co. v. Bailey, 1913, 102 N.E. 970, 54 Ind.App. 370.
11. Artificial Ice & Cold Storage Co. v. Martin, 1935, 198 N.E. 446, 102 Ind.App. 74.
12. Klenberg v. Russell, 1890, 25 N.E. 596, 125 Ind. 531.

**Negligence**
Turning a horse loose in streets of a populous city is negligence, and one who does so is liable for personal injuries caused by horse, without allegation or proof that he knew that horse was vicious.—Weaver v. National Biscuit Co., 1942, 125 F.2d 463.
13. Page v. Hollingsworth, 1855, 7 Ind. 317.
14. Frammell v. Little, 1861, 16 Ind. 251.
15. Gordan v. Kaufman, 1900, 89 N.E. 898, 44 Ind.App. 603.

*Footnotes Identify Source Authority*

***The A.L.R. Index.*** Currently a five-volume alphabetical subject index, *Index to Annotations*, covers all the A.L.R. series. It is an easy index to access. There is also a word book and a digest that can be used to index the annotations. However, because the subject index is so effective, there is seldom any reason to resort to these alternative indexes.

Let's work through the dog-bite problem with the A.L.R. In this index, under Dog the reader finds references to a number of A.L.R. annotations including to 64 A.L.R.3d 1039. Notice, as you use this subject index, there is a pocket part to the index volumes. The pocket part to this subject index reveals additional A.L.R. articles, including one entry for absolute or strict liability for a dog bite, located at 51 A.L.R.4th 446.

***Content of A.L.R. Annotations.*** The 64 A.L.R.3d 1039 article illustrates the typical A.L.R. format. When the A.L.R. editors identify a new area, they

**FIGURE 3-3 EXCERPT FROM POCKET PART IN *INDIANA LEGAL ENCYCLOPEDIA***

## § 17. — Notice of Viciousness

9. I.L.E. quoted at length in Doe v. Barnett, 1969, 251 N.E.2d 688, 693, 145 Ind.App. 542.
10. Burgin By and Through Akers v. Tolle, 1986, App. 4 Dist., 500 N.E.2d 763.

Williams v. Pohlman, 1970, 257 N.E.2d 329, 146 Ind.App. 523.

**"Vicious propensity"**

A "vicious propensity" on part of animal is a propensity or tendency of animal to do any act which might endanger safety of person or property in given situation.—Doe v. Barnett, 1969, 251 N.E.2d 688, 145 Ind.App. 542.

**Act of animal**

It is act of animal and not state of mind of animal from which a dangerous propensity must be determined.—Doe v. Barnett, 1969, 251 N.E.2d 688, 145 Ind.App. 542.

**Playful conduct**

Dangerous propensity on part of animals may be deduced from very playful conduct.—Doe v. Barnett, 1969, 251 N.E.2d 688, 145 Ind.App. 542.

**Cattle**

Cattle are not naturally ferocious or dangerous animals and owner of cattle is not strictly liable for injuries caused by animal unless owner had knowledge of vicious propensity of particular animal. Thompson v. Lee, 1980, App., 402 N.E.2d 1309.

11. Williams v. Pohlman, 1970, 257 N.E.2d 329, 146 Ind.App. 523.
12. Puckett v. Miller, 1978, 381 N.E.2d 1087, 178 Ind.App. 174.

**General and particular propensities**

Owner of domestic animal is bound to take notice of general propensities of class to which it belongs, and also of any particular propensities peculiar to animal itself of which he has knowledge or is put on notice; insofar as such propensities are likely to cause injury, he must exercise reasonable care to guard against them and to prevent injuries reasonably anticipated therefrom.—Borton v. Lavenduskey, 1985, App., 4 Dist., 486 N.E.2d 639, reh. den. 488 N.E.2d 1129, transfer den. ← *Citation to Case*

**Natural propensities**

Owner of domestic animal must use reasonable care to prevent injuries caused by natural propensities of that particular class of animals, if propensities might reasonably be expected to cause injury.—Burgin By and Through Akers v. Tolle, 1986, App. 4 Dist., 500 N.E.2d 763. ← *Citation to Case*

Owner of domestic animal, who has no knowledge of vicious tendency, is bound to know natural propensities of that particular class of animals.—Burgin By and Through Akers v. Tolle, 1986, App. 4 Dist., 500 N.E.2d 763. ← *Citation to Case*

14. Williams v. Pohlman, 1970, 257 N.E.2d 329, 146 Ind.App. 523.
16. Keane v. Schroeder, 1970, 264 N.E.2d 95, 148 Ind.App. 131.

**FIGURE 3-4 EXCERPT FROM INDEX IN *AM. JUR.* 2d**

GENERAL INDEX

**FIGURE 3-5 EXCERPT FROM DISCUSSION IN *AM. JUR.* 2d**

4 Am Jur 2d ANIMALS §95

This does not mean, however, that such knowledge is limited to actual notice or actual knowledge by the owner;[1] knowledge that the disposition of the animal was such that it would be likely to commit an injury similar to the one complained of is sufficient.[2] The owner is liable if he knew or should have known its dangerous propensities or that it was a probable source of harm,[3] and proof that the owner of a vicious dog had notice of his vicious propensities may be made by introducing evidence of facts and circumstances from which an inference of knowledge arises.[4] Knowledge of one attack by a dog is generally held sufficient to charge the owner with all its subsequent acts.[5] There need be, however, no notice of injury actually committed, and therefore it is unnecessary to prove that a dog had ever before bitten anyone.[6] In this respect, it is stated that the old doctrine that every dog is entitled to "one bite" is out of harmony with a modern humanitarian society.[7] The owner or keeper of a dog must observe manifestations of danger from him to human beings from other traits than viciousness alone, short of actual injury to some person, and cannot neglect to keep him in restraint until he has effectually killed or injured at least one person.

*Text*

1. Perazzo v Ortega, 32 Ariz 154, 256 P 503; Buck v Brady, 110 Md 568, 73 A 277; Miller v Prough, 203 Mo App 413, 221 SW 159; Benke v Stepp, 199 Okla 119, 184 P2d 615; Thompson v Wold, 47 Wash 2d 782, 289 P2d 712.

2. Domm v Hollenbeck, 259 Ill 382, 102 NE 782; Twigg v Ryland, 62 Md 380; Brune v De Benedetty (Mo App) 261 SW 930; Emmons v Stevane, 77 NJl, 570, 73 A 544; Hyland v Cobb, 252 NY 325, 169 NE 401; Tubbs v Shears, 55 Okla 610, 155 P 549; Crowley v Groonell, 73 Vt 45, 50 A 546; Godeau v Blood, Vt 251; Thompson v Wold, 47 Wash 2d 782, 289 P2d 712.

3. Andrews v Jordan Marsh Co. 283 Mass 158, 186 NE 71, 92 ALR 726.

4. § 124, infra.

5. Ayers v Macoughtry, 29 Okla 399, 117 P 1088.

In Tubbs v Shears, 55 Okla 610, 155 P 549, knowledge of a previous attack on a person was held sufficient to charge the owner with knowledge of the dog's viciousness irrespective of the circumstances under which the previous attack was made, it being said that self-defense does not justify a dog bite.

Where one keeps on his premises a dog which has attacked or bitten a considerable number of persons and is notoriously cross and vicious, it may be presumed that the owner has some knowledge of this fact; hence, in an action to recover for injuries inflicted by such dog, evidence of his general reputation for viciousness is admissible, not to prove the particular fact of the dangerous propensity of the animal, but the public notoriety, as tending to support the inference of knowledge of such propensity on the part of its owner. Fake v Addicks, 45 Minn 37, 47 NW 450.

Where, in an action for injuries sustained when he was bitten by the defendant's dog, the plaintiff introduces proof of two prior instances tending to show that the dog was vicious, but the evidence is not such as to constitute conclusive proof that the dog had a vicious propensity to bite people, and that the defendant knew it, it is error to refuse to permit the defendant to rebut such evidence on the issue of notice, by proof that the dog was not vicious and that it never manifested any dangerous propensities, but had been always friendly, both to children and human beings in general. Domm v. Hollenbeck, 259 Ill 382, 102 NE 782.

***Practice Aids.***—Complaint for injury by dog known to be vicious, with allegation of specific previous attacks. I AM JUR PL & PR FORMS, 1:1093.

6. Rider v White, 65 NY 54; Tubbs v Shears, 55 Okla 610, 155 P 549; Missio v Williams, 129 Tenn 504, 167 SW 473; Plummer v Ricker, 71 Vt 114, 41 A 1045; Robinson v Marino, 3 Wash 434, 28 P 752.

7. Perkins v Drury, 57 NM 269, 258 P2d 379.

In Mungo v Bennett, 238 SC 79, 119 SE2d 522, the court said that the popular notion that "a dog is entitled to one bite" was exploded in the early case of M' Caskill v Elliot, 36 SCL (5 Strobh) 196.

The doctrine that every dog is entitled to "one free bite," if it ever prevailed in this state, is no longer followed. Kennet v Sossnitz, 260 App Div 759, 23 NYS 2d 961, affd 286 NY 623, 36 NE2d 459.

*Footnotes to Source Authority*

select a lead or representative case and place it at the beginning of the article. In the dog-bite article 64 A.L.R.3d 1039, the annotation begins with the case of *Bramble v. Thompson*, 264 Md. 518, 287 A.2d 265 (1972). See Figure 3-6.

**FIGURE 3-6 EXCERPT FROM LEAD CASE IN A.L.R. ANNOTATION**

Henry Claude BRAMBLE et al.

v

Herman THOMPSON et ux.

Court of Appeals of Maryland
February 16, 1972
264 Md 518, 287 A2d 265, 64 ALR3d 1031

*Lead Case*

**SUMMARY OF DECISION**

The Circuit Court for Queen Anne's County, Maryland, B. Mackett Turner, Jr., and James A. Wise, JJ., sustained defendants' demurrers to plaintiffs' declaration in an action for personal injuries sustained when plaintiffs, as inadvertent trespassers, were attacked by defendants' dog on defendants' property. The attack occurred when the plaintiffs, during a boating outing, docked at a pier used by defendants in their business.

The Court of Appeals of Maryland, Digges, J., affirmed, holding that the demurrers were properly sustained in view of the absence of any legal duty, on the part of owners of property, to trespassers to protect them from animals known to be vicious.

After the case begins the article. See Figure 3-7. Immediately after the title is a box used throughout all Lawyer's Co-operative books. It is entitled ''Total Client-Service Library References'' and contains a listing of other Lawyer's Co-operative publications relevant to this question.

As you read the article, notice that there is a topic index for each article and a separate subject-matter index for each topic in the article itself. This technique helps you to pinpoint the parts of the article you need to read. See Figure 3-8. If you are concerned only with the law of a particular state, a ''Table of Jurisdictions Represented'' even tells you what subsections of the A.L.R. article to read. See Figure 3-9. A.L.R. articles also reference readers to other similar A.L.R. articles. It gives practice pointers with tips on how to deal with common problems encountered in these types of cases (Figure 3-10). There follows the substance of the article, an excerpt of which is shown in Figure 3-11.

***Updating A.L.R.*** The remaining step is to update this information. The first and second series have their own methods for updating. Articles in the first A.L.R. series (A.L.R.) are updated by a set of books called the *Blue Book of Supplemental Decisions*, which references citations to cases that were decided after the article was written. This set is updated by an annual pamphlet as well. It is not

**FIGURE 3-7 BEGINNING OF AN ARTICLE IN A.L.R. ANNOTATION**

**ANNOTATION**

**LIABILITY OF OWNER OF DOG KNOWN BY HIM TO BE VICIOUS FOR INJURIES TO TRESPASSER**

*by*

*Thomas R. Trenkner, J.D.*

*Title of Annotation*

---



*Table of Contents*

**TOTAL CLIENT-SERVICE LIBRARY® REFERENCES**

4 AM JUR 2d, Animals §§ 94-98, 105
1 AM JUR PL & PR FORMS (Rev ed), Animals, Forms 121-133
1 AM JUR PROOF OF FACTS 597, Animals, Proof 3 (Knowledge of Vicious Propensities)
US L ED DIGEST, Animals § 5
ALR DIGESTS, Animals §§ 27-31
L ED INDEX TO ANNO, Animals; Trespass
ALR QUICK INDEX, Animals; Dogs; Nuisances; Trespass
FEDERAL QUICK INDEX, Animals; Dogs; Nuisances; Trespass

*References to other Lawyer's Co-operative Publishing Company Publications*

**Consult POCKET PART in this volume for later cases**

Total Client-Service Library is a registered trademark of Lawyer's Co-operative Publishing Company.

**FIGURE 3-8 EXCERPT FROM A DESCRIPTIVE-WORD INDEX IN A.L.R. ANNOTATION**

INJURY TO TRESPASSER FROM VICIOUS DOG 64 ALR3d
64 ALR3d 1039

* * *

B. APPLICATION OF PRINCIPLES IN PARTICULAR CIRCUMSTANCES



---

INDEX

**FIGURE 3-9 TABLE OF JURISDICTIONS REPRESENTED EXCERPT FROM A.L.R. ANNOTATION**

64 ALR3d INJURY TO TRESPASSER FROM VICIOUS DOG § 1[b]
64 ALR3d 1039

* * *

**TABLE OF JURISDICTIONS REPRESENTED**
**Consult POCKET PART in this volume for later cases**

| | | | |
|---|---|---|---|
| Cal | §§ 2[a, b], 9[a, b], 11[a] | Mo | § 2[b] |
| Colo | §§ 2[a], 3-5[a], 6[a, b] | NJ | §§ 3, 5[a], 7, 9[c] |
| Conn | §§ 2[a], 3-5[b], 6[a] | NY | §§ 2[a], 3, 7-9[a], 11[b] |
| Ca | §§ 2[a], 9[a], 10, 12 | Ohio | §§ 2[a, b], 3, 6[a] |
| Ky | §§ 2[a], 3, 4, 8 | Tenn | §§ 2[a], 3, 5[a], 6[b], 7 |
| Md | §§ 2[a, b], 9[a, c], 13 | Wash | §§ 2[a], 3-5[a], 6[a] |

---

**I. Preliminary matters**

**§ 1. Introduction**

**[a] Scope**

This annotation collects the cases in which the courts have decided whether, or under what circumstances, the owner of a dog[1] known by him to be vicious[2] will be liable for injuries to a trespasser[3] upon the dog owner's real property.

Relevant statutory provisions are discussed only to the extent that they are reflected in the reported cases within the scope of this annotation. Thus, the reader is advised to consult the latest enactments in his jurisdiction.

**[b] Related matters**

Animals as attractive nuisance. 64 ALR3d 1069.

Liability of owner or operator of business premises for injuries to patron caused by insect or small animal. 48 ALR3d 1257.

Liability for injury inflicted by horse, dog, or other domestic animal exhibited at show. 80 ALR2d 886.

Contributory negligence, assumption of risk, or intentional provocation as defense to action for injury by dog. 66 ALR2d 916.

Liability for injury to property inflicted by wild animal. 57 ALR2d 242.

---

1. The rules as to liability for injuries inflicted by domestic animals have generally been held to apply to persons who keep or harbor such animals upon their premises, regardless of whether they own them. Thus, for the purposes of this annotation, the keeper, harborer, or possessor of a dog is regarded as included within the term "owner." For a general discussion of the liability of the keepers of domestic animals, see 4 Am Jur 2d, Animals §92.

2. For the purposes of this annotation, a "vicious" dog is any dog expressly concluded by the court to possess dangerous propensities not ordinarily present in domestic animals. For a general discussion as to when domestic animals are regarded as "vicious" or "dangerous," see 4 Am Jur 2d, Animals § 86.

3. There appears to be widespread disagreement as to the precise definition of the word "trespasser," and no attempt at a definition is made here. Rather, this annotation collects only the cases in which the courts have expressly concluded that the victim of a dog attack was a trespasser.

**FIGURE 3-10 PRACTICE POINTERS EXCERPT FROM A.L.R. ANNOTATION**

§ 2[a] INJURY TO TRESPASSER FROM VICIOUS DOG 64 ALR3d
64 ALR3d 1039

* * *

exercised reasonable care in the manner in which he had employed his animal.[42] However, in most of the cases decided under the negligence theory, the courts have made no mention of the time of day at which the attack occurred. And in one case, the court, observing that in today's world landowners are frequently away from their property during the day, expressly rejected the view that a person's right to keep a vicious dog to defend his property is dependent upon whether the dog is used during the day or at night.[43]

It was also suggested in one case decided under the negligence theory that the fact that the injured person

**[b] Practice pointers[47]**

The potential impact of state statutes in cases involving liability for injuries caused by dogs cannot be overemphasized. Many, if not most, jurisdictions have now enacted "dog bite" statutes which impose liability on dog owners without regard to the former viciousness of the dog and without proof that the owner knew that the animal was vicious.[48] But a number of these statutes further provide that the owner is not liable for injuries to a person who, at the time of the attack, was committing a trespass on the owner's property or was teasing, tormenting, or abusing the dog on the

---

**39.** § 11, infra.

**40.** § 11[a], infra.

**41.** Weber v Bob & Jim, Inc. (1969) 59 Misc 2d 249, 298 NYS2d 854, infra § 11[b].

**42.** Woodbridge v Marks (1897) 17 App Div 139, 45 NYS 156, infra § 11[b].

**43.** Bramble v Thompson (1972) 264 Md 518, 287 A2d 265, 64 ALR3d 1031, infra § 13.

**44.** Conway v Grant (1891) 88 Ga 40, 13 SE 803, infra § 12.

**45.** All of the cases decided under the negligence theory involved noncriminal trespassers, and in 40 percent of these it was held that the liability of the dog owner was not established or supportable.

**46.** Bramble v Thompson (1972) 264 Md 518, 287 A2d 265, 64 ALR3d 1031, infra § 13.

**47.** See generally I Am Jur Pl & Pr Forms (Rev ed), Animals, Forms 121-133.

**48.** 4 Am Jur 2d, Animals § 97.

**49.** See, for example, Hirschauer v Davis (1955) 163 Ohio St 105, 56 Ohio Ops 169, 126 NE2d 337.

**FIGURE 3-11 EXCERPT FROM A.L.R. ANNOTATION ARTICLE**

§ 2[b] INJURY TO TRESPASSER FROM VICIOUS DOG 64 ALR3d
64 ALR3d 1039

Even in the absence of evidence that a dog misbehaved on other occasions, counsel may be able to establish that the owner of a vicious dog had knowledge of its propensities by introducing evidence of facts and circumstances from which an inference of knowledge arises. For example, evidence that the dog was unusually large, that it was used as a watchdog, that its owner kept it chained or muzzled most of the time, and that there were "Beware of Dog" signs on the premises, would all tend to establish that the owner had knowledge of the dog's viciousness.[61] Moreover, testimony regarding the general characteristics of the dog's breed may be admissible as tending to prove that the dog had a propensity for vicious behavior.[62] But while testimony as to the type, size, and use of the dog may be admissible, even when given by a lay witness, as tending to show the dog's training and capabilities, testimony as to general characteristics of a breed will usually be admitted only when given by experts.[63]

**II. Strict liability theory**

**A. General principles**

**§ 3. View that dog owner is strictly liable for injuries to trespassers**

The following cases support the view that an owner of a dog known by him to be vicious is liable for the injuries which the dog inflicts upon a trespasser, regardless of the care exercised by the owner in confining the dog.

**Colo**—Swerdfeger v Krueger (1960) 145 Colo 180, 358 P2d 479.

Melsheimer v Sullivan (1891) I Colo App 22, 27 P 17.

**Conn**—Woolf v Chalker (1862) 31 Conn 121 (under state "dog bite" statute).

**Ky**—Dillehay v Hickey (1902) 24 Ky LR 1220, 71 SW 1 (under state "dog bite" statute).

**NJ**—Eberling v Mutillod (1917) 90 NJL 478, 101 A 519.

**NY**—For New York cases, see

**61.** 1 Am Jur Proof of Facts 597, Animals, Proof 3.

**62.** See, for example, Radoff v Hunter (1958) 158 **Cal** App 2d 770, 323 P2d 202, infra § 11[a].

**63.** 1 Am Jur Proof of Facts 597, Animals, Proof 3.

very helpful to a researcher because the diligent researcher would have to look up all of the citations and read these cases to find out how the law has changed since the article was written.

Articles in the second A.L.R. series (A.L.R.2d) are updated in separate volumes called the *Later Case Service.* These volumes are updated annually by pocket parts.

A.L.R.3d, A.L.R.4th, and A.L.R. Fed. use pocket parts to update the annotations. In each of these later series, the updating materials give summaries of the later-decided cases along with citations so the reader can scan to see how these later cases impact the research. Figure 3-12 shows a pocket part page from the dog-bite article.

**FIGURE 3-12 EXCERPT FROM A.L.R. ANNOTATION POCKET PART**

64 ALR3d 1039-1064

**64 ALR3d 1039-1064**
§ 1 [64 ALR3d 1041]

**[b] Related matters**

Landlord's liability to third person for injury resulting from attack by dangerous or vicious animal kept by tenant. 81 ALR3d 638.

Personal injuries inflicted by animal as within homeowner's or personal liability policy. 96 ALR3d 891.

Liability of owner of dog for dog's biting veterinarian or veterinarian's employee. 4 ALR4th 349.

Liability of dog owner for injuries sustained by person frightened by dog. 30 ALR4th 986.

Liability for personal injury or death caused by trespassing or intruding livestock. 49 ALR4th 710.

Modern status of rule of absolute or strict liability for dogbite. 51 ALR4th 446.

ALR3d

Knowledge of Animal's Vicious Propensities. 13 Am Jur Proof of Facts 2d 473.

VERALEX™: Cases and annotations referred to herein can be further researched through the VERALEX electronic retrieval system's two services, **Auto-Cite®** and **SHOWME™**. Use Auto-Cite to check citations for form, parallel references, prior and later history, and annotation references. Use SHOWME to display the full text of cases and annotations.

§ 3 [64 ALR3d 1048]

Also supporting view that owner of dog known by him to be vicious is liable for injuries which dog inflicts upon trespasser, regardless of care exercised by owner in confining dog:

**Ark**—Hamby v Haskins (1982) 275 Ark 385, 630 SW2d 37.

**NJ**—DeRobertis v Randazzo (1983) 94 NJ 144, 462 A2d 1260 (citing annotation).

A paralegal who began with the A.L.R. in researching the dog-bite problem would have seen a reference to the Indiana cases and been able to answer the question as to the law in Indiana. The A.L.R. annotations break down legal problems into subissues and point out factual differences that change results in the cases. A.L.R. can provide a quick background analysis of relevant cases from various jurisdictions. The research is current and topical. Many times it provides a quick answer to the research problem.

**Treatises.** Experts write books on particular areas of the law. Known as **treatises**, some of these works give invaluable insight and analysis of the legal problems arising in the areas they cover. In fact, certain treatises contain some of the classic explanations of the law. A treatise by a noted expert might be very persuasive to a court on some issues. Most treatises are used like encyclopedias. They contain subject-matter indexes and individual topical headings. The text material references the researcher to footnotes that cite to the source law. Treatises are typically updated by pocket parts, although some treatises are published in a loose-leaf format.

Some lawyers read treatises for both background and analysis information on problems. Paralegals may not have access to treatises in the law libraries they use, but where treatises are available they can provide a depth of treatment unparalleled in other secondary sources.

**Legal Periodicals.** Law schools and law associations publish journals of articles written by experts, professors, students, and others on various legal topics. As you walk through a large university library, the number of these law journals is overwhelming.

However, the paralegal who has researched magazine articles through the *Readers Guide to Periodical Literature* will feel comfortable with the *Index to Legal Periodicals.* This index is broken down into three categories: a subject and author index, a table-of-cases index, and a book review index. There is a cumulative index for the period 1926 to 1976, with supplemental volumes covering the period after 1976, including monthly pamphlets for the most recent year.

Some of these journal articles are arcane and pedantic. Some are legal classics. Some are written by law school students with little practical information. Some are written from a practical rather than a theoretical standpoint.

**POINTER: As you read a legal periodical, treatise, or encyclopedia, learn to read the footnotes. The footnotes contain citations to cases and other legal reference materials that support the text. Footnotes are a valuable finding tool for locating primary source materials.**

Journal articles offer a wealth of background information. Although rarely will you initiate your research with law review articles, some scholars do, and they find them effective for this purpose. Unfortunately, paralegals do not have the opportunity to use the full range of legal periodicals unless they have access to a law school with a large library. Where available, legal periodicals can provide unique insight or problem-solving approaches that the researcher might never have thought of.

## Digests

Over four million legal cases have been reported in the United States. Each case may discuss anywhere from one to more than a hundred points of law. Cases are published in chronological order, and there is no way to look up a particular case or point of law from a particular case without a finding tool of some sort. Paralegals can use an encyclopedia, the A.L.R., or a treatise for finding cases. A digest, however, is designed solely for this purpose. To locate a specific case or to locate a series of cases, use a digest.

**Indexing for Digests.** A digest is an index of cases. It is an outline of all legal points covered by case law. As courts develop new rules of law, the digest is expanded. West Publishing Company has the most extensive digests for use in case-law research. West's outline of legal points covered by their digest system consists of seven major headings, over 400 topics, and over 40,000 subtopics. When a case is decided, West Publishing is sent a copy of the slip opinion from the court. A West editor reads the slip opinion and summarizes each legal point covered by it. Then the editor checks the 40,000 subtopics and assigns each summary a key number from the West outline. Each summary is then placed under the appropriate key number in the West digests.

**Finding the Digest Topic.** Although a digest is simply an index for finding cases, it is so large that West needs separate indexes for the digest. There are several ways to access information from a digest.

***Descriptive Word Index.*** First, there is a subject or descriptive-word index. This descriptive-word index is like the index used by legal encyclopedias or the A.L.R. except that it gives the researcher a key number to look under. To locate the topic and key number, use the TAPP rule. Digest entries are listed in alphabetical order. Under each alphabetical entry are each of the subtopics (Figure 3-13). So if the descriptive-word index referred you to Anim 🔑 53, then simply go to the main volume that contains the topic Animals and look under 🔑 53. There the researcher will find cases decided during the period covered by the digest that discuss this point of law. Under Animals 🔑 53, the researcher will find a summary of various cases with their citations.

***The Table of Contents in Each Digest Volume.*** Second, instead of using the descriptive-word index, you could have simply gone to the main volume and looked directly under Animals to find the precise key number. See Figure 3-14. The topics are arranged alphabetically so you would find Animals in the volume that begins with the topic Abandonment. Each digest volume has on its spine the first and last topic covered in that volume. This approach is usually helpful if the researcher knows exactly what heading to look under or becomes frustrated with the descriptive-word index.

***West Headnotes.*** Third, sometimes you will find the key number when you are reading a case. In the front of each case are the headnotes that appear in the digest. Look again at *Mauller v. City of Columbus* on page 234 of the Appendix and cited in Chapter 2 of this text. It has headnotes at the beginning of the case. If you had discovered this case by using another secondary tool, you could have used the headnote number for the rest of your research. The key number system is the same in each of the West digests and case reporters; therefore, once you have located the right key number, you use it in every West digest.

***Table of Cases.*** Fourth, sometimes you will remember a name of a case dealing with a precise legal point but you do not remember the citation for the case. Digests have a Table of Cases by plaintiff and by defendant. So if you know only the name of one party, you can still locate a case citation. After locating the case, the researcher can find the key number for the point of law.

***Words and Phrases.*** Fifth, a digest has a section on words and phrases. Whenever a word or phrase is defined, it is listed alphabetically in this section of the digest under the word or phrase.

**FIGURE 3-13 EXCERPT FROM THE DESCRIPTIVE-WORD INDEX IN THE *INDIANA DIGEST***

DOCUMENTS 1 Ind D—606

**References are to Digest Topics and Key Numbers**

**FIGURE 3-14 EXCERPT FROM THE TABLE OF CONTENTS IN THE *INDIANA DIGEST* VOLUME**

**ANIMALS**

*Scope-Note.*

INCLUDES animals the subjects of property or of legal protection or regulation, other than game and fish; nature and incidents of rights of property in animals, and liabilities for injuries by them; regulations for their protection from disease, ill treatment, etc., and relating to estrays; contracts for feeding, care, and use or hire; and the offense of cruelty to animals.

**Matters not in this topic, treated elsewhere, see Descriptive-Word Index.**

*Analysis.*

1. Nature of property.
2. Animals subjects of ownership.
3. Evidence of ownership in general.
4. Licenses.
5. Marks and brands.
6. ———— Adoption and use in general.
7. ———— Statutory regulations.
8. ———— Recording.
9. ———— Transfer.
10. ———— Evidence of ownership.
11. ———— Destroying or altering.
12. ———— False marking or branding.
13. ———— Criminal prosecutions.

* * *

The keynote appearing in this illustration is used in connection with the key numbering and index system of West Publishing Company.

The West digest uses each of these case location methods, methods that are not much different from indexes used in nonlegal research. A digest is just an index of cases. It is unique only in that there is an index for this index. Otherwise there would be no effective way to access the points of law covered by the millions of cases.

Sometimes there may be more than one key number dealing with a point of law. If the case is indexed under only one of these points, the researcher can miss finding a case or cases. Try different key numbers if the case summaries do not appear to be on point. Look at other key numbers under the same topic to see if more precise cases can be located on the subject. Remember, the same key number system is used in each West digest. Once you find a key number, it works for each digest published by West. Store this information if more research will be necessary later in the case. Read the entire case. Cases are not always summarized under the correct key number. That is why it is always a good idea to use alternative finding tools such as the A.L.R. or an encyclopedia.

**Updating for Digests.** Digests are generally updated by annual pocket parts. In fact, each of the West digests except the *American Digest System* uses pocket parts for updating. These pocket parts are supplemented by pamphlets usually quarterly or biannually. Do not forget to look in the pocket parts as well as the pamphlets to find more recent cases. Note that cases will be decided even after these pocket parts and pamphlets have been sent to the subscribers. To find even more current cases, go directly to the latest volumes of the jurisdiction's reporter system. Each volume of a West reporter and each West advance sheet will have a digest for that volume as well.

The *American Digest System* is updated by the General Digest Series. Each month a new volume will be sent to the subscribers containing the cases most recently decided. A researcher must look in every volume of the General Series of this *American Digest System* to find cases decided during the relevant period. This is a laborious process.

**Variety of Digests.** The sole function of a digest is to locate case authority. There are different digests for different jurisdictions. Although most states have their own digest, a few states rely instead on a regional digest. There are digests for some specialized courts (such as bankruptcy), and in specialized areas (such as Social Security). There is a separate digest for finding federal cases. Two other digests are designed solely for finding cases of the U. S. Supreme Court. The *American Digest System* is a national digest for all cases dating from the inception of our country to the present.

The paralegal starts a case search by looking for a binding precedent. So begin looking for state cases in a state digest if one is available and in a regional digest if no state digest is available. Begin looking for federal cases in the *Federal Digest*, which is now in its fifth series. The *Federal Digest* covered cases prior to 1939; *Modern Federal Practice Digest* covered cases from 1939 to 1961; *Federal Practice Digest* 2d covered cases from 1962 to 1975; and *Federal Practice Digest* 3d covered cases from 1975 to the present. West now has started the *Federal Practice Digest* 4th, which is not complete. Begin looking for bankruptcy cases in the *Bankruptcy Digest*. Look for U.S. Supreme Court cases through either the *U.S. Supreme Court Digest*, West, or *U.S. Supreme Court Digest*, Lawyers Co-operative.

Only if you cannot find any binding precedent in that jurisdiction's digest would you use any other digest. To expand the search, you might use the *American Digest System*, although this process is time-consuming and takes considerable effort. Each of these digests is published by West except for the *U.S. Supreme Court Digest*, which is published by Lawyers Co-operative.

There is a digest to find cases for every jurisdiction. Pinpointing what digest to use initially saves research time. Figure 3-15 shows how to make this choice.

**Use of State Digests.** Let's study a typical state digest. By now you are well aware that the first research step is the use of an index. In consulting a digest, the researcher usually begins with the descriptive-word index, commonly contained in separate volumes at the beginning or the end of the digest set. This index will provide the key number reference. Merely look under the appropriate

FIGURE 3-15 GUIDELINES FOR SELECTING THE APPROPRIATE DIGEST

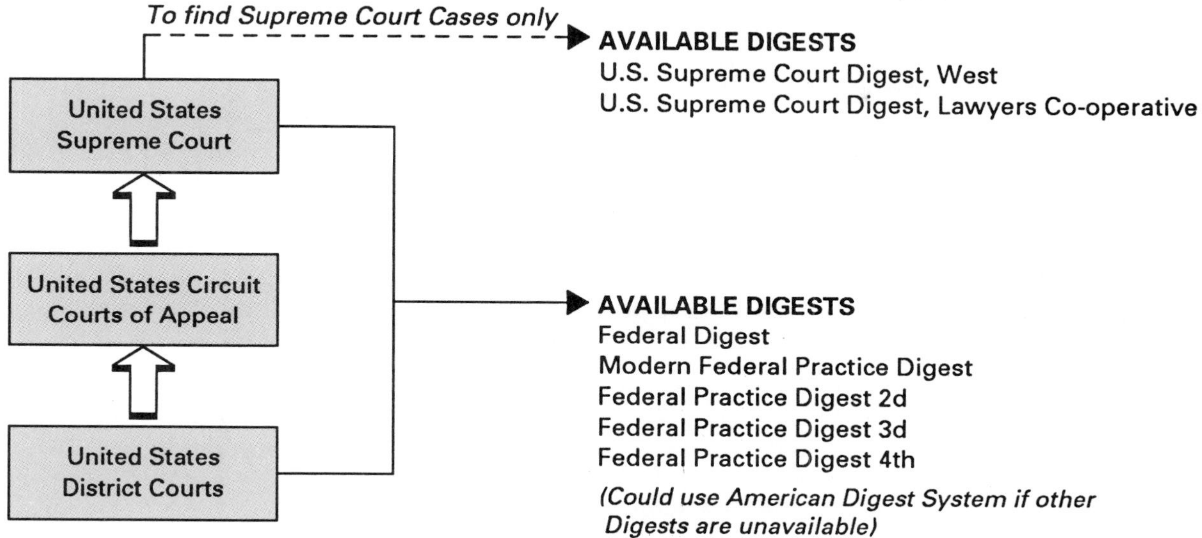


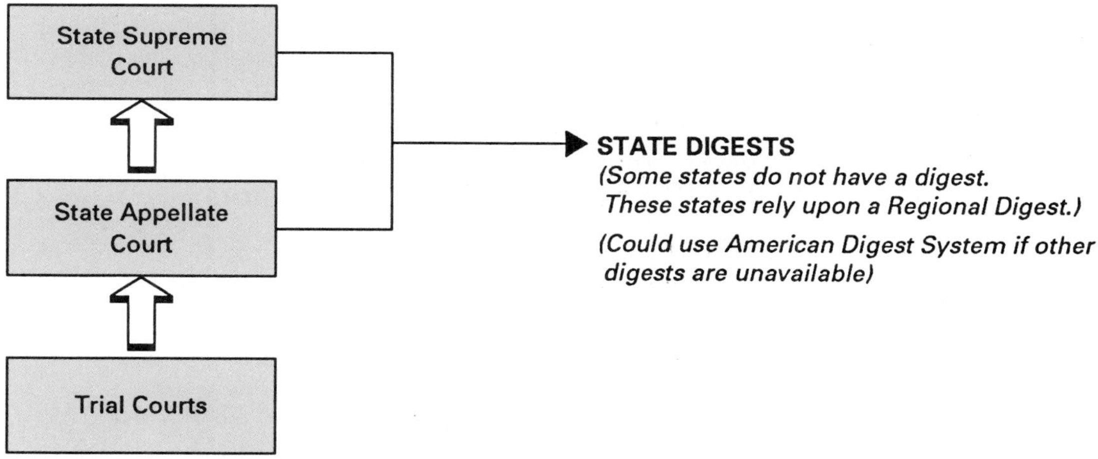


topic and key numbers in the main volume. In some states you will find more than one series or set of main volumes. In these cases, look under the appropriate topic and key number in both sets of volumes. Look then in the pocket parts. Pamphlets are put out to update the pocket parts, so check for pamphlets as well.

Try the one-bite/two-bite question using the Indiana digest. In the index, under Dogs (Figure 3-13), we find a key number reference to Anim ⚷ 53, 68. Under this topic and key number 53 in the main volume there are a number of cases cited. See Figure 3-16. You can find more recent information in the pocket parts and pamphlets.

**FIGURE 3-16 EXCERPT OF CASES CITED IN A DIGEST**

3 Ind D—375 **ANIMALS ⚷ 55**

**For references to other topics, see Descriptive-Word Index**

thorizing peace officers to kill any dog running at large unmuzzled in locality where muzzling of dogs is authorized, were not repealed by Acts of 1923, p. 243 (Burns' Ann. St. §§ 16-301, 16-302), declaring that dogs are personal property and requiring dogs to be listed for taxation the same as other personal property.

1925-1926 Op.Atty.Gen. 447.

**⚷ 53. — Injuries by animals at large.**

Ind. 1890. In an action to recover damages for personal injuries sustained by the plaintiff by being attacked by a cow belonging to the defendant, which he permitted to run at large, a complaint is defective that fails to allege that the animal possessed a vicious disposition, or propensity, which inclined it to attack mankind. Without such allegation there is necessarily no charge that the defendant had notice of any such evil disposition. And as the wilful conduct of the animal in attacking the plaintiff was not such as the defendant had a right to expect, or might anticipate, he is not responsible for the injury caused by such unexpected and wilful conduct.

Klenberg v. Russell, 25 N.E. 596, 125 Ind. 531.

Ind. 1884. In the absence of the passage by the county commissioners of an order, under Rev.St.1881, § 2637 (Burns' Ann.St. § 16-101), allowing cattle to run at large, the owner of cattle running at large and doing damage is liable, without regard to their habits or to the quality of fences through which they break.

Stone v. Kopka, 100 Ind. 458.

App. 1909. Owner of cows wrongfully allowing them to run at large on highway is not liable for injuries caused by horse frightened at the cows and running away; there being no special circumstances, such as allowing them to run at large during nighttime, or that they so obstructed the beaten part of highway that a horse would be frightened.

Anderson v. Nesbitt, 88 N.E. 523, 43 Ind. App. 703.

**⚷ 54. — Persons liable for injuries.**

Persons liable for injuries by and to animals. C.J.S. Animals, §§ 164-167, 224.

**⚷ 55. — Actions.**

Ind. 1888. If the gates at the crossing are left open by the land-owner, or by a wrong-doer other than the railroad company, that is a matter of defence.

* * *

The keynote appearing in this illustration is used in connection with the key numbering and index system of West Publishing Company.

Because there may have been additional cases decided since West sent out the most recent digest pocket parts or pamphlets, the careful researcher will also look in the most recent advance sheets to the applicable regional reporter. Indiana is in the North Eastern region, so the paralegal would check the most recent volumes of the *North Eastern Reporter.* Each *North Eastern Reporter* has a digest of cases for that volume.

Regional digests are used the same way state digests are used. So are the specialized digests such as those for bankruptcy and Social Security cases.

**Use of Federal Digests.** Use federal digests the same way you use state digests. Start with the descriptive-word index and locate a key number. Because the *Federal Practice Digest* will soon consist of five series, the paralegal must look under the main volume in each series to find all federal cases dealing with any point of law. Accordingly, the researcher would look under the appropriate topic and key number in all four (soon to be five) series. In *Federal Practice Digest* 4th there are pocket parts and quarterly pamphlets to update them. To complete the research, look in the most recent advance sheets for the *Federal Supplement* (F. Supp.), the *Federal Reporter* (F.2d), and the *Supreme Court Reporter* (S. Ct.). You should now have all recent federal cases as well.

We can now give the paralegal a process to follow for most digest research:

**Step one:** Select a digest for the appropriate jurisdiction. (For example, use a state digest for state cases, a federal digest for federal cases.)

**Step two:** Use the descriptive-word index to find the appropriate topic and key number.

**Step three:** Look in the main volume of each series under the topic and key number.

**Step four:** Examine the pocket parts under the same topic and key number.

**Step five:** Look at the pamphlets, if any, under the topic and key number.

**Step six:** Look in the advance sheets for the reporters covering cases for that jurisdiction.

**Use of the *American Digest System*.** West has published a digest called the *American Digest System* to cover all cases in the United States. It is cumbersome to use, although the technique for using this set is not much different from the other sets. The *American Digest System* begins with the *Century Digest*, covering cases from the beginning of the set until 1986. The *Century Digest* is followed by sets called *Decennials*, each covering a ten-year period. For example, the *First Decennial* would cover cases from 1896 to 1906. This practice was followed until the *Ninth Decennial*. The *Ninth Decennial* is divided into two parts, each spanning a five-year period. Finally, there is a *General Digest*. Volumes are added to the *General Digest* series on a monthly basis. A researcher must consult each volume of the *General Digest* for more recent cases—not an insignificant task, since it will consist of sixty volumes at the end of a five-year period.

This is clearly time-consuming and burdensome. It is also an expensive set because at five-year intervals West Publishing will combine all cases with the same topic or key number in one volume and issue another set. The subscribers then are instructed to discard the *General Digest* Series—which might consist of sixty volumes. The main difference between other digests and the *American Digest System* is the updating methodology. The *American Digest System* does not use pocket parts. Instead, it is updated monthly by a new bound volume.

Use this set only if your search is broad-based. You will not use it frequently, but it is effective for locating all cases under a specific point of law. A national encyclopedia or the A.L.R. will sometimes be more effective than the *American Digest System* for finding cases in other jurisdictions. The process for finding every case under a specific key number in the *American Digest System* will follow these steps:

**Step one:** Locate topic and key number reference from descriptive-word index. (Remember, key numbers have been added at different times. You may need to look at the descriptive-word index for different series.)

**Step two:** Look under the topic and key number for *each* volume of the *General Digest.*

**Step three:** Look under the topic and key number for the *Ninth Decennial* in both Parts I and II.

**Step four:** Look under the topic and key number in the appropriate volume in each of the remaining eight *Decennials.*

**Step five:** Convert the topic and key number by using the table in the *First Decennial* to a topic and key number for the *Century Digest,* which has a key numbering system different from the later sets.

**Advantages and Disadvantages of Digests.** Remember, a digest is just an index. It is an excellent finding tool for locating citations to cases. It even includes alphabetical tables of cases. If you know the name of a party to the case, you can locate the full citation, which is another valuable function of a digest. But a digest has many shortcomings. Sometimes a point of law is improperly summarized or put under the wrong heading. Sometimes two key number headings contain the cases dealing with the same point of law. Sometimes the index is difficult to use. If the researcher starts with the wrong key number, considerable search time can be wasted. Yet digests pinpoint cases better than other tools do. Sometimes they reveal citations to cases factually similar to the researched problem when no other tool does so. And digests identify series of cases more accurately than other available tools.

A digest gives no explanation as to how cases interrelate. A digest does not tell the researcher if a trend is developing or unraveling or whether the cases are contradictory or consistent. The digest just helps *find* cases. The analysis comes from you. To explain trends or apparent inconsistencies, you will have to use other tools, such as encyclopedias, the A.L.R., or treatises.

Often, more than one case will relate to the issue presented. Try different key numbers if the case summaries do not appear relevant. Look at other key numbers under the same topic to verify that the correct key number has been found.

When you begin a research project using a digest, your inclination may be to stop too soon. Keep plugging away. Usually a case quite similar to yours has already been decided. Finding that one case among more than four million decisions is not always simple. But keep trying. Law research is an area in which perseverance leads to success.

## Annotated Codes

Constitutions, statutes, and court rules are researched according to a common technique. Start with an annotated code. Usually it is safe to assume a federal problem begins with one of these source authorities rather than a case, as there is no substantial body of federal common law. At the federal level, the *United States Code Annotated* (U.S.C.A.) and *United States Code Service* (U.S.C.S.) both annotate the U.S. Constitution and the rules for the federal courts. Most annotated state codes include references to that state's constitution as well as to the rules for that state's courts. The technique for using a state or federal annotated code is almost always the same.

**Researching a Statute.** If you do not already know the citation, begin with the index volumes in any annotated code to find the cite to the applicable statutes. (Again the TAPP rule will be helpful.) Read the statute. Then read the annotations for summaries of cases construing the statute.

Sometimes you will already know the citation to the statute. Most civil rights attorneys and their paralegals, for example, look automatically at 42 U.S.C. Section 1983 for certain types of cases. When the practitioner needs supporting case law, the researcher simply starts the process by looking under Title 42, Section 1983.

Using an annotated code like U.S.C.A. or U.S.C.S. is easy if you can overcome the sometimes poor indexing. In Chapter 2, we looked at a mail theft statute. Now let's assume you work in an attorney general's office as an investigator. Your supervisor has asked for your opinion as to whether a person could be charged with a crime for opening mail found on her apartment floor but belonging to her roommate. The mail had been dropped by the mail carrier onto the hallway floor through a slot in the door.

We will start with the U.S.C.A. (The process is the same if you start with U.S.C.S.) Naturally you open the index to Theft. You find nothing that answers the inquiry. At this stage you apply the TAPP rule and, redefining the search, open the index to Mail (see Figure 3-17).

This leads you to the statute shown in Figure 3-18.

The next step is to look at the summaries in the annotation. A code is a grouping of laws by subject matter. In an annotated code, the publisher adds relevant information and authority after each individual statute. Typically, it provides historical information such as how the statute has been amended. After this historical commentary, the publisher summarizes the cases that have discussed the statute. These cases are categorized under subtopics. In the mail theft situation, note 79 deals with "mail slots." See Figure 3-19.

**FIGURE 3-17 EXCERPT FROM U.S.C.A. INDEX**



Now consult the pocket parts under the same statute and under the same subtopic reference. See Figure 3-20. You find a more recent case listed under this subtopic.

**FIGURE 3-18 EXCERPT FROM MAIL THEFT STATUTE, 18 U.S.C. 1708**

**§ 1708. Theft or receipt of stolen mail matter generally**

Whoever steals, takes, or abstracts, or by fraud or deception obtains, or attempts so to obtain, from or out of any mail, post office, or station thereof, letter box, mail receptacle, or any mail route or other authorized depository for mail matter, or from a letter or mail carrier, any letter, postal card, package, bag, or mail, or abstracts or removes from any such letter, package, bag, or mail, any article or thing contained therein, or secretes, embezzles, or destroys any such letter, postal card, package, bag, or mail, or any article or thing contained therein.

* * *

**FIGURE 3-19 ANNOTATION SHOWING CASES ADDRESSING "MAIL SLOTS"**

**18 § 1708**
**Note 79** **CRIMES Pt. 1**

**79. — Mail slots**

This section covering mail receptacles and authorized depositories of mail includes mail slots. Wade v. U.S., C.A.Cal.1972, 457 F.2d 335.

A floor in a private home where mail was delivered to several persons, equally accessible to all, and was delivered by dropping mail through a small letter slot in wall at left of door, was not an "authorized depository for mail matter" within this section stating penalty to be imposed against a person who steals, takes, or abstracts a letter from authorized depository for mail matter, or who removes any article or thing therein from such letter. U.S. v. Askey, D.C.Tex.1952, 108 F.Supp. 408.

**80. — Mail trucks**

A mail truck in a railroad terminal was an "authorized depository for mail," within former section 317 of this title, which penalized the stealing from an authorized depository for mail. Burton v. U.S., 1948, 169 F.2d 969, 83 U.S.App. D.C. 369.

**81. — Porches**

Where evidence clearly showed that check was taken from porch, defendant could not be convicted of possessing check stolen from authorized depository of mail even though package of checks was placed on porch because it was too big to go into mailbox. U.S. v. Thomas, D.C.Tex.1973, 361 F.Supp. 978.

**82. — Receptacles**

Even assuming that rod attached to mail box was not a "mail receptacle" within meaning of this section's prohibition against taking a letter "from or out of a mail receptacle," such would not preclude finding that check, which was "clothes-pinned" to rod attached to mail box, was stolen from "mail route" as also prescribed by this section, which prescribed offense of unlawful possession of stolen mail matter. U.S. v. Douglas, C.A.Okl.1982, 668 F.2d 459, certiorari denied 102 S.Ct. 2908, 457 U.S. 1108, 73 L.Ed.2d 1317.

Act of defendant in taking a letter which was clipped to a clothespin hooked or fastened to the lid of a mailbox fell within statutory prohibition against taking a letter from or out of a mail receptacle. U.S. v. White, C.A.Colo.1975, 510 F.2d 448.

**83. — Store counters**

While, in view of evidence that postman mistakenly left another's letter containing money orders on front counter of

FIGURE 3-20 POCKET PART WITH CASES ADDRESSING "MAIL SLOTS"

**CRIMES AND CRIMINAL PROCEDURE** **18 § 1708 Note 262**

L.Ed.2d 715, certiorari denied 104 S.Ct. 1314, 465 U.S. 1038, 79 L.Ed.2d 711.

**78. — Mail routes**

University office was clearly delivery point on mail route and receptacle where mail was customarily placed, for purposes of prosecution for possession of contents of letter which had been stolen from mail, regardless of whether distribution of mail from office to dormitories by university employees was considered further extension of "mail route," where postal authorities themselves delivered mail to the office. U.S. v. Cochran, D.Me.1985, 646 F.Supp. 7.

**79. — Mail slots**

Mail which had been placed through mail slot in outer door of two-family residence and which fell to floor in common area was in authorized depository for mail matter and, thus, defendant who removed mail from common area which was not addressed to her could be convicted of possessing checks stolen from the mail. U.S. v. Nolan, C.A.3 (Pa.) 1986. 784 F.2d 496, certiorari denied 106 S.Ct. 2257, 476 U.S. 1144, 90 L.Ed.2d 702.

**119. — Entrapment**

U.S. v. Rhodes, 713 F.2d 463 [main volume] certiorari denied 104 S.Ct. 535, 464 U.S. 1012, 78 L.Ed.2d 715, certiorari denied 104 S.Ct. 1314, 465 U.S. 1038, 79 L.Ed.2d 711.

**131. — Inferences**

In prosecution for possession of stolen mail based upon defendant's possession of stolen item 13 months after its theft, trial court did not err in instructing jury regarding inference which could be drawn from possession of recently stolen property, where judge carefully explained that inference of guilty knowledge based on possession was merely permissible and not mandatory, and that inference became more doubtful with passage of time. U.S. v. Johnson, C.A.Mich.1984, 741 F.2d 854, certiorari denied 105 S.Ct. 573, 469 U.S. 1075, 83 L.Ed.2d 512.

**133. — Knowledge**

Instruction defining knowledge required for conviction for possessing check from United States mail which allowed jury to infer defendant's knowledge that check was stolen merely from fact that she possessed it was proper where charge referred to defendant's unexplained possession of check, and defendant disputed that she had ever possessed check. U.S. v. Peterson, C.A.2 (N.Y.) 1987, 808 F.2d 969.

**135. — Possession of stolen mail matter**

U.S. v. Rhodes, 713 F.2d 463 [main volume] certiorari denied 104 S.Ct. 535, 464 U.S. 1012, 78 L.Ed.2d 715, certiorari denied 104 S.Ct. 1314, 465 U.S. 1038, 79 L.Ed.2d 711.

Are you finished? This is the hardest question in research. A new case might have been decided since these pocket parts were issued or the publisher might not have properly summarized a case. You might consult the advance sheets or even some secondary sources.

**Researching a Constitutional Issue or Court Rule.** Researching a constitutional issue or a court rule follows the same procedure. In Chapter 2, we discussed *Griswold v. Connecticut*, which held that there was a right of marital privacy. We saw how this right was extended to the abortion area. Suppose that you want to expand your research on related constitutional issues. If you want to learn what a state can or cannot do prior to viability, for example, you should look under the annotated headnotes to the Fourteenth Amendment. Health Headnote 3807 (viability) in the pocket parts would lead you to *Webster v. Reproductive Services*, 109 S. Ct. 3040 (1989). See Figure 3-21.

The process for using an annotated code is quite simple:

**Step one:** Select the annotated code for the appropriate jurisdiction. For federal law use either U.S.C.A. or U.S.C.S.

**Step two:** Use the descriptive-word index to find the information for the relevant statute.

**Step three:** Read the statute.

**Step four:** Read the annotated summaries after the statute to locate cases or other authority relevant to the inquiry.

**Step five:** Read the pocket parts.

## Loose-Leaf Services

Some paralegals work in specialized areas such as tax or labor law. Loose-leaf sets are published for many of these specialized areas of practice. Publishers use a loose-leaf format because as the law changes or needs updating, the publisher can simply rewrite the applicable pages. Then the outdated pages can be removed and the new pages inserted.

Loose-leaf services try to provide in one specialized set of volumes everything the researcher will need for answering problems. These sets copy all relevant statutes, regulations, and cases, together with an explanation of these materials. Loose-leaf services may have topical indexes but will almost always have a subject index as well. Typically, loose-leaf services implement a paragraph numbering system rather than page numbering. A sample page from a loose-leaf service is seen in Figure 3-22.

Often the loose-leaf service may collect related cases from administrative agencies or the courts and publish these cases as a set of books along with the loose-leaf set. The loose-leaf set will provide an index digest for the cases.

## Words and Phrases

Courts will often decide cases as to the meaning of a word in a statute or transaction document. West Publishing Co. has published a set called *Words and Phrases*, which collects these cases. West Publishing then provides a summary of the case and a citation to each case. It is updated by pocket parts. *Words and Phrases* is designed to help find cases and define words. When a word has a doubtful meaning in a statute or other authority or in a transaction document, *Words and Phrases* helps you locate cases that may have settled the meaning of the word.

**FIGURE 3-21 EXCERPT OF ANNOTATIONS CONCERNING CONSTITUTIONAL ISSUE**

**Amend. XIV, § 1**
**Note 3804**

**CONSTITUTION**

could conclude that abortions were immoral ''injuries to be avoided'' under necessity statute, except insofar as *Roe v. Wade* established absolute constitutional bar to all state regulation of abortion during first trimester. People v. Archer, N.Y.City Ct.1988, 537 N.Y.S.2d 726.

**3805. — Second trimester**

Ragsdale v. Turnock, 625 F.Supp. 1212 [main volume] vacated in part and affirmed in part 841 F.2d 1358.

Statute which provided that physician who failed to submit second trimester abortion tissue remains to qualified pathologist shall be charged with third-degree misdemeanor was not unconstitutional; section was directed at attending physician rather than patient, and thus, did not pose unacceptable risk of deterring woman's choice to have abortion. Northeast Women's Center, Inc. v. McMonagle, E.D.Pa.1987, 665 F.Supp. 1147.

**3807. — Viability**

State's interest in protecting potential human life does not come into existence only at point of viability and thus, there should not be rigid line allowing state regulation of abortion after viability but prohibiting regulation before viability. (Per Chief Justice with two Justices concurring). Webster v. Reproductive Health Services, Mo. 1989, 109 S.Ct. 3040.

**3810. — Informed consent**

Thronburgh v. American College of Obstetricians and Gynecologists, 106 S.Ct. 2169 [main volume] 476 U.S. 747, 90 L.Ed.2d 779.

**3812. — Spouses**

Spouse of pregnant woman does not have legal right to prevent abortion and require child to be carried to term. Arnold v. Board of Educ. of Escambia County Ala., C.A.11 (Ala.) 1989, 880 F.2d 305.

Provision of Georgia Parental Notification Act that requirement that minor's parent be notified of abortion must be waived if unemancipated minor is mature and well educated enough to make intelligently the decision on her own means that minor must be mature enough to make intelligently the abortion decision in consultation with her physician but without participation of parents, not that minor must meet higher standard of competence than adult women whose right to abortion is the right to make their decision in consultation with their physicians, and thus, standard is not unconstitutional. Planned Parenthood Ass'n of Atlanta Area, Inc. v. Harris, N.D.Ga.1987, 670 F.Supp. 971.

**3814a. — Corecion**

Coercing a minor to abort fetus violates the minor's constitutionally protected freedom to choose whether to abort or bear her child. Arnold v. Board of Educ. of Escambia County Ala., C.A.11 (Ala.) 1989 880 F.2d 305.

**3816. — Judicial consent**

Rule intended to provide for expedited appeal of action brought by pregnant woman under 18 who was not emancipated, or who has been adjudged incompetent, to obtain judicial authorization for abortion, but which does not provide for appeal in case in which trial court fails to act

**FIGURE 3-22 EXCERPT FROM *SOCIAL SECURITY LAW AND PRACTICE, A LOOSE-LEAF SERVICE PUBLISHED BY THE LAWYERS CO-OPERATIVE PUBLISHING COMPANY***

**ANALYSIS OF PARTICULAR IMPAIRMENTS** **§ 42:26**

tions, and that the claimant's severe pain could make frequent doctors visits useless.[19]

**II. MUSCULOSKELETAL DISORDERS**

General References

20 CFR Part 404, Subpart P, Appx 1 (Listings) §§ 1.00-1.13, 101.00-101.08
L Ed Index to Annotations: Disability; Physical Disability; Social Security and Unemployment Compensation
15 Federal Procedural Forms, Social Security and Medicare § 60:63
16A Am Jur Legal Forms 2d, Social Security and Medicare § 235:93
24 Am Jur Trials 699, Social Security Hearings and Appeals in Disability Cases §§ 57-59
ALR Digest, Social Security § 12.5
Gilbert & Peters, Social Security Disability Claims § 22:2 (Form 34), Appendix 30
What constitutes "disability" within Federal Social Security Act. 77 ALR2d 641.
VERALEX™; Cases and annotations referred to herein can be further researched through the VERALEX electronic retrieval system's two services, AUTO-CITE® and SHOWME™. Use Auto-Cite to check citations for form, parallel references, prior and later history, and annotation references. Use SHOWME to display the full text of cases and annotations.

A. GENERAL CONSIDERATIONS

**§ 42:26. Introduction.**

Various bone disorders, including spinal disorders, arthritis, and fractured, deformed, or lost limbs, may be found disabling on the basis of medical evidence alone, thereby relieving a claimant of the necessity to prove inability to work.

The evaluation of musculoskeletal impairments as disabling mainly involves the determination of the effect such an impairment has on the individual's loss of function. An individual's capacity for movement (motility) may be restricted by amputation, deformity, pain, or a combination of these factors.[1] Loss of function, and factors involved in establishing loss, are discussed at §§ 42:30-42:35.

Pain is recognized as an important factor causing functional loss in musculoskeletal impairments by the SSA and is specified as one of the elements which must be met in many of the listed categories (§§ 42:33-42:34). Nevertheless, the SSA's general rule concerning pain as a symptom (§§ 42:1 et seq.) applies in the evaluation of musculoskeletal impairments, so that pain must be associated with applicable abnormal signs and laboratory findings.[2]

Additionally, the SSA has specified the objective criteria required under the musculoskeletal listings for evaluating the claimant's impairment and for corroborating the claimant's statements regarding his impairment (§§ 42:36-42:37).

19. Mitchell v Schweiker (1982, WD Mo) 551 F Supp 1084.

1. 20 CFR Part 404, Subpart P, Appx 1 (Listings) § 1.00(A).

2. 20 CFR Part 404, Subpart P, Appx 1 (Listings) § 1.00(A).

**SOCIAL SECURITY LAW AND PRACTICE** **35**

### Regulations

By law, every regulation must be published in the *Federal Register* before its enactment. The *Federal Register* lists regulations in chronological order. Like session laws, it is not an effective research tool. The federal regulations are also contained in the *Code of Federal Regulations* (C.F.R). Like the *U.S. Code* and individual state codes, the C.F.R. arranges the regulations by subject matter and the same title arrangement used by the *U.S. Code*. The C.F.R. is poorly indexed, although recent editions have made some improvements. Often the paralegal will need to peruse the topic headings of the applicable volume to find the appropriate regulation. Alternatively, the researcher can find the *U.S. Code* citation authorizing the regulation through the *U.S. Code*. The *Code of Federal Regulations* contains a table converting U.S.C. citations to C.F.R. citations. This method sometimes proves effective, but most of the time the researcher must simply persevere. At the end of the C.F.R. is a volume entitled *LSA: List of C.F.R. Sections Affected*. This volume informs the reader which *Federal Register* citations affected what regulations during the most recent year. The *Federal Register* also contains another table in the most recent monthly publication, detailing the same information for the past month. This is the update methodology for C.F.R. users. Each year the government replaces the current C.F.R. with a new set.

## EXPANDING THE LEGAL RESEARCH

In most legal research courses, the paralegal is given a problem and expected to find an answer. In some situations, as we have seen, there may be no source authority that answers the query for your jurisdiction, or the answer may be unclear because case results conflict or no pattern emerges in the cases. At first, paralegals have difficulty with fuzzy answers. They also have difficulty with situations where the search reveals there is *no* source law specifically answering the query. However, each of these situations presents a real research possibility. Imagine if a legal research student were assigned a research problem that had no answer. The diligent student would spend many frustrating hours in the law library and find nothing. Then the teacher would announce that there was no answer! This happens repeatedly in legal research.

If there is no binding authority answering the inquiry in your jurisdiction, the next step is to look for persuasive precedent in other jurisdictions or for general principles from the existing body of law within the same jurisdiction to answer the inquiry. In these situations, the researcher may look for analogous law for patterns in the existing law.

Before expanding the search for persuasive precedents in other jurisdictions, however, double-check the law by using alternative finding tools. If a digest was used first, use an encyclopedia to see if the answer is the same. Look at the A.L.R. or a treatise. Sometimes this will expose errors in the method used. Assuming no error, the search should then be expanded to look for persuasive precedents or analogous law in the same or other jurisdictions.

## COMPLETING THE LEGAL RESEARCH

At some point, the research must stop, perhaps because the researcher has answered the query or perhaps because there is no answer to the query. At this point, the updating process begins. However, there is no reason to quit researching. A new law review article may provide a new perspective or approach. The paralegal might stumble across a treatise that suggests a different result. Research can direct the thought process, but your thought process will often redirect your research as well.

As I teach legal research strategies to my paralegal students, I emphasize the wide range of available updating techniques. I have seen too many lawyers and students who stopped their research too soon. The lawyers go to court and are embarrassed when opposing lawyers tell them they are relying on cases that have been overruled or statutes that have been repealed. In most instances, the updated information could have been found by following only a few simple steps.

Most updated information will be found by simply using the pocket parts or pamphlets for one set of books in which you did your research. For example, if the statute was found in an annotated code, look at the pocket parts or pamphlets to that set. If you located the case in a digest, encyclopedia, or A.L.R., look in the pocket parts and pamphlets to these sets. This is a process that must become automatic. It prevents the researcher from overlooking the most obvious changes in the source authority.

### Shepard's

Third-year law students like to impress first-year law students by asking if they have "shepardized their cases" yet. The first-year students have no idea what this means. However, if all of law school were as simple as learning about **Shepard's**, then law school would be quite easy. Shepard's Citations is a division of McGraw-Hill Book Company that exclusively publishes updates of cases and other authority. Almost any source authority discussed in this chapter can be updated by a *Shepard's*.

Law changes constantly. The paralegal cannot assume a case or statute will remain the same. All legal researchers must keep their work current to make sure there has been no change in the law. A case you found could have been appealed and reversed by a higher court. Another decision in another case could have overruled the case or limited its application in some fashion. Shepard's has developed a method for providing this history on every reported case.

There is a *Shepard's* to update every case, statute, constitutional provision, and regulation. Each regional case reporter has a *Shepard's* for that set. Each state's statutes have a set of *Shepard's*. The federal supplements and federal reporters each have a *Shepard's*. The federal Constitution, statutes, and regulations all have their Shepard's. In fact, there is even a *Shepard's* for law review articles.

Whenever a source authority is material to the result of your analysis, it should be **shepardized**. The appropriate *Shepard's* gives the researcher the history of the authority being updated. It lists every time a case has been cited in another case. It tells the subsequent history of a case or statute.

*Shepard's* is not designed to be used in the initial phases of legal research. It is not generally used as a finding tool for cases or statutes. Often you will locate additional cases by using *Shepard's*, however. The purpose of *Shepard's* is to update a case, statute, or other authority after it has been located through other sources.

**How to Use Shepard's.** In the front of each volume of a *Shepard's*, there is a table of symbols used to describe the changes in the law. For cases, *Shepard's* tells if a case has been reversed, overruled, distinguished, explained, followed, or harmonized. See Figure 3-23. For statutes, *Shepard's* tells if a statute has been repealed, modified, nullified, or affected by the case law. See Figure 3-24.

**FIGURE 3-23 *SHEPARD'S* ABBREVIATIONS FOR HISTORY AND TREATMENT OF CASES**

**ABBREVIATIONS—ANALYSIS**

| | |
|---|---|
| **History of Case** | |
| a (affirmed) | Same case affirmed on appeal. |
| cc (connected case) | Different case from case cited but arising out of same subject matter or intimately connected therewith. |
| D (dismissed) | Appeal from same case dismissed. |
| m (modified) | Same case modified on appeal. |
| r (reversed) | Same case reversed on appeal. |
| s (same case) | Same case as case cited. |
| S (superseded) | Substitution for former opinion. |
| v (vacated) | Same case vacated. |
| Cert den | Certiorari or appeal denied or dismissed by Illinois Supreme Court. |
| US cert den | Certiorari denied by U.S. Supreme Court. |
| US cert dis | Certiorari dismissed by U.S. Supreme Court. |
| US reh den | Rehearing denied by U.S. Supreme Court. |
| US reh dis | Rehearing dismissed by U.S. Supreme Court. |
| **Treatment of Case** | |
| c (criticised) | Soundness of decision or reasoning in cited case criticised for reasons given. |
| d (distinguished) | Case at bar different either in law or fact from case cited for reasons given. |
| e (explained) | Statement of import of decision in cited case. Not merely a restatement of the facts. |
| f (followed) | Cited as controlling. |
| h (harmonized) | Apparent inconsistency explained and shown not to exist. |
| j (dissenting opinion) | Citation in dissenting opinion. |
| L (limited) | Refusal to extend decision of cited case beyond precise issues involved. |
| o (overruled) | Ruling in cited case expressly overruled. |
| p (parallel) | Citing case substantially alike or on all fours with cited case in its law or facts. |
| q (questioned) | Soundness of decision or reasoning in cited case questioned. |

### FIGURE 3-24 *SHEPARD'S* ABBREVIATIONS FOR HISTORY OF STATUTES

**ABBREVIATIONS—ANALYSIS**

**Form of Statute**

| | | | |
|---|---|---|---|
| Amend. | Amendment | Proc. | Proclamation |
| App. | Appendix | Pt. | Part |
| Art. | Article | Res. | Resolution |
| Ch. | Chapter | § | Section |
| Cl. | Clause | St. | Statutes at Large |
| Ex. Ord. | Executive Order | Subch. | Subchapter |
| H.C.R. | House Concurrent Resolution | Subcl. | Subclause |
| | | Subd. | Subdivision |
| No. | Number | Sub ¶ | Subparagraph |
| ¶ | Paragraph | Subsec. | Subsection |
| P.L. | Public Law | Vet. Reg. | Veterans' Regulations |
| Pr.L. | Private Law | | |

**Operation of Statute**

**Legislative**

| | | |
|---|---|---|
| A | (amended) | Statute amended. |
| Ad | (added) | New section added. |
| E | (extended) | Provisions of an existing statute extended in their application to a later statute, or allowance of additional time for performance of duties required by a statute within a limited time. |
| L | (limited) | Provisions of an existing statute declared not to be extended in their application to a later statute. |
| R | (repealed) | Abrogation of an existing statute. |
| Re-en | (re-enacted) | Statute re-enacted. |
| Rn | (renumbered) | Renumbering of existing sections. |
| Rp | (repealed in part) | Abrogation of part of an existing statute. |
| Rs | (repealed and superseded) | Abrogation of an existing statute and substitution of new legislation therefor. |
| Rv | (revised) | Statute revised. |
| S | (superseded) | Substitution of new legislation for an existing statute not expressly abrogated. |
| Sd | (suspended) | Statute suspended. |
| Sdp | (suspended in part) | Statute suspended in part. |
| Sg | (supplementing) | New matter added to an existing statute. |
| Sp | (superseded in part) | Substitution of new legislation for part of an existing statute not expressly abrogated. |
| Va | (validated) | |

**Judicial**

| | | | |
|---|---|---|---|
| C | Constitutional. | Vp | Void or invalid. |
| U | Unconstitutional. | Va | Valid. |
| Up | Unconstituional in part. | Vp | Void or invalid in part. |

There is a *Shepard's* for every state. Each state's *Shepard's* covers statutes, cases, constitutional provisions, and administrative regulations. The coverage for federal authority is the same. Hence the questions you ask before selecting a *Shepard's* are parallel to the ones you asked at the beginning of the research project: What is the source authority that needs shepardizing? In what jurisdiction is this authority that needs shepardizing? The answer to the first question ensures you use a case *Shepard's* rather than a statute *Shepard's*, and the answer to the second question ensures you use a New York *Shepard's* to look up a New York case.

The *Shepard's* are color coded. The burgundy volumes are the permanent books. Yellow pamphlets are semi-permanent volumes. Red and white pamphlets change quarterly. The researcher must look in the most recent quarterly edition (the red or white pamphlets), any yellow pamphlet, and each of the burgundy sets that have been published since the date your authority was decided or passed.

Every *Shepard's* is used in essentially the same way. The most frequently used sets of *Shepard's* are those dealing with case law. If you shepardize a state case, for example, look up the citation to the case in the *Shepard's* for that regional reporter. There is a *Shepard's* for Supreme Court cases, for the *Federal Reporter*, and for the *Federal Supplement*. A *Shepard's* works with either an official or unofficial citation to the case.

To use a *Shepard's* for case law, you need only a citation for the case to be shepardized. Then, using the volume number, turn to the page of the *Shepard's* that references this volume number. Then locate the page reference of the citation. See Figure 3-25. Every time the case you are shepardizing is cited in another case, there is an entry in *Shepard's*. *Shepard's* also tells if the case appears in an A.L.R. article or a law review article.

If you shepardize a statute, look up the citation to the statute following the same process as for a case. Let's look at the *Shepard's* entry for Title 18, Section 1708 (the mail theft statute) in Figure 3-26. Under this entry, the researcher can see the subsequent treatment of this statute. If a statute had been amended or modified this will be noted. If a later case held this statute as unconstitutional, this would likewise be noted. Follow the same process for a constitutional provision (Figure 3-27) or a regulation. The researcher uses the color-coded volumes in the same manner as in the case law research.

Let's look at *Griswold v. Connecticut* in *Shepard's*. First, note the year that the case was decided. *Griswold* was decided in 1965. The first time this case appears in the main volume is in Volume 4 of *Shepard's*. Under that entry, there are five and one-half pages of cases. Figure 3-28 is an excerpt from one of them. Second, look at the yellow, red, and white pamphlets, which reveal even more cases. Third, examine the symbols to see the various ways *Griswold* has been treated. Some cases limited *Griswold*; others explained it. Sometimes it is cited in a dissenting opinion. This implies that the shepardized case is not being followed as some judges think it should.

*Shepard's* is a means to check the status of a law or other authority. Before a case is cited as authority, the researcher must make sure the case has not been reversed by a higher court or overturned in a subsequent decision. Before a statute

## FIGURE 3-25 EXCERPT FROM THE *SHEPARD'S* ENTRY FOR A CASE

**CALIFORNIA REPORTER** **Vol. 50**

15A4234n
27A4985n
28A4929n

**—391—**
(241CA2d
[149)
2A21033s

**—397—**
(241CA2d85)
101CaR655
103CaR[5]41
109CaR[2]52
114CaR40
123CaR[5]493
144CaR[1]239
j149CaR[3]78
181CaR[1]677
181CaR[2]678
539P2d[5]61
41JBC650
30A21108s

**—402—**
(241CA2d
[237)
83CaR[2]230
91CaR[3]126
91CaR[4]126
93CaR[3]529
123CaR[2]913
130CaR[3]385
167CaR47
185CaR[4]230
c189CaR[3]189
194CaR559
197CaR[2]700
f208CaR[1]491
Mo
622SW758
37HLJ598

**—408—**
(241CA2d93)
s68CaR59
51CaR[4]644
52CaR[4]790
53CaR[8]797
54CaR56
68CaR[13]539
68CaR[14]539
76CaR556
79CaR[9]845
89CaR[5]294

**—414—**
v54CaR385
v419P2d641
60CaR[9]553
76A2502s
95A21122s

**—429—**
(241CA2d
[289)
54CaR[3]492
54CaR[4]492
14CLA100

**—437—**
(241CA2d
[189)
55CaR[1]549
65CaR[4]110
73CaR[4]707
78CaR[2]442
92CaR[4]212
98CaR[3]69
98CaR726
d118CaR[2]588
Ark
541SW921
Ill
261NE434
308NE16
NJ
232A2d143
264A2d737
10A3314s
10A3331n
10A3345n

**—440—**
(241CA2d
[200)
61CaR[5]781
61CaR[2]782
65CaR[7]57
68CaR[6]463
68CaR[7]463
68CaR[8]463
68CaR[9]463
70CaR[8]486
74CaR[1]212
75CaR[9]202
d76CaR[3]197
78CaR[3]55
78CaR[1]903
78CaR[10]904
83CaR[10]728

**—444—**
(241CA2d
[158)
s34CaR232
j53CaR[2]627
105CaR108
176CaR[1]140
27CLA954
46SCL779
10SFR376
22A2774s

**—448—**
(241CA2d
[164)
60CaR[5]637
d88CaR292
94CaR[5]161
q94CaR161
189CaR[5]30
483P2d[5]777
q483P2d777
43JBC695

**—452—**
(241CA2d
[186)
52CaR[3]306
75CaR[1]826
95CaR[2]135
152CaR[3]289
159CaR[3]874
d194CaR[3]721

**—454—**
(241CA2d
[195)
55CaR[3]874
150CaR[1]609

**—457—**
(64C2d423)
(412P2d801)
s46CaR903
52CaR[5]523

**—460—**
(64C2d437)
(412P2d804)
s47CaR117
64CaR[1]156
j64CaR[3]159
72CaR[3]372
74CaR[4]249
74CaR[5]249

**—462—**
(64C2d412)
(412P2d806)
55CaR[9]228
57CaR[7]606
60CaR[9]675
67CaR[9]446
72CaR[1]913
80CaR[6]80
82CaR[6]660
83CaR[7]174
89CaR[14]239
95CaR[13]273
95CaR[6]273
95CaR[7]763
j95CaR772
96CaR[9]379
97CaR[9]821
102CaR[7]144
102CaR757
105CaR[7]221
109CaR[14]72
109CaR[5]73
113CaR367
114CaR[9]200
119CaR[6]433
120CaR[9]579
122CaR[10]766
122CaR[13]927
123CaR[10]707
e123CaR[14]
[708
124CaR[14]425
126CaR[5]532
126CaR[7]532
130CaR[9]136
135CaR[13]646
146CaR[7]823
f148CaR[5]702
149CaR[1]95
149CaR[10]420
149CaR[9]420
154CaR[9]115
156CaR[10]107
166CaR[14]227
166CaR[14]797
167CaR261
172CaR[13]366
175CaR[13]784
175CaR[11]785
176CaR[5]169
177CaR[6]873
178CaR[13]211
178CaR[13]333
e179CaR[13]
512P2d[14]296
512P2d[5]297
421P2d103
534P2d[9]67
537P2d[10]886
549P2d[9]1232
636P2d[13]22
Cir. 9
291FS[3]113
312FS[7]1255
341FS[7]300
407FS[6]564
Tenn
566SW873
58CaL388
60CaL1524
9Pcf99

**—468—**
(64C2d432)
(412P2d812)
s47CaR250
53CaR362
53CaR[6]408
e55CaR[6]487
e55CaR[7]487
63CaR[1]173
63CaR[2]173
63CaR[3]173
374CaR774
91CaR[5]905
139CaR[2]807
158CaR[1]849
165CaR[1]168
165CaR[2]168
226CaR[1]713
226CaR[2]713
63FRD534
Cir. 9
296FS[1]447
296FS[2]447
296FS[4]447
19HLJ657
23HLJ1078
54MnL134
98A2726s

**—471—**
(241CA2d
[352)
57CaR[1]123
57CaR[2]123
57CaR[1]392
f57CaR[4]418
58CaR[2]69
29A2171s
72A3761n
72A3785n

**—483—**
(241CA2d
[320)
cc307P2d976
72CaR[3]365
73CaR[3]700
73CaR[4]700
73CaR[5]700
Wash
716P2d861
49A2982s

**—489—**
(241CA2d
[229)
85CaR[1]252
104CaR871
108CaR[1]692
109CaR[1]24
141CaR[1]477
j141CaR[1]480
e157CaR[1]128
e160CaR[1]795
203CaR[1]25
Cir. 9
720F2d[1]1139
26HLJ106
2PLR330

**—495—**
(241CA2d
[410)

**—499—**
(241CA2d
[338)
(31CC473)
US cert den
in385US931
67CaR[11]433
79CaR[1]673
105CaR[4]52
108CaR[1]112
f118CaR[3]516
182CaR[4]873
Cir. 8
302FS[4]639

**—508—**
(241CA2d
[303)
534P2d51
740P2d897
78A21404s
93A3454n

**—515—**
(241CA2d
[278)
84CaR[4]430
84CaR[3]431
121CaR[5]663
52VaL998
91A2857s

**—518—**
(241CA2d
[401)
(31CC347)
104CaR[2]616
23A2710s

**—520—**
(241CA2d
[330)
52CaR[2]603
77CaR[1]614
110CaR[7]609
d118CaR[5]698
d118CaR[6]698
208CaR[8]36
208CaR[8]726
234CaR720
690P2d[8]6
691P2d[8]274

**—526—**
(241CA2d
[397)
91CaR[1]809
100CaR[1]563
123CaR743
123CaR[1]744

**—529—**
(64C2d447)
(413P2d129)
e50CaR[1]532
60CaR[1]21
63CaR[1]370
75CaR[1]205
141CaR[1]436
e413P2d[1]132
433P2d[1]162
450P2d[1]597
139CaR[1]491
141CaR[4]77
151CaR[1]38
159CaR[1]338
169CaR[1]893
191CaR[1]447
210CaR[1]443
223CaR[1]126
229CaR[1]817
516P2d[1]3
601P2d[1]570
724P2d[1]503
Cir. 9
719F2d[1]1006
W Va
351SE380

**—538—**
(64C2d487)
(413P2d138)
53CaR[2]167
58CaR[2]114
426P2d[2]514

**—539—**
(64C2d454)
(413P2d139)
s47CaR818
125CaR[1]699
125CaR[8]699
150CaR[1]599
162CaR[3]546
195CaR[1]221
d195CaR[3]222
Cir. 7
297FS[1]41
Cir. 9
502F2d[7]810
668F2d[3]1050
577FS[3]1306
NC
194SE529
W Va
328SE156
54A21187s
67A332n
67A359n
41A4621n
41A4682n

**—546—**
(64C2d428)
(413P2d146)
s47CaR302
e58CaR[1]863

***

**FIGURE 3-26 EXCERPT FROM THE *SHEPARD'S* ENTRY FOR A STATUTE**

| UNITED STATES CODE '82 Ed. | | | | | | | T.18 § 1708 |
|---|---|---|---|---|---|---|---|
| 567F2d580 | Cir. 1 | **§ 1708** | 315F2d715 | 591F2d219 | 342F2d971 | 566F2d944 | 548F2d632 |
| Cir. 4 | 151F2d46 | 85US178 | 327F2d656 | 601F2d96 | 343F2d540 | 569F2d270 | 550F2d1058 |
| 410F2d752 | Cir. 2 | 159US663 | 349F2d863 | 607F2d49 | 355F2d81 | 577F2d886 | 567F2d677 |
| 85FS558 | 74F221 | 194US462 | 378F2d812 | 617F2d348 | 355F2d344 | 582F2d900 | 570F2d616 |
| Cir. 5 | 162F2d169 | 245US472 | 414F2d766 | 619F2d294 | 356F2d39 | 583F2d1311 | 571F2d352 |
| 343F2d542 | 517F2d969 | 345US565 | 420F2d306 | 625F2d466 | 356F2d104 | 585F2d101 | 583F2d819 |
| Cir. 6 | 26FS770 | 346US513 | 421F2d687 | 680F2d295 | 356F2d425 | 585F2d746 | 607F2d758 |
| 28F2d929 | 237FS317 | 412US847 | 422F2d1199 | 704F2d702 | 356F2d918 | 588F2d157 | 620F2d130 |
| 620F2d130 | 335FS90 | 419US980 | 423F2d1166 | 715F2d100 | 357F2d140 | 598F2d994 | 620F2d587 |
| Cir. 7 | 413FS137 | 423US413 | 424F2d49 | 85FS405 | 358F2d140 | 600F2d554 | 635F2d527 |
| 84F2d919 | Cir. 3 | 431US793 | 428F2d593 | 156FS757 | 360F2d568 | 604F2d923 | 640F2d857 |
| Cir. 8 | 1F2d170 | 448US85 | 434F2d640 | 224FS972 | 363F2d24 | 608F2d1039 | 741F2d855 |
| 14F2d280 | Cir. 4 | 453US107 | 441F2d655 | 331FS1182 | 368F2d463 | 610F2d230 | 52FS150 |
| 466F2d622 | 246F118 | 21LE879 | 441F2d1092 | 361FS129 | 372F2d481 | 614F2d85 | 422FS1056 |
| 137FS301 | 139F2d431 | 40LE297 | 442F2d296 | 372FS1226 | 378F2d647 | 625F2d1175 | 573FS1204 |
| Cir. 9 | 326F2d389 | 48LE1077 | 442F2d1019 | 378FS45 | 379F2d906 | 631F2d393 | 586FS27 |
| 421F2d183 | 361F2d579 | 62LE409 | 443F2d381 | 397FS1079 | 380F2d20 | 632F2d501 | Cir. 7 |
| 455F2d505 | 141FS531 | 97LE1250 | 445F2d1328 | 448FS827 | 384F2d926 | 632F2d645 | 33F26 |
| 17MJ787 | 215FS476 | 98LE258 | 457F2d396 | 470FS469 | 385F2d46 | 633F2d691 | 142F907 |
| **§ 1706** | Cir. 5 | 37LE380 | 459F2d471 | Cir. 4 | 387F2d641 | 635F2d449 | 285F803 |
| 237US625 | 193F504 | 42LE191 | 460F2d465 | 29F705 | 389F2d685 | 639F2d269 | 84F2d919 |
| 284US303 | 294F78 | 46LE598 | 463F2d488 | 35F60 | 389F2d728 | 649F2d370 | 114F2d982 |
| 59LE1151 | 168F2d765 | 52LE761 | 482F2d140 | 41F130 | 392F2d220 | 656F2d1205 | 182F2d252 |
| 76LE309 | 391F2d191 | 65LE624 | 486F2d1035 | 44F593 | 401F2d532 | 659F2d550 | 186F2d847 |
| 35SC710 | 411F2d522 | 69LE523 | 510F2d496 | 272F585 | 404F2d333 | 734F2d1065 | 213F2d242 |
| 52SC182 | 431F2d961 | 16SC136 | 515F2d644 | 26F2d676 | 409F2d827 | 5FS113 | 214F2d595 |
| Cir. 1 | 505F2d894 | 24SC732 | 515F2d1077 | 157F2d1013 | 415F2d638 | 63FS731 | 215F2d630 |
| 151F2d46 | 66FS243 | 38SC150 | 516F2d391 | 193F2d720 | 418F2d440 | 108FS409 | 218F2d898 |
| 676F2d15 | 217FS519 | 73SC911 | 517F2d584 | 286F2d516 | 418F2d1223 | 142FS533 | 233F2d647 |
| 728F2d45 | 304FS844 | 74SC253 | 517F2d969 | 326F2d737 | 422F2d1318 | 211FS680 | 251F2d421 |
| Cir. 2 | Cir. 6 | 93SC2358 | 519F2d413 | 402F2d264 | 423F2d1215 | 269FS30 | 297F2d179 |
| 74F221 | 239F711 | 95SC241 | 531F2d1134 | 422F2d290 | 428F2d1210 | 272FS687 | 318F2d676 |
| 517F2d969 | 258F398 | 96SC821 | 532F2d200 | 423F2d1195 | 433F2d947 | 304FS844 | 323F2d406 |
| 179FS448 | 186F2d713 | 97SC2045 | 537F2d16 | 423F2d1222 | 436F2d1305 | 320FS461 | 334F2d781 |
| 192FS860 | 329F2d686 | 100SC2549 | 545F2d301 | 431F2d244 | 449F2d752 | 361FS979 | 339F2d976 |
| 237FS317 | 585F2d182 | 101SC2679 | 563F2d46 | 446F2d201 | 450F2d339 | 429FS1037 | 341F2d44 |
| Cir. 4 | Cir. 7 | Cir. DC | 565F2d229 | 447F2d1383 | 450F2d1207 | 501FS183 | 360F2d906 |
| 148F2d521 | 251F2d421 | 169F2d969 | 613F2d30 | 453F2d634 | 455F2d968 | 573FS166 | 374F2d755 |
| 62FS798 | 253F2d458 | 265F2d820 | 635F2d175 | 478F2d846 | 455F2d974 | Cir. 6 | 402F2d172 |
| Cir. 5 | Cir. 8 | 307F2d678 | 700F2d884 | 500F2d376 | 456F2d195 | 11F225 | 420F2d1097 |
| 168F2d768 | 168F785 | 312F2d888 | 703F2d674 | 514F2d618 | 456F2d217 | 33F865 | 430F2d1240 |
| 461F2d88 | 198F72 | 372F2d911 | 730F2d896 | 529F2d194 | 456F2d1312 | 34F316 | 452F2d533 |
| Cir. 6 | 209F816 | 421F2d1132 | 736F2d851 | 540F2d204 | 457F2d371 | 37F108 | 489F2d873 |
| 274F2d306 | 231F886 | 469F2d579 | 8FS883 | 569F2d208 | 460F2d1251 | 50F414 | 489F2d980 |
| 52FS150 | 270F768 | 486F2d1295 | 159FS210 | 615F2d1021 | 461F2d83 | 55F476 | 489F2d983 |
| Cir. 7 | 15F2d40 | 510F2d776 | 163FS685 | 620F2d415 | 462F2d1376 | 60F1006 | 493F2d1282 |
| 81F2d76 | 17F2d572 | 569F2d63 | 164FS329 | 650F2d532 | 463F2d1180 | 61F204 | 499F2d1383 |
| 84FS450 | 19F2d195 | 598F2d170 | 173FS281 | 85FS558 | 466F2d237 | 294F475 | 501F2d487 |

* * *

**FIGURE 3-27 EXCERPT FROM THE *SHEPARD'S* ENTRY FOR A CONSTITUTIONAL PROVISION**

**UNITED STATES CONSTITUTION** **Amend. 14**

| | | | | | | | |
|---|---|---|---|---|---|---|---|
| 718FS1112 | 885F2d363 | 890F2d340 | 107SC2808 | USDk 88-608 | 724FS534 | 107SC2626 | 479US539 |
| 720FS41 | 886F2d851 | 891F2d802 | 107SC2951 | USDk | 727FS1117 | 108SC2755 | 479US572 |
| 720FS343 | 888F2d530 | 891F2d831 | 108SC1358 | [88-1150 | 728FS1350 | 109SC719 | 479US891 |
| 721FS1578 | 889F2d757 | 892F2d1511 | 108SC1720 | 128FRD315 | 730FS77 | 109SC2319 | 479US894 |
| 722FS952 | 891F2d138 | 894F2d1538 | 110SC1061 | Cir. DC | 730FS1406 | 109SC2711 | 479US900 |
| 726FS418 | 891F2d144 | 896F2d480 | 58USLW | 895F2d800 | Cir. 7 | USDk | 479US902 |
| 726FS456 | 893F2d148 | 719FS1052 | [4265 | Cir. 1 | 891F2d166 | [87-2084 | 479US919 |
| 727FS825 | 894F2d219 | 720FS1570 | 58USLW | 888F2d940 | 718FS1397 | Cir. DC | 479US941 |
| 727FS848 | 894F2d930 | 721FS1302 | [4483 | 889F2d1197 | 719FS1422 | 886F2d339 | 479US955 |
| 728FS1069 | 895F2d413 | 723FS1497 | USDk | 890F2d536 | 719FS1430 | 725FS42 | 479US972 |
| 729FS321 | 897F2d897 | 727FS1566 | [88-1150 | 895F2d18 | 720FS1335 | Cir. 2 | 479US1044 |
| 730FS1267 | 718FS25 | 730FS421 | Cir. 1 | 897F2d9 | 723FS1306 | 885F2d1064 | 479US1049 |
| Cir. 3 | 718FS1381 | 29MJ705 | 719FS26 | 719FS54 | 725FS1034 | 724FS153 | 479US1306 |
| 885F2d1103 | 719FS688 | 1ExER207 | 108BRW871 | 721FS21 | 726FS193 | 724FS1100 | 480US2 |
| 886F2d621 | 720FS117 | 75ABA(4)78 | Cir. 2 | 721FS384 | 726FS698 | 726FS954 | 480US18 |
| 886F2d1393 | 724FS547 | 73A4630n | 718FS128 | 721FS401 | 726FS1135 | 728FS993 | 480US43 |
| 887F2d1209 | 726FS699 | 73A4651n | Cir. 3 | 724FS28 | 727FS456 | 730FS588 | 480US106 |
| 889F2d457 | 726FS1146 | 73A4684n | 723FS236 | 728FS841 | 729FS601 | Cir. 3 | 480US137 |
| 892F2d1171 | 727FS1179 | | Cir. 4 | 728FS848 | 730FS1459 | 725FS248 | 480US153 |
| 897F2d105 | 728FS496 | **Amend. 9** | 722FS1265 | 729FS202 | 730FS1477 | 128FRD196 | 480US230 |
| 719FS293 | 730FS162 | | 722FS1305 | 730FS462 | 103BRW994 | 103BRW517 | 480US479 |
| 719FS383 | 731FS273 | 478US189 | 730FS681 | 108BRW875 | Cir. 8 | Cir. 4 | 480US620 |
| 719FS1260 | Cir. 8 | 486US596 | Cir. 5 | Cir. 2 | 886F2d159 | 889F2d1353 | 480US627 |
| 720FS423 | 884F2d1054 | 100LE640 | 720FS570 | 887F2d420 | 886F2d1044 | Cir. 5 | 480US714 |
| 720FS477 | 884F2d1089 | 106LE425 | 727FS42 | 889F2d437 | 887F2d170 | 720FS570 | 480US923 |
| 728FS359 | 885F2d1332 | 108SC2050 | Cir. 9 | 893F2d500 | 887F2d896 | 729FS41 | 480US926 |
| 729FS1064 | 886F2d1044 | 109SC3048 | 884F2d450 | 895F2d69 | 888F2d547 | Cir. 6 | 481US6 |
| 730FS1319 | 887F2d136 | 110SC1061 | 889F2d923 | 896F2d665 | 896F2d1133 | 722FS382 | 481US148 |
| 106BRW80 | 888F2d538 | 58USLW | 895F2d1280 | 718FS141 | 725FS1053 | Cir. 7 | 481US189 |
| Cir. 4 | 889F2d801 | [4265 | 896F2d413 | 718FS194 | 730FS980 | 895F2d346 | 481US206 |
| 885F2d153 | 890F2d96 | USDk 88-605 | 896F2d1218 | 720FS41 | Cir. 9 | 720FS702 | 481US225 |
| 885F2d162 | 890F2d1419 | Cir. DC | Cir. 10 | 724FS1432 | 885F2d640 | Cir. 8 | 481US271 |
| 885F2d183 | 891F2d1371 | 893F2d372 | 729FS750 | 725FS786 | 885F2d1442 | 730FS225 | 481US288 |
| 885F2d1214 | 893F2d153 | Cir. 2 | Cir. 11 | 725FS787 | 886F2d252 | 730FS989 | 481US394 |
| 886F2d709 | 893F2d1557 | 885F2d1064 | 727FS1568 | 726FS1407 | 891F2d718 | Cir. 9 | 481US499 |
| 886F2d723 | 894F2d976 | 718FS129 | 75ABA(3)67 | 728FS307 | 896F2d413 | 896F2d1218 | 481US521 |
| 889F2d1343 | 894F2d987 | 719FS90 | 73A4636n | 105BRW196 | 896F2d1159 | Cir. 10 | 481US554 |
| 891F2d498 | 895F2d440 | 728FS253 | | Cir. 3 | 718FS1462 | 892F2d1458 | 481US613 |
| 892F2d1203 | 896F2d307 | Cir. 3 | **Amend. 11** | 885F2d32 | 720FS1414 | Cir. 11 | 481US657 |
| 895F2d142 | 718FS728 | 720FS51 | | 885F2d1112 | 730FS310 | 891F2d1558 | 481US748 |
| 896F2d831 | 719FS1473 | Cir. 4 | 479US100 | 893F2d1445 | 108BRW273 | 724FS869 | 481US840 |
| 896F2d850 | 724FS664 | 726FS1494 | 482US130 | 895F2d118 | Cir. 10 | | 482US84 |
| 718FS1294 | 727FS1287 | Cir. 5 | 483US470 | 719FS296 | 885F2d1487 | **§ 2** | 482US307 |
| 719FS436 | 730FS989 | 719FS1351 | 483US597 | 719FS1261 | 885F2d1493 | | 482US347 |
| 719FS1324 | Cir. 9 | Cir. 6 | 486US613 | 721FS634 | 721FS272 | 101LE803 | 482US370 |
| 724FS380 | 884F2d1247 | 722FS382 | 96LE115 | 721FS646 | 724FS858 | 105LE160 | 482US473 |
| 724FS1194 | 885F2d641 | 730FS83 | 97LE394 | 722FS1189 | 727FS585 | 108SC2758 | 482US501 |
| 730FS1368 | 885F2d645 | Cir. 7 | 97LE499 | 724FS346 | 727FS1405 | 109SC2381 | 482US582 |
| Cir. 5 | 885F2d1359 | 725FS947 | 99LE522 | 726FS538 | 728FS1520 | Cir. 2 | 482US644 |
| 889F2d1394 | 886F2d1169 | 730FS1441 | 100LE651 | 729FS1101 | 730FS348 | 724FS1099 | 482US732 |
| 890F2d724 | 891F2d242 | Cir. 9 | 102LE8 | 103BRW644 | 730FS1035 | Cir. 3 | 482US921 |
| 891F2d91 | 896F2d365 | 889F2d923 | 103LE281 | 105BRW789 | Cir. 11 | 128FRD201 | 482US924 |

* * *

**FIGURE 3-28 EXCERPT FROM THE EARLIEST *SHEPARD'S* NOTATIONS FOR *GRISWOLD***

**SUPREME COURT REPORTER** **Vol. 85**

| | | | | | | | |
|---|---|---|---|---|---|---|---|
| **—1678—** | j87SC[10]1659 | 91SC[10]1299 | j92SC[10]1046 | j93SC[4]2127 | j94SC[5]3019 | 97SC875 | 97SC2108 |
| (381US479) | j885SC[10]332 | j91SC[8]1302 | 92SC[10]1213 | 93SC[2]2639 | 95SC[1]2211 | 97SC[5]876 | 97SC[10]2109 |
| s85SC328 | 88SC510 | j91SC[8]1491 | j93SC[10]404 | d93SC[10]2639 | j96SC[8]838 | 97SC[10]877 | 97SC2286 |
| s151Ct544 | j88SC523 | 91SC[10]1822 | j93SC[3]626 | j93SC[10]2648 | d96SC[10]1444 | 97SC[10]881 | j97SC2289 |
| s153Ct725 | j88SC[5]1462 | j91SC[10]1837 | j93SC[10]637 | j93SC[5]2662 | j96SC[10]1448 | j97SC[10]1487 | j97SC2822 |
| Conn | j88SC[1]1968 | j91SC[8]1949 | d93SC[8]715 | 93SC[4]2676 | j96SC[8]1584 | f97SC[10]1935 | e98SC[10]680 |
| s200A2d479 | 89SC847 | j91SC[10]1950 | d93SC[9]728 | j93SC[10]2716 | 96SC[4]1823 | c97SC1937 | 98SC[10]684 |
| s213A2d525 | 89SC[4]1247 | j91SC[8]2055 | d93SC[5]730 | 93SC[10]2826 | 96SC[8]2598 | j97SC1953 | 99SC[8]1064 |
| j86SC833 | 89SC[8]1248 | j92SC705 | e93SC[10]734 | 93SC[10]2829 | 96SC[10]2598 | j97SC1954 | 99SC[10]1064 |
| j86SC[10]956 | j89SC[1]1399 | 92SC[8]723 | 93SC[8]745 | 94SC[10]2841 | 96SC[10]2841 | j97SC1957 | d99SC[10]1871 |
| j86SC[1]1086 | j90SC1025 | 92SC[10]1033 | 93SC[1]746 | f96SC[1]2874 | f96SC[1]2874 | 97SC[1]2015 | j99SC2636 |
| j86SC[10]1839 | j90SC[9]1082 | 92SC[1]1034 | 93SC[8]756 | j96SC[1]2881 | j96SC[1]2881 | e97SC[8]2015 | 100SC[10]2688 |
| j87SC[10]439 | j90SC1922 | 92SC[3]1040 | 93SC[10]757 | 97SC[1]455 | 97SC[1]455 | e97SC[10]2015 | 100SC[5]2829 |
| 87SC[10]538 | j91SC392 | 92SC[10]1042 | 93SC[10]1174 | j97SC466 | j97SC466 | d97SC2026 | j101SC1181 |
| j87SC[10]555 | j91SC[10]1180 | 92SC[9]1043 | 93SC[10]1297 | 97SC[1]466 | 97SC[1]466 | 97SC[10]2026 | d101SC1211 |

* * *

is cited, the researcher must make sure the statute has not been amended or modified by a later statute or even repealed. The researcher must also make sure the statute has not been held unconstitutional or given a narrow interpretation. From a research standpoint, whenever you believe a change in the authority would disturb your conclusion, shepardize.

## Blue and White Books

Paralegals are often asked to find a parallel citation for a case. Perhaps the lawyer has a citation to the unofficial version of the case and needs the official version. *Shepard's* provides the information the first time an entry from the case appears in one of its volumes. An even easier way is to consult the *National Blue and White Book*. The sole purpose of this set is to provide parallel citations. See Figure 3-29. Correct citation form is the mark of professionalism. The *National Blue and White Book* can provide parallel citations in less than a minute. It contains a table converting an official citation to a parallel unofficial citation and another table converting an unofficial citation to an official citation. There are also Blue and White Books for particular states.

## Legal Dictionaries

A number of dictionaries are published solely for legal professionals. Because paralegals want to write like lawyers, frequently they will try to use legal terms with which they are only slightly familiar. Do not use a legal word or phrase unless you are sure of its meaning. Take a simple word like "verdict." Some paralegals have been known to write that a court issued its "verdict." Wrong. Juries—not courts—render verdicts. Be precise. If a legal term is new to you, look it up in a legal dictionary. The two most popular legal dictionaries are *Black's Law Dictionary*, 5th Ed. (West, 1979) and *Ballentine's Law Dictionary*, 3d Ed. (Laywers Co-op, 1969).

**FIGURE 3-29 EXCERPT FROM THE *NATIONAL BLUE AND WHITE BOOK***

**69 NEW YORK REPORTS, SECOND SERIES**

| N.Y.2d | N.Y.S.2d | | N.E.2d | | N.Y.2d | N.Y.S.2d | | N.E.2d | | N.Y.2d | N.Y.S.2d | | N.E.2d | | N.Y.2d | N.Y.S.2d | | N.E.2d | |
|---|---|---|---|---|---|---|---|---|---|---|---|---|---|---|---|---|---|---|---|
| Page | Vol. | Page | Vol. | Page | Page | Vol. | Page | Vol. | Page | Page | Vol. | Page | Vol. | Page | Page | Vol. | Page | Vol. | Page |
| 1 | 511 | 216 | 503 | 681 | 199 | 513 | 95 | 505 | 605 | 343 | 514 | 682 | 507 | 275 | 509 | 516 | 166 | 508 | 901 |
| 8 | 511 | 219 | 503 | 684 | 208 | 513 | 348 | 505 | 914 | 355 | 514 | 689 | 507 | 282 | 514 | 516 | 168 | 508 | 903 |
| 20 | 511 | 559 | 503 | 990 | 211 | 513 | 349 | 505 | 915 | 365 | 514 | 694 | 507 | 287 | 525 | 516 | 174 | 508 | 909 |
| 32 | 511 | 565 | 503 | 996 | 225 | 513 | 356 | 505 | 922 | 376 | 514 | 701 | 507 | 294 | 536 | 516 | 179 | 508 | 914 |
| 56 | 511 | 580 | 503 | 1011 | 232 | 513 | 359 | 505 | 925 | 382 | 515 | 212 | 507 | 1068 | 547 | 516 | 186 | 508 | 920 |
| 66 | 511 | 808 | 503 | 1345 | 246 | 513 | 367 | 505 | 932 | 406 | 515 | 418 | 508 | 130 | 559 | 516 | 451 | 509 | 51 |
| 89 | 511 | 821 | 503 | 1358 | 255 | 513 | 372 | 505 | 937 | 418 | 515 | 424 | 508 | 136 | 570 | 516 | 614 | 509 | 309 |
| 103 | 512 | 652 | 504 | 1079 | 265 | 513 | 656 | 506 | 187 | 426 | 515 | 428 | 508 | 140 | 576 | 516 | 616 | 509 | 311 |
| 141 | 512 | 794 | 505 | 237 | 281 | 513 | 954 | 506 | 525 | 432 | 515 | 733 | 508 | 645 | 585 | 516 | 619 | 509 | 314 |
| 144 | 512 | 796 | 505 | 239 | 290 | 514 | 191 | 506 | 901 | 437 | 515 | 735 | 508 | 647 | 593 | 516 | 623 | 509 | 318 |
| 148 | 512 | 797 | 505 | 240 | 302 | 514 | 197 | 506 | 907 | 448 | 515 | 740 | 508 | 652 | 621 | 511 | 227 | 503 | 692 |
| 154 | 513 | 73 | 505 | 584 | 310 | 514 | 200 | 506 | 910 | 459 | 515 | 745 | 508 | 657 | 623 | 511 | 227 | 503 | 692 |
| 159 | 513 | 75 | 505 | 586 | 313 | 514 | 201 | 506 | 911 | 469 | 515 | 750 | 508 | 661 | 625 | 511 | 227 | 503 | 692 |
| 166 | 513 | 79 | 505 | 590 | 321 | 514 | 205 | 506 | 915 | 478 | 515 | 753 | 508 | 665 | 628 | 511 | 226 | 503 | 691 |
| 174 | 513 | 83 | 505 | 594 | 329 | 514 | 209 | 506 | 919 | 490 | 515 | 761 | 508 | 672 | 630 | 511 | 228 | 503 | 693 |
| 185 | 513 | 87 | 505 | 598 | 339 | 514 | 324 | 506 | 1177 | 497 | 516 | 159 | 508 | 894 | 632 | 511 | 228 | 503 | 693 |
| 191 | 513 | 91 | 505 | 601 | | | | | | | | | | | 635 | 511 | 229 | 503 | 694 |

* * *

## The Restatements

Sooner or later, every paralegal will encounter some reference to a "restatement." ***Restatements of the Law*** is a set of books written by a panel of experts—lawyers, judges, and professors—who have developed principles of how the law should be decided.

The American Law Institute has published the *Restatements* in two editions. The first edition presented the panel's formulation of what the law ought to be on the simple basis of the majority trend on the particular issue. If a majority of the states had decided a law a certain way, then the panel wrote the principle mirroring the majority approach.

In the second edition of *Restatements*, however, the panel wrote the principles the way its members thought the law should be decided. For example, *Restatement* Section 402 (A) said if a defective product injured a party, then the manufacturer of the product would be liable to the injured party. This was different from the common law, which required negligence on the part of the manufacturer. In fact, at the time this restatement provision was drafted, no state had adopted such an interpretation. Thereafter, a California lawyer cited Section 402 (A) in successful support of his client's case, and California adopted the *Restatement* position. This position is known today as **products liability law** or **strict liability in tort**. Almost every state has adopted it.

You can consult a **Restatement** to guide your research or thought process. Restatement opinion is excellent persuasive authority.

## Lexis and Westlaw

Computers have begun to change the way we approach many research projects. At present, the computer has not replaced the traditional research strategies discussed in this chapter. In some cases, the traditional research tools are more effective either from a cost standpoint or from the standpoint of being able to pinpoint the applicable source authority. This will probably change as computers become more sophisticated. To understand the similarities and differences between the traditional research tools and computers, you need to first understand how to use computers for legal research.

At present, there are two main legal computer databases: Westlaw (put out by West Publishing Company) and Lexis (put out by Mead Data Control, Inc.). Basically, both databases contain cases and other source authority from about 1970 to the present. You search for some authority in Lexis or Westlaw by telling the computer to look through a database for a certain word or phrase or certain combinations of words or phrases.

For example, suppose you want to use the computer in your dog-bite research to find out whether Indiana is a one-bite or two-bite state. You will be using either Lexis or Westlaw. First, as in traditional research, you determine what jurisdiction's law will control the answer to your query. In this case it will be Indiana. On either Westlaw or Lexis, Indiana cases appear in a separate database. When you tell the computer to look at the Indiana database, this limits the scope of the computer's search. Now it is up to you to try to tell the computer what to look for in the Indiana database. Suppose you tell the computer to look for all Indiana cases with the word "dog" in them. The computer will tell you that there are at least 231 Indiana cases containing the word "dog." The computer will list these cases for you, or you can actually read each of them on the screen. But because there are so many cases containing the word "dog," you redirect your search and ask the computer for only those "dog" cases that include the word "bite." The computer will tell you that there are at least 16 such cases in Indiana with both of these words.

Suppose you know that there are three possibilities: Indiana is either a one-bite, a two-bite, or a dangerous propensity state. You can enter these words, asking the computer to list each case that uses any of them, and soon the computer will retrieve this information. Automated research works well when you use the correct search words. However, suppose the only Indiana dog-bite case had never mentioned the word "dog" but had used "basset hound" throughout the opinion. It would be unlikely that you could ever locate that case by means of the computer.

Both Westlaw and Lexis provide a way to check citations on the computer. Westlaw has incorporated the Shepard's system as part of its database. Lexis has incorporated "Auto-cite," a system developed by the research department of Lawyers Co-operative Publishing Company, as a means to check citations.

A computer research system offers many advantages. In traditional research, you are limited to the indexing tools provided by the publisher. In computer research, you create the index by devising words or phrases for the computer to look for. When you formulate a query, you choose the terms. The disadvantage is that computers lack intelligence. The computer looks only for the specific words you tell it to and for no others. Hence, to use a computer effectively, you must have some familiarity with the vocabulary used in the researched cases.

The computer is quick. It is also current. A case decided by the Supreme Court yesterday is probably already entered into both Westlaw and Lexis.

Paralegals now entering the job market will be expected to have some familiarity with the use of computer research systems. A good reference is *The Process of Legal Research* (Little, Brown & Company, 1986).

# 4 LEGAL MEMORANDA

If wishes were horses, then beggars would ride. If rules were results, there would be little need of lawyers. (K. N. Llewellyn, *The Bramble Bush* [New York: Oceana Publications, 1960]).

In England there are two types of lawyers: **barristers** present oral arguments to the court, while **solicitors** advise clients and prepare written memoranda to assist barristers with their arguments. The memorandum that educates a British barrister on the legal points of a case serves essentially the same function in American law. Lawyers and paralegals prepare memoranda to educate other members of their firm about legal situations. The first writing experience of many paralegals is preparing a legal memorandum.

## WHAT IS A MEMORANDUM?

A memorandum is a written opinion on a legal matter usually prepared for intraoffice use. Rarely will a memorandum leave the law office. The memorandum is an informative and descriptive form of writing.

There are many reasons to write memoranda. A memorandum may be prepared to help with decision making: Should the firm accept a certain case? Should the client pursue or defend a claim? What action should a senior partner take in a problem case? A client may ask how a law applies to a given fact situation, and this query will be addressed by writing a memorandum.

Legal memorandum writing involves applying rules of law to fact problems. When a memorandum is prepared, the legal professional goes through the same thought process as a court may later go through to decide this particular problem.

The difference, of course, is that the memorandum writer renders an opinion as to what the result may be, whereas the judge actually decides the result. Most memorandum writers never recognize the similarity between what they do and what a court does.

## PREPARING TO WRITE A MEMORANDUM—SOME GENERAL GUIDELINES

Because most memoranda are read only by clients and other members of the law firm, the details of preparation vary from firm to firm. Nonetheless, several general guidelines are applicable to all facets of memorandum writing.

### Give A Neutral Analysis

A memorandum should be written from a neutral point of view. Always keep in mind that a client may not appreciate a theoretical answer to an abstract question. A good memorandum explores problems and finds acceptable solutions. The more you research and think about a situation, the more likely you are to discover new approaches and favorable arguments for your client. Explore each argument and approach, and use the memorandum as a springboard for developing solutions.

Do not make the mistake of betraying your own feelings about whether a particular law is good or bad. Editorializing is not the mark of a professional. A paralegal asked to prepare a memorandum on an abortion question, for example, should describe the law, not what the paralegal feels the law ought to be.

### Get Sufficient Instructions

Paralegal students like direction. If a teacher gives vague instructions, the students typically complain. Most paralegal students want the comfort of structure, but paralegals work with attorneys who frequently give poor or inadequate instructions. The lawyer assigning the memorandum may have given vague instructions to you because the client's request was vague or because there was inadequate time to give a more detailed explanation. Unfortunately, sometimes poor instructions will be all the instructions you receive. However, whenever you are assigned a memorandum to write, try to find out as much information as possible.

### Ascertain the Objectives of the Memorandum

Clarify the purpose of the memorandum. Find out why the memorandum is necessary. Before writing, learn as much about the background of the memorandum as possible: the client objectives, the facts, the law, and the issues. Is it a preliminary assessment of the merits of a case? Will the contents be shown to the client or to other firm members? How much time should you devote to the memorandum? Spending a few extra minutes at the preliminary stage to ascertain as much of this background information as possible will save hours of work later in the project.

### Learn the Facts

Find out the facts about the client's problem. Often the reason you become stymied in researching a problem is because you have an incomplete picture of the facts. When this happens, you seldom appreciate the subtleties of the problem. Spending extra time to learn about the facts will save many research hours.

### Gather the Source Authority

The next step is to gather the relevant source materials as discussed in Chapters 2 and 3. If the problem is governed by a statute or regulation, make a copy of this law. Some firms prefer that you copy the relevant authority in the body of the memorandum. The writing process begins as you research, but the writing process will not end until the research is complete. As you research, pay attention to the legal questions arising from the facts. If you uncover new issues, research these issues as well.

### Organize the Issues

After you have gathered the source law and reviewed any secondary sources necessary to understand the problem, organize the issues. In fact, it is usually a good idea to make an outline of the main points of a memorandum. Only then will you be ready to start the actual writing.

## FORM OF THE MEMORANDUM

Unlike the brief, which may have strict requirements as to form, there is no standard form that paralegals must follow for a memorandum. The form of the memorandum will differ from firm to firm and even from lawyer to lawyer. Of course, a memorandum should contain pertinent client identification, a date, your name, and a title. (See the sample memorandum on page 237 in the Appendix to this text.) The memorandum will also contain the question or questions addressed by the memorandum, a statement of relevant facts, a discussion section, and a conclusion. In this regard, the structure of a memorandum is similar to that of a case brief, which you learned to prepare in Chapter 2. The fact section of a case brief is the same as the statement of facts section in a memorandum. The questions addressed are the legal issues. The discussion section is similar to the legal reasoning section, and the conclusion is similar to the holding. Because of these similarities, legal memoranda require the same thought processes discussed in Chapter 2.

The reader must understand the scope of the memorandum. In all memoranda, state explicitly any limitations. If certain issues have not been covered, say so. If alternative arguments might lead to the same result, describe the alternatives. In more complex memoranda, you may include an introduction or summary section to describe the main points of the memorandum. This section might include an outline of the memorandum or other background information.

## Facts of the Memorandum

Clients come to lawyers with problems. The client tells the lawyer a story. The story may involve a dispute, or the story may only involve a potential dispute. On the other side of the dispute might be an individual, a company or a governmental agency. The other party to the dispute may also be seeking legal advice. This is the peculiar work of the legal system: to prevent or resolve disputes, to plan around problems, and to structure relationships or to undo them.

**The Importance of the Facts.** Our legal system resolves disputes by applying rules of law to them. There are hundreds of thousands of rules of law. The facts determine what rule of law applies. New facts may create new rules of law or may result in an old rule being applied in a new way. Consider the law as a catalog with hundreds of thousands of rules. As the paralegal is given the facts, the paralegal consults the catalog and selects the rule that best fits this problem. You cannot select the right principle without knowing the factual dimensions of the problem. Sometimes the catalog will not have a rule that fits the facts. Then a new rule will have to be created. This is how important facts are to the legal professional.

Legal problems are fact-sensitive—even a slight fact variation may change the rule or principle used to decide a case. Times change the facts as well. Consider *Roe v. Wade*—the case addressing the right to abortion. *Roe* was decided in 1973. At that time, neonatal care was not as advanced as it is in the 1990s. Changes in modern medicine have advanced the date of viability, and this fact could affect a current analysis of *Roe*. As facts change, so does the analysis of issues. Fact analysis might change a result.

Too many legal professionals pay too little attention to the facts. The facts should be written as clearly and completely as a novelist tells a story. Paralegals in particular tend to overemphasize the importance of legal principles when they are developing memoranda. Pay as much attention to the facts as you do to the legal principles. It is facts that determine what principles apply to a dispute. Facts may bend principles or reshape them. Facts determine the outcome of cases.

Legal professionals may be tempted to abbreviate the facts section of the memorandum because they assume the client and their supervisors already know the facts. There are several reasons why the facts should be thoroughly stated. First, remember your opinion is based on a certain fact pattern. The fact pattern you relied on should be clear to anyone who reads the memorandum. Second, your supervisor should not have to reread the entire file to learn the key facts of the case.

**Present the Facts in Narrative Form.** The facts should be presented in a narrative form. Tell a story. Write the facts in the third person and in the past tense unless the events are still occurring when the brief is written. As you narrate the story, relate the facts in an organized manner. You can develop the facts by chronology or by cause and effect. For example, a cause-and-effect outline in a personal injury case might separate the accident details from the injury details. You might put the most important facts first and the least important facts later. Whatever method you use do not present the facts haphazardly.

**Present the Facts Objectively.** Do not be judgmental of the facts. The facts in a memorandum should be presented neutrally. The fact section of the memorandum should not assess the merits of the facts. Any comment on how an assessment of the facts would change the analysis should be reserved for the discussion section of the memorandum. Pay attention to facts that might cause a court to be sympathetic to the opponent's case as well as your client's case.

Remember that a client will often relate a biased version of the facts. Recall the dog-bite situation discussed in Chapter 3. This problem was presented from a victim's perspective. Perhaps the dog's owner will bring in witnesses to show how lovable and peaceful this dog is. These neighbors might explain the only time the dog was ever aggressive was when someone teased it. The facts may be evenly balanced, making it difficult to predict the outcome.

**Develop All the Facts.** Often the inability to make progress on researching or writing a memorandum stems from the lack of factual development of the case. Nothing is more crucial to the analysis than the development of the facts. On some occasions the facts will be given to you. On other occasions the facts may be hotly controverted. You may not know whether your client's version or the opposing party's version is correct. Present both sides of the facts.

## Issues in the Memorandum

Memoranda are much easier to write once the writer has focused the issues. As the research continues, what began as a one-issue problem may have turned into a multiple-issue problem. Consider the dog-bite case. The original issue was whether Indiana was a one-bite or two-bite state. As the case is prepared for trial, the lawyer might look to see if the client was a trespasser, licensee, or invitee. The owner of a dog may owe a different duty to a trespasser than to a guest. Another issue might be whether different standards of care apply to children and adults.

Issues will splinter as the research continues. It is not unusual to research one issue, only to discover several other important issues as you research. Issues can also narrow. Your research may reveal that the law is too settled to be contested. It would be useless in that situation to pursue the issue any further. You might also find that you fit a narrow exception to a rule; by phrasing the rule more specifically, you can better position the argument. Issues can also be combined. You will find that several issues really pertain to a broader question.

**The Importance of the Issues.** Nothing focuses and organizes a memorandum better than well-written issues. How issues are grouped or splintered and how issues are ordered will determine structure better than the most detailed outline. Pay attention to the issues, and structure will fall into place.

The presentation of the issues can even change the analysis of a problem. A good illustration of this point comes from Judge David Souter's testimony before the U.S. Senate during confirmation hearings prior to his appointment to the Supreme Court. Souter noted the tension between the right-to-exercise-religion clause and the establishment-of-religion clause of the First Amendment. On the one hand, the First Amendment to the U.S. Constitution guarantees the free exercise of religion. On the other hand, it ensures separation of church and state. A landmark Supreme Court case said Amish children could not be forced to attend high school against their religious beliefs. Judge Souter suggested this landmark case might have been decided differently had a state passed a law exempting the Amish child from attending high school. Then it might be argued the state was favoring one religion over another! How issues are framed determines the outcome of cases. Many experienced legal writers believe issue writing is crucial to the analysis.

**The Format of the Issues.** Issue writing is an art. Usually issues are written in a question form. An issue should emphasize the facts or law as appropriate. An issue should not be written as a sterile question but should incorporate the key facts of the problem. When you incorporate facts into the statement of the issue, the issue becomes more concrete and less abstract. Consider this statement of an issue, which does a good job of combining the facts with the legal problem:

> Was an indigent defendant charged with attempted robbery deprived of the assistance of counsel as protected by the due process clause of the Fourteenth Amendment when appointed counsel did not see or talk to the defendant until thirty minutes before trial, did not ask but one question at trial, did not interview or call witnesses, did not speak on the defendant's behalf at sentencing and did not inform the defendant of his right to appeal?

The issues in memoranda, like the facts, should be neutrally written. The issue in a memorandum should also not suggest the result. This is not true in the preceding statement of the issue.

## The Discussion Section of the Memorandum

The discussion section of a memorandum explains the reasoning process from the issue to the conclusion. Before preparing the discussion section, consider how a judge thinks.

A judge hears a story—often he or she hears more than one version—and as the story unfolds, the judge is presented with issues or questions to resolve. The judge must select the legal principles (a statute or case law) applicable to the dispute and then must apply these rules to the facts of the case in order to reach a conclusion or holding (the *ratio decidendi*). Most discussion sections follow this same approach.

**The Format of the Discussion Section.** The discussion section can involve the analysis of very simple questions or very complex legal questions. The general approach, however, is the same.

***Simple Issues.*** If the issue is simple and the rule of law to be applied to the dispute is fairly obvious, then the discussion section of the memorandum can be structured as follows:

1. Issue
2. Rule of law

3. Application of Rule
4. Conclusion

In law school this approach is sometimes referred to by the acronym IRAC: Issue, Rule, Application of Rule, and Conclusion.

Now we will apply these principles to the dog-bite problem from Chapter 3 by writing a short memorandum, but let's give the hypothetical a few more facts. The lawyer who assigned the original problem to be researched has just learned that although the dog has never bitten anyone before, the dog has snarled at the mail carrier and has snapped at the ankles of several small children. Your supervisor is concerned because the dog has never actually bitten anyone before. Your client has been seriously injured. Examine this short discussion.

| | |
|---|---|
| **Issue** | The sole issue discussed is whether an owner of a dog that has demonstrated dangerous propensities can be held liable for damages caused by a dog bite even if the dog has not bitten anyone before |
| **Rule** | this incident. The law is settled in Indiana that owners are liable for a dog bite if the dog has dangerous propensities. A dog can demon- |
| **Application of Rule to facts** | strate dangerous propensities without actually biting someone. Once an owner notices a pet may pose a threat to others, the owner is under a duty to prevent injury. When a dog has snarled and and snapped at children and others, the owner is on notice the dog |
| **Conclusion** | poses a possible threat. In this case the owner was on notice of the dangerous propensities and should be held liable. |

Notice how the issue, rule, analysis, and conclusion are developed. The format that starts with the issue, identifies the rule, applies the rule of law to the facts, and arrives at the conclusion is an effective format to follow.

This format need not be followed precisely in every case, however. At times you can state the rule or principle, or even the conclusion, first. As the rules to be applied become more complex, you will need to expand some sections more than others. For example, as the facts become more controverted, more of the memorandum must address the factual differences on the conclusion. Your memorandum should describe how the result will change if the court believes one version of the story over the other version. At times both the rule of law and the facts can be in doubt, and in such situations the analysis can be quite lengthy.

***Complex Issues.*** In many instances, a memorandum will analyze more than one issue. Each issue should be discussed under a separate subhead. In other words, if you develop three issues in the memorandum, then insert three subheadings in the discussion section. Each subhead should be written in a declarative sentence combining the key facts and the legal principle in the sentence. Examine the subheads in the *Griswold* appellant brief on pages 199–228 in the Appendix to the Resource Manual.

When legal issues become more complex, usually it is because the legal principles are more abstract. In many cases, the best advice is to recognize the likelihood that a more definite or concrete answer is not possible. Recognizing the fact that you cannot possibly provide a clear-cut answer takes considerable pressure off of the writer in formulating the discussion section in the memorandum.

No matter how complicated the problem, you will be trying to apply the appropriate legal principle to the facts of your case. How you organize and state the issues can help considerably in dealing with complex problems. Break the issues into narrower issues or into subparts. Try to reduce general principles into narrower principles. These techniques will aid the analysis process.

**The Use of Logic in the Discussion Section.** Paralegals develop and apply legal principles using deductive and inductive logic.

***Deductive Logic.*** A memorandum in the dog-bite situation, for example, can be developed like a syllogism in logic. The rule of law is the major premise. The facts are the minor premise. The conclusion flows from these statements. Let's put the dog-bite problem into a syllogism form:

| | |
|---|---|
| **Major Premise** | Owners of dog with vicious propensities are liable to dog-bite victims. |
| **Minor Premise** | A dog who has snapped and snarled at children has vicious propensities. |
| **Conclusion** | Owner of dog that bit client is liable to client. |

This approach uses **deductive logic**.

Deductive logic is a form of reasoning by which specific conclusions are inferred from accepted general principles. Hence, if an accepted legal principle states that a contract cannot be entered into in jest (major premise) and a court decides marriage is a contract (minor premise), then a court could deductively conclude a couple who married in jest did not enter into a valid contract. Legal rules are often deduced by such syllogisms.

***Inductive Logic.*** **Inductive logic**, on the other hand, is a form of reasoning by which general conclusions are drawn from particular situations. A good example of the use of the inductive approach is polling. A poll samples a few opinions and then draws a general conclusion. You use the inductive method when you work a jigsaw puzzle and notice the pattern after putting a few pieces together. This method is often applied in case-law situations.

Sometimes there are no rules for certain fact problems. Then the person using the catalog must look to see if there are any trends in the law. If so, a new rule could be made for this new fact pattern following the trend of other jurisdictions. This is an inductive approach.

In *Griswold*, for example, the rule of law was not apparent. There was no right of marital privacy recognized in the case law. The appellant in *Griswold* had to construct the foundation of such a right of privacy from the pattern of rights protected by the U.S. Constitution. The lawyer in *Griswold* identified a pattern and convinced a court that the facts fit this pattern.

Look at the Appendix to the resource manual that accompanies this text and read the brief prepared on this issue by the appellant. Notice how much of the content of the brief was devoted to developing the legal principle. Then reread Justice Douglas's opinion. Notice how much of his opinion was devoted to finding a right of privacy. This is a good example of the inductive approach.

**Identifying the Legal Principle.** Although there are four different steps in the discussion section (identify the issue, identify the legal principle, apply the principle to the facts, and reach the conclusion), most of the discussion section will focus either on identifying the legal principle or on applying the principle to the facts, or on both.

A memorandum is about law. The paralegal will research the law and select rules or principles from the research that pertain to the factual dispute. At times, such as in the dog-bite situation, the rules may be derived easily from good research techniques. Yet there are instances when no case or statute will directly answer the question presented. Then the paralegal must explain why persuasive precedents from lower courts or precedents from other jurisdictions should be used or extrapolated.

At other times, the paralegal must use persuasive authorities such as treatises, legal periodicals, or the *Restatements*. These authorities, in the absence of binding authority, may suggest a cogent approach. The paralegal should always buttress legal statements with a citation to the authority on which the statement is based. Use appropriate quotes from a case if it adds to the presentation, but don't overquote material.

Lawyers use citations in the body of the memorandum rather than in footnotes. Using correct citation form will make your memorandum look more professional. Using incorrect citation form will detract from its professionalism. *A Uniform System of Citation,* 15th ed. (The Harvard Law Review Association, 1991) tells you how to cite all legal authority. Use this work, popularly known as the **Blue Book**, until you learn how to cite cases, statutes, and other authority.

If you rely on *dicta*, say so. Give cases both for and against the reasoning if applicable. Explain doubts. Detail the reasoning. A discussion section takes a snapshot of the law at the time the memorandum is written and explains the snapshot to the reader. Sometimes the rule can be derived only by analogy. Sometimes other rules will be used to illustrate the situation. The rule might be a mixture of several rules. Rules may conflict. In each of these cases, the paralegal must not only identify the rules, but also explain the reason why rules have been selected.

***How to Incorporate Case Law.*** Read and cite the actual case, not a summary of the case. Although you will be reading summaries of cases from secondary sources such as encyclopedias or treatises, these summaries should not be relied on in preparing a memorandum; summaries may be inaccurate or incomplete. The summary of a case will not suggest factual similarities or differences. Only a careful reading of the case will enable you to appreciate the legal implications of the source authority. Paralegals' difficulty digesting the meaning of cases results partly from their inexperience, partly from their failure to prepare case briefs of all important cases, and partly from their tendency to rely on secondary sources. You must understand what these cases say.

***How to Incorporate Secondary Authority.*** In writing their first memorandum, many paralegals make the same mistake many grade school students make in writing their first report: they copy from an encyclopaedia or other secondary source. Worse yet, some paralegals actually copy the West headnotes or summaries as original material in their memorandum. Read and cite the source law, not the secondary sources. Secondary sources normally should not be cited (much less copied) in a brief or memorandum unless the citation is on a background issue over which there is no real dispute. Never cite or copy West headnotes. The paralegal student is always amazed to be "caught" copying from a West headnote and wonders how the instructor knew. The answer is that only West headnotes are written in sentences like this:

> Although decedent and man claiming to be her common-law husband and sole next of kin had lived together in one of homes maintained by decedent, and decedent had sometimes referred to him as her husband in city where that home was located, in view of absence of evidence of an express agreement to marry in praesenti, and in view of fact that decedent had been known as a single person in city where she had worked and where she had maintained another residence, and had held herself out as a single person in all of her business transactions, existence of a common-law marriage was not established. (*Marriage* ⚿13, from *Borton v. Burns*, 11 Ohio Misc. 200, 230 N.E. 2d 156 [1967].

While this extended sentence structure is typical of West headnotes, it is certainly not typical of a student paralegal's writing style.

The paralegal can cite an A.L.R. annotation in a memorandum if it is especially relevant to the question presented. The paralegal should recognize that A.L.R. articles will present cases on both sides of the question. The person who assigned the memorandum probably wants an answer, not a citation to an A.L.R. article. If you cite an A.L.R. article, take the time to explain any conflicts addressed by the annotation. Again, apply the case to your facts.

***How to Develop the Discussion.*** New legal professionals, whether law students or paralegals, have a difficult time writing their first several memoranda. Most inexperienced writers develop the memorandum discussion as if they were writing a book report on each case they have read; they tend to summarize case after case in their discussion section. However, a memorandum is about law. It is not about individual cases. You can describe tree after tree, or you can describe the forest. The paralegal must realize that cases are parts of larger principles or rules. You *must* write about the rules or principles, not just about the cases.

A good way to spot whether you are developing the discussion correctly is to look at the paragraphing. Do you begin each paragraph with a different case, write about the case, and then go to the next case in the next paragraph? If so, you are writing about cases, not principles. When each paragraph in a memorandum discusses a different case, then the writer is probably writing case summaries and not deducing principles from the cases.

There is also an easy way to help overcome this thought process. Make yourself use "signals" in your memorandum.

**Signals** are ways to tell the reader how legal authority supports the argument. The standard signals are described in *A Uniform System of Citation* (Figure 4-1). Look at how these signals are used. If a case fully supports the statement you made, simply cite the case without any signal. If the case is merely an example of how a case supports the statement you made, then write "See, *e.g.*, . . ."

When you use signals in your discussion section, the reader will look at the cases as principles rather than as isolated cases. Using signals helps you, the writer, to begin synthesizing the cases. As you begin to group cases, you begin to look for common threads or principles. Your final product will appear more professional. Peruse the first draft of your memorandum to see how signals are used. This will tell more about the extent to which your thinking is developed on the subject. If the memorandum appears to discuss case after case, rewrite it using signals.

In summary, the discussion section must initially identify and justify the legal principle used to reach the conclusion of the memorandum. Then this rule is applied to the facts.

**Applying the Principle to the Facts.** Law is not just abstract principles. Law is not just rules. Law is a way to solve problems. Memorandum writing involves the application of rules to problems. This means you must discuss how the facts affect the principle. The facts distinguish one case from another. Facts show how rules can conflict with one another.

Consider a parent who tells a child not to leave the house until the parent returns from work. This is a rule. Yet if a fire breaks out, the child must make a judgment. Facts can change rules. In some cases, the facts fit the rule. In such cases the paralegal need only describe how the facts fit within the rule.

The point is that the memorandum writer must first deduce principles from the primary source law and then apply the principles to the facts of the problem. A major flaw in the writing of some paralegals is their failure to address the facts of the case and relate the facts to the legal principles.

If the facts are unclear, say so. If you need more facts, say so. If the facts are disputed, tell how believing one version over another version might affect the outcome. In a memorandum, the paralegal will try to do what a court will do: distinguish the facts, harmonize cases, and narrow or expand a rule.

Most general principles of law can be narrowed to more precise principles, and narrow principles can be expanded to general principles. A precedent may be expanded or limited in subsequent cases. The facts will often be the reason why the court finds it necessary to change a rule or to change the scope of the rule. You need to show why your situation is unique.

Applying the principles to the facts is the step most paralegals forget in their discussion section.

**Explaining Your Reasoning.** Your conclusion is given in a separate section of the memorandum. However, the discussion section explains how you reach the conclusion. If facts are disputed, explain how the outcome of this dispute affects your analysis. If the principle applicable to the dispute is uncertain, explain the choices. State your reservation or doubts about the conclusion.

**FIGURE 4-1 SIGNALS THAT INDICATE HOW LEGAL AUTHORITY SUPPORTS YOUR ARGUMENT**

**Introductory Signals**

**(a) Signals that indicate support.**

[no signal] Cited authority (i) states the proposition, (ii) identifies the source of a quotation, or (iii) identifies an authority referred to in text.

*E.g.,* Cited authority states the proposition; other authorities also state the proposition, but citation to them would not be helpful. "*E.g.,*" may also be used in combination with other signals, preceded by a comma:

*See, e.g.,*
*But see, e.g.,*

*Accord* Cited authority directly supports the proposition, but in a slightly different way than the authority(ies) first cited. "*Accord*" is commonly used when two or more cases are on point but the text refers to only one; the others are then introduced by "*accord*." Similarly, the law of one jurisdiction may be cited as in accord with that of another.

*See* Cited authority directly supports the proposition. "*See*" is used instead of "[no signal]" when the proposition is not stated by the cited authority but follows from it.

*See also* Cited authority constitutes additional source material that supports the proposition. "*See also*" is commonly used to cite an authority supporting a proposition when authorities that state or directly support the proposition have already been cited or discussed. The use of a parenthetical explanation of the source material's relevance (rule 2.5) following a citation introduced by "*see also*" is encouraged.

*Cf.* Cited authority supports a proposition different from the main proposition but sufficiently analogous to lend support. Literally, "*cf.*" means "compare." The citation's relevance will usually be clear to the reader only if it is explained. Parenthetical explanations (rule 2.5), however brief, are therefore strongly recommended.

**(b) Signal that suggests a profitable comparison.**

*Compare . . . with . . . [and] . . .* Comparison of the authorities cited will offer support for or illustrate the proposition. The comparison's relevance will usually be clear to the reader only if it is explained. Parenthetical explanations (rule 2.5) following each authority are therefore strongly recommended.

**(c) Signals that indicate contradiction.**

*Contra* Cited authority states the contrary of the proposition. "*Contra*" is used where "[no signal]" would be used for support.

*But see* Cited authority directly contradicts the proposition. "*But see*" is used where "*see*" would be used for support.

*But cf.* Cited authority supports a proposition analogous to the contrary of the main proposition. The use of a parenthetical explanation of the source material's relevance (rule 2.5) following a citation introduced by "*but cf.*" is strongly recommended.

"*But*" should be omitted from "*but see*" and "*but cf.*" whenever the signal follows another negative signal:

*Contra* Blake v. Kline, 612 F.2d 718, 723–24 (3d Cir. 1979); *see* C. Wright, Law of Federal Courts § 48 (3d ed. 1976).

**(d) Signal that indicates background material.**

*See generally* Cited authority presents helpful background material related to the proposition. The use of a parenthetical explanation of the source material's relevance (rule 2.5) following each authority introduced by "*see generally*" is encouraged.

**(e) Signals as verbs.** When "*see*," "*compare*," "*see generally*," or another signal word is used as the verb of an English sentence, the word should be printed in ordinary roman type:

For a discussion of limits on the property power, see Note, *The Property Power, Federalism, and the Equal Footing Doctrine*, 80 Colum. L. Rev. 817 (1980).

For a related view, compare Note, *The Rights of Sources*, 88 Yale L.J. 1202 (1979), which discusses the rights of reporters' sources.

---

*A Uniform System of Citation*, 14th ed. (Harvard Law Review Association, 1986)

A memorandum predicts what happens when you apply legal principles to certain factual situations. The paralegal is simply doing what most professionals do: giving an informed opinion. An appraiser tells a homeowner what real estate is worth, and a physician makes a diagnosis. Legal professionals tell what the law is on a given subject.

The legal professional leads the reader to a conclusion in the discussion section. The conclusion may be full of doubt. If so, the legal professional tells the reader why there is so much doubt.

## The Conclusion of the Memorandum

A memorandum must give an answer to the questions presented. This answer is given in a formal way in a section headed Conclusion or Brief Answer.

Most students are accustomed to giving concrete answers rather than abstract answers. Paralegal students like concrete answers, yet the law does not always permit certainty. The law does not always have ascertainable answers. Two judges who study the same legal problem may reach different conclusions. Paralegals should approach legal problems as they approach other abstract problems; there will not always be a single solution or answer.

Legal conclusions cannot always be definite, but any legal conclusion should be made as definite as possible. Certainly, if the conclusion can be stated definitely, answer it definitely. However, experience in the legal process will teach you that the "sure winner" can be lost. There is room for judgment in making conclusions.

Remember that case law changes, judges retire, and an overlooked fact may become crucial to the outcome of a case. The composition of a court can change—a court may become more conservative or more liberal. A judge might change his or her mind. The more memoranda you write, the more you will see both sides to a controversy and the more likely your opinion will be more hedged and balanced. But do not double-talk. Explain the basis for any reservations. In short, give a direct conclusion, if possible; if not, explain the reservations.

Remember that your supervisor or the client is asking for your opinion. The client is even paying a fee for the opinion. Your supervisor may decide whether to try a case or to settle it based on the conclusion you give. A client may decide to appeal or not to appeal on the basis of your conclusion. Frame the conclusion in the most definitive or reasonable way possible, given the law and facts.

A memorandum writer has to balance probable results, given a new set of facts, given a law that might be modified or even changed by this case, and given the existing trends in the law. But a memorandum writer does not have an advocate to argue the opposite side of the question as a court will have. Although a memorandum writer cannot know whether the same judge or judges will be on the court when the researched problem is actually decided, the writer should be able to spot trends in the cases. Trends may develop because of societal pressures or because of changes in philosophy of judges. Thus the memorandum should develop both sides of the argument.

At times you may have to write a memorandum without receiving all of the material facts. In such situations it is difficult to give unequivocal opinions.

Unless the law is certainly fixed and the facts have been carefully developed, the discussion section should be written flexibly to explore the legal and factual uncertainties. Even when the law is seemingly fixed, the memorandum might not anticipate an eroding precedent or a new trend.

Legal rules blur at the edges. Legal rules conflict. New facts change rules. Many such variables affect case or statutory analysis. If you want precision, the best advice is to find another line of work. The fuzziness of law is part of its intrigue. When you prepare a legal memorandum you cannot pretend this fuzziness does not exist. You cannot pretend conflicting cases actually are consistent.

A paralegal must learn to state hard and fast rules where possible, but also to acknowledge uncertainty where it exists. There is nothing wrong with saying the result is unclear "because . . ." or to say the principles of several cases are contradictory.

As you state the conclusion, do not write, "I believe," "I feel," or "I guess." As a professional, simply state the conclusion without injecting yourself into it. Some paralegals forget they are representing the interests of clients. This text tells you to write the facts neutrally and to make the conclusion as objective as possible. In the real world, facts are not neutral. Parties see events from different perspectives. There is much room for judgment in making conclusions. Memorandum writing is not a theoretical exercise. The writer should use the memorandum as a springboard for developing theories and approaches for the client. The writer should always be scouting for an advantage for the client, given the factual situation. Yet in the final analysis, the reasoning of the memorandum must constitute the best judgment of the writer.

## The Style of the Memorandum

**Style** is the individualized way you write. Look at a letter you write to a friend. The personality you show in the letter is your style. Because much legal writing is written impersonally, legal professionals sometimes think this means there is no room for style.

However, consider these two passages:

**Before:** The Appellee's argument that appellee is not responsible under the dangerous propensity standard is specious because an animal which has nipped or growled at others has demonstrated a dangerous propensity.

**After:** Appellee is wrong. When a dog has previously snapped and snarled at other people, the dog has shown a dangerous propensity.

The first passage is dull; the second passage is written so the reader appreciates the situation. Both make the same point, yet one is more direct and more readable. Legal writing does not have to bore the reader.

It is not unusual to see a clever courtroom attorney write a drab brief. This occurs when an attorney who is unafraid to use wits in the courtroom is afraid to use these same wits in a brief. Each writer has a different personality. Some writers are methodical, some are flamboyant, others are scholarly. You need to recognize your personality strengths and weaknesses. If you make points best with a scholarly development, use that style. If you are effective with a lighter style, use that method. But if you tend to be hurried or careless or to leave projects uncompleted, do not carry those personality traits to your work.

Legal writing is a precise art. It must be practiced carefully. Your personality changes with your audience. You act differently among peers than you act with your parents or your employer. You may be more formal with one person, less formal with another. Briefs and memoranda are written in a formal style, although some law firms permit less formality in memoranda than in briefs.

Formal style does not mean a stuffy style or a style filled with legalese. It does mean avoiding familiar or informal expressions. It means writing in third person (using he, she, or it, not I, we, or you) like most novels are written. Write "the plaintiff argues . . .," "the petitioner asserts . . .," or "the appellee contends . . ." Even better, use the parties' names; write "the Bank argues . . .," "the Roes assert . . ." or "the X Corporation contends . . ."

The point here is to use a style with which you are comfortable. That style should not interfere with the reasoning process but should enhance the way the reasoning process is presented to the reader. Chapter 11 will help you with style technique.

## A SAMPLE MEMORANDUM

Now that we have seen the process of writing a memorandum, let's prepare a memoranda on the law before *Griswold v. Connecticut* was decided. The year is 1963. Assume you are a paralegal in the law firm defending Estelle Griswold and Lee Buxton, who were just indicted for selling contraceptives in Connecticut. Your supervisor has just related these facts to you and said: "It doesn't seem right that they can arrest someone for this in our country. I don't know if there is a right to privacy in the Constitution, but there should be. Would you prepare a memo for me on this federal constitutional issue?" You might prepare the memorandum that appears on pages 237–243 of the Appendix to this text.

# 5 LEGAL BRIEFS

> For judges think that they must follow rules, and people highly approve of that thinking. (Llewellyn, *The Bramble Bush* [New York: Oceana Publications, 1960]).

A lawsuit is our society's way of resolving disputes between parties. A court resolves disputes by applying rules of law to the facts of the dispute. An adversary court system works best when both parties to a dispute are allowed an opportunity to fully argue their respective cases. Many legal arguments are presented to courts in written documents called briefs. A brief is written to persuade a court to rule favorably for a particular party. Many paralegal students who have never seen a brief may be mislead by its name. In fact, briefs can be hundreds of pages in length. A brief does not mean a short document:

> Originally, the American legal brief was brief in fact; it was the lawyer's summary of the evidence offered and the legal position taken, something to inform the court of what was coming or remind it of what had passed. Today, the legal brief is hardly ever short and often terribly long; oral argument is ordinarily much briefer than the brief. This is partly because litigation has become more complicated. The procedure has in a sense been simplified, but the issues in litigation—both the facts and the law of the usual lawsuit—have become vastly more elaborate. (C. Rembar, *The Law of the Land*. [New York: Simon and Schuster, 1980], p. 179.)

**POINTER: Sometimes lawyers refer to a brief as a memorandum when it is filed with a trial court. Be careful not to confuse such a memorandum with the intra-office memorandum discussed in Chapter 4.**

Much of what has been discussed about memoranda writing is applicable to writing briefs. Briefs, like memoranda, are organized around issues. As in a memorandum, issues are developed in a brief by identifying the legal principles applicable to the dispute and by applying these legal principles to the facts of the case. However, instead of predicting a conclusion to a legal question as the writer does in a memorandum, a brief writer *argues* for a particular conclusion. The brief writer will use both deductive and inductive logic in that argument.

Beyond the similarities lie significant differences between writing a brief and writing a memorandum. A memorandum is designed to give advice. In giving advice the main concern is objectivity. Good advice weighs risks and benefits. Certainly a brief writer is giving advice to the court in a brief, but this is not the document's main function. The main function of a brief is to persuade. The writer attempts to persuade a court regardless of whether the advice is the best advice under the circumstances. Whereas the memorandum is characterized by objectivity and neutrality, neither characteristic is expected in a brief, although the brief writer owes an ethical duty not to misrepresent the law or facts of a case.

## TYPES OF BRIEFS

The attorney/paralegal team files various types of briefs, depending on which court is hearing the case. A brief filed with a trial court differs in some respects from a brief filed with an appellate court or administrative agency.

### Trial Briefs

An attorney may file a brief with a trial court to support a procedural motion or to argue the merits of the case. For example, a party who files a motion to dismiss a case in a trial court might be required to file a brief explaining the basis or reasoning for the motion. The opposing party will respond with a brief. If the motion to dismiss is overruled, then the party might file a motion for summary judgment. Again a brief may be filed with the motion. The opposing party will respond with its own brief in opposition to the motion. The same parties may later have a dispute over a discovery question. One party may then file a motion to compel discovery. A brief may be filed with that motion. The other party may respond with another brief. The parties may also file briefs at trial or even after trial with a motion to amend the judgment or to correct errors made at trial.

### Appellate Briefs

The idea of allowing parties to appeal the decision of a lower court dates to 700 B.C., when Athens set up the Court of Areopagos to review homicide and sacrilege cases. Now most decisions of a lower court can be reviewed by an appeals court. For example, federal circuit courts of appeal review decisions of the U.S. district courts (the federal trial courts). The Supreme Court of the United States reviews the decisions of federal circuit courts of appeal. If an appeal is filed in a case, the parties will file appellate briefs.

It is through the briefs filed with the court that an appellate judge becomes acquainted with the contentions of the parties to an appeal. An appellate brief is typically more formal in both form and content than a brief filed with a trial court. Most appellate courts have strict rules as to the content and length of a brief, as well as to the color of its cover, the width of its margins, and the length of each page, to name just a few typical requirements. If an appellant files a brief one day late, many appellate courts will simply dismiss the appeal. Appellate rules vary for each court, so familiarize yourself with the relevant rules of the court before starting any briefing project.

### Other Briefs

Briefs are not filed only with courts. A brief might be filed with a labor arbitrator in a labor-management arbitration proceeding. Briefs may be filed in a variety of administrative situations: a black-lung claim, a Social Security disability claim, a merit system proceeding. Although such briefs may be less formal in their structure and presentation, the writer uses the same thought process used to prepare a brief for filing with a court.

Briefs frame disputes. Briefs debate disputes. A good brief helps the court see your client's version of the case. A brief serves as a reminder to the court of facts of the case if the case is taken under advisement. A good brief will be used by a court to write a good decision. This is how case law is made in this country. Remember that you are a professional writer. The brief is your work of art.

## BRIEF WRITING PROCESS

Brief writing is a fluid process. The first stage, like the first stage of writing a legal memorandum, begins with legal research. This is the time to gather the relevant primary authority (cases and statutes) as well as the various secondary sources (treatises, law review articles, encyclopedias) that support or contradict your client's position.

During the initial stage comes the assessment of strengths and weaknesses of the issues. As the writing process begins, the writer decides which issues are stronger than others, which issues can be ignored, and which issues should be grouped with other issues. Faced with one strong issue and one very weak issue, a writer may elect to omit the weaker argument altogether, rather than lose credibility with the court by presenting it. The writing process continues until the brief is filed with the court.

## THE FORM AND CONTENT OF A BRIEF

The form of the brief differs from the form of a memorandum in some respects. The parts of a brief will vary from court to court. Some courts are quite strict as to the format of a brief. Figure 5-1 illustrates the rules merely for the appendix portion of an appellate brief to one of the federal circuit courts. Requirements for a typical appellate brief include a table of contents, a table of authority, a jurisdictional statement, a statement of facts, a statement of the case (which is a review of the procedural steps in the case), the issues presented for review, an argument section (including perhaps an additional summary of this argument), and a conclusion section detailing the relief sought.

**FIGURE 5-1 SOME OF THE REQUIREMENTS FOR AN APPENDIX TO A BRIEF TO BE FILED IN A FEDERAL CIRCUIT COURT**

## RULES OF APPELLATE PROCEDURE

### Rule 30. Appendix to the Briefs

**(a) Duty of Appellant to Prepare and File; Content of Appendix; Time for Filing; Number of Copies.** The appellant shall prepare and file an appendix to the briefs which shall contain: (1) the relevant docket entries in the proceeding below; (2) any relevant portions of the pleadings, charge, findings or opinion; (3) the judgment, order or decision in question; and (4) any other parts of the record to which the parties wish to direct the particular attention of the court. The fact that parts of the record are not included in the appendix shall not prevent the parties or the court from relying on such parts.

Unless filing is to be deferred pursuant to the provisions of subdivision (c) of this rule, the appellant shall serve and file the appendix with his brief. Ten copies of the appendix shall be filed with the clerk, and one copy shall be served on counsel for each party separately represented, unless the court shall by rule or order direct the filing or service of a lesser number.

**(b) Determination of Contents of Appendix; Cost of Producing.** The parties are encouraged to agree as to the contents of the appendix. In the absence of agreement, the appellant shall, not later than 10 days after the date on which the record is filed, serve on the appellee a designation of the parts of the record which he intends to include in the appendix and a statement of the issues which he intends to present for review. If the appellee deems it necessary to direct the particular attention of the court to parts of the record not designated by the appellant, he shall, within ten days after receipt of the designation, serve upon the appellant a designation of those parts. The appellant shall include in the appendix the parts thus designated. In designating parts of the record for inclusion in the appendix, the parties shall have regard for the fact that the entire record is always available to the court for reference and examination and shall not engage in unnecessary designation.

Unless the parties otherwise agree, the cost of producing the appendix shall initially be paid by the appellant, but if the appellant considers that parts of the record designated by the appellee for inclusion are unnecessary for the determination of the issues presented he may so advise the appellee and the appellee shall advance the cost of including such parts. The cost of producing the appendix shall be taxed as costs in the case, but if either party shall cause matters to be included in the appendix unnecessarily the court may impose the cost of producing such parts on the party.

**(c) Alternative Method of Designating Contents of the Appendix; How References to the Record May be Made in the Briefs When Alternative Method is Used.** If the court shall so provide by rule for classes of cases or by order in specific cases, preparation of the appendix may be deferred until after the briefs have been filed, and the appendix may be filed 21 days after service of the brief of the appellee. If the preparation and filing of the appendix is thus deferred, the provisions of subdivision (b) of this Rule 30 shall apply, except that the designations referred to therein shall be made by each party at the time his brief is served, and a statement of the issues presented shall be unnecessary.

If the deferred appendix authorized by this subdivision is employed, references in the briefs to the record may be to the pages of the parts of the record involved, in which event the original paging of each part of the record shall be indicated in the

**FIGURE 5-1 SOME OF THE REQUIREMENTS FOR AN APPENDIX TO A BRIEF TO BE FILED IN A FEDERAL CIRCUIT COURT (Cont.)**

appendix by placing in brackets the number of each page at the place in the appendix where that page begins. Or if a party desires to refer in his brief directly to pages of the appendix, he may serve and file typewritten or page proof copies of his brief within the time required by Rule 31(a), with appropriate references to the pages of the parts of the record involved. In that event, within 14 days after the appendix is filed he shall serve and file copies of the brief in the form prescribed by Rule 32(a) containing references to the pages of the appendix in place of or in addition to the initial references to the pages of the parts of the record involved. No other changes may be made in the brief as initially served and filed, except that typographical errors may be corrected.

**(d) Arrangement of the Appendix.** At the beginning of the appendix there shall be inserted a list of the parts of the record which it contains, in the order in which the parts are set out therein, with references to the pages of the appendix at which each part begins. The relevant docket entries shall be set out following the list of contents. Thereafter, other parts of the record shall be set out in chronological order. When matter contained in the reporter's transcript of proceedings is set out in the appendix, the page of the transcript at which such matter may be found shall be indicated in brackets immediately before the matter which is set out. Omissions in the text of papers or of the transcript must be indicated by asterisks. Immaterial formal matters (captions, subscriptions, acknowledgments, etc.) shall be omitted. A question and its answer may be contained in a single paragraph.

**(e) Reproduction of Exhibits.** Exhibits designated for inclusion in the appendix may be contained in a separate volume, or volumes, suitably indexed. Four copies thereof shall be filed with the appendix and one copy shall be served on counsel for each party separately represented. The transcript of a proceeding before an administrative agency, board, commission or officer used in an action in the district court shall be regarded as an exhibit for the purpose of this subdivision.

**(f) Hearing of Appeals on the Original Record Without the Necessity of an Appendix.** A court of appeals may by rule applicable to all cases, or to classes of cases, or by order in specific cases, dispense with the requirement of an appendix and permit appeals to be heard on the original record, with such copies of the record, or relevant parts thereof, as the court may require.
(As amended Mar. 30, 1970, eff. July 1, 1970.)

## Table of Contents

Most appellate briefs contain a table of contents. Most trial briefs do not have such a section. The table of contents includes all the main headings to the brief (Jurisdictional Statement, Statement of Facts, Issues Presented for Review, etc.) with appropriate page references. For an example of a table of contents from the appellant's brief, refer to the *Griswold* brief on pages 199–202 in the Resource Manual Appendix. The table of contents in a brief is quite similar to the table of contents in a textbook.

## Table of Authority

The **table of authority** contains an alphabetical list of every case cited in the brief, noting the page on which each case appears. A separate list of every statute or regulation cited likewise indicates the page on which each appears in the brief. A section entitled ''Other Authority'' lists periodicals, restatements, and other secondary authorities cited in the brief along with a page reference for each. For an example of the table of authority, refer again to the *Griswold* brief in the Resource Manual Appendix. Most trial briefs do not have a table of authority.

The table of authority serves the same function as the index contained in the back of a textbook—namely, to cite the reader to an exact page for a reference. However, the table of authority references legal sources cited in the brief, not general terms and subjects.

## Jurisdictional Statement

Jurisdiction is the power of a court to hear and decide a case. The jurisdictional statement usually includes a statement of how the case was decided below, the type of appeal (interlocutory, emergency, or on the merits), and a citation to the statute or court rule giving the appellate court the right to hear the case. This section of the brief is usually routine and straightforward. In this section the writer tells the court how the dispute arose and how the court has the power to resolve such a dispute. In most instances, briefs filed with a trial court will not include a jurisdictional statement unless a jurisdictional question is at issue.

## Statement of the Facts

The facts of the case are the events that relate to the dispute between the parties. The party filing the initial brief is usually expected or required to recite the facts in that initial brief. In a trial court, the initial brief is usually filed by the moving party (the party making a request for the court to do something or not to do something). In an appeals court, the initial brief is usually filed by the appellant. Usually the other party (the nonmoving party in the trial court and the appellee in an appeal) will be given an opportunity to file a response brief. Next, the moving party or appellant will file a reply brief. Although the party filing the initial brief writes the facts, the party filing the response brief will restate any omitted or misrepresented facts in the response brief.

**How the Facts Change in the Course of a Lawsuit.** Between the initiation of a case and the time that case is decided by a court or a jury, the facts will change.

Begin with the filing of a lawsuit. One party files a complaint. The party being sued files a motion asking the court to dismiss the case. At this point, the court has no evidence before it. The only document the plaintiff has filed is a complaint. What are the facts in the situation? The facts on a motion to dismiss are the allegations in the complaint and anything that can reasonably be inferred from these allegations. The court will assume the facts of the complaint are true for purposes of ruling on such a motion. In preparing a brief in support of a motion to dismiss, the fact section would consist of the allegations made in the complaint.

Suppose the court overrules the motion to dismiss, and the opposing party then files a motion asking the court for summary judgment. Now the parties file affidavits with the court giving their versions of the dispute. The facts are now set out in the affidavits. Usually at this point the court still has not heard any testimony. The court cannot tell from the affidavits which side is telling the truth. The facts on a motion for summary judgment are the statements made in the affidavits. In order to prevail on a motion for summary judgment, a party must convince a court that there is no genuine issue remaining in the case. In these situations, the party says to the court: "Even if the other side's facts are true, my client should win."

At trial the court does hear testimony of witnesses. These are the facts in a trial brief. In trial briefs, the parties frequently argue over which version of the facts is more credible. In deciding a case, the court or the jury decides that one version of the facts is more credible. After such a decision or verdict, the prevailing party's version of the facts is usually accepted for purposes of an appeal. Thus the procedural posture of the case determines the facts.

In most appeals, the parties will retell the facts to the court in the fact section of the appellate brief as the facts were told to the trial court. If the case had been dismissed without a trial in the lower court, then the facts would again be the allegations in the complaint. If the lower court granted a motion for summary judgment, then the facts on the appeal would be the facts set out in the affidavits. If there was a trial, the facts would be the testimony and exhibits presented at trial. A court reporter would have transcribed the testimony and attached the exhibits to a transcript to be used by the lawyers in preparing the case for the appeal.

**How to Organize the Statement of Facts.** If you are asked to prepare the fact section of an appellate brief, you will need to read the transcript and summarize in narrative form the testimony of the witnesses. A narrative statement presents the facts in a story form as opposed to presenting them in a witness-by-witness fashion.

At trial, witnesses are sometimes called ad hoc, as they are available. Their stories are not necessarily told in chronological or sequential order. Do not tell the story as the testimony was presented. Tell the story with a plan in mind.

In most cases, you will need to cite the page from the transcript to support each fact so the court and your adversary can check the statements if necessary. Thus you will need to put a page reference for each factual statement. This is usually done by referring to a transcript page "(t.p.____)" or to a page of the record "(r.p.____)."

The facts are the events that relate to the dispute. If the case involves an automobile accident, the facts include the events leading up to the accident, the accident, and the post-accident investigation. Further facts have to do with the alleged injuries or damages, including treatment at a hospital, medical bills, and any resulting disability.

**How to Present the Facts Objectively and Favorably.** In a memorandum, the facts are recited neutrally. In a brief, the court expects the facts to be described fairly but knows the perspective is that of an advocate. The most effective factual statement will appear to have been written neutrally but actually will slant the facts favorably to your client's side. For example, a brief written on behalf of the wrongdoer might simply say this:

> As a result of this accident, John Roe sustained an injury to his right arm.

If you represent the injured party, however, you might be more specific:

> As a result of this accident, Joe Roe's right arm was mangled in the punch press and is now nearly paralyzed. Despite extensive rehabilitative therapy, Mr. Roe has regained only 30 percent of the use of his right arm. Before the accident, the plaintiff was right-handed.

A rule common to writing both case briefs and memoranda is to include all relevant and material facts and to omit any facts not relevant or material to the dispute. This rule works well when the goal is to achieve neutrality or objectivity.

The decision to include or exclude a marginally relevant fact is more subjective. Some facts naturally evoke sympathy with judges. Decisions to include or exclude facts in the fact section of the brief should be made from an adversarial perspective.

Less-experienced lawyers and paralegals frequently ignore facts that negatively impact their case. This is a mistake. If damaging facts are ignored in a brief, a good opponent highlights this "oversight" repeatedly in a response brief, stressing how important these facts are to the disposition of the case. Remember that a good opponent exploits any unfair presentation of the facts. The court then wonders why facts were omitted. Do not ignore bad facts.

Leave out facts that do not affect the outcome of the issues being briefed. Include all facts that are relevant to the outcome—stress the favorable ones and downplay the unfavorable. Although this advice is inherently contradictory, the best way to write the facts in a brief is to write them fairly but slant them in favor of your client.

**How to Downplay Unfavorable Facts.** Different brief writers use different techniques to downplay unfavorable facts. Some writers like to bury unfavorable facts in the middle or at the end of a long paragraph. Others downplay unfavorable facts by the order in which the facts are presented, by sentence structure, by association with more favorable facts, or by word selection. For example, in the following passage, the plaintiff was drunk at the time of the accident. See how this fact is played down:

> *Facts of the Collision*: On April 1, 1990, Alex Martin was the owner and operator of a 1985 Buick Regal Sedan. He was traveling in a southerly direction on Pennsylvania Avenue. As he approached the parking lot of Duffy's Tavern in Evansville, Indiana, Juanita White pulled directly into the path of his vehicle, intending to execute a left turn. She completely blocked Mr. Martin's lane of travel and he had nowhere to go to avoid the collision.
>
> Immediately after the collision, Juanita White stated that she looked both ways but did not see Mr. Martin. She acknowledged that she pulled

directly into his path and that the accident was her fault. Sometime later, when someone told her that Mr. Martin may have been drinking, was the first time she attributed any fault to him.

**The Importance of the Statement of Facts.** The fact statement of a brief is more important than the fact statement of a memorandum. The fact section tells the court what the dispute is about. If the brief is filed with a trial court, the fact statement may be used by the judge to refresh his or her recollection of the evidence in the case if a ruling is not made promptly. If the brief is filed with an appellate court, the fact statement explains to the appellate judges what the dispute is about. Remember that the appellate judges do not hear testimony of witnesses. The appellate judges learn about the case only from reading the briefs and perhaps by reviewing the transcript of the trial proceedings. In some cases, the only way the appellate court knows what happened in the lower court is by reading the factual statement of the brief. The factual statement should be written as favorably as possible for your client. Spend some extra time with this section of the brief. Reread the facts after the argument is finished. A little extra care with the facts can be very productive.

## Statement of the Case

In a case brief, there is usually a section called **procedural posture**. The procedural posture tells us at what stage of the case the dispute was decided. The case may have been decided by the lower court in dismissing a complaint or by granting a motion for summary judgment. The lower court may have granted or denied an injunction. The case may have been decided after a trial or after an appeal to various other courts.

The statement of the case serves a similar function. The statement of the case gives the history of what the parties did prior to filing the brief. It tells about the complaint, the answer, discovery disputes, and about the trial. With this background, the statement of the case also sets the stage for the present brief. It tells how the parties have reached this particular juncture in the case.

But there is another important role for this section of a brief. This section tells how the issues will be defined. As we noted in our discussion of the fact section of a brief, the facts of the case considered relevant differ at various stages of a case. The statement of the case pinpoints the way the court will look at your client's version of the facts.

Assume a traffic accident where vehicles heading in cross directions collide at an intersection and both parties claim a green light. One party files a lawsuit. If the other party files a motion to dismiss, the court must assume the truth of the plaintiff's allegations. If this case is dismissed and later appealed, the statement of the case will tell the appellate judges how the facts must be reviewed. The appellate court, like the trial court, must assume the truth of the allegations of the complaint.

The defendant might file a motion for summary judgment with an affidavit saying he had the green light. The plaintiff might then file an affidavit saying she had the green light. On a motion for summary judgment the court cannot tell who is telling the truth, but will only determine if a genuine dispute exists as to the material facts of the controversy. In this hypothetical there is a genuine issue of fact, so the court should deny this motion.

At trial, the court or jury might find for the plaintiff. Then, on appeal, the appeals court would accept the plaintiff's version of the incident, not the defendant's version.

An example of a statement of the case might read as follows:

> This is a personal injury action brought by the plaintiffs, Steve Smith and Mary Ann Smith, for injuries they received in an automobile accident on May 17, 1975. The plaintiffs sued Lu Chang, the driver of the automobile they occupied. The suit against him was on the basis that he was guilty of wilful and wrongful misconduct as set forth in the Automobile Guest Statute as it exists in Indiana. The plaintiffs also sued the defendant, Hideaway Tavern, on the theory that it sold alcoholic beverages to minors (the plaintiffs and the defendant driver) and that the consumption of these beverages contributed to the automobile accident. The owners of Hideaway Tavern denied that any sale took place and further contended that even if a sale took place, the consumption of alcoholic beverages did not contribute to the automobile accident.
>
> The case was filed in Vanderburgh County on October 19, 1975, and was tried to a jury in the Vanderburgh Superior Court with the Honorable Wilbur Williams presiding. The trial commenced on October 7, 1977, and on October 8, 1977, the jury returned a verdict for the defendants. On October 8, 1977, the Court entered judgment on that verdict. The plaintiffs timely filed their Motion to Correct Errors, which was denied on February 1, 1978, and on March 1, 1978, the plaintiffs filed their transcript and proceeded with this appeal.

## The Issues

Issues are the legal questions the court must answer. Issues arise in many different ways. A party who loses at trial may believe the case was not correctly decided. The party may claim errors were made in pretrial rulings. The party may claim errors were made in the discovery process. The party may believe the trial was not conducted fairly. The party may believe the court did not consider all the evidence in the case. In fact, the loser may believe the judge made repeated errors in the case.

If the appellate court agrees, it will either **remand** the case (send it back to the trial court for a new trial) or reverse the case and enter judgment for the prevailing party. A plaintiff must identify the legal question presented to a trial court, and an appellant must identify the alleged errors presented to the appeals court. Legal questions and errors are identified by stating the issues. The issues define the questions that the parties are arguing about in a case.

The issue section usually appears early in the brief, although it may actually be prepared late in the writing process. Editors will tell you the preface of a book is often written last, although it appears in the front of the book. Issues and prefaces are written late in the process because you can write both better when you know the strengths and weaknesses of your product.

**The Importance of the Issues.** The issue section is perhaps the most important section of the brief. Many times it is how you ask the question that suggests the answer to the court. However, framing the issue requires substantial background in how legal precedent decides such questions. That is why this section will be written only after much research and often much rewriting. In fact, that is why this section is frequently written last.

If an issue is not raised on appeal, the issue may be waived. In other words, if a party does not include an issue in the appeal, then the court will not permit the party to raise the issue later. Consequently, a common error is to include an issue with little merit or to include two issues when one issue would suffice. Such a practice may compromise or detract from meritorious issues. Therefore a critical question is whether a marginal issue should be presented in the brief.

**How to Present the Issues.** Issues are written in a question form. In *Griswold*, for example, the issues were written by the appellant as follows:

> 1. Whether Sections 53-32 and 54-196 of the General Statutes of Connecticut, on their face or as applied in this case, deprive these appellants of liberty or property without due process of law in violation of the Fourteenth Amendment to the Constitution of the United States.
>
> 2. Whether Sections 53-32 and 54-196 of the General Statutes of Connecticut, on their fact or as applied in this case, deprive these appellants of their rights to freedom of speech in violation of the First and Fourteenth Amendments to the Constitution of the United States.

Some brief writers begin each issue with the word "whether." Never use the redundant "whether or not. . ."

Issues that are related should be combined. Splinter issues if doing so will help the argument flow better. Parties are given wide latitude in determining how issues are grouped or divided. However, a court does not want to reread the same argument stated three different ways, nor does it want to read an awkward brief in which issues have been combined unnaturally.

In preparing an issue, write the question by combining key facts with the legal principles. Inexperienced brief writers tend to ignore the facts in the statement of the issues. However, each case is different because of its unique facts. Use both facts and law in framing issues.

Keep in mind that although the issues may be written late in the process, the judge may read them first. Write them so the judge will want to rule in your client's favor before reading the argument section. Issues identify for the court the nature of the dispute. It cannot be overemphasized that how a dispute is framed often will determine the way the dispute is resolved. Even if you do not write the issues last, read them last to ensure that they are worded in the most favorable light possible, given the facts and legal posture of the case.

In summary: incorporate the facts into the statement of the issues in a way that suggests a favorable answer for your client.

## Argument

The argument section is the main part of the brief. Structurally, the argument section is divided into subsections that usually correspond with the number of issues, although at times several issues may be grouped under one subsection. Each subsection is given a subhead. These subheads serve the same function as headlines in a newspaper. A well-written subhead capsulizes the argument for that subsection. If written correctly, the subhead might be adopted as the rule of law or *ratio decidendi* of the case.

There is no rigid formula for structuring or ordering subtopics in an argument section. Sometimes the issues or subtopics are placed in the order they arose in the lower court, and sometimes the more important issues are placed before the less important ones. Sometimes issues are ordered so as to educate the court by presenting more basic issues before more complicated issues.

Under each subhead the writer presents the argument relating to the particular issue. In Chapter 4, we saw how a writer developed the discussion section of a memorandum by identifying the issue, identifying the legal principle applicable to that issue, applying the legal principle to the facts of the case, and then reaching a conclusion. As in the discussion section of a memorandum, each subsection of the argument in a brief should address each of these steps of the legal thought process. However, as in memoranda, the process may not be developed in the same sequence in every brief.

As you begin to develop a subtopic, remember that the judge deciding the case may have little knowledge of the facts or law of the case. A brief must first educate and then persuade the court on the merits of the issues. The first sentence under a subtopic is sometimes the most difficult sentence to write, especially for an inexperienced brief writer. Sometimes writer's block occurs because you have not carefully thought out the argument before beginning the writing process, but even an experienced brief writer occasionally encounters writer's block. Develop the habit of writing that first sentence as a journalist writes the lead sentence of a news story: to capture the attention of the reader. This first sentence might begin with a recitation of certain key facts or with a critical legal principle. Lead with strength if possible.

There is an old adage among lawyers: If the law is on your side, argue the law. If the facts are on your side, argue the facts. If neither the law nor the facts are on your side, then pound the table. In brief writing, there is some truth to this adage. If the facts enhance your argument, emphasize the facts. If the law favors your argument, concentrate on legal principles. However, if neither the law nor the facts advance your argument, consider not making it.

**Arguing the Facts.** The most common mistake of an inexperienced brief writer is to ignore the facts of a case in preparing the argument section of the brief. Many inexperienced writers concentrate too much of their argument on legal principles. Yet the facts caused the dispute. The facts are why the parties are in court. The key facts relating to each subtopic should be included in the discussion so the court can appreciate the relationship of the facts to the issue.

The court may not decide the case immediately after hearing the testimony. In fact, the case might be taken under advisement and decided months later. Then the trial brief will be used to refresh the judge's recollection of the case. Accurate factual accounts may be adopted by a court in its findings or decision.

In every brief the facts set the stage for selecting the applicable legal principles. The argument section should create the most favorable picture possible of the relevant facts related to the issue being argued. Too often this picture is omitted. Don't let this happen to the briefs you write.

In summary, the argument section of the brief should emphasize the factual strengths of the client's position while effectively minimizing the factual strengths of the opposing side. The single most common mistake of inexperienced legal professionals in preparing briefs is leaving the facts behind in the fact section of the brief. The argument section of a brief must explain how the facts impact the legal principles. The argument section must also explain how the different versions of the facts may affect the outcome of the case. An effective brief explains how facts are unique. Which set of facts is used by the court may determine what rules of law are selected to decide the case.

**Arguing Legal Principles.** In some cases it may not be clear what legal principles will be used to decide the case. The common law is premised on the concept of evolving principles to meet changing situations. Legal principles change. There might not be a principle to deal with a new problem, or the existing principles might be contradictory. As new cases are decided, legal principles grow into general principles or splinter into narrower principles. Existing legal principles are rejected or approved. The function of a legal professional in preparing an argument is to demonstrate which rule of law ought to be applied to solve the dispute. Lawyers argue the applicability of one rule versus another rule.

When I prepared my first brief, an attorney told me that if he had an old precedent supporting his position, he would argue, "This precedent has remained a settled principle for over a century." If the old precedent was against him, he would argue, "This antiquated principle has no validity in the twentieth century." If a recently decided case was favorable to his position, he would say, "This recently decided precedent has now settled this issue." If the recently decided case was unfavorable to his position, he would say, "This issue is still unsettled."

As the research phase is completed, the brief writer assesses what legal principles are applicable to the dispute and how those principles will likely affect the outcome of the case. Like the writer of a memorandum, the brief writer must first locate any binding authority. When there is binding authority, the issue is usually simple to argue. More commonly, though, there is uncertainty as to the applicable legal principle or how that principle should be applied.

In some jurisdictions, courts may have already settled questions that are only now being litigated in your case. These courts may have found problems with expanding a principle or with narrowing the principle. Another jurisdiction may already have grappled with alternative approaches. These persuasive precedents may help a court decide on an approach in your case.

On occasion, one case might contradict other cases in the same jurisdiction. This can happen when a court decides a case without completely researching the law. A court will then have to decide which case to follow.

As you identify the principle applicable to a dispute, assess why a principle should be applied to your case. Are there sound logical or policy reasons justifying the use of the principle? For example, in the early 1900s, many states passed so-called **guest acts**. These laws prevented a guest (a passenger) in an automobile from suing the driver for negligence. At the time most of these laws were passed, there were few automobiles. Giving a passenger a ride was considered a treat. These guest laws were based on the belief that a person should not be allowed to sue someone who was doing them a favor. Today many families have two or three automobiles, and in most situations damage claims are paid by insurance. The rationale for guest acts has eroded. There is little justification for permitting someone to be careless with the modern automobile. Today it is not a special treat to ride in a car; it is something we do daily. As a result, many states have held their guest laws unconstitutional. Some states have not. However, in each situation, the courts reassessed the rationale for these laws—the same as you should do in every brief.

***When the Principle Is Ripe for Change.*** Presented with facts that strongly suggest a change in the way a legal principle is applied, a court will sometimes be reluctant to change settled authority no matter how sympathetic those facts may be. In such a case the brief writer must provide an argument that explains the rationale for a change in the principle. The principle may be changed because other jurisdictions have confronted similar situations and have made the change. The principle may be changed because the logical extension of the rule leads to absurd results. The principle may need to be changed because of changes in society. When a court sees a distinction or a rationale for changing a principle, it will more readily conform the principle to the changed environment. This is how the common law system is intended to work.

***When There Is No Decided Authority.*** As they did in memorandum writing, sometimes legal professionals will find there is no decided authority on a subject. The brief writer must then construct an argument telling the court what principles *ought* to be used by the court in deciding the case. In *Griswold*, we saw there was no marital right of privacy before the decision of the Supreme Court in that case. Refer to brief filed by the appellant with the Supreme Court in *Griswold* (see the Resource Manual Appendix). Notice how most of the argument section under Point III was spent developing the principle that Griswold felt was dispositive of the case.

***When There Is Authority For and Against Your Position.*** At times there are cases both for and against your position. Although you will focus on the supportive precedent, do not ignore the authority against your position. Explain why these cases should not be followed. Harmonize the cases if possible. If the cases cannot be harmonized, then criticize the result of the contrary cases. When you ignore contrary authority, the court sometimes infers that those decisions are more harmful to your client's position than is actually so.

***When the Law Is Contrary to Your Position.*** If the principle of law is clearly contrary to your position, then the party must decide whether the argument should even be presented. A party is permitted to argue for a good-faith change in authority. However, make sure a good-faith argument is possible. Otherwise sanctions can be taken against your client. No brief should ever present a frivolous argument. Although a brief writer is an advocate, the lawyer who signs the brief is an officer of the court. That lawyer has certain ethical duties that transcend the adversary relationship.

**Arguing the Application of Law to Fact.** Many brief writers quit after they discuss the facts and legal principles. Yet this is when most legal arguments begin. In appellate briefs, for example, the facts have already been decided. The parties may even have agreed on the legal principles applicable to the dispute. In many of these cases, the parties are arguing over the way rules are applied.

We saw such a situation earlier in this text when we looked at the mail theft statute. A person steals mail from an apartment floor after the mail had been dropped there by a postal employee through a slot in the apartment door. This statute read as follows:

> Whoever steals, takes, or abstracts, or by fraud or deception obtains, or attempts so to obtain, from or out of any mail, post office, or station thereof, letter box, mail receptacle, or any mail route or other authorized depository for mail matter, or from a letter or mail carrier, any letter, postal card, package, bag, or mail, or abstracts or removes from any such letter, package, bag, or mail, any article or thing contained therein, or secretes, embezzles, or destroys any such letter, postal card, package, bag, or mail, or any article or thing contained therein . . . .

Assume this is the first case on the subject. The parties file briefs arguing over whether this statute fits their situation. The parties have agreed on the facts. The rule (the mail-theft statute) is also a given. However, the issue is whether the rule fits the facts.

Brief writers develop an argument by the same inductive or deductive approaches used in developing the discussion section of a memorandum. The brief can use analysis or illustrations to argue the conclusion. The analysis should explore the rationale for the legal principle or rule. In the mail theft situation the government might argue that the statute is intended to ensure the intended recipient receives the mail and that the statute should be broadly read to meet that objective. The defendant might argue that criminal statutes are narrowly construed and once the mail is inside the apartment it can no longer be considered within the realm of the post office authority.

The brief writer shows how facts of the case differ from those of other decided cases (distinguishing your case from other cases). The brief writer might describe how a favorable decision for your client would make other cases or statutes consistent (harmonizing the rules). In arguing the application of law to facts, the object is to convince a court that the most logical and wisest approach is to fit the rule to your client's position.

The facts of your case are usually unique in some way. New facts bend rules. The brief writer who can draw a word illustration of how facts are different or distinguishable from other decided cases or how facts are outside the scope of a statute will start with a decided advantage in the brief-writing process.

### The Conclusion Section

The conclusion section of the brief tells the court what the party wants. Do you want the court to grant an injunction, to award damages, to order a party to produce a document, or to reverse a case? In short, this section tells the court what ruling the party is seeking. Be specific. It is useless to present a brilliant argument if the court is unsure after reading the argument what relief is appropriate.

## THE STYLE OF A BRIEF

Style is the personalized way you write. A brief is written in a formal style, but formal does not mean stuffy or boring. As in any form of writing, the writer should use a style consistent with his or her personality. A writer cannot educate or persuade a court by using stuffy language or convoluted principles a judge cannot comprehend.

The most important principle for a brief writer is to write so the court understands and appreciates your client's position. The brief must be readable. If the court consists of judges who are sophisticated students of the law, the argument can explain the subtleties of the law. If the court is less sophisticated, you must write the argument more to the point.

Chapter 11 of this text addresses how to develop a more readable style. You can adjust sentence length or word length, depending on the audience. Shorter sentences are generally easier to understand, as are shorter words. Do not search for longer words to impress the court. Search for shorter words to make the brief more understandable. The most brilliant argument is useless if the court does not understand it. The goal is to develop an argument in readable language. Yet readability is just one concern of the brief writer. A brief must also persuade.

Law deals with human problems. Although brief writers cannot inject personal opinions into their arguments, they need to present briefs with their clients' interests in mind. Your style should not be detached from your client's position. A brief writer presents an argument as a novelist tells a story. The novel is a story about events that occur, not about the novelist's opinion of the events. A brief is an argument. A novel develops a story with a plot; a brief develops an argument by combining facts and law. This is the design of a brief. The way the legal professional tells these facts and law can affect the decision in a case.

### Rules for Effective Brief Writing

Here are some rules to help you present the facts and law in an effective way:

**1. Do not simply rephrase legal authority.** The study of law requires the ability to derive legal principles from primary source materials. Inexperienced legal professionals tend to read a case or secondary source and simply repeat or rehash the language in their brief without really understanding the material. (This is the same problem teachers see in lower grades when students paraphrase material from an encyclopedia.)

The point is to read and understand the source law materials. Then explain the legal principle with readable style without losing the meaning of the original principles.

**2. Do not discuss case after case in paragraph after paragraph.** Cases are precedents to be followed. However, it is the principle or holding in the cases, not the case itself, that is important. One of the best diagnostic clues as to whether you are handling the principles correctly is to look at your paragraphs. If you begin one paragraph with ''In *Smith v. Jones* the court said . . .,'' and begin the next paragraph with ''In *Doe v. Roe* the court said . . .,'' and begin a third paragraph with ''In *Barber v. Martinez* . . .,'' it suggests you are only discussing the cases you found and not synthesizing those cases. The cure for this problem is to review the signals set out in Chapter 4 (especially Figure 4-1) to see if you can combine the paragraphs into a single principle.

**3. Do not inject your opinion.** The court does not care how *you* feel on this issue. It cares about precedent and the merits of the case. The court does care about the logic of the position. Your opinion does not belong in a brief.

**4. Do not write in first person.** The brief is written formally. Do not use ''I believe . . .,'' or ''I think . . .'' A brief, like most novels, should be written in the third person.

**5. Do not exaggerate or misrepresent your client's position.** If the court feels you are not relating your client's position accurately, the result is usually unfavorable to your client.

**6. Do not ignore the facts in the issue and argument sections.** In their first efforts to write a brief, many students ignore the facts when they get to the argument section. But facts are what makes one case different from others. The writer who includes the facts only in the fact section and forgets the facts in the argument section of the brief is generally an inexperienced brief writer.

**7. Do not ignore correct citation form.** There are rules for citing cases and statutes, and a brief that fails to follow the correct citation form creates a poor impression on a court. Follow the citation form in *A Uniform System of Citation*, unless the rules of the court dictate otherwise.

**8. Do not ignore precedents that obviously impact a decision in your case.** An argument cannot omit relevant information. If certain decisions will obviously be relevant to a decision, discuss these cases.

**9. Do not ignore the court rules.** Even if you read the rules before you started, it is a good practice to reread the rules when you finish. It is easier to see if you have complied with the court rules when the project is complete. The rules will be different for each court, so you must familiarize yourself with the relevant rules before starting a particular brief-writing project.

**10. Do not neglect to proofread the brief carefully.** A judge will read the brief. If there are grammatical or spelling errors, for instance, the court will be inclined to think that you did not feel the case was important enough to proofread. When you say, "My clients right's" the judge will cringe and wonder who is protecting that client.

**11. Do not say "the law is clear . . ." or "it is obvious . . ."** Unless the law is "clear" or unless it is "obvious," the brief writer should avoid blanket conclusions. Most of the time these statements are red flags that the law is not clear or that it is not obvious. You lose credibility with the court when this happens.

POINTER: Too much legal work is done under the pressure of a deadline. Allow plenty of time. If you rush against a deadline, you do not have sufficient time to proofread carefully and check the rules.

## THE RESPONSE OR REPLY BRIEF

Briefs argue disputes. Although there are instances where briefs are submitted simultaneously to a court, usually the parties take turns, particularly with lengthy briefs. One party (the moving party or the appellant) writes the first brief, and the opposing side (the nonmoving party or the appellee) then files a response brief. The party filing the first brief may have to file a reply brief to the response brief.

Before preparing a response or reply brief, outline the strengths of your client's case. Try to ascertain how the original brief handled these strengths. Did the other party omit facts or fail to discuss the facts in the argument section? Did the original brief omit a statement or case? Did the original brief minimize or exaggerate facts or the law? By identifying the strategy of the opponent, you should be able to refocus the dispute.

Some judges may read thousands of pages of briefs in a year. A judge soon learns whether a party is fairly stating the case. If the original brief omitted key facts, you should note the omission without saying the opposing side was less than honest. The court will draw the conclusion. If the original brief misstated a key legal principle, give the exact quote from the court decision. Compare the quote with the misstatement. An effective technique is to quote the misrepresented material in your brief. Then show why it is wrong. Again the court can tell whether the party correctly stated the applicable principles. Seldom, if ever, should the brief attack the other brief writer.

At times a brief writer may personally attack your client. Do not respond to such an *ad hominen* argument. Instead, simply point out that the other side prefers to avoid the legal and factual arguments in the case but would rather focus on nonlegal and personal issues.

At other times the original brief will have fairly stated the opponent's case. In those situations, your duty is to state your client's position as forcefully and fairly as possible.

Briefs are intended to present disputes in a civilized manner. Both sides air their arguments. Then a court will make a decision. The decision becomes part of our common-law tradition. Good decisions are made when good briefs are filed. As you write a brief, remember your importance to the process.

## A SAMPLE BRIEF

*Griswold v. Connecticut* was decided by the United States Supreme Court. Before the decision in that case, both parties filed briefs with the Supreme Court. Both briefs are reprinted in the Resource Manual Appendix. Read these briefs, and see how the writers applied the principles of effective brief writing.

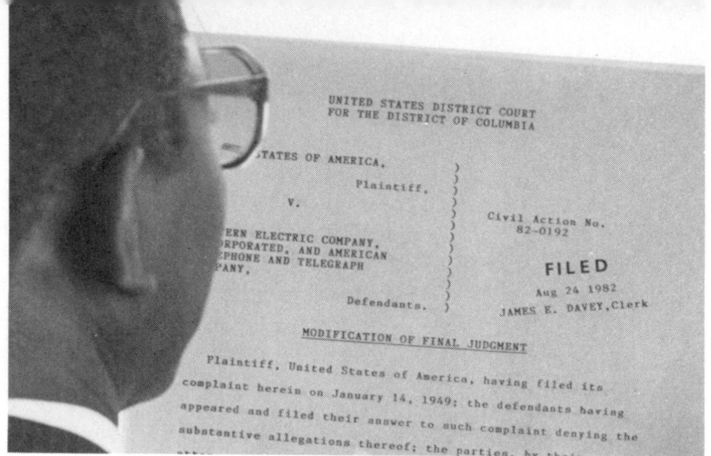


# 6 LITIGATION DOCUMENTS

> Success in solving the problem depends on choosing the right aspect, or attacking the fortress from its accessible side. (George Polya, *How to Solve It*, 2d ed. [Garden City, NY: Doubleday, 1957], p. 209)

In England, there once were nonlawyer experts called ''special pleaders not at the bar.'' These special pleaders would prepare litigation documents for filing with the courts in both civil and criminal proceedings. They had mastered the highly technical pleading rules required by the common law. Today paralegals working in a litigation practice often perform a similar function.

## BACKGROUND OF PLEADING PRACTICE

In the early colonies, there were no strict rules as to how pleadings should be worded; however, by the nineteenth century, pleading practice became very technical. As recently as the early 1960s pleading practice in most state courts was subject to highly complex rules. A party's failure to follow a particular pleading rule could lead to dismissal of the case.

### Code Pleading

Prior to the adoption of the current rules of civil procedure, a plaintiff would file a complaint or declaration, and the defendant would file an answer or plea. The plaintiff then would file a replication, the defendant a rejoinder, the plaintiff a surrejoinder, the defendant a rebuttal, and so on. These pleadings were used to frame in detail the issues in cases. These pleadings were referred to as **code pleading**. Under code pleading, claims had to be asserted by making the allegations fit within prescribed categories. Many cases would not fit into any precise pleading category. Numerous valid claims were defeated because the pleadings had not complied with the technical requirements of the pleading rules.

## Notice Pleading

In the 1950s, the federal courts adopted the Federal Rules of Civil Procedure, and most state courts followed the direction of the federal courts in the 1960s. The philosophy of these new rules was to permit cases to proceed to trial without the strict pleading requirements of code pleading. Thus the primary purpose of a pleading is no longer to frame issues but to notify another party of a claim, which is why a pleading under the modern rules is called **notice pleading**.

Under the modern rules, most of the technical requirements of the common law have been eliminated. For example, Subpart (e) of Rule 8 of the Federal Rules of Civil Procedure simply says

> (e) *Pleading to be Concise and Direct; Consistency.*
>
> (1) Each averment of a pleading shall be simple, concise, and direct. No technical forms of pleading or motions are required.

Hence the only requirement is that a pleading contain a ''short and plain statement of the claim.''

Under code pleading, there were complaints, answers, pleas, replications, rejoinders, surrejoinders, and rebuttals. The Federal Rules of Civil Procedure have simplified the types of pleadings allowed. Rule 7 says

> *Pleadings.* There shall be a complaint and an answer; a reply to a counterclaim denominated as such; an answer to a cross-claim, if the answer contains a cross-claim; a third-party complaint, if a person who was not an original party is summoned under the provisions of Rule 14; and a third-party answer, if a third-party complaint is served. No other pleading shall be allowed, except that the court may order a reply to an answer or a third-party answer.

Under Rule 7, a party states the initial claim in a complaint. The defendant's responsive pleading is an answer. A defendant who asserts a claim against a plaintiff files a counterclaim. The plaintiff's response is a reply. A party stating a claim against another party (e.g., co-plaintiff against co-plaintiff) files a cross-claim. Parties against whom cross-claims are filed state their defenses in an answer.

**Practice Under Notice Pleading.** Let's look at an example of the change in pleading practice from the old rules. In *Conley v. Gibson*, 355 U.S. 41 (1957), a plaintiff filed a simple complaint in the federal district court claiming race discrimination. This was all this plaintiff said. He was not represented by any attorney. The district court dismissed this complaint saying the plaintiff had not alleged a sufficient basis for a claim. The United States Supreme Court heard this case and said this simple complaint had alleged sufficient facts to state a claim.

Most states have followed this practice of notice pleading. There is now little formality required for pleadings filed in civil cases, although courts continue, of course, to expect professional documents.

The current Federal Rules of Civil Procedure also radically changed the way trials were conducted. Prior to the adoption of these rules, trial lawyers withheld information about their case until the witnesses were on the witness stand. Under the new rules, parties are given various ways to discover information about the other party's case. This is what we referred to earlier as the discovery process.[1] Parties may request the opposing party to produce documents; they may take depositions of witnesses and send interrogatories to the opposing party. A litigation paralegal will often be asked to draft pleadings for filing with a court. Many litigation paralegals are also involved in the discovery process.

## DISTINCTION BETWEEN PLEADINGS AND MOTIONS

The rules of most jurisdictions make a distinction between pleadings and motions. Generally, a pleading asserts a claim against another party or is used to defend against a claim. A motion asks the court to take some action against one party or in favor of the moving party.

### Pleadings

A pleading is a document filed in a lawsuit to assert a claim against another party or to defend against a claim. A party begins a lawsuit by filing a complaint. A complaint is a pleading. The complaint describes the claim of a plaintiff. Rule 3 of the Federal Rules of Civil Procedure simply says

> *Rule 3. Commencement of Action.*
> A civil action is commenced by filing a complaint with the court.

When a complaint is filed, it stops (or tolls) the statute of limitations. Other pleadings used to make a claim against a party in a civil lawsuit include counterclaims, cross-claims, and third-party claims.

When a complaint is filed, the defendant is required to file an answer. In an answer the defendant admits or denies every allegation made in the complaint. The defendant may also respond that it is "without information" to answer the allegations.

The defendant might also have a claim against the plaintiff. In such a case, the defendant files a counterclaim. A counterclaim is a complaint in which the original defendant takes the role of plaintiff and the original plaintiff takes the role of defendant. The plaintiff must answer the counterclaim by filing a reply.

There might be two defendants in a lawsuit. A defendant might also have a claim against another party. That defendant could file a cross-claim. A cross-claim is a complaint. The defendant who is named in the cross-claim would have to answer the cross-claim. A third-party complaint is a complaint against a nonparty to an existing lawsuit.

The function of a pleading is to notify the adverse party of the nature of a claim or defense. Pleadings are still used to frame issues in a lawsuit, although this is not the main purpose of pleadings under the modern rules. Issues are formulated more fully through pretrial procedures and the discovery process.

Pleadings are filed in noncivil cases as well. In criminal cases, a charge is made by an indictment or information. If a grand jury is called, an indictment is used. If a charge is filed by a prosecutor, an information is used.

POINTER: In some states, a petition rather than a complaint is used to initiate such proceedings as divorces or will contests.

### Motions

A motion is a document filed with a court to ask the court for an order against another party or in favor of the moving party. For instance, a motion might be made to request a court to grant a restraining order against another party, to dismiss the case, or to order a party to answer a question at a deposition.

Parties file motions at every stage of a lawsuit. Courts today generally encourage the use of short and concise documents. The technical requirements of the common law no longer apply to motions. Although some litigation documents still have strict requirements (a criminal indictment is one example), most motions have few rigid form or content imperatives.

## FORM OF COURT DOCUMENTS

The court rules encourage the drafting of short and plain pleadings and motions. Rule 8(a) of the Federal Rules of Civil Procedure provides

> (a) Claims for Relief. A pleading which sets forth a claim for relief, whether an original claim, counterclaim, cross-claim, or third-party claim, shall contain (1) a short and plain statement of the grounds upon which a court's jurisdiction depends . . . (2) a short and plain statement of the claim showing the pleader is entitled to relief, and (3) a demand for judgment for the relief the pleader seeks . . .

In addition, Federal Rules of Civil Procedure 10 states the general form requirements:

> **Rule 10. Form of Pleadings**
>
> **(a) Caption; Names of Parties.** Every pleading shall contain a caption setting forth the name of the court, the title of the action, the file number, and a designation as in Rule 7(a). In the complaint the title of the action shall include the names of all the parties, but in other pleadings it is sufficient to state the name of the first party on each side with an appropriate indication of other parties.
>
> **(b) Paragraphs; Separate Statements.** All averments of claim or defense shall be made in numbered paragraphs, the contents of each of which shall be limited as far as practicable to a statement of a single set of circumstances; and a paragraph may be referred to by number in all succeeding pleadings. Each claim founded upon a separate transaction or occurrence and each defense other than denials shall be stated in a separate count or defense whenever a separation facilitates the clear presentation of the matters set forth.

Further, Federal Rules of Civil Procedure 7(b)(2) provides that the form requirements in Rule 10 apply also to motions.

### Caption

Most court documents must begin with a caption (Figure 6-1). A caption contains the names of the parties, the court in which the pleading is filed, the

**FIGURE 6-1 SAMPLE CAPTION FOR ACTION BROUGHT IN THE SOUTHERN DISTRICT OF NEW YORK**

UNITED STATES DISTRICT COURT
SOUTHERN DISTRICT OF NEW YORK

| | | |
|---|---|---|
| JOHN E. HEAD,<br>Plaintiff,<br><br>vs.<br><br>DONALD LEGG,<br>Defendant. | )<br>)<br>)<br>)<br>)<br>)<br>)<br>)<br>)<br>)<br>) | CAUSE No. ______________ |
| | | COMPLAINT |

docket number assigned to the case by the court, and a heading or title identifying the pleading. The title might simply be "Complaint" or "Answer." The legal secretary will usually know how to format the caption.

## Introductory Paragraph

Following the caption, a litigation document might contain an introductory paragraph. The first paragraph of the pleading might say:

> John Doe, by counsel, Maria Lawyer of Lawyer and Lawyer, for his complaint against the defendant, Mary Roe, alleges and says:

This introductory paragraph usually identifies the parties involved in the pleading or motion and the nature of the document.

## Recitation of Basis of Relief Sought

Following the introductory paragraph comes a recitation of the facts supporting the pleading as well as the basis for the pleading. The basis for the pleading is usually a court rule or a statute that gives the party the right to ask the court for the relief sought by the pleading. The pleading explains in simple terms the facts and the rule of law that entitle the party to the relief sought. Rule 8 of the Federal Rules of Civil Procedure states that "[E]ach averment of a pleading shall be simple, concise, and direct." These paragraphs are usually separately numbered. Sometimes they are referred to as **rhetorical paragraphs**.

## Demand or Prayer

The pleading or motion typically ends with a "demand" or a "prayer." The **demand** of a pleading asks the court for a specific relief—for example, damages, injunctive relief, or mandamus. The **prayer** of a motion asks the court for a specific order—for example, dismissal of the case, an order to produce a document, or an order to show cause. The pleading is signed by an attorney, whose address and telephone number must appear on the document. A certificate of service follows.

### Certificate of Service

Any pleading filed with a court must be mailed or served on the other parties to the case. The **certificate of service** at the end of the pleading certifies you have mailed or otherwise served all other parties with the pleading at the time the pleading is filed. See Figure 6-2.

POINTER: No certificate of service is included in a complaint. Instead the defendant is issued a summons, which shows that the defendant received the complaint.

**FIGURE 6-2 A CERTIFICATE OF SERVICE**

**CERTIFICATE OF SERVICE**

The undersigned, attorney for the plaintiff (defendant) herein, certifies that a copy of the foregoing instrument was served upon the attorneys of record of all parties to the above cause by enclosing same in an envelope addressed to such attorneys at their business address as disclosed by the pleadings of record herein, with postage fully prepaid, and by depositing said envelope in a U.S. Post Office mailbox this _____ day of ___________, 19____.

______________________
Signed by attorney

## THE IMPORTANCE OF DEADLINES

Paralegals may be responsible for filing and mailing pleadings or motions, so it is essential for them to understand the importance of filing pleadings on time. Most legal work must be completed before a deadline. Inexperienced paralegals sometimes fail to appreciate the critical nature of deadlines: *A case can be lost if a deadline is missed.* If a complaint is filed beyond a statute of limitations, the lawsuit is barred. If an answer is not filed within the allotted time period, a party can be defaulted. If a party misses a deadline for filing a brief on an appeal, the appeal may be dismissed or decided without the brief.

New paralegals are likely to be accustomed to an academic environment where deadlines are excused. Courts are less tolerant than your least tolerant professor. Mail litigation documents on time. Read the court rules as to how the time periods are calculated. The most common mistake of a legal professional is missing a deadline. Many of these mistakes are caused by miscalculating the time period. Usually the first day is not counted. Usually the rule provides how to calculate the period when the period ends on a weekend or holiday. If the other party served the documents on you by mail, the rules may give you additional time for filing.

The Federal Rules of Civil Procedure also tell how the documents are to be filed or served. For example, Rule 6(a) makes the following provision:

> **(a) Computation.** In computing any period of time prescribed or allowed by these rules, by the local rules of any district court, by order of court, or by any applicable statute, the day of the act, event, or default from which the designated period of time begins to run shall not be included. The last day of the period so computed shall be included, unless it is a Saturday, a Sunday, or a legal holiday, or, when the act to be done is the filing of a paper in court, a day on which weather or other conditions have made the office of the clerk of the district court inaccessible, in which event the period runs until the end of the next day which is not one of the aforementioned days. When the period of time prescribed or allowed is less than 11 days, intermediate Saturdays, Sundays, and legal holidays shall be excluded in the computation. As used in this rule and in Rule 77(c), "legal holiday" includes New Year's Day, Birthday of Martin Luther King, Jr., Washington's Birthday, Memorial Day, Independence Day, Labor Day, Columbus Day, Veterans Day, Thanksgiving Day, Christmas Day and any other day appointed as a holiday by the President or the Congress of the United States, or by the state in which the district court is held.

## PREPARING LITIGATION DOCUMENTS

Every artisan must learn to use the available tools of the profession. The tools of a paralegal for preparing court documents are the court rules and legal form books. Both types of tools are critical to the litigation paralegal.

### Court Rules

No legal professional should ever draft any court document without first reading the court rules pertaining to that pleading. If the pleading is to be filed in a federal district court, the paralegal must consult the Federal Rules of Civil Procedure. These rules apply to all actions filed with a federal district court, and can be found in the *U.S. Code* and the annotated codes, as well as in commercial publications.

Each state also has trial rules for practice in its courts. These state court rules are usually found in an annotated code. In addition, West Publishing Company and other publishers publish booklets containing these rules. If you are in a litigation practice, keep one of these booklets at your desk. Court rules are like the rules to a board game. Unless you consult these rules, you will not understand the function of the pleading.

The Federal Rules of Civil Procedure set out the rules for filing complaints, answers, discovery, pretrial motions, trial motions, and post-trial motions. However, different district courts have rules that supplement the federal rules. These rules are referred to as **local rules**. Figure 6-3 is an example of a local rule of the Southern District of Indiana. Earlier we introduced you to the discovery process. Suppose one party asks for the production of documents and the opposing party refuses to produce the documents requested. The requesting party now needs to ask for a court order to force compliance with the request. In some district

**FIGURE 6-3 A LOCAL RULE OF THE SOUTHERN DISTRICT OF INDIANA**

**Rule 13**

**Attorney's Conference**
**Concerning Motions and Objections Relating to Discovery**

To curtail undue delay in the administration of justice, the court shall refuse to rule on any and all motions having to do with discovery under Rules 26 through 37 of the Rules of Civil Procedure unless moving counsel shall first advise the court in such motion that after personal consultation and a good faith effort to resolve differences, they are unable to reach an accord. This statement shall recite, in addition, the date, time, and place of such conference and the names of all parties participating therein. If counsel for any party advises the court in writing that opposing counsel has refused or delayed meeting and discussing the problems covered in this Rule, then the court may take such action as is appropriate to avoid delay.

courts the judge would not order the production of the documents if the motion did not allege that the attorneys have personally met and tried to resolve the issue. The Federal Rules of Civil Procedure do not require such a meeting, but local rules of some federal courts do. The court might send the parties back for the meeting. Pleading practice is so much easier if you follow the rules.

Read the applicable rules before you begin to draft, and review the rules before you file the document. No paralegal should draft any court pleading unless the paralegal first consults the rules of the court in which the pleading is to be filed. Look at Figure 6-4, which is a chart of the federal rules matched with the appropriate courts.

## Form Books

In addition to the court rules, the paralegal should consult a good form book before preparing any court document. You do not have to draft court documents without help, but neither do you have to ask an attorney for assistance. Help can be found in good forms. Private publishers prepare pleading form books, some of which pertain to particular states or jurisdictions and others to certain types of cases. For example, Lawyer's Co-operative Publishing Company has published a multivolume set entitled *American Jurisprudence Pleading and Practice Forms,* rev. ed. The forms contained in this set include litigation documents pertaining to almost any type of case. For an automobile accident claim, for example, there are forms for a complaint, a cross-claim, and the affirmative defenses needed for pleading such cases. Form books contain representative motions for filing. Bender's *Federal Practice Forms* is a similar set designed for use in the federal district courts. Many publishers have compiled form books for practicing in the various state courts.

There is no reason to draft original pleadings for every case. If a form has already been prepared, then use the form. But do not be afraid to change the

**FIGURE 6-4 MATCHING THE FEDERAL RULES WITH THE APPROPRIATE COURTS**

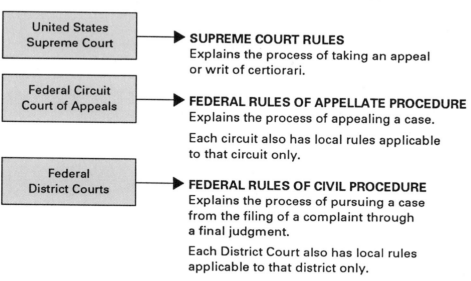

| COURT | APPLICABLE RULE |
|---|---|
| United States Supreme Court | **SUPREME COURT RULES** Explains the process of taking an appeal or writ of certiorari. |
| Federal Circuit Court of Appeals | **FEDERAL RULES OF APPELLATE PROCEDURE** Explains the process of appealing a case. Each circuit also has local rules applicable to that circuit only. |
| Federal District Courts | **FEDERAL RULES OF CIVIL PROCEDURE** Explains the process of pursuing a case from the filing of a complaint through a final judgment. Each District Court also has local rules applicable to that district only. |

form to conform to your situation. When you can improve the form, do so. In fact, it is important to tailor the form to the facts of your case.

POINTER: Often you will find more appropriate forms by consulting other files in your office in similar cases.

## CONTENT OF THE PLEADINGS

The substantive content of a litigation document will vary with the function of the document. However, several comments about content are appropriate.

First, claims or defenses in pleadings can be stated either alternatively or hypothetically. For instance, a complaint for personal injuries caused by a defective product can plead that the manufacturer breached a warranty, was negligent, or was liable under a strict liability theory. These are alternative theories of recovery.

Second, a litigation document should usually specify the rule or other authority it relied on. If the complaint is based on a violation of a particular statute, cite the statute in the pleading paragraphs. If a motion to compel is based on a particular rule, cite the rule in the motion.

Third, lay out the factual basis for the pleading or document. A pleading makes a claim. Claims arise from transactions or occurrences. Develop the facts in pleadings or motions as you would any story, so the court can understand the dispute. A court will be more inclined to rule favorably on the pleading or motion if the court understands the nature of the dispute.

Fourth, describe how your client has been or will be affected by the dispute. In a complaint, describe the injuries or damages. In a motion, tell the court why an order is necessary.

Finally, tell the court the relief your client is seeking. Remember that a pleading or motion is asking for relief. Be specific, if possible. The court needs to know what your client is seeking through the pleading or motion.

## CONSTRAINTS ON LITIGATION PRACTICE

Rule ll of the Federal Rules of Civil Procedure is a rather recent change in trial practice. What it does is provide a mechanism for sanctions for pleading practice that a court finds inappropriate. Rule 11 of the Federal Rules of Civil Procedure provides in part as follows:

> The signature of an attorney or party constitutes a certificate by the signer that the signer has read the pleading, motion, or other paper, that to the best of the signer's knowledge, information, and belief formed after reasonable inquiry it is well grounded in fact and is warranted by existing law or a good faith argument for the extension, modification, or reversal of existing law, and that it is not interposed for any improper purpose, such as to harass or to cause unnecessary delay or needless increase in the cost of litigation. If a pleading, motion, or other paper is not signed, it shall be stricken unless it is signed promptly after the omission is called to the attention of the pleader or movant. If a pleading, motion, or other paper is signed in violation of this rule, the court, upon motion or upon its own initiative, shall impose upon the person who signed it, a represented party, or both, an appropriate sanction, which may include an order to pay to the other party or parties the amount of the reasonable expenses incurred because of the filing of the pleading, motion, or other paper, including a reasonable attorney's fee.

It is not the paralegal's responsibility to decide whether a particular pleading is to be filed, so the point is not that the paralegal will face sanctions. The point is that the paralegal must use good faith and be extremely careful to ensure accuracy in any court document the paralegal is asked to prepare. If the paralegal is drafting an answer to a complaint, drafting an affidavit for the client to use, or answering a discovery request, accuracy is a paramount concern.

There is a second reason why accuracy in litigation is important. If your client does not carefully read an affidavit you prepare, that affidavit may be used to impeach the client at a later hearing. This happens more frequently than you expect.

When a client signs an affidavit or answers to interrogatories, it is done under oath. When a lawyer signs a pleading, there is a verification of accuracy. Remember this fact while preparing any pleading for filing with a court. In fact, striving for accuracy makes sense when drafting any legal document.

## PLEADING STYLE

Throughout this text, we have stressed the need to abandon archaic expressions and to write clearly and understandably. Pleading practice is no exception. The rules specify "short and direct" court documents. Nevertheless, some lawyers continue to prepare pleadings in stilted legalese. This problem is a remnant of the practice of earlier generations of lawyers who were required to deal with the technical rules for litigation documents. Some lawyers who never practiced under the old rules use forms passed down from lawyers who did. Other lawyers use outdated form books.

Earlier in this chapter we saw the Supreme Court tell the lower courts that pleadings do not need to be technical to comply with the rules. This discussion should not lead to the conclusion that pleadings should be written informally. That conclusion would be wrong. Courts expect a professional product. A legal writer should write clearly, not informally.

Any professional writer understands the demands of the audience. Your audience is a judge. That judge is highly educated. A pleading will be subtly educating that judge about your client and your client's case. Read and reread the pleading with this principle in mind.

Write the facts plainly. Write in short sentences. Use your language. Some lawyers have an annoying habit of beginning every pleading paragraph with the word "that." There is no reason for you to do this. Some lawyers draft pleadings using the abomination "and/or." Certainly there is no reason for you to do that.

When you begin to work as a paralegal, don't be tempted to write pleadings with legalese. If your pleading is written in a professional manner, your supervisor should have no objection. When you begin to draft pleadings, write them so you can understand them. The rules require nothing more.

## SAMPLE PLEADINGS AND MOTIONS

It is helpful to trace a lawsuit through its course from a drafting perspective. We will examine some actual court documents used in an important civil case.

In 1965, Ralph Nader wrote a book entitled *Unsafe At Any Speed.* This book was about automobile design safety. During the 1960s the courts began grappling with an issue of whether a car manufacturer could be held liable for producing enhanced injuries in motor vehicle accidents even if its motor vehicle did not cause the collision. In other words, if a vehicle was not safely designed to survive a crash, then can its manufacturer be held responsible for the "secondary impact" (sometimes referred to as a "second accident")?

The pleadings (with minor editing) in this section are from *Evans v. General Motors*, 359 F.2d 822 (7th Cir.), *cert denied*, 385 U.S. 836 (1966), the first case to test this theory of liability in court. *Evans* was ultimately decided in favor of General Motors. However, shortly thereafter, the 8th Circuit decided *Larsen v. General Motors Corp.*, 391 F.2d 495 (8th Cir. 1968) in favor of the plaintiff. Numerous states had to decide this question that led to the following comment:

> *Evans* and *Larsen*, continuing their national battle for supremacy . . . have enunciated "second collision" principles precisely poles apart. Their clashing concept as to the appropriate legal principle controlling manufacturers' liability for design defects producing enhanced injuries in motor vehicle accidents but not causing or contributing to the initial collision, has led to a new "War between the States" unsurpassed since 1865.[2]

The facts of *Evans* are best recited by paraphrasing the facts from the appellate briefs filed by the parties with the Seventh Circuit:

> Roy L. Evans was driving a 1961 Chevrolet station wagon and was struck on the driver's side in an intersection collision. The complaint alleged the driver's side of the vehicle collapsed into Evans. He was killed as a result of the accident. The complaint alleged the 1961 Chevrolet vehicle did not have side rails but instead used an x-frame, which created an unreasonable risk of injury to the occupants of this vehicle. The complaint stated claims for negligence, strict liability in tort, and implied warranty. The complaint was brought by Barbara F. Evans, Evans' widow, on behalf of his surviving children.

## The Complaint

A civil case is initiated by filing a complaint. It is not unusual for the paralegal to prepare a complaint for the attorney's review. The amended complaint from *Evans* set out on pages 244–248 in the Appendix to this text is a good example of a complaint.

**Composition of the Complaint.** Like other pleadings, a complaint has a caption. When the complaint is filed, the clerk will assign a number to the case. This number will be written on the complaint.

The heading might simply say "Complaint." The first paragraph of the complaint, like the first paragraph of any pleading, typically begins by identifying the party filing the complaint.

There is no precise formula for the contents of a complaint. Usually the complaint will recite the jurisdictional facts (the facts that give the court the power to resolve this particular controversy). The complaint also recites the facts that give rise to the alleged wrong, the legal theory of the claim, and the damages sought. The complaint closes with a "prayer" for relief. The prayer is simply a request for specific relief: money damages, an injunction, a declaratory judgment, or the like.

A complaint can be quite brief. Two or three short sentences can meet the legal minimum. Yet it is not usually in the plaintiff's interest to file such an abbreviated complaint. A complete statement of the claim will educate the court about the nature and extent of the plaintiff's claim. If you set out the theories in detail, you will save much effort later when the court requires a detailed statement of the claim as part of a pretrial order.

The defendant will be required to answer the averments in the complaint. Writing short sentences can make it more difficult for the defense in good faith to deny the allegations of the complaint. A court will be able to appreciate the significance of its rulings when the complaint sets out a detailed statement of the claim.

## The Summons

The complaint is served with a summons. The summons is a form that tells the defendant that a response to the complaint must be filed, usually within twenty days of the receipt of the complaint. Defendants generally retain legal counsel shortly after they receive a summons.

A complaint tells the court what a lawsuit is about. It places the other party on notice of the lawsuit and provides some information about the claim that must be defended. Some court proceedings are commenced by the filing of a petition. Petitions are often used for divorce, adoption, guardianship, and estate proceedings. A petition is quite similar to a complaint.

After a lawsuit is filed, the party who is sued may want to file a counterclaim against the plaintiff or a claim against another party alleging that party is responsible for the wrongdoing. A sample counterclaim appears on page 249 in the Appendix to this text. These documents are structured almost identically to a complaint.

## Responding to the Complaint

Depending on the jurisdiction, a response to the complaint must be filed within twenty days of service of the complaint and summons. Parties can be defaulted and substantial damages taken against them if they ignore a pleading deadline. When a complaint is filed against a party, the party must respond either by filing a motion with the court to extend the time to file an answer to the complaint or by filing a responsive pleading. A responsive pleading is either a motion to dismiss or an answer. Before preparing a motion to dismiss, you must review the trial rules to see if your motion conforms to the rule. This is the attorney's ultimate responsibility. Some important choices are made at this stage. If a defendant fails to file a timely motion to dismiss, the defendant waives certain of these defenses.

In answering the complaint, the paralegal will go through the complaint (preferably with the client) and make an initial decision whether to admit or deny the allegations. Of course, the attorney must review the decisions to admit or deny. Admitting an allegation will remove that issue from the controverted questions to be tried in the lawsuit. By denying an allegation in a complaint, the party puts that allegation in dispute.

A party may also need to file certain affirmative defenses with the answer. Rule 8(c) of the Federal Rules of Civil Procedure provides the following:

> **Affirmative Defenses.** In pleading to a preceding pleading, a party shall set forth affirmatively accord and satisfaction, arbitration and award, assumption of risk, contributory negligence, discharge in bankruptcy, duress, estoppel, failure of consideration, fraud, illegality, injury by fellow servant, laches, license, payment, release, res judicata, statute of frauds, statute of limitations, waiver, and any other matter constituting an avoidance or affirmative defense. When a party has mistakenly designated a defense as a counterclaim or a counterclaim as a defense, the court on terms, if justice so requires, shall treat the pleading as if there had been a proper designation.

If these affirmative defenses are not claimed in the answer, they could be waived.

Often only a few sentences are sufficient to meet the minimum requirements for filing an answer. However, if your investigation is fairly complete, the answer can map out the defense. A detailed answer can help educate the court about the merits of the defense, although at times a party might tactically decide to file a skeleton document to avoid educating the other party about its knowledge of the case. The answer filed in *Evans* is on page 250 in the Appendix.

## DISCOVERY PRACTICE

Lawyers typically do not like the day-to-day discovery practice. As we noted at the beginning of this chapter, a generation ago trials were conducted by ambush, with neither side disclosing information to the oppposition. Now, with the liberal rules of discovery, almost the reverse is true. Parties are required through the discovery process to disclose their entire case to the other side.

One method for conducting discovery is sending interrogatories to the adverse party. The paralegal might draft these questions. There are form books to help, but the questions should be tailored to your particular case. The party answering these interrogatories (perhaps another paralegal) will often answer these questions by providing as little information as possible while still complying with the rules. Interrogatories should be worded with this reality in mind.

In *Evans*, the plaintiff filed an extensive set of interrogatories. Some of them have been included on pages 253–254 in the Appendix.

In many cases, rules limit the number of interrogatories a party can file. Hence the use of this scarce resource should be tailored to aid other discovery devices. Asking a party to itemize bills or other damages in a personal injury lawsuit may provide more information than simply asking the party to explain the accident. The paralegal who answers these interrogatories should remember that the client will be signing the answers. The client may be confronted with these answers at a trial. Prepare the answers with this thought in mind.

The paralegal will prepare requests for production of documents to serve on the other party to the lawsuit. This is a request for the other side to produce exhibits and other documents that can be used in the lawsuit. In a substantial case that involves a major corporate client, the paralegal can spend months reviewing documents that must be produced pursuant to such a request. If a document is requested and if there is no basis for objection, the document must be produced. Under no circumstances should it be concealed. The risk is that sanctions will be taken against your client. From a practical standpoint it is not unusual for a discharged employee to give this information to the other side of a case. Then the effects on the lawsuit could be devastating.

In drafting discovery responses, the paralegal must understand that even inadvertent failure to produce a document might be construed by a jury or the court as an attempt to subvert the process. If a paralegal placed in charge of answering a request has any questions as to whether some item should be produced, the paralegal must ask the supervising attorney. Always err on the side of caution.

## OTHER PRETRIAL MOTIONS

Parties will file numerous types of motions prior to a trial. Most of these motions are catalogued by the Federal Rules of Civil Procedure. Remember that a motion is simply a request to a court to take a particular action.

A commonly filed pretrial motion is a motion for summary judgment. It asks the court to rule for a particular party without a trial. Technically the motion claims there is no genuine issue of material fact that needs to be tried. Normally a summary judgment motion is filed with affidavits and other discovery information.

The paralegal may be asked to prepare the supporting affidavits. An affidavit is a sworn written statement. Paralegals routinely prepare affidavits. Also, the parties will usually file a brief with the motion.

I have always stressed to my paralegal students how carelessly prepared pleadings might be used at a trial against a party. In one of my first paralegal classes I emphasized how important it is to draft accurately. Several years later I was involved in a case in which one of my former paralegal students had prepared the pleadings. The cross-claim he had written for his client contradicted his client's position in the case. Improperly prepared pleadings can haunt a case.

## PREPARATION FOR TRIAL

The court will order disclosure of witnesses' names and addresses as well as proposed exhibits. The paralegal will often prepare these lists for trial. They are important. If a witness or exhibit is omitted, the court might not permit the witness to testify or might exclude an exhibit. Motions will be made at trial such as a **motion in limine** (a motion to prevent a party from introducing prejudicial evidence during the trial).

At trial, written motions will usually be prepared for a directed verdict (a request that the trial be terminated because the other party has not adduced sufficient evidence to warrant a finding) at the close of the adverse party's case and at the close of all of the evidence.

Jury instructions will need to be prepared. Remember your audience. It is the jury. Write the instructions so they can be understood by the jurors. Many states have developed pattern jury instructions to be used in various types of cases. Consult these pattern jury instructions before starting to draft your own.

Motion practice carries with it serious responsibilities. Courts expect ethical behavior. Remember that the lawyer is an officer of the court. While it is the lawyer's ultimate responsibility to review pleadings for filing with a court, not all lawyers are as diligent as they should be. Lawyers are sometimes in a hurry. They may be worrying about another case. Therefore you should prepare documents with great care and urge your supervising attorney to review the documents with equal care.

Also remember to write understandably but formally. Apply the rules of drafting that we will discuss in Chapters 7 through 9. Be accurate. Be careful.

## ENDNOTES

1 Discovery is governed by Rules 26–37 of the Federal Rules of Civil Procedure.

2 *Frericks v. General Motors Corp.*, 20 Md.App. 518, 317 A.2d 494, 495 (Ct. Spec. App. 1974) (footnotes omitted).

# 7 LEGAL CORRESPONDENCE

> If you scribble your thoughts any which way, your readers will surely feel that you care nothing for them. (Kurt Vonnegut, "The Practical Writer," *The Royal Bank Letter*, January/February 1981, p 1.)

Legal professionals generate a lot of correspondence—to clients, lawyers, opposing parties, and other professionals. Legal professionals may use correspondence to give opinions, to gather or provide information, to demand action, or to settle cases. At times their letters will be used to make important business decisions. For example, many insurance companies require the attorneys who represent them in a lawsuit to write monthly or quarterly reports concerning the progress of litigation. One insurance company might receive its attorney's progress report plus a settlement proposal concerning the same case from the opposing lawyer. Based on the monthly report, the settlement correspondence, and other independent information, the insurance company will decide to settle or not to settle the lawsuit.

## FUNCTIONS OF LEGAL CORRESPONDENCE

In the general practice of law, a lawyer may use correspondence for various purposes. Correspondence will be used to seek information, to persuade, to provide information, to threaten, or to make a record of a position. Often a letter will combine several of these functions. A settlement letter, which is intended primarily to persuade, may also contain a threat. A letter demanding that a tenant surrender possession of an apartment may attempt to reason with the tenant to avoid litigation. A legal professional should be aware of the function of the letter before sending it.

## To Seek Information

Legal professionals are always gathering information for their clients. In a personal injury case, for example, the legal professional may write to the client's physicians to request reports. The legal professional may also write to other persons to request weather information, engineering reports, police reports, or background information about the opposing party.

It is not unusual for a law firm to have a standard form for requesting information such as medical reports. However, it is important to tailor your letters to the facts of your case. In just a few minutes you can change the form to fit your particular case, and your change will result in a more specific reply that may produce information the expert would not normally have provided.

Some professionals such as engineers or physicians may charge a fee for providing the information you request. Thus it is certainly worthwhile to tailor the request for the particular situation rather than using a form request.

## To Persuade

Legal professionals write letters to convince other parties to take action or to refrain from taking action on a specific matter. For example, a legal professional might write a governmental agency on behalf of a client to convince the agency not to take some action against the client. Lawyers write other lawyers arguing the merits of a case. Lawyers also write letters to clients to convince them of the merits of a course of action.

Persuasive letters written by legal professionals emphasize the legal and factual merits of a client's position much as the argument section of a brief does. A settlement letter that has good facts but a tenuous legal argument will obviously showcase the facts and may deemphasize the legal problems. It is significant to note that tactical concerns often dictate the contents of persuasive letters. You might be trying to keep from disclosing some information to the other side, or you could be trying to elicit a particular response.

Legal professionals can persuade by various techniques. At times, the logic of the position alone can be used to persuade. At other times, a threat of the consequences is necessary. Certainly sympathy is sometimes used to persuade. The point is to identify the objective and select the best way to achieve that objective given the parties involved.

## To Provide Information

Just as lawyers seek information, they are often asked to provide information to clients and others. At times this information is merely factual. A letter may report the status of a case or the result of an investigation; it may report the significance of a recently decided case or a recently passed law. In many of these situations, accuracy is the paramount concern, and the letter should be read and edited with this concern in mind.

Providing accurate information means including all the relevant or material information. It may involve choosing whether to provide detailed information or to delete entirely any mention of a particular matter.

The legal professional may also render an opinion on a matter. The opinion may be a legal opinion, such as an assessment for a client as to whether a lawsuit is advisable. An opinion letter may address the advisability of pursuing a case that may have economic, political, or practical implications. In writing opinion letters, the process is quite similar to that discussed in Chapter 5 for writing memoranda. In fact, in many cases, the processes are almost identical. In an opinion letter, as in a memorandum, the legal professional addresses all the pertinent facts and law and gives an objective assessment of the strengths and weaknesses of a legal position.

## To Threaten

Some letters are intended merely to communicate a threat of action. A demand letter to a debtor is a good example of such a letter. However, these types of letters are also used in a variety of other situations. A client may want to start negotiations under a contract or over a custody arrangement in a divorce-related case. In such cases, a threat might open the negotiation process.

Many factors govern the content of demand letters. For example, federal, state, or local laws may prescribe what is appropriate and what must be included in letters to debtors. The same is true of letters to evict tenants. It is important to research any applicable laws before writing such letters.

As with other correspondence, your first concern should be to recognize the real objective of the letter. If you send a demand letter to collect a debt for a client, you obviously want payment. Yet any experienced collection attorney will tell you that there are often other objectives. You might be seeking only to remind the debtor of the obligation. The debt simply might not be a high priority with the debtor until the letter is received. A gentle reminder rather than a threat may be all that is needed in these cases. In other cases, you might be seeking an acknowledgement of the debt or you might be seeking a response to the letter so that you can learn more information about the debtor. For instance, you may be seeking employment information so garnishment proceedings can be instituted. The letter may be intended solely as a record of a demand for payment to comply with a statutory prerequisite to an action.

The tone of the letter can vary from debtor to debtor. Hence a demand letter can be written as a friendly reminder, as a prodding letter, as an appealing letter, or as a threatening letter. There are many ways to write a demand letter.

## To Record Information

At times, the sole purpose of a letter is to serve as a record of an event or transaction. In such cases, the letter may be intended for use in a future litigation between the parties or to ensure that the other party is aware that a paper trail has been made to document a situation. Examples of such letters may be the demand letter, a letter written to verify a meeting or phone conversation, or a letter written to record a deal made between the parties. In these cases, many of the rules and guidelines for drafting transaction documents (Chapters 8–10) will be helpful.

## EFFECTIVE LETTER WRITING

The most important advice about letter writing is that you recognize the objective of the letter. One helpful way is to consider why you are writing a letter rather than telephoning. After you recognize the objective of the letter, try to fulfill it as effectively as possible.

Often a client's main impression of a law firm is formed by reading letters from that firm. A misspelling, a grammatical error, or a typographical error in a letter detracts from the favorable impression the client may have formed from a personal conference. Such errors sometimes suggest that the client's case is not receiving proper care from the firm. Therefore it is important to proofread each letter carefully before it is sent.

Letter writing involves more than careful proofreading. Style is the personalized way you write. Too many legal professionals hide their style by using canned letters or language. No rule says that your letter must begin with "In reply to your letter of . . ." or end with "Thanking you for your attention in this matter, I remain. . ." No rule says that a letter from a legal professional must be crammed with legalese. Your letter should strive to deliver the message in the best words possible, given the intended reader.

My former law partner uses contractions and colloquial expressions in his letters. He avoids all formality and legal terms. He is a writer when he is not practicing law. Some lawyers would never use any informality in their correspondence. However, this lawyer's letters are readable, accurate, and reflect his personality. The reader seldom misses the message. The point is not necessarily to incorporate contractions—or even informality—into your letters; the point is to use your own writing style.

### Guidelines for Effective Letter Writing

What follows are some guidelines to use in writing effective legal correspondence.

**1. Address the letter to a specific person, if possible.** Paralegals write letters to governmental entities and large corporations. If you know the person who is responsible for taking the action you seek, address it to that person. Otherwise your letters bounce from bureaucrat's desk to bureaucrat's desk. Even if you address a letter to the wrong person, that person will be responsible for handling it and channeling it to the right place.

**2. Keep sentences and paragraphs short.** A letter is not a treatise. Readability studies show short sentences and paragraphs aid the reader in understanding the message. Your letter will be more readable if you pay attention to sentence and paragraph length.

**3. Write personally.** Do not be afraid to write with pronouns. Use "I," "you," or "us" in your correspondence. The letter should not center the attention on you, the writer, but the reader. Write to that reader.

**4. Simplify the language.** A partner of mine asked a governmental agency if garbage trucks needed to have a certain permit. Here is the reply:

> Per your August 21, 1990 correspondence, received August 21, 1990, our agency has authorization to exercise discretion in the termination of policy, as well as the power to adopt applicable codes and statutes of other administrative/legislative bodies. In so doing, the Department uses as policy regarding the nonregulation of commodities with negative value (trash), 62.12 of the Federal Carrier Reports, where Administrative Rules No. 130, paragraph 25.130 is cited as authority for the non regulatory finding. If you have any further questions regarding this matter, please do not hesitate to call me.

The writer could have said, "No, our agency does not require a garbage truck owner to obtain a permit." The earth will not move and the National Guard will not be called out if you write so that the reader understands your letter.

**5. Tell clients what they need to know.** If you want the client to take some course of action, do not equivocate or give vague instructions. Lay out your instructions in a direct way. Otherwise you will only receive a phone call asking for clarification.

**6. Write what you mean.** So much miscommunication with clients occurs because legal professionals write letters to impress the client rather than to provide the pertinent information. The letter on the garbage truck permit issue is a good illustration of writing to impress the reader rather than to answer the question. A good means to accomplish a direct approach is by writing using active rather than passive voice. (We will discuss this in Chapter 11.)

**7. Write to the reading level of the reader.** The vocabulary and reading ability of your clients will vary incredibly. Do not write the same type of letter to all clients. In some ways, letter writing should be easier than other forms of legal writing. Visualize your targeted reader. Consider the reader's level of education and the level of background knowledge that the reader may already have. Some clients will expect formality. Formality does not mean a canned response. You can write formally but clearly. You can also write informally but clearly. Choose the style most appropriate for the particular client.

**8. Keep your emotions out of the letter writing.** Keeping this advice in mind almost always prevents letters written in anger or on impulse. It will prevent you from making insults and facetious comments in your letters. Seldom will you accomplish either a short-term or long-term goal by sending out a nonprofessional letter. If you are a target of such a letter, put it away before responding. This may not ease your anger, but it should ensure a more appropriate response.

**9. Proofread the letter.** Letters are often dictated in a hurry and signed with a glance. Spend a few minutes to proofread the letter before it is mailed.

**10. Check for enclosures.** Probably the most common mistake made in connection with letters is to refer to an enclosure with the letter and then fail to enclose it. Check the letter for enclosures *before* it is sent out.

**11. Mail the letter on time**. A mistake made repeatedly in the law office is neglecting to mail a letter on time. When a student misses an assignment, the student can anticipate a lower grade. When a legal professional fails to make a deadline, the result can be costly to the client. The client's bail might be revoked. The client might fail to attend a hearing or to review a pleading on time. As a result of your mistakes, the client might lose the case and be required to pay damages he or she otherwise would not owe.

## THE FORMAT OF LETTERS

As a paralegal, you will write thousands of letters in your career. This means you will make thousands of impressions. When a client shows one of your letters to friends and relatives, their judgment of your law firm's ability will be influenced by the appearance of that correspondence. Make every letter professional.

### The Legal Business Letter

Legal correspondence tends to resemble other business letters, although the exact format may vary from law firm to law firm. The essential elements of a business letter include the date, the address, the salutation, the body of the letter, and the signature. Legal correspondence may also include a reference line, a complimentary close, identification notations, enclosure notations, and copy notations. In the following discussion we will examine the important elements of a basic legal business letter, which are illustrated in Figure 7-1.

**Date.** Usually the date is placed two to six lines (three is standard) below the printed letterhead. The date includes the month, day, and year.

Legal correspondence is often used to make a record of an event or transaction. In Chapter 6, we emphasized the importance of complying with deadlines. Dates are important in most phases of the legal practice. Do not predate or postdate letters, and do be sure to mail each letter when it is supposed to be mailed.

**Special Mailing and Handling Notations.** If the correspondence is sent by other than regular mail (e.g., certified, registered, express, or priority mail), this is noted about two lines below the date and two lines above the address. If the letter is addressed "Confidential" or "Personal," this information is also placed below the date and above the address.

**Address.** The inside address of a business letter is usually placed two lines below the date or two lines below the special notations, if there are any. The inside address follows this format:

| | |
|---|---|
| **For an individual:** | Name<br>Business or title<br>Full address |
| **For a business:** | Name of entity<br>Department information if applicable<br>Full address |

**FIGURE 7-1 THE BASIC FORMAT OF A LEGAL BUSINESS LETTER**

**Law Offices of**
**Cheng, Long and Fortini**
**506 Samson Blvd.**
**Evansville, Indiana 47708-1234**

| | |
|---|---|
| *DATE* | May 17, 1991 |
| *MAILING NOTATION* | CERTIFIED MAIL, RETURN RECEIPT REQUESTED |
| *ADDRESS* | UNIVERSAL INSURANCE SOCIETY<br>One Bank Plaza<br>Suite 1187<br>P.O. Box 7007<br>Hartford, Connecticut 46240-7007 |
| *ATTENTION* | Attn: Ms. Samantha Rice |
| *SUBJECT* | RE: Claim Number: 39625<br>Insured: Tommie Thomas<br>Claimant: Terri Hunt<br>Date of Loss: May 17, 1990 |
| *SALUTATION* | Dear Ms. Rice: |
| | As you know, I submitted a settlement demand to you on February 6, 1991. You said that you would be contacting me to see if this matter can be resolved without litigation. Unless I hear from you before June 1, 1991, I will have no choice but to recommend to my client that suit be filed. |
| *COMPLIMENTARY CLOSE* | Yours very truly,<br><br>CHENG, LONG AND FORTINI |
| *SIGNATURE* | Jo Long |
| *INITIALS* | JL/jw |
| *ENCLOSURE*<br>*COPIES* | Enc.: Copy of Feb. 6, 1991 Settlement Demand<br>cc: Terri Hunt |

It does not do much good to mail a letter properly dated to the wrong address. Check the address on all correspondence. Do not rely on the secretary. If at all possible, address the letter to a specific person rather than simply to a company or agency, especially if the letter is going to a large corporation or a governmental entity. Otherwise the letter may be shuffled from person to person until it ends on the right desk. When you address it to a particular person, that person then has the responsibility for seeing that it gets to the right desk.

If the letter is addressed to a business but to the attention of a particular individual, this information is typed below the inside address.

**Reference or Subject Information.** Following the address, many business letters include a signal as to their subject matter. The information reads like this:

Re: Sale of Smith Property

Some companies prefer that you reference a file, billing information, an insurance policy number, or other information. This might read as follows:

Insured: John Doe
Date of Accident: April 13, 1990
Claim Number: XYZ-1334

In most legal correspondence this information is placed two lines below the address or attention line and two lines above the salutation.

**Body of Letter.** The body of the letter contains the contents of the communication (the message). Legal correspondence serves many purposes. The opening paragraph should identify the purpose of the letter, if possible. Often the lead sentence can state the purpose. If the message is quite lengthy, outlining the body of the letter may be helpful to both you and the reader. Such an outline will, of course, vary with the type and objective of the letter.

**Complimentary Close and Signature.** Most business letters end with a complimentary close such as ''Very truly yours,'' ''Yours truly,'' or ''Sincerely.'' The complimentary close is followed by your signature, under which your name is typed.

As a paralegal, you will use the firm's letterhead in your correspondence. Make sure that the designation ''Paralegal'' or ''Legal Assistant'' always follows your name so that the recipient will neither assume that you are an attorney nor infer that you are trying to pose as one.

**Copies of Letters.** When indicating that copies of a letter were sent to other individuals, the most common notation is this:

c: John Doe

For more than one recipient, add a ''c'':

cc: John Doe
Mary Roe
Atlas Corporation

It is acceptable to type "Copies:" or "Copies to:" and then list the individuals receiving the copies. This is typed two lines below any other notation. You might want someone to receive a copy of the letter without showing that information on the original letter. This is typed on the file copy of the letter as "bcc: John Smith."

**Enclosures.** Again there is more than one way to indicate that the writer of a letter has included enclosures: "enc.," "Enclosure," and "Enclosures (2)," are all acceptable. Sometimes the enclosures are also listed by typing "Enclosures:" and listing each item separately. When identification initials of the letter writer and typist are given, these are placed two lines below the last line of the signature block. The enclosure information follows one or two lines below.

## EXAMPLES OF LEGAL CORRESPONDENCE

A good way to learn how to write effective legal correspondence is to look at some examples of different forms of letters commonly written by attorneys. We have selected a settlement letter, a progress letter on a case, a demand letter, and an opinion letter. All can be found in the Appendix to this text.

### Settlement Letters

A settlement letter or brochure is usually written to persuade an insurance company to settle a claim. Although the letter will naturally strive to make the strongest case possible, it must not oversell the case and tarnish the firm's credibility with the adjuster handling the claim. It should be realistic. If there is some information that your client is not ready to disclose—perhaps a witness or an exhibit—you must be careful not to misstate your case.

A settlement letter is a cross between a brief and a final argument. On the one hand, the letter may need to address the legal merits of the case. On the other hand, the letter must also be sensitive to the factual strengths and weaknesses of a claim.

The purpose is to maximize the recovery in the lawsuit. The letter must use facts and law to convince the adjuster the case is worth settling with the demand. An insurance adjuster is a professional who investigates and adjusts claims. The adjuster and the adjuster's supervisor are your audience. Remember to tailor the writing to your audience. An insurance adjuster is familiar with the insurance laws. Although the adjuster does not have the in-depth legal training of a lawyer, the adjuster has more insight than many people will have in this area.

The adjuster may have personally investigated the facts and should already have made an assessment of the insured's position. Adjusters also know there are costs and risks associated with litigation. They will usually be more sensitive to factual problems than to legal theories. Therefore you should highlight the facts of your claim. Neutralize but do not ignore unfavorable facts.

The facts of an accident usually can be categorized as the events of the accident (both before and after). These facts include the details of the accident as well as the injuries and damages incurred.

Descriptions of injuries should be reduced to understandable terms. Consult a medical reference such as R. Gray, *Attorney's Textbook of Medicine* (Matthew Bender & Co., 1984) if you do not understand the medical terms. Explain the injuries graphically. Emphasize the pain and suffering. Itemize medical bills, lost wages, and hospital bills (so-called special damages). Itemize the details of treatment and the reports of the treating medical experts. Include the projected future medical care and lost wages as well.

Detail the physical limitations and emotional consequences of the injury. Describe a typical day in your client's life. Stress day-to-day activities that are no longer possible because of the injuries.

If there are unique legal questions raised by the case, state these theories so the adjuster will understand the implication of your theory of the case. State the law so the adjuster understands the law. It is sometimes beneficial to show comparable verdicts in similar cases. *Verdicts, Settlements and Tactics* (Shepard's/McGraw Hill, monthly), for instance, reports this information to its subscribers.

A typical settlement letter without exhibits appears on pages 255–259.

## Report Letters

Lawyers are typically asked by sophisticated clients to provide routine reports on the status of ongoing litigation. The main goal of report letters is to give an accurate accounting of the main points of the case. These reports are used by the client to assess the merits of a claim. The letter on pages 260–269 is a good illustration of such a report.

## Demand Letters

Some clients may consult your firm because they have a substantial number of delinquent accounts payable. Paralegals sometimes do the collection work for these clients, who usually have tried to collect the debts themselves. They hope the lawyer will be more successful. A similar situation arises when a landlord must evict a tenant from a rental property. In these situations the legal professional will be asked to prepare a demand letter.

Too often the legal professional reaches into a file and pulls out the first available form. Before you do this, take a few moments to try a few alternatives. First, find out the facts. Try to see why the debt has not been paid. Are there extenuating circumstances? Second, find out the law. Many laws deal with this facet of your firm's practice. A demand letter may be subject to fair debt-collection practice laws. Failure to obey these laws can be quite costly. A typical demand letter is illustrated on page 270.

## Opinion Letters

The U.S. Attorney General is routinely asked to give legal opinions to various governmental agencies. These opinions are published in a set of books called the *Opinions of the Attorney General*. Most states similarly publish the opinions of their attorneys general. These opinions can be used as persuasive authority.

Most attorneys are asked almost daily for their opinions on various legal matters: the marketability of real estate, for example, or how the antitrust laws apply to a particular transaction, or the validity of a noncompetition clause in a business contract. Often the opinions are given in writing.

An opinion letter is structured and written like a memorandum. In fact, the main difference between the two documents is that the client will read the letter, whereas most memoranda are read by other legal professionals.

On the basis of the legal opinion, the client may make significant business decisions. If there are doubts as to the opinions, these doubts need to be clearly stated so that the client can reasonably appraise the business risks and benefits.

The sample legal opinion letter on pages 271–278 in the Appendix concerns the marketability of a real estate title. We chose this letter not so much for the way the opinion itself is written but to show you how the lawyer spelled out all his reservations on matters he was not giving an opinion.

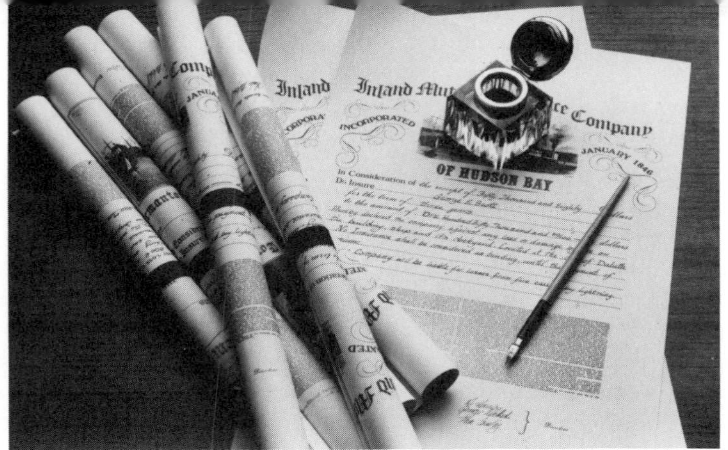

# 8 TRANSACTION DOCUMENTS

*DRAFTING*: I know no art more difficult. I know no art more fascinating. The law is given; we will presuppose you understand it. The situation, too, is given. We will presuppose you understand this, too. Not only what your client *wants*, but what he *can get*. Now, with these things in mind, to turn them into action; to find the words, to make the words clear-cut, precise in outline; to steer the words around the legal dangers; to keep them self-consistent as between the first paragraph and the fourth; to read them with an eye not only to where you want to get, but keenly, from opposing counsel's outlook, with an eye to what they will seem to have said if fifteen unanticipated troubles happen to arise. This is drafting. I recommend it to you. (K. N. Llewellyn, *The Bramble Bush* [New York: Oceana Publications, 1960], p. 98.)

Legal professionals often refer to the preparation of transaction documents as **legal drafting.** Legal drafting of contracts, leases, and other transaction documents is unlike most other forms of writing, and it has even been said that there is no other comparable form of writing. In preparing a transaction document, the paralegal will sometimes be a mere scrivener reporting the transaction or the deal. At other times, the drafter will be an architect of the transaction itself. One paralegal may rely on a form to prepare a contract; another paralegal may need to write an entirely unique document to complete a transaction. This chapter will explore the process of preparing transaction documents.

## PUTTING TOGETHER LEGAL RELATIONSHIPS

Transaction documents describe and memorialize the agreement parties reach as to how they will carry out a transaction. Adverse parties sometimes enter transactions with different perspectives. Parties will look for opposite interpretations in documents governing a transaction. Writing under these circumstances is different from other forms of writing.

The role of the legal drafter is more than just that of a writer and observer of a transaction. The legal drafter is also an integral part of the negotiation process. When you draft a contract, for instance, you will have the opportunity to choose to include or omit provisions to benefit a client. You can select a particular word to favor one side over another.

The way you draft documents can affect the outcome of the negotiations as well. It is not unusual for a legal professional to present to the opposing side a draft that sours the deal because the documents arouse suspicion or distrust. Distrust of the legal drafter can cause harm to a client.

Parties negotiating a contract or lease may be far apart in their negotiating positions until a short time before the execution of the documents, and after the execution of the documents the parties may never again reach amicable terms. In such cases, the document must be written flexibly enough to permit the parties to agree and soundly enough to prevent future controversies.

In putting together legal relationships, the drafter must be sensitive to the objectives of the parties, to the function of the document, to any legal or ethical constraints on the transaction, to the details of the transaction, and to various other practical considerations.

## Objectives of the Parties

Parties enter into transactions with different assumptions. A person selling a business usually wants to ensure that the price will be paid. The seller wants security. The person purchasing the business may be taking a risk and may want some flexibility in the relationship. Accordingly, parties do read agreements looking for opposite interpretations. The drafter must recognize the objectives of each of the parties to the transaction. As a drafter begins to put a transaction on paper, the drafter must be able to see how the objectives of the parties may conflict in the future. Understanding the objectives of the parties enables paralegals to anticipate future problems with the relationship created by the document.

## Functions of Transaction Documents

Legal drafting serves three different functions. First, the writing may record an event (a **fulfilling document** such as a deed). A fulfilling document is prepared merely to memorialize an event. It is intended to serve as evidence of a transaction. In preparing this type of document, your main objective is to ascertain the facts and to record them in compliance with applicable legal requirements.

A fulfilling document is used as a receipt where property of value exchanges hands or as a memorial for an event that the parties want recorded. For example, when you go to the supermarket, you pay money and get a receipt. The receipt is a record of a transaction. Similarly, when you graduate from high school, you get a diploma. This is a record of an event. Many legal transaction documents serve the same function as a receipt or diploma—to record a transaction or event.

Second, the writing may anticipate and provide for future eventualities (an **achieving document**, such as a lease, option, or contract). An achieving document, like a fulfilling document, will memorialize a transaction, but the achieving document also lays out a framework for a future relationship. In preparing this type of document, the drafter must not only ascertain facts and comply with legal requisites to the transaction, but also anticipate various events that might occur during the transaction. Then the drafter must chart the response to those events.

An achieving document envisions an ongoing transaction. The parties have already agreed to the details of that relationship and have anticipated most of the situations that might occur during the relationship. For instance, the parties may be selling a house on contract with payments to be made over a period of time. This relationship may continue for years.

The achieving document must anticipate the future problems of the parties and then accurately deal with these contingencies.

Third, the writing may provide for a means or method to resolve future problems (a **regulating document**, such as a collective bargaining agreement or the bylaws of a corporation). A regulating document develops procedures to resolve future problems without necessarily directing a particular result. A regulating document is prepared when there will be an ongoing relationship between parties. For example, the bylaws of a corporation provide a way for shareholders to hash out problems without necessarily telling how a particular problem will be resolved. A grievance procedure in a collective bargaining agreement is a means to resolve disputes between labor and management.

## Legal and Ethical Considerations

Legal and ethical considerations impose constraints on all legal documents. The most cleverly drafted transaction document is useless if it violates legal or ethical constraints.

**Legal Considerations.** An important concern of every legal drafter is compliance with any legal requisites. How competently a document is drafted is unimportant if you ignore the applicable rules. Ask any attorney who tries to file a complaint using legal-size paper when the local rules mandate letter-size paper. Explain to your client's heirs how competently you drafted the will, when you cannot probate it because it has not been properly witnessed. Try to record a deed or mortgage that is not properly notarized.

Some jurisdictions mandate certain "magic" language for certain types of transactions. A statute may require that a warranty deed contain the words "convey and warrant." An option may need to be "irrevocable." Spend the necessary time to check the statutes and case law applicable to the transaction. The extra time that you take to educate yourself will make the next effort easier.

The law permits a wide latitude to parties in structuring transactions and relationships. We refer to this latitude as **freedom of contract**. An unorthodox way of structuring a deal may become the way of doing business in the future. However, the drafter must recognize that there are some limits on the right to freedom of contract. For example, a contract is not permitted to have an illegal purpose such as gambling or prostitution. But even if there is a legal purpose, a contract cannot violate the **doctrine of unconscionability** or the rule respecting contracts of adhesion. The basic test of unconscionability is whether the provisions at issue are so one-sided as to be oppressive and unfair.

A **contract of adhesion** is a standardized contract drafted by parties of superior bargaining strength who present the contract on a take-it-or-leave-it basis. Many insurance contracts and warranty agreements of major retailers fit this criteria. The lesson here is that the drafter has much flexibility in structuring relationships, yet this flexibility is not without limits. Obviously, no matter how skillfully the documents have been prepared, if the court decides that you have drafted an unconscionable document or a contract of adhesion, your efforts were for naught.

**Ethical Considerations.** There are ethical constraints on your role as a drafter. Ethically, you generally cannot represent conflicting interests to a transaction. This means that a lawyer may not represent, for example, both the buyer and the seller to the same transaction.

Ethics rules require that attorneys supervise the work of nonlawyer assistants. Ethics rules and statutes forbid the unauthorized practice of law. Therefore, when paralegals work with clients, they must make sure that the clients are aware that their work is being supervised by an attorney.

At times, one party to a transaction will be unrepresented. If the other side is unrepresented, you should be cautious not to overreach. However, at the same time you try to advance the best interests of your client.

POINTER: You must identify yourself as a paralegal in your communications with clients and others. When you make a telephone call, identify yourself as a paralegal at the beginning of the conversation. Be sure to designate under your signature on letters that you are a paralegal.

## The Details of the Transaction

Perhaps the biggest mistake of the novice drafter is failing to gather sufficient factual information about the transaction. If factual information is not ascertained, the legal professional has little basis for predicting future complications. In any area of the legal practice, legal professionals must know as much about the applicable transaction as the parties (and their experts). Drafting requires as much time acquainting yourself with the details of the transaction and the applicable law as it does time spent writing.

When a transaction document is complete, it should embody the deal as accurately as possible. The highest compliment for a drafter is to be told that the document accurately reflects the transaction contemplated by the parties. The drafter is engineering a transaction, and the documents are the blueprint for that deal. To put a transaction together, you must understand the dynamics of the relationship between the parties. Although the deal should be workable, this does not mean that the documents will be ironclad. There are no ironclad documents.

Nevertheless, the more you know about the details of the transaction, the more likely the transaction can be completed successfully.

Finally, you must familiarize yourself with the jargon and practices of the client's business. You should draft in language used in your client's business so that your client can help spot problems that you may have overlooked. If you use language your client can understand, the parties will be able to work out differences long after the execution of the documents, rather than resorting to attorneys or other third parties.

## Practical Considerations

Paralegals must embrace many practical considerations when they draft transaction documents. Practical considerations can impose constraints that paralegals must consider from the outset of the drafting process.

**Time and Money Constraints.** It is important to understand that not every client can afford a fifty-page contract—nor is it always necessary. Some clients want to pay a minimal fee for a simple document. Other clients are not so concerned with cost but want the document to provide as much security as possible.

However, you have only so much time to satisfy clients' demands. You cannot satisfy every client's demand if you focus all your energy on one case or transaction. While law is a profession, it is also a business.

**The Parties' Personalities.** A skilled legal professional will draft a simple one-page agreement for a wary client who distrusts lawyers and a fifty-page agreement for a nit-picking client who wants every detail spelled out. A legal professional can build trust with a difficult party by keeping the agreement simple and may solidify a difficult deal with comprehensive provisions.

**Be Creative but Selective.** A skilled drafter can patch together difficult negotiations with creative solutions. An imagination can solve drafting dilemmas when parties are working toward completion of an agreement. Language bridges many misunderstandings. However, at times a skilled drafter will choose not to broach a subject, either knowing how the law will resolve the problem, or fearing that the negotiations could be stalemated. The skill is in knowing when to take the appropriate course of action.

**Anticipate Future Problems.** The writer must anticipate future problems likely to be encountered in the parties' relationship. Every legal professional has been blamed for adding "legal complications" when the parties "had everything worked out." Sometimes the personality of the legal professional frustrates the process. More often problems arise because the transaction is more complicated than the client originally envisioned. Even in simple transactions parties fail to anticipate many potential problems. Few people worry about termites or water damage, for example, until these problems affect them personally. However, experience tells us that such problems are common enough that a contract for sale of real estate should contain provisions for them. Such are the typical situations confronted daily by drafters of transaction documents.

**Avoid Making Business Judgments.** Normally the drafter of transaction documents should avoid making business judgments. In an attempt to solve problems you may suggest alternative courses of action, but making business decisions is not ordinarily within the scope of the legal professional's expertise. The drafter should usually allow the client to steer the course of the negotiations. The business client knows the economics of the transaction better than most legal professionals.

**Avoid Overreaching Conduct.** Although the drafter of documents is obliged to represent a client's "best interests," such representation does not include **overreaching conduct**—that is, outwitting the opponent through trickery or deceit. From a practical standpoint, overreaching may kill the deal. It may also lead to a tumultuous relationship between the parties. If you view the agreement as a treaty between the parties, you may have a signed treaty—but you may have created an unworkable relationship.

## VOLUNTEERING TO DRAFT THE DOCUMENT

An experienced drafter will gain as much for the client through the drafting process as through the negotiation process. In fact, seldom is the negotiation process completed until the drafting process is completed.

### Advantages of Drafting the Document

The skilled drafter as a matter of strategy will frequently opt to prepare the first draft of the documents relating to a transaction. To appreciate the advantages of preparing the first draft, consider the fact that many issues are preempted by this process. Choices made by the drafter may not even be considered by opposing counsel who later reviews the documents on behalf of the opposing party. Rather than suggesting alternative courses of action, many reviewing attorneys will overlook important options and may suggest only cosmetic language changes. The party who drafts the documents has much control over how the transaction is structured.

### Disadvantages of Drafting the Document

Writing the first draft of a transaction document also has some disadvantages. Earlier we saw that ambiguities are construed against the party who prepared the document—the so-called *contra proferentem* doctrine.

Moreover, if not carefully written, the first draft can scuttle negotiations. As we suggested earlier, when the other side reviews a twenty-page document and recalls that she had spent only thirty minutes discussing the transaction, distrust can surface. This distrust may kill a project that your client has dreamed about for years. All too often, lawyers will be blamed for losing a deal when the first draft fails to mirror the original understanding reached during negotiations. However, the clients fail to understand that in many of these cases the parties had never reached any agreement on most of the basic provisions of a transaction. Finally, writing the first draft can be time-consuming and therefore more expensive to your client.

## CONSULTING CHECKLISTS AND FORM BOOKS

Many transactions, such as leasing an apartment, are executed over and over again. When you interview the client, you will ask certain standard questions. There are various checklists you can consult before you conduct an interview, and many form books are available to help you start the writing process.

### Use of Checklists

On arrival in your office, many clients will announce that they have "arrived at a deal" and that you should "prepare the papers." More times than not, the "deal" is nothing more than an agreement as to price. The plethora of other terms customarily included in the agreement have not been discussed, much less negotiated. Your task is to put the entire transaction together.

Before meeting with any client concerning any drafting task, make at least a cursory check of the applicable law and prepare a checklist. Many form books contain sample checklists of areas to cover. Review the checklist just before the meeting even if you do not adhere to it rigidly in your interview. No legal professional can draft a document properly unless he or she knows what the client knows and what the client wants. A drafter must listen to the client and rely on the checklist only to double-check to make sure that nothing was missed. Reed Dickerson summarizes what to do during client interviews:

> Find out what the client wants to accomplish and what specific problems it involves. Explore the detailed possibilities with him and help him think the problem through. . . At this stage, the draftsman pumps the client for information. He points out any substantive inconsistencies that he thinks he sees in the idea. . . He mentions any . . . practical problems, and any drafting problems, that he thinks the client ought to know about.[1]

A good legal professional asks questions carefully, listening and following up on the answers given. A checklist is used as a guide, not as an immutable agenda.

### Use of Forms

Most paralegal students are introduced to the law library in sessions that are brief and sometimes rather spotty. Often their introduction to legal form books is completely ignored in the paralegal curriculum. Yet almost any transaction document you draft has been written before and probably is in a form book. In fact, when inexperienced paralegals begin to prepare transaction documents, they are likely to be overwhelmed by the number of available form books. Many paralegals—and many rookie attorneys—fail to recognize the unevenness of the available forms. Not all forms are well written or well designed.

**Types of Form Books.** Form books can be substantive, procedural, or a combination of the two. A **substantive form book** will provide forms dealing with various legal transactions (wills, trusts, leases, contracts). A **procedural form book** deals with court-related documents (complaints, answers, motions, interrogatories, jury instructions). Form books may be combined with textbook materials explaining the applicable law, may cover the entire spectrum of legal instruments, or may cover only a single subject such as contracts or torts. Form books may include tax advice or may incorporate tax information directly into the forms. Form books may be premised on the law of a particular jurisdiction, such as you find in many Continuing Legal Education materials.

**Other Sources of Forms.** Lawyers and their secretaries may have kept applicable forms from previous transactions, and you will inevitably collect forms from other lawyers. Recently a significant market has developed in computer-stored forms. Instead of in a form book, the documents are stored on software.

**The Importance of Modifying Forms.** When you first look for a client checklist, you should scan alternative forms as well. As a checklist, as a guide, and as a means to begin the drafting project, a form is helpful. However, to rely only on a form is seldom good practice.

Too many legal professionals simply convert an existing document to fit the client's situation rather than create a new document for the transaction. While forms are an excellent starting point, forms should not dictate the substance of the transaction.

Paralegals tend to rely too heavily on "canned" documents or so-called boilerplate. In some situations, of course, a document that has evolved through several lawsuits may prove to be more accurate than a hastily drafted original document. However, too frequently the canned forms are infested with problems. Before relying on one form, consider that many are outdated or simply inappropriate. Seldom will you find a form that will fit a particular transaction perfectly. Remember that every form can be improved.

***The Use of Litigated Forms.*** Some form books are filled with forms copied from cases that have been litigated. One reason why the form ended up in litigation may have been because the form was not well drafted. As one writer noted:

> An adjudicated form is a form that has attached to it a certificate that there is something terribly wrong with it. If there were not something terribly wrong with it, it would not have been adjudicated.[2]

Another commentator offered these words regarding the use of litigated forms:

> At this point we should like to inject a parenthesis on "annotated" forms. After examining and checking a vast number of footnotes, we are convinced of one fact: case citations for substantive forms consume valuable space for very little purpose. For one thing, it has been said with some justice that a good form would not have been litigated in the first place; if the issue was truly one of construction or interpretation, the fault usually lay in a missing or ambiguous clause. Why, therefore, perpetuate the omission or ambiguity, with the chance that some other court will reject the interpretation in the cited case? A clear English sentence is worth volumes of precedent. In the second place, it is rare that an entire agreement should be in issue in litigation. Perhaps the case has turned on a single phrase in paragraph

> 15; perhaps there are a dozen other latent ambiguities or contingencies which have not happened to arise. Nevertheless, the entire document is soberly reprinted as an "adjudicated" form. Moreover, even if the point has been in issue and if the interpretation is reasonably reliable as precedent, what about the time factor? Is a 1910 agreement adequate for 1948 problems? In most cases, the economic background is so different, the changes in common and statute law have been so great (e.g., the income tax!), that the cited form is frequently more misleading than helpful. Weighing these factors, we have so altered most of the usable forms in the reported cases that the product is unrecognizable; and we have therefore refrained from cloaking them in the mantle of "authority."[3]

In determining whether to use an adjudicated document, ask yourself if the use of the selected provision expresses the intent of the parties better than what you are able to draft. This test alone should determine whether to use any adjudicated form—or for that matter whether to substitute any other person's work for your own.

A document should be designed to prevent litigation between the parties. Although this is not always possible, you should hesitate before adopting a form that obviously failed the litigation-avoidance test. Repeating the mistakes of others is not a skillful way to practice any craft.

***The Fear of Modifying Forms.*** It is my experience that most legal professionals modify a form only with trepidation. I am reminded of the day when a sign was placed on the Interstate announcing the closing of the State of Delaware.[4] Most drivers turned around. Why? Because anything that looks official is unlikely to be questioned. If you hand a printed lease to a tenant, usually it will be signed with no change. If you hand a typewritten lease to a tenant, it is likely to be changed. Tell someone that something is "standard policy" and it is very seldom questioned:

> Twenty years ago I was involved in the legal end of real estate. People came to me to sign their leases and have them countersigned. Most paid their security deposits and moved along without reading the forms. On rare occasions someone would say, "I'd like to read this lease before signing it. I have a constitutional right to do so!"
>
> I'd always reply, "Of course you have a right to do so. Go right ahead and read it!"
>
> Halfway through the form the person would exclaim, "Wait a second! Hold it! This document practically makes me an indentured servant for the duration of the lease!"
>
> I'd reply, "I doubt that. This is a standard form. There's the form number in the lower left corner."
>
> The person usually responded, "Oh . . . a standard form. Well, in that case . . ." and he or she would sign, bullied into submission by several printed digits that apparently possessed some magical property.[5]

Legal professionals approach forms from form books the same way the tenant reads the standard contract—reluctant to make any modifications. Whenever you pick up a form, you should immediately make a substantial change to it. After you have made a substantial change, you will have the necessary confidence to begin drafting the remainder of the transaction. Every competent drafter will experience "printer phobia"—the fear of changing anything that has been printed. The cure is to change the form just for the sake of change and then start rewording the document.

**Integrating a Variety of Forms.** You should gather a variety of forms. One form may overlook some needed language or may more closely mimic the relationship that you are structuring. But a word of caution: whenever you integrate forms, check for consistency in the language. A surprising number of disputes arise because the language of one form conflicts with the language of another, or because the language used in one clause may suggest a different meaning when different language is used to express the same concept in another clause.

***Maintaining Consistency.*** Too many disputes are generated by handwritten changes to a printed document. When one form contains the part of the necessary information and another form contains the remaining necessary information, these forms are sometimes spliced together. The danger of inconsistency becomes a very real problem. A blank in a printed contract is an invitation to litigation. Make sure when you insert language into the blank that the words are consistent with the printed language. Otherwise, you will be courting litigation. Maintain consistency among any forms that have been spliced together as well as in your own language in the particular document. Inconsistencies created by handwritten changes to printed forms have been frequent enough for the courts to develop a rule: ambiguity is resolved in favor of the interpretation suggested by the handwritten provision.

In drafting a simple truck lease, for example, when students are told to provide that the lessee cannot assign the lease, they repeatedly make the mistake of ending the lease with a boilerplate clause that declares the lease to be "binding upon the heirs, successors and *assigns of the parties*." While a court might reach the intended result in this situation, the inconsistency is not worth the risk of litigation. Substitute provisions inserted into an existing form must be revised to read consistently with the other language of the document. The following quote best sums up the use of forms:

> Should lawyers refrain from using legal boilerplate? They cannot operate efficiently without it. Indeed, they cannot operate even inefficiently without it. The danger in prefabricated legal text is not that all forms are bad, but that even good forms can be bad if they are used indiscriminately or without a thorough grasp of the specific objectives that they are intended to serve in the particular case.[6]

But consider what one form-book editor wrote:

> In short, a good form book is a good tool for a good lawyer; it never can be a good substitute for a good lawyer.[7]

A good drafter develops good forms. The best writers are always improving form books.

## THE COMPONENTS OF THE DOCUMENT

Organizational principles will not prove difficult to apply in the early stages of drafting legal documents because no particular structure is required. This point cannot be overemphasized. There is no "right" way that an agreement must be structured. You can draft a perfect document without using a single "witnesseth," without a "whereas," without beginning "Know all men by these presents . . ." or ending with "In witness whereof . . ." Nevertheless, agreements do tend to follow a certain pattern.

### Preamble

Typically, a legal document will begin with a **preamble** that recites the parties to the transaction and identifies the type of document being created. For example, a lease might begin this way:

> This lease is made this ________ day of ________________, 199____, by ____________________ ("lessor") and ____________________ ("lessee").

The same format would be used to start a contract, an option, or another multiparty document. While this approach is not mandated, it does tell the reader at the start the type of transaction contemplated and the parties to the agreement.

### Recitals

**Recitals** usually follow the preamble. The recitals provide the purpose of the agreement or a brief background for the reader. Recitals are intended to give some background information related to the formation of the agreement:

> Recitals which usually follow the description of the parties are designed to store the background or purposes of the agreement and often set forth matters of inducement or representation to create an estoppel. They are used to foreclose inquiring into the surrounding circumstances and previous negotiations. If the recitals are clear and the operative part is ambiguous, the recitals govern the construction. If the recitals are ambiguous, and the operative part is clear, the operative part must prevail. If both the recitals and the operative part are clear, but they are inconsistent with each other, the operative part is to be preferred. But recitals should be used with caution and a skillful draftsman will rarely resort to their use. A contract should explain itself and if a preamble or recital is required to make it clear, it is generally a sign that the draft requires revision.[8]

In older documents (and in documents copied from older documents), these recitals might begin with the archaic expression "Witnesseth . . ." Certainly there is no reason to use this term or any other particular expression. You might choose a heading such as "Recitals" or "Background.

Courts vary as to whether they will interpret the recitals as part of the agreement; but if you remember that in preparing an agreement you are writing the part of the transcript of the trial involving this agreement, then it cannot hurt to pad the recitals. However, many defense firms will prepare lengthy recitals in release documents. Often these recitals will greatly exaggerate the potential claims that are asserted. If the release is voided for some reason, these padded recitals may not be the actual script that they want written for the jury.

In many cases the drafter will begin each new recital with a whereas. For example:

> Whereas the lessor is the owner of certain real estate described by Exhibit A hereto; Whereas the lessee is desirous of leasing this real estate;

There is no reason other than custom to begin the clauses with a whereas, but many legal professionals do.

### Consideration

Usually the document will then recite that there is **consideration** of some sort, in language such as the following:

> NOW, THEREFORE, in consideration of the mutual promises and agreements of the parties hereto, the parties now agree as follows:

Consideration is an act, forebearance, or promise that has an economic value and is used to create an enforceable contract. In some situations the consideration must be recited in the body of the contract. Even where the consideration is not required to be stated, it is almost always a good practice to do so.

### Operative Provisions

The next section contains the operative provisions of the agreement. If there are definitions or preliminary terms, these will usually be placed first. Boilerplate and housekeeping provisions, such as the provisions dealing with the assignability of the document, applicable law, notice provisions, and so on, usually are found at the end. Boilerplate provisions are the routine provisions found in all similar contracts.

### The Parties' Signatures

Finally, the document will typically end with a sentence evidencing the signature of the parties. For example:

> In witness whereof, the parties hereto have set their hands on the date first written.

Certainly a much simpler ending would be appropriate; again, no particular form is usually required.

### The Importance of Logical Structure

Although the drafter has considerable latitude in the design of legal documents, the experienced drafter soon discovers that you can test the logic of an agreement by study of its structure. Some writers cannot begin to write without a structured outline, and no writer should end the writing process without a careful concern for the elementary principles of arrangement.

## EXAMPLES OF TRANSACTION DOCUMENTS

A paralegal may be asked to prepare many different types of transaction documents. In this section we will examine some of the more commonly drafted documents.

### Bill of Sale

A bill of sale is used when personal property is sold. The bill of sale is a simple receipt. Figure 8-1 is an example of a bill of sale.

### Deed

When real estate exchanges hands, the transaction is recorded by a deed. There are various types of deeds. A warranty deed is used when the party selling the real estate warrants title to the property. A quit-claim deed is used when the party sells whatever the party owns without a warranty. A corporate deed is used when a corporation conveys real estate. A sheriff's deed is used in cases such as foreclosures. An example of a warranty deed appears as Figure 8-2.

### Corporate Documents

When a corporation is formed, **articles of incorporation** are prepared. The articles of incorporation serve as a record that the corporation is properly incorporated. An example of articles of incorporation is shown in Figure 8-3.

When a corporation is formed, the shareholders must set up rules for handling the affairs of the corporation. These rules are called **corporate bylaws**. The bylaws establish a board of directors, identify officers for the corporation and their duties, and set forth requirements regarding voting or shareholder issues and various other matters. Figure 8-4 shows an excerpt from a set of bylaws. The board of directors and the shareholders hold meetings. The records of these meetings are called minutes. An example of corporate minutes is found on page 279 in the Appendix to this text.

### Promissory Notes

One of the simpler achieving documents is a promissory note. A promissory note is a promise to pay a certain sum over a period of time. An example of a promissory note is included as Figure 8-5.

When preparing a promissory note, as when preparing bills of sale or deeds, the drafter usually starts with a form and fills in the blanks.

### Leases

Many paralegal students are familiar with leases. A **lease** is a bilateral agreement that sets forth the terms for the rental of real estate. The lease is an excellent example of an achieving document. The lease maps out the rights of the tenant and the rights of the landlord. It structures a relationship that continues over time. It anticipates problems that might occur over the course of the relationship.

**FIGURE 8-1 A BILL OF SALE**

THIS FORM HAS BEEN APPROVED BY THE INDIANA STATE BAR ASSOCIATION FOR USE BY LAWYERS ONLY. THE SELECTION OF A FORM OF INSTRUMENT, FILLING IN BLANK SPACES, STRIKING OUT PROVISIONS AND INSERTION OF SPECIAL CLAUSES, CONSTITUTES THE PRACTICE OF LAW AND MAY ONLY BE DONE BY A LAWYER.

## BILL OF SALE

**This Indenture Witnesseth,** That

("Transferor") of ______________________ County, State of ______________________

in consideration of

Dollars ($ ), the receipt of which is

acknowledged by Transferor, grants, sells, transfers and delivers to

("Transferee") of ______________________ County, State of ______________________

the following described personal property ("Property"):

SAMPLE

The Property is transferred to and for the benefit of Transferee and Transferee's successors, assigns and personal and legal representatives. Transferor makes the following representations under oath: (1) Transferor is the lawful owner of the Property; (2) the Property is free from all encumbrances and lawful claims for possession of others; (3) Transferor has the legal right to sell the Property; and (4) Transferor will warrant and defend the Property against the lawful claims and demands of all persons.

STATE OF )
) SS:
COUNTY OF )

Before me, the undersigned, a Notary Public, in and for said County and State, this __________ day of __________, 19__________, personally appeared:

and acknowledged the execution of the foregoing Bill of Sale. In witness whereof, I have subscribed my name and affixed my official seal.

My Commission Expires: __________ __________

______________________
NOTARY PUBLIC

Resident of ______________________ County

Dated this __________ day of __________, 19____

______________________

______________________

______________________

______________________

______________________

This instrument was prepared by ______________________, Attorney at Law.

**FIGURE 8-2 A WARRANTY DEED**

THIS FORM HAS BEEN APPROVED BY THE INDIANA STATE BAR ASSOCIATION FOR USE BY LAWYERS ONLY. THE SELECTION OF A FORM OF INSTRUMENT, FILLING IN BLANK SPACES, STRIKING OUT PROVISIONS AND INSERTION OF SPECIAL CLAUSES, CONSTITUTES THE PRACTICE OF LAW AND MAY ONLY BE DONE BY A LAWYER.

**Mail tax bills to:** **Tax Key No.:**______________

**WARRANTY DEED**

**This indenture witnesseth that**

*of* *County in the State of*

**Convey and warrant to**

*of* *County in the State of*
*for and in consideration of*
*the receipt whereof is hereby acknowledged, the following Real Estate in* *County*
*in the State of Indiana, to wit:*

SAMPLE

**State of Indiana,** **County, ss:**
*Before me, the undersigned, a Notary Public in and for said County and State, this* *day of*
*19* *personally appeared:*

*An acknowledged the execution of the foregoing deed. In witness whereof, I have hereunto subscribed my name and affixed my official seal. My commission expires* ____________________ *19*

________________
*Notary Public*

**Dated this** ________ **Day of** __________ **19**___

______________________________

______________________________

______________________________

______________________________

______________________________

______________________________

*Resident of* ____________________ *County.*

**This instrument prepared by** ________________________________ *Attorney at Law*

**MAIL TO:**

**FIGURE 8-3 ARTICLES OF INCORPORATION**

**ARTICLES OF INCORPORATION**
State Form 4159 (R6 / 3-88)

*INSTRUCTIONS:* *Use 8½ x 11 inch white paper for inserts. Filing requirements - Present original and one copy to the address in the upper right corner of this form.*

Provided by: EVAN BAYH
Secretary of State
Room 155, State House
Indianapolis, Indiana 46204
(317) 232-6576
Indiana Code 23-1-21-2
**FILING FEE $90.00**

**ARTICLES OF INCORPORATION OF**

(Indicate the appropriate act)
The undersigned desiring to form a corporation (herein after referred to as "Corporation") pursuant to the provisions of:

☐ Indiana Business Corporation Law ☐ Indiana Professional Corporation Act 1983

As amended, executes the following Articles of Incorporation:

**ARTICLE I NAME**

Name of Corporation

(The name must contain the word "Corporation," "Incorporated," "Limited," "Company" or an abbreviation of one of those words.)

**ARTICLE II REGISTERED OFFICE AND AGENT**

(The street address of the corporation's initial registered office in Indiana and the name of its initial registered agent at that office is:)

Name of Agent

| Street Address of Registered Office | ZIP Code |
|---|---|
| | |

**ARTICLE III AUTHORIZED SHARES**

Number of shares: ______________________________
If there is more than one class of shares, shares with rights and preferences, list such information on "Exhibit A."

**ARTICLE IV INCORPORATORS**
(The name(s) and address(es) of the incorporator(s) of the corporation:)

| NAME | NUMBER and STREET OR BUILDING | CITY | STATE | ZIP CODE |
|---|---|---|---|---|
| | | | | |

In Witness Whereof, the undersigned being all the incorporators of said corporation execute these Articles of Incorporation and verify, subject to penalties of perjury, that the statements contained herein are true,

this ____________ day of ______________________ 19 ______ .

| Signature | Printed Name |
|---|---|
| Signature | Printed Name |
| Signature | Printed Name |

This instrument was prepared by (Name)

| Address *(Street, Number, City and State)* | ZIP Code |
|---|---|
| | |

**FIGURE 8-4 CORPORATE BYLAWS**

BYLAWS
of
*XYZ CORPORATION*

ARTICLE I. OFFICE

*SECTION 1.1. PRINCIPAL OFFICE.* The principal office of the corporation shall be located in the City of Evansville, Vanderburgh County, State of Indiana. The corporation may have such other offices, either within or without the State of Indiana, as the Board of Directors may designate, or as the business of the corporation may from time to time require.

*SECTION 1.2. REGISTERED AGENT AND OFFICE.* The name of the first registered agent of the corporation is ________________. The office of the resident agent of the corporation, required by the Indiana General Corporation Act to be maintained in the State of Indiana, may be, but need not be, identical with the principal office of the corporation, and the address of the registered office where the resident agent is located may be changed from time to time by the Board of Directors as provided by law.

ARTICLE II. MEETINGS OF SHAREHOLDERS

*SECTION 2.1. ANNUAL MEETING.* An annual meeting of the shareholders, for the purpose of electing directors and for the transaction of such other business as may come before the meeting, shall be held on the 31st day in the month of December in each year, beginning with the year ________ or on such other day within such month as shall be fixed by the Board of Directors. If the day fixed for the annual meeting shall be a legal holiday in the State of Indiana, such meeting shall be held on the next succeeding business day. If for any reason the annual meeting has not been called within six (6) months after the time designated for the meeting, any shareholder may call the annual meeting. If the election of directors shall not be held on the day designated herein for any annual meeting of the shareholders, or at any adjournment thereof, the Board of Directors shall cause the election to be held at a special meeting of the shareholders as soon thereafter as may be convenient.

*SECTION 2.2. SPECIAL MEETINGS.* Special meetings of the shareholders which may be held for any purpose or purposes, unless otherwise prescribed by law, may be called by the President, by a majority of the Board of Directors and must be called by the President or Secretary at the request of the holders of not less than twenty-five percent (25%) of all outstanding shares entitled to vote at such meeting.

**FIGURE 8-5 A PROMISSORY NOTE**

THIS FORM HAS BEEN APPROVED BY THE INDIANA STATE BAR ASSOCIATION FOR USE BY LAWYERS ONLY. THE SELECTION OF A FORM OF INSTRUMENT, FILLING IN BLANK SPACES, STRIKING OUT PROVISIONS AND INSERTION OF SPECIAL CLAUSES, CONSTITUTES THE PRACTICE OF LAW AND SHOULD BE DONE BY A LAWYER.

**PROMISSORY NOTE**

*Indiana, 19*

**I promise to pay to the order of**

*the sum of*

*as follows:*

*payable at*

*With interest at the rate of per cent per annum payable from date during such period when there shall be no delinquency, but with interest at the rate of ________ per cent per annum during such period of any delinquency, and with attorney's fees, without any relief whatever from Valuation or Appraisement Laws. The drawers, sureties, guarantors and endorsers severally waive presentment for payment, protest, notice of protest and non-payment of this note and agree that on default in payment of this note or any part, prinicipal or interest when due, the whole amount remaining unpaid shall, without notice of non-payment or demand of payment immediately become due and payable. The receipt of interest in advance or the extension of time shall not release or discharge any endorser, surety or guarantor on this note.*



________________________

________________________

________________________

**This instrument prepared by** ________________________ *Attorney at Law*

PRINTED BY THE ALLEN COUNTY INDIANA BAR ASSOCIATION, INC.

The lease will usually include basic information as to the following:

- The parties
- Identification of the premises
- Term of the lease
- Amount of rent and when rent is to be paid
- Insurance
- Taxes
- Security deposit
- Parking
- Utilities

Some clients want a simple lease; others want every contingency covered. Be sure to find out how detailed a lease your client wants.

### Contract for the Sale of Real Estate

Another commonly prepared achieving document is a contract for the sale of real estate. Like the lease, the real estate contract structures the terms of an ongoing real estate relationship. However, the principal difference between a real estate lease and a contract is that at the end of the term the purchaser will own the property. Hence many of the basic terms are similar to that of a lease.

## ENDNOTES

1 Reed Dickerson, *The Fundamentals of Legal Drafting* (Boston: Little, Brown, 1965), p. 36.

2 C. A. Beardsley, ''Beware of, Eschew, and Avoid Pompous Prolixity and Platitudinous Epistles,'' 16 *Cal. S.B.J.* (1941), pp. 65, 66.

3 J. Rabkin and M. H. Johnson, *Current Legal Forms with Tax Analysis*, Vol. 1 (New York: Matthew Bender, 1979), p. viii.

4 Herb Cohen, *You Can Negotiate Anything* (New York: Bantam Books, 1980), p. 59.

5 Id. at 28.

6 Reed Dickerson, ''Some Jurisprudential Implications of Electronic Data Processing,'' 18 *Law & Contemp. Probs.* (1963), p. 61.

7 J. Rabkin and M. H. Johnson, *Current Legal Forms with Tax Analysis*, Vol. 1 (New York: Matthew Bender, 1979), p. ix.

8 J. G. Thomas, ''Problems in Drafting Legal Instruments,'' 39 *Ill. B.J.* (1950), pp. 51, 55.

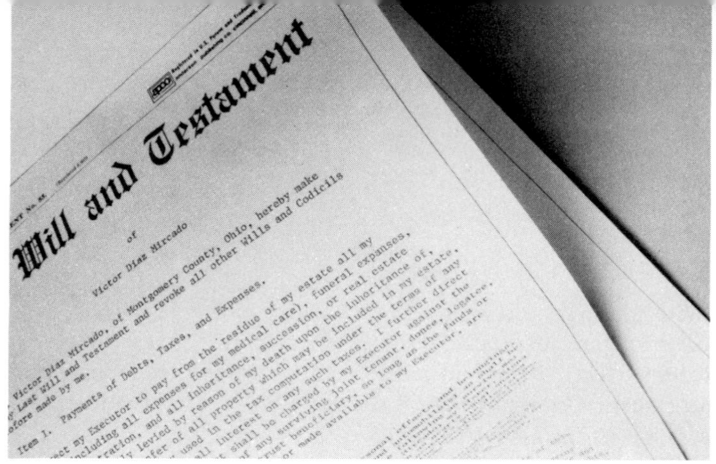


# 9 STRUCTURE IN LEGAL DOCUMENTS

> If I had eight hours to cut down a tree, I would use six of them sharpening my axe. (Abraham Lincoln)

At some point in the writing process, usually at the beginning, every writer must pay attention to structure. More than any other writing focus, structure determines how coherently you communicate your message. In fact, checking the structure of a document often will be an internal check of logic. Unfortunately, many legal professionals spend too much time on the particulars of a document at the expense of its overall design.

## THE DESIGN OF A LEGAL DOCUMENT

The **design** of a legal document is the format in which ideas are organized within the document. Design is an important concern in all forms of writing. The design should omit nothing important and add nothing superfluous.

### Omit Nothing Important

First, you must be careful not to leave out anything material to the document. In construing legal documents, courts presume that if you left something out, you intended to do so. They don't make allowance for carelessness. A legal writer cannot leave out ideas any more than a mechanic can leave out a few nuts and bolts when assembling a machine.

### Add Nothing Superfluous

Second, you must not add material that is extraneous to the thought being communicated. Paralegal students often find it difficult to cut a paragraph or to strike a sentence, but unnecessary verbiage will only diminish the clarity of your document. Cutting is necessary if there is any superfluous material.

## PARALLEL STRUCTURE

Parallel ideas should be presented using parallel structure: words with words, phrases with phrases, clauses with clauses, adjectives with adjectives, participial phrases with participial phrases, prepositional phrases with prepositional phrases, noun clauses with noun clauses. In the Bible, the beatitudes (Mt. 3:3–10) exemplify the virtue of parallel structure:

> Blessed are the poor in spirit: for theirs is the kingdom of heaven. Blessed are they that mourn: for they shall be comforted. Blessed are the meek: for they shall inherit the earth. Blessed are they which do hunger and thirst after righteousness: for they shall be filled. . . .

Notice the difference in clarity had the beatitudes not been written with parallel structure:

> Blessed are the poor in spirit; for theirs is the kingdom of heaven. They that mourn are also blessed, for they shall be comforted. The earth shall be inherited by the meek. Those who hunger and thirst after righteousness shall be filled, and they are also blessed.

Caesar said: "I came, I saw, I conquered." Again, look at the parallel structure. Sentences expressing parallel ideas should be given parallel structure. So should paragraphs expressing parallel ideas. When correcting for parallel structure, you have two choices: either put words into the same grammatical structure or eliminate the need for the structure by reorganizing the ideas.

### Make Words Joined by Conjunctions Parallel

When you join words together with conjunctions such as *and* or *but*, the words should be the same part of speech. Verbs should be joined with other verbs, nouns with other nouns and participial phrases with other participial phrases. Disparate parts of speech should not be joined together by conjunctions. This principle that words joined by *and* and *or* should be grammatically compatible applies also when you use correlative conjunctions such as *either . . . or, neither . . . nor.*

### Make Lists Parallel

Whenever you make a list or enumerate ideas, check for parallel structure. Consider this list:

1. apples
2. the oranges
3. bring the laundry
4. did I buy a gift for my wife?

To rewrite with parallel structure to conform to 1, then each entry needs to be a noun. To conform to 2, each entry needs to be a noun preceded by an article. To conform to 3, each entry would start with a verb. To conform to 4, each entry would ask a question.

### Make Headings Parallel

Parallelism is particularly important when you write headings for contracts or for a brief. Each heading should be of the same grammatical structure as each other heading. Do not use one heading that begins with a verb and another that begins with a noun phrase.

### Use Parallel Structure to Provide Eloquence

Parallel structure also can be used to provide eloquence to your writing. Consider this example:

> That plaintiff's argument is contrary to law is seen simply by reading *Smith v. Jones*. That plaintiff's argument is absurd is seen by the countless contradictions in plaintiff's brief. These contradictions include. . .

Be conscious of parallel structure. Parallel structure tells the reader that you are discussing parallel ideas. Parallel structure adds emphasis to your writing. When you present similar ideas, use parallel structure.

## OUTLINE: THE BASICS OF DESIGN

The design should begin with an outline. An outline consists of three components: division, classification, and sequencing.

### Division

**Division** means the main headings of your outline. Remember when you were taught in math class that the whole must equal the sum of the parts. In an outline, each heading or grouping is exclusive, but when considered together the headings must constitute a whole. Let's say you are writing about sports. You might decide to divide your material according to different types of sports; if so, the main headings might be Basketball, Baseball, Football, Tennis, and so on. Of course you might decide to divide your material chronologically or by individual or team sports. There is no restriction on how to divide your writing so long as the divisions constitute a whole.

**Division in Transaction Documents.** When preparing a transaction document, you will find division important for outlining its main points. In a will, for example, an outline might be based upon a sequence of events:

- Pay the debts and taxes.
- Give A a piano.
- Give B a sum of money.
- Give C all the residuary.

A contract may be broken down by responsibilities:

- Rent payments.
- Possession.
- Payment of taxes and insurance.
- Security deposit.

- Contingencies (default, eminent domain).
- Pets.

A good way to write headings for transaction documents is to base the headings on the actions the parties will be taking under the agreement. After all, an agreement governs a relationship between parties.

It is generally helpful to use numbers and letters for paragraphs and subparagraphs, especially for purposes of cross-referencing a document. Just as there is no particular outline that must be used, there is no particular numbering or lettering system that must be used.

**Division in Briefs and Memoranda.** Sometimes the main components of a brief are specified by court rule. A court rule might require you to include a jurisdictional statement, the statement of facts, the issues, the argument, and a conclusion.

In the discussion section of a memorandum and in the argument section of a brief, you will use headings corresponding with the issues presented. Hence these sections are divided by legal issues. Look at the headings used in the briefs filed in *Griswold v. Connecticut,* which are set out in the Resource Manual Appendix.

## Classification

**Classification** is the arrangement of the information under the appropriate grouping or subgrouping. Whether a concept fits under heading A or heading B is a classification concern.

**Use Correct Classification in Contracts.** In a contract, whether information fits under paragraph 1.1 or paragraph 9.5 is a classification concern. If you classify under headings, fitting the information under the appropriate heading obviously aids access and clarifies the terms of the agreement. For instance, all provisions relating to a default should be put under one heading, not scattered throughout the document. If the same concern is addressed in several sections of the agreement, a court might not give proper consideration to the displaced terms.

**Check Classifications When You Edit.** In editing a document, cross-checking for classification problems can help you spot conflicting language. You may find that you have addressed an issue in two separate parts of a document or that you have made conflicting statements.

## Sequencing

Sequencing simply refers to the order of your outline. Whether heading A or heading B comes first is a sequential concern.

**Sequencing in Transaction Documents.** You must decide what provision of a lease or contract should come first. In most cases you have complete freedom as to how the provisions are ordered. However, some common sense guidelines apply. First, put the provisions that have the most financial impact near the beginning. Put the rent provisions, for instance, near the beginning rather than at the end. Second, place the provisions that the parties will most likely use most frequently before provisions that the parties will least likely use. Third, put the exceptions or conditions nearer the end and after the general provisions. In other words, the general comes before the specific. Fourth, put provisions in the order the events will occur. For instance, put a provision dealing with the length of the lease before a provision dealing with the renewal of the lease. Fifth, put a provision dealing with a default nearer the end. Finally, put the boilerplate language common to all such agreements toward the end of the document.

Although these rules are sometimes contradictory, try to arrive at a reason for the way you sequence in transaction documents.

**Sequencing in Briefs and Memoranda.** In writing briefs and memoranda, you must decide what issue to present first. The general rule is that you should present stronger issues before weaker ones. If the issues are equal, then those that will benefit your client the most should be presented first. For example, in a criminal case, two issues might be of equal merit but one issue might result only in a remand and a new trial, whereas the other might result in your client going free through a reversal. Obviously, the second issue would be more beneficial to your client.

However, these are just general rules. There are many reasons why you might select a different sequencing approach. You might even decide to lead with a weak issue if, by developing it, you can paint a sympathetic picture of your client's situation and prompt a court to rule for your client on another issue.

## The Importance of Headings

A headline in a newspaper is used to capture your attention. For years, legal professionals were more concerned with the content than with the layout of a document. Now we know that the format and layout of a document can enhance readability. Type size, margins, and typefaces are important factors. Headings break up the material and make reading the page more pleasant.

**Use Headings as a Road Map.** Headings provide a context for the material that follows. Headings in a contract can lead the reader directly to a specific provision. Headings in a brief can help the reader follow your argument.

**Develop Customized Headings.** Spend some time on headings; do not simply write generic ones. Legal documents deserve headings that are just as well thought out as newpaper headlines. For example, consider these headings for an apartment lease:

| **Before** | **After** |
|---|---|
| Term | Length of this lease |
| Rent | Rent owed for apartment |
| Security deposit | How the security deposit is handled |
| Taxes | Taxes that must be paid |
| Insurance | Insurance that must be paid |
| Maintenance | Your duty to maintain apartment |

| | |
|---|---|
| Default | What happens if a default occurs? |
| Pets | No pets! |
| Subleasing | How to handle subleasing the apartment if you must move |

**Review Headings to Check Structure and Readability.** Headings play a significant role both in checking structure and in aiding readability. Pay attention to the headings in a legal document.

## A Basic Outline for Memoranda and Briefs

General outlines serve as guides in legal writing. As you analyze a legal issue in a memorandum or develop an argument in a brief, you might follow an outline similar to this:

1. Background or introduction
   - Set the tone for the discussion
   - Focus the discussion
   - State the theme or purpose
   - Give the theory
2. Statement of the issue
3. Discussion of the applicable rule of law
   - Show how rule was derived
   - Show reader that the correct rule is used
4. Apply rule to facts of your case
5. Disprove opponent's position or argument
   - Distinguish cases of opponent
   - Show logical inconsistencies of opponent's position
   - Show how facts change the analysis
6. Give your conclusions

**Multiple Issues.** If there are more than one issue, then each issue can be discussed according to this outline. (Notice that it follows the IRAC principle discussed in Chapter 4.)

**Customized Outlines.** Although the generic outline is useful, cases differ from one another; often you may find it better to develop your own outline. You have considerable freedom to develop that outline in whatever way enables you to best present your ideas. The important thing is that you do prepare an outline for any complex document you write.

## Paragraph Design

The basic unit of structure in legal writing is the paragraph. How paragraphs are sequenced can add to or detract from how effectively an idea is communicated. Transitions between paragraphs can also add to or detract from readability. In fact, the strength or weakness of an argument can be detected by looking at the topic sentences in each paragraph. Isolating the individual topic sentences in a brief, for example, can help you trace your opponent's logic. Although there are no fixed rules on paragraph structure, there are some general rules that can lead to better development of your ideas.

**Paragraphs Should Flow in Logical Sequence.** In expository or argumentative writing, such as memoranda and briefs, the first paragraph should set the tone or provide a background to the reader. It might set out the theories or outline the development of an argument. The opening paragraph might even lead with the most persuasive statement (an anticlimactic approach) as opposed to building the argument to a climax. The anticlimactic approach presents the reader with the gist of the argument at the outset, and the remainder of the writing attempts to reinforce this conclusion.

The middle paragraphs should develop or prove the concepts outlined in the opening paragraph. These paragraphs may follow a chronological or historical development, use a compare/contrast approach, follow a general-to-specific or specific-to-general development, or focus on cause and effect.

A good way to make transitions in the middle paragraphs is through the use of adverbs. When you want to express emphasis you can use adverbs such as *indeed*, *that is*, or *certainly*. In introducing an illustration or example use *for example*, *for instance*, or *namely*. To express a contrast of ideas, use *however*, *nevertheless*, or *on the contrary*. You can, of course, number the points by using such words as *first*. . ., *second*. . ., and *finally*. . . .

The final paragraph should finish what you told the reader you were going to do in the first paragraph. In other words, the final paragraph should prove the point of the discussion. The final paragraph can be used to summarize the point of the discussion or to detail an opinion or course of action. Transition adverbs such as *accordingly*, *consequently*, *thus*, *therefore*, or *as a result* might be used in a concluding paragraph. In any event, always read the first and last paragraphs to see if the development has been completed. One of the most common mistakes of inexperienced paralegals is not following through on the idea started at the beginning of a document, especially when preparing briefs or memoranda. The same principles, of course, apply when writing correspondence.

**A Paragraph Should Contain a Topic Sentence.** As in other forms of writing, a paragraph in a legal document should contain a topic sentence, although the topic sentence does not necessarily have to be the first sentence of the paragraph. In legal writing, a topic sentence may summarize a proposition of law. Then, in the remainder of the paragraph, you can show how the legal proposition was derived or the effect of the legal proposition on the facts of a case. The topic of a paragraph can be implied. Opening each paragraph with a rigid topic sentence will only result in a boring piece. A topic sentence aids structure, but there is no set formula for writing topic sentences.

**Paragraphs Should Vary in Length.** No standard rule dictates paragraph length. A one-sentence paragraph may be appropriate, especially to make a transition between two adjacent paragraphs. Correspondence typically contains paragraphs shorter than those of briefs. Paragraphs break up the material for the reader. Shorter paragraphs often are easier to read. If paragraphs are too short, however, it usually means that the ideas are not being covered adequately. If paragraphs are too long, it usually means that the discussion is too convoluted.

The rule is that a paragraph should complete the thought of the topic sentence. Each paragraph should deal with only one topic. If the topic is finished, move to the next paragraph.

**Paragraphs Should Utilize Transitions.** Paragraphs should be unified. Each paragraph should be connected to each adjacent paragraph. If you connect each of the paragraphs to the others, then the reader is better able to grasp your logic. Transitions lead the reader through your thought process. Don't fall prey to the common error of writing isolated rather than connected paragraphs, a poor practice that usually stems from failure to think the position through sequentially. Remember that adverbs can aid the transition between paragraphs.

## SENTENCE STRUCTURE

There is more to writing sentences than starting with a capital letter and ending with a punctuation mark. There is more to it than avoiding dangling modifiers and ensuring that subject and verb agree. A sentence is used to communicate an idea or—as you were taught years ago—a complete thought. Like the paragraph, the sentence can either add or detract from an argument. Your sentence structure can cause a reader's attention to drift from your analysis, or it can cultivate great interest in your theory. Here are some guidelines for using sentence structure to help the writing process.

### Vary Sentence Length

The movement to simplify legal documents tends to advocate shorter sentences. Although the skillful use of short sentences does aid readability, the advantage is lost when a document consists entirely of short sentences. The best practice is to vary your sentence length, a technique that serves to accent an argument well. Use a series of longer sentences and end the paragraph with a brief one. Or lead with a series of short sentences for cadence, building up to a point that is made with a longer sentence.

Don't hesitate to use shorter sentences when they will do the same job as longer sentences, but develop the habit of varying sentence length.

### Vary Sentence Type

You should favor the simple sentence. However, as it does in sentence length, variety in sentence type aids the presentation of thought. You already know that there are simple sentences, compound sentences, and complex sentences.

> I like simple sentences. (simple sentence)
>
> I like simple sentences, but I do not like compound sentences. (compound sentence)
>
> I like sentences that read like this. (complex sentence)

A simple sentence contains a subject and predicate. A compound sentence contains two or more independent clauses, both of which are complete sentences. A complex sentence contains one independent clause and one or more dependent clauses. In other words, a complex sentence contains a complete sentence and at least one clause that is not a complete sentence. Compound-complex sentences combine the properties of the two types.

**Avoid Overloaded Sentences.** Do not cram several ideas into one sentence. A good way to check on how many ideas are crammed into a sentence is to look for the verbs (including the different verb forms such as infinitives and participles). The presence of several verbs is a sign of too many ideas in a sentence.

## Use Sentences to Create Special Effects

Strategically placed sentences create special effects. An exclamatory sentence can drive home a legal argument. A parenthetical sentence can highlight an aside. (So can a footnote.) A rhetorical question can focus a dispute.

A sentence is used to communicate an idea. The main idea of the sentence should be in the main clause. Subordinate ideas should be placed in subordinate clauses. A sentence that contains the main idea at its beginning is called a **loose sentence**. A loose sentence is usually more readable. A sentence that contains the main idea at its end is called a **periodic sentence**. A periodic sentence is used to build suspense.

You can make a sentence easier to understand by opening with a familiar idea before introducing an unfamiliar idea. You can provide emphasis by putting a key word at the end of a sentence. You can bury an idea by placing it in a dependent or restrictive clause. Learn to use sentences creatively to drive home your points. Understanding sentence structure will broaden your writing ability.

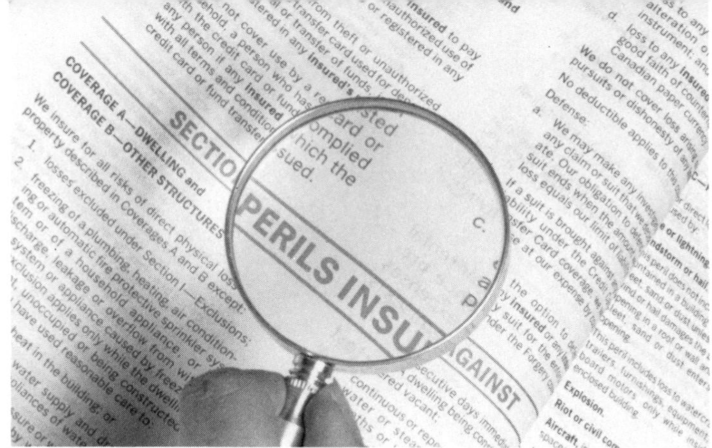


# 10 DISEASES OF LEGAL WRITING

> The difference between the right word and almost the right word is the difference between lightning and a lightning bug. (Mark Twain)

A paralegal is a professional writer. In many situations the legal writer must be concerned with problems that are not of concern to other professional writers. For example, the wrong word in a legal document can lead to an expensive dispute. In fact, too many legal disputes are actually caused by poor legal drafting. One survey found that 25 percent of all contract disputes arose from poor drafting.

A paralegal will prepare many types of technical documents. Although certain rules that apply to technical writers also apply to legal writers, many problems are unique to the legal professional. This chapter explores the unique problems of legal writing.

## AVOID AMBIGUITY

Avoiding ambiguity is a critical concern of the legal professional. Ambiguity develops when two different interpretations are possible.

### Words with Multiple Meanings

Words with multiple meanings can be ambiguous. For instance, the word *ton* can mean a short ton or a metric ton. Similarly, the word *profit* can refer to either gross or net. A *quart jar* can mean a jar that holds a quart of liquid or a jar that displaces a quart of liquid. Ambiguity will also arise from the misuse of the simple words *and* and *or* and the words *shall* and *may.*

> Does "P or Q" mean "P or else Q or else both," "P or else Q, but not both" or "P, that is to say Q"? Does "P and Q" mean "only both P and Q" or "P or else Q or else both"?[1]

The classic example of this problem is seen in an old English case that involved a charter party who was required "to load a full and complete cargo of sugar, molasses, and/or other lawful produce."[2] What can be loaded? There are at least seven different combinations. For example, the ship can be loaded with only sugar or only molasses—or the ship could be loaded with no sugar or molasses. However, words with multiple meanings are not the only source of ambiguity.

### Syntax Problems

Ambiguity can arise from syntax problems. Syntax is the relationship of words to one another. For example, consider an insurance policy that covers any "disease of organs of the body not common to both sexes."[3] Does this policy cover a fibroid tumor (which can occur in any organ) of the womb?

Ambiguity can even arise from the punctuation of a sentence. Consider a contract for sale of "approximately 10,000 (heaters), all in perfect condition."[4] Is this a warranty of the heaters (all heaters must be in perfect condition, as the buyer would argue)? Or is it a limitation of quantity (you can buy all the heaters that are in perfect condition)?

### Vagueness

Ambiguity is the situation where two different interpretations are possible; vagueness is the situation where there is a question of degree. Exactly when yellow turns into orange on a color wheel is an illustration of vagueness.

In most cases, ambiguity is an undesirable disease of legal writing. In contrast, vagueness in legal drafting is sometimes appropriate. In fact, conscious use of vagueness is a necessary and sanctioned practice in certain forms of legal drafting. The parties to a proposed agreement may believe that a stumbling block in negotiations may never arise, but they want a means to cover the contingency satisfactorily for both parties if it does. Inserting a vague term in the agreement can resolve the dispute, so parties sometimes "agree to be vague." Judicious use of vagueness can be an effective bargaining technique—but you should remember that if a dispute later arises, the controversy has only been delayed, not resolved.

In child-custody agreements, lawyers frequently provide for "reasonable visitation" for the noncustodial parent. Reasonable visitation is a vague concept. By using the word "reasonable," the lawyer has made an assumption that the parties themselves can discover through the process of trial and error what will be reasonable for them under the circumstances. Those parties may apply that concept differently from other parties, yet the phrase "reasonable" visitation is a concept that a court can enforce if the circumstances warrant. Rather than working out detailed specific visitation hours, the attorneys, or in some cases the courts, delegate responsibility to the parties. The concept of reasonableness in any case is vague, but it can be an appropriate problem-solving approach.

An able legal professional will frequently complete a transaction by finding solutions to stagnated negotiations. Often the use of vague or elastic terms such as "reasonable," "as soon as practical," "appropriate," "good faith," or "proper" will provide a vehicle for resolving an impasse. Again, the use of vagueness in this context is neither improper nor inappropriate. If the client has been cautioned that a vague concept has been inserted, the client can complete a transaction by assuming the risk. If the eventuality occurs and intervention is necessary, a court can resolve the conflict. That is a business risk accepted by the client to reach the agreement in the first place.

## AVOID INCONSISTENCY

Grade school teachers want students to explore a variety of words and urge their students not to use the same words again and again. Students who use a word repeatedly are likely to find it circled boldly in red on their papers.

The consistency principle in legal writing is contrary to this early lesson. The consistency principle tells us to use the same word, phrase, or clause in the legal document whenever the same meaning is intended and to use a different word, phrase, or clause when a different meaning is intended. Word variation offends the consistency principle. No principle of drafting is more important than being consistent throughout the document. The consistency principle is immaterial to students in disciplines other than law; but in legal drafting, inconsistency of expression courts litigation.

The rationale for this rule is that the drafter has carefully and logically selected the words for a legal document. Although this may or may not be the situation, paralegals must pay attention to the consistency rule.

The ultraquistic subterfuge and the elegant variation are two examples of the consistency principle.

### The Ultraquistic Subterfuge

Many words have more than one dictionary meaning. When you use a word with multiple meanings to express different ideas in the same document, it is termed an **ultraquistic subterfuge** or legerdemain with two senses. An example of an ultraquistic subterfuge is seen in this sentence:

> The real *property* shall be the *property* of the wife.

Here the first *property* refers to a specific piece of land. The second *property* refers to ownership. Another example is seen from an actual case:

> A defendant is not *responsible* if at the time of his unlawful conduct his mental or emotional processes or behavior controls were impaired to such an extent that he cannot be held *responsible* for his act.[5]

Here the word *responsible* is used in two different contexts. The first *responsible* means "able to discharge one's obligations." The second *responsible* means "accountable for one's actions." The ultraquistic subterfuge results from using homonyms in the same document. Homonyms are two words that have the same spelling but different meanings. This often results in confusion because the same word is used with two different meanings in the same document. Avoid the use of homonyms in legal documents.

### The Elegant Variation

The converse of the rule that applies to homonyms applies to the use of synonyms. The error of using synonyms to mean the same thing is termed an **elegant variation**. Courts assume that if you use different words, you intend different meanings. When you use synonyms, the courts assume you intend different shades of meaning.

Unfortunately, most legal professionals who use elegant variations do not intend any difference in meaning. They are simply practicing what they were taught to do long ago—using different words for the sake of variety or to show off their vocabulary. Again, the rule is that if you intend the same meaning, then use the same word. Less-experienced writers believe that repetition of words means lack of imagination. They do not understand that each word has a specific meaning and function. The elegant variation—changing words for the mere sake of change—is a flaw of inferior writers. But in legal drafting, the flaw creates ambiguity.

Do not substitute synonyms. Choose an appropriate word, and use that word throughout the document.

## AVOID REDUNDANT PAIRS

Consider the words "last will and testament." What is the difference between "will" and "testament"? Historically, some experts believe that a will dealt with real estate and a testament dealt with personal property, but today a will disposes of all property. Yet legal professionals continue to use the redundant "will and testament."

There is no legal or logical reason to use redundant pairs. Choose the one word that accomplishes your objective. For example, instead of saying "I authorize and direct you," say "I direct you." You cannot direct someone to do something without giving authority to that person. Consider this list of redundant pairs and notice how one word can always be used:

| | |
|---|---|
| alter or change | assumes and agrees |
| convey and transfer | covenant and agree |
| deemed and considered | due and owing |
| each and all | each and every |
| for and during the period | full and complete |
| full force and effect | kept and performed |
| made and entered into | mentioned or referred to |
| null and void | remise and release |
| sole and exclusive | give and devise |
| then and in that event | true and correct |

## AVOID NOUN AND VERB STRINGS

A problem related to redundant pairs is the problem of **encircling** the concept. This situation frequently occurs when you are unsure of the right word so you use a string of words to capture the concept.

This pattern is seen, for example, in a string of verbs such as "The trustee shall serve until he *resigns*, *dies* or *leaves* the country." What happens if the trustee becomes incompetent? The simple solution would be to say, ". . . until he is unable or unwilling to serve."

Another example is seen in the string of nouns in this provision:

> Seller assumes no liability for interruptions to service due to strikes, riots, war, floods, fire, or acts of God.

What happens if vandalism prevents service? A proper solution might be to rephrase the clause to read, "Seller is not liable for service interruptions due to events beyond Seller's control." Trying to anticipate every eventuality without meeting the problem head-on frequently results in missing an eventuality. This problem often arises in statutes, especially where the substantive law requires that the statutes be strictly construed. Does the following include bank accounts?

> Business and all furniture, fixtures, and personal property used in connection thereof, and all accounts receivables . . .[6]

Does the phrase "personal effects, jewelry, and furniture" include silverware? Does "all jewelry, wearing apparel, silver, silverware, china, pictures, paintings, books, house furniture and furnishings, and articles of household or personal use or ornament of all kinds" include statues?

In these examples, the drafter attempted to exhaustively provide for every possible eventuality and in each of these situations the drafter overlooked a pertinent fact. In each of these examples, the drafter did not anticipate all eventualities. However, each of these oversights could have been avoided by recognizing that whenever encircling is used in a document, the danger of missing an important possibility exists. The danger is not a product of laziness because the drafter may have spent an agonizing time attempting to enumerate all eventualities. But that time can usually be spent more constructively in trying to reconceptualize the problem. Whenever you begin to use a string of words to define a concept, consider whether you are creating a conceptualization problem. Overspecificity does not enhance conceptualization.

Consider this example:

> . . . to prevent garbage from leaking, spilling, falling, or blowing out of such vehicle.

Now substitute the word *escape* for "leaking, spilling, falling, or blowing." You do not lose any substance.

You can substitute the word *convey* or the word *assign* for the following string of words: "grant, bargain, sell, alien, release, confirm, and enfeoff." You can make the same change to the following string: "bargain, sell, assign, transfer, give over, and conform." Again you lose no substance. The fact that most high school sophomores know these strings are redundant has not kept them from fogging the pages of legal documents. Don't be afraid to break that habit.

## AVOID THE VAGUE REFERENT

Most attorneys recognize that words such as *it, there,* and *this* when used as a pronoun should be avoided because they are vague referents. These words are meant to refer to "closely adjacent antecedent nouns" but in legal documents they cause problems for readers and, worse, create ambiguity. Yet the same legal professional who will avoid using the pronouns *it, there* and *this* to begin a sentence will use *said, such,* or *hereabove* without hesitation in legal drafting. Vague referents are frequently utilized by attorneys out of intellectual laziness.

When you use any of these terms, the reader will not know whether you are referring to the preceding clause, sentence, paragraph, or the entire agreement. A case will best show this point:

> In a California case the phrase, "except as herein expressly provided," was the subject of litigation. It went through three courts: trial court, an intermediate appellate court, and the Supreme Court of California. The trial court held that "herein" in that phrase meant *in the entire statute,* that is, "except as expressly provided in this statute." In the intermediate appeal court consisting of five judges, it was held by a three-to-two vote that "herein" meant "in this particular section," not in the statute. Then it went up to the Supreme Court of California, a court of seven judges. And that court held, by a four-to-three vote, that "herein" meant "in the statute itself." Here we have trial court holding one way, a three-to-two decision in the appellate court holding the opposite, and a four-to-three decision in the Supreme Court of California holding the way the trial court held.
>
> The District Court of Appeals explained its holding with the following reasoning:
>
> "In the expression 'Except as *herein* expressly provided' the term 'herein' means 'in this section,' and the words that follow, 'the provisions *of this act* shall not apply, . . .' refer to the entire statute. The placing of the words 'herein' and 'of this act' in the same sentence and their proximity in the sentence make it manifest that the Legislature did not intend and did not achieve vagueness or obscurity. Hence the section means that the provisions of the entire act, except as provided in that section, are not applicable to the sale of the vendor's own securities . . . ."
>
> "*The conclusion expressed above is affirmed, if confirmation is necessary, by the legislative history of subdivision 3 of section 2(c)*" (italics supplied).
>
> But the majority in the California Supreme Court reasoned:
>
> "It is argued that the introductory phrase in that section, 'Except as herein expressly provided' does not refer to the remainder of the act, but is confined to section 2 in which it appears. The meaning of the term 'herein' is determined by the context of the statute in which it is used (see In re Pearsons, 98 Cal. 603, 608, 33 P. 451). *Here it is clear that the word refers*

> *to the entire act.* If the reference were to section 2, the language would be meaningless since no exceptions appear in that section. *The all-embracing application is compelled by the manifest purpose of the act* which discloses a comprehensive scheme for controlling the issuance and sale of corporate securities. It is also indicated in the codification of section 2(c). In rephrasing the section for inclusion in the Corporation Code there is substituted for the words 'Except as herein expressly provided,' the phrase: 'Except as expressly provided in this division.' The reference is to division 1, title 4 of the Corporations Code (secs. 25000-26104; Stats. 1949, ch. 384, p. 698) which comprises all of the Corporate Securities Act. It is therefore significant that the intended application of the word 'herein' in Section 2(c) is likewise to the entire act'' (italics supplied).[7]

### Specific Troublesome Words and Phrases

The paralegal who uses words like *aforesaid, such,* and *hereinabove* evidently believes that they sound professional. But these words create the same problem that *it* and *there* create at the beginning of a sentence. Certain words and phrases invariably cause problems. Avoid them.

**''Such.''** From a readability standpoint, it is almost always preferable to substitute the articles *a*, *an*, and *the* for the word *such*. *Such* is a demonstrative adjective that should be used with *as*. Using *such* as a synonym for *the* is an illiteracy.

**''Notwithstanding the Foregoing.''** Legal professionals love the phrase *notwithstanding the foregoing*. But like other relics of legalese, the phrase raises an immediate question. Does it mean the preceding sentence, paragraph, or the entire document? The mystery deepens when this phrase becomes a double negative. I once reviewed a statute concerning leases of public property; the first sentence excepted ''not-for-profit entities.'' In the succeeding sections, all other leases of public property required an appraisal before the public authorities could lease the property. Then a section provided that ''notwithstanding anything else,'' no lease could be for a rental value less than two-thirds of the fair market value of the property. Question: Did this section apply to a ''not-for-profit entity''?

## AVOID LEGAL JARGON

Too many paralegals believe there is a certain way lawyers must write. These paralegals will use archaic legal jargon to make their documents seem ''legal.'' Only infrequently must certain words be used to meet legal requirements. For example, a warranty deed might require use of the words ''warrant and convey,'' and an option might require the words ''irrevocable and binding.'' In most cases, however, a legal professional has considerable freedom in preparing a legal document. Exercise this freedom to write so that both you and your client can understand the document, if possible.

Ideally, the words in a legal document should express the idea of the parties. The words should be within the vocabulary of the audience. The words should not cause confusion or ambiguity. Choosing the right word, however, requires more than using the common—or dictionary—meaning of words.

In any profession there develops a specialized language. For instance, the language of the physicist has dramatically changed in the past fifty years. There is no reason why legal language should not change also. There is no reason why legal professionals should continue to use multisyllable words when simple words will suffice. This is, of course, good advice for any technical writer, not just legal drafters. Find a simple word instead of the more difficult word, if possible. Here are some sample words that legal professionals can avoid entirely:

above (as an adjective)
above-mentioned
aforementioned
aforesaid
henceforward
herein
hereinabove
same (as a substitute for *it*, *he*, *him*, etc.)
thenceforth
thereunto
therewith
to wit
unto
wheresoever

You must appreciate the legal connotations in choosing words; but just because a word has an established legal meaning does not mean that you must use that particular word. Just because legal professionals of an earlier era used certain language does not suggest that you need to reuse that language today. Yet it is that logic that leads to the use of many archaic expressions in legal instruments. Language usage changes outside the legal community, and there is no reason to believe that it will not change inside the legal community as well.

## LEARN THE DIFFERENCE BETWEEN "SHALL" AND "MAY"

A sentence in a legal document will either command, authorize, or declare a result. Legal writers must choose their words carefully in order to ensure the proper result.

### The Proper Use of "Shall"

Many legal professionals think that every sentence in a transaction document must use the word *shall*. However, *shall* should be used only to impose a duty. In practice, this word is overused in legal documents.

Paralegals think that *shall* is a legal word to use. Whenever you use the word *shall*, however, test whether that word is really proper by substituting the phrase "has a duty" for the word *shall*. If this substitution does not work, then select another appropriate word. *Shall* should not be used in legal drafting to express future tense but should be used only to impose a duty. In some cases, the writer is trying to create a condition rather than a duty. If this is your intent, use the word *must*.

In many cases, *shall* and *may* are unfortunately interchanged by the parties, leading to unintended results. In legal drafting,

> "shall" is always used to impose a duty, regardless of whether the duty is affirmative or negative, and "may" is always used to convey authority (but not to deny authority).[8]

Learn to recognize the difference between *shall* and *may*.

### The Proper Use of "May"

The word *may* also causes problems. First, there is the potential ambiguity of *may* as authorization and as possibility. *May* can be read to mean that you are giving someone the authority to act, or you may be describing a possibility. In the sentence "I may go to the store," you can mean either that someone has given you permission to go to the store or that you are considering whether to go to the store. *May* can mean either permission or a possibility. Read each sentence containing the word *may* with both definitions in mind.

A second dimension of the problem with *may* is the use of the negative, or *may not*. *May not* does not negate authority:

> A second difficulty in the use of "may" is that the negative of authority is not expressed by "may not"; rather, the negative of authority is expressed by the negative duty, "shall not." Thus, if a provision reads, "if a person does not have a license. . ., he may not exhibit a sign. . .," there is doubt about whether the phrase "may not exhibit" means (1) "may possibly not exhibit," (2) "is authorized not to exhibit" or (3) "is not authorized to exhibit."[9]

In summary, the legal professional should be aware of these dimensions of the use of the word *may*. Remember that *may not* does not negate authority. Remember also that the word *may* can mean either permission or possibility. Always ask yourself: Is *may* meant to confer authority or is it used to connote a possibility?

This concise synopsis solves many problems:

> 1. To create a right, say "is entitled to."
> 2. To create discretionary authority, say "may."
> 3. To create a duty, say "shall."
> 4. To create a mere condition precedent, say "must" (e.g., "To be eligible to occupy the office of mayor, a person must * * *").[10]

## KNOW HOW TO USE "AND" AND "OR"

Choosing between the conjunction *and* and the conjunction *or* appears to be rather simple: *and* is used in the conjunctive sense and *or* is used in the disjunctive sense. The conjunctive sense connotes "togetherness," whereas the disjunctive sense connotes "take your pick." Although this choice seems simple, consider these problems:

> You are told to pick up the red and white flags. If there is a red flag, a white flag and a red and white flag, which do you pick up?
>
> You are told to pick up the red or white flags. What flags do you pick up?

A statute says that a city may build a skating rink or a swimming pool. Can the city build both?

A statute says that a city may build a skating rink and a swimming pool. Can the city build just a skating rink?

You are given an invitation that says "husbands and wives may attend." Can one party go without the other?

A statute says that a tax is imposed on manufacturers of bows and arrows. Is the tax imposed on a manufacturer that makes only bows?

These situations demonstrate that the words *and* and *or* can have different meanings. These words also have a joint or inclusive sense as well as a several or exclusive sense. To prevent confusion, say, "A and B or either of these" or "either. . . or. . . (but not both)." Be precise when you use either *and* or *or*. Too many drafting problems are created when *and* or *or* are used. Pay attention to the different meanings of these words.

### Do not use "and/or"

Although the courts have condemned the use of *and/or*, lawyers continue to claim the right to use it in legal instruments. The use of *and/or* is an invitation to a lawsuit. Consider some comments of one court on this subject, which held that and/or:

> should not be used in an affidavit and threatened to order costs against anyone so using it. In *Bonitto v. Fuerst Bros.*, Viscount Simon, in discussing the confusion in the pleadings, spoke of "the repeated use of that bastard conjunction 'and/or' which has, I fear, become the commercial court's contribution to basic English."
>
> In *Millen v. Grove*, a notice to quit under the National Security (Landlord and Tenant) Regulations gave as the ground that the premises were reasonably required by the lessor "for her personal occupation and/or for the occupation of some person who ordinarily resides with and is wholly or partly depended upon her." Gavan Duffy J. said that "the draftsman invited trouble by the common and deplorable affection for the form "and/or"; but he thought that the notice substantially stated the two grounds provided for in the Regulations, namely the premises being required for her personal occupation *and* for the occupation of some person, etc.[11]

Or as another commentator put it:

> A custom has grown among many lawyers to use the words "and/or" in many documents. The expression is an anachronism and should be avoided. Either the word "and" or the word "or" is proper but never both. Don't be an "andorian."[12]

## AVOID PROBLEM MODIFIERS

A modifier limits the meaning of a word or phrase: "It is the function of a modifier to limit the scope of the idea that is communicated by an unmodified word."[13] Many problems are caused by misuse of modifiers.

## The Unnecessary Modifier

Both the Thirteenth and Fourteenth Amendments to the U.S. Constitution provide that Congress has the power to enforce the provisions "by appropriate legislation." Notice that the word *legislation* is modified by the word *appropriate*. Why add the adjective *appropriate?* Logically, this implies that some legislation is inappropriate. The word *appropriate* incorporates an undefined standard. The courts must tell us what is appropriate legislation on a case-by-case basis.

Another example is from a jury instruction that provided that the plaintiff was to prevail if a "fair preponderance of the evidence" was in the plaintiff's favor. Is there an unfair preponderance? Or if you say "duly licensed physician," is there an unduly licensed physician? In drafting, a modifier that incorporates an undefined standard can cause vagueness.

Further, in some instances, a modifier will create a double standard. This situation occurs when you attempt to define the modifier. Consider this example:

> A second modifier fault arises out of an attempt to be clear; the draftsman says too much. If he writes that a hauler of garbage "shall properly cover the vehicle," the provision is defective, as has been suggested, in that the term "properly" calls for a judgment for which no standard is provided. If, on the other hand, the draftsman writes that the hauler "shall keep the vehicle properly covered so as to prevent the contents from leaking, spilling, falling or blowing out of the vehicle," the phrase which begins "so as to prevent" offers a standard for interpreting "properly"; but it also offers the possibility of a double standard. The question is whether "properly" means the same thing as "so as to prevent the contents from leaking. . ." If the draftsman intended by the word "properly" to say something different from "so as to prevent. . .," there is the ambiguity of a double standard. If not, the word "properly" is superfluous and should be omitted to avoid the risk of ambiguity. Thus, one would say, the hauler "shall keep the vehicle covered so as to prevent the contents from leaking. . ."
>
> Usually the risk of a double standard is created by use of a modifier, such as "properly," to precede a word, such as "cover," which it modifies, plus some "purpose" which is added for clarification. In most instances, the "purpose" states the draftsman's idea more clearly and accurately than the modifier does.[14]

The initial concern of the legal drafter is to determine whether the modifier is even necessary. When you say "the landlord may by his designated representative. . .," the adjective *designated* connotes something other than just a representative. The representative somehow must have a designation. The problem is that the tenant can cause a delay by asking for a designation.

Another example of an unnecessary modifier is the adjective intensifier (e.g., *very, extremely, greatly*). Seldom do these intensifiers add anything meaningful to the document. In the context of legal drafting, adjective intensifiers can almost always be deleted.

Sometimes we can have problems telling whether a word is a modifier or is part of a noun. Consider the following:

Cow killer (a wasp or a killer of cows)

NCAA basketball (a game sponsored by the NCAA or a basketball with an NCAA trademark)

To the extent that modifiers are necessary to provide flexibility for a transaction, there is no reason not to use them. However, the legal drafter is cautioned that many modifiers are unnecessary.

## The Squinting Modifier

You learned in grammar class that a misplaced modifier appears to modify the wrong referent and a dangling modifier is one that has no referent in the sentence. To a legal drafter, a misplaced modifier is a problem only if it causes equivocation. Most drafting experts agree, for example, that splitting an infinitive is acceptable practice if it prevents ambiguity of reference.

However, legal drafters must be aware of a special kind of misplaced modifier—a **squinting modifier**, which is a modifier ambiguously placed between two possible referents. A squinting modifier presents a problem as to what word or group of words another word or group of words attaches. Consider the following examples:

"No child may be employed on any weekday when the school is not open for more than four hours."

"No person may molest an animal on the highway."[15]

These sentences show squinting-modifier problems. In the first example, the question is whether the child may be employed on days when school *is* open for less than four hours or whether the child can be employed for more than four hours on weekdays. In the second example, it is a question whether it is the animal or the person that must be on the highway to make the provision operative.

Squinting modifiers are caused by recurrent sentence patterns. The simplest examples are seen in sentences having adjectives or adjective phrases that can modify two nouns. Sometimes more difficult to spot are squinting modifiers involving (1) successive prepositional phrases, (2) problems with the conjunctions *and* and *or,* (3) the terminal *because* clause, and (4) the vague participle. We will look at examples of each of these situations.

## Successive Prepositions

The use of two successive prepositional phrases routinely causes squinting-modifier problems. The following is the classic example of this problem:

Every shareholder of a company in Canada.

Does the phrase *in Canada* relate to *shareholder* or to *company*? The phrase relates to a noun, and there are two, namely, the subject *shareholder* and the object of the first preposition. One remedy is to convert one of the phrases to a clause.

> A shareholder of a company who is in Canada.

The pronoun *who* is personal and must refer to *shareholder.* Another remedy is to convert a prepositional phrase to a participial phrase.

> A shareholder of a company incorporated in Canada.

The word *incorporated* can refer only to company; but *domiciled*, for example, could refer to both.[16]

My own acquaintance with ambiguity resulting from two successive prepositional phrases is from *Alvey v. G.E.*[17], when the Seventh Circuit Court of Appeals, in reversing and remanding the case, wrote the following:

> In the context of this case under the present complaint, . . .[18]

Because the case was remanded, we were concerned whether the plaintiff could file a new complaint to remedy the pleading problem. After remand, we filed leave to amend our complaint arguing that "under the present complaint" implied that an amended complaint could be filed. The defendants argued that "in the context of this case" meant that the facts of this case foreclosed an amendment. Both interpretations were plausible. The district court granted leave to amend, and the Seventh Circuit upheld the district court's decision.

## The Use of "and" or "or" with Adjectives or Adjective Phrases

Consider this sentence:

> I give you the black cows and horses.

Did you give me the black cows and *all* the horses, or did you give me the black cows and *just* the black horses? You have the same situation when you say "charitable institutions or organizations." Do you mean a charitable institution or any type of organization? Or do you mean charitable institutions or charitable organizations?

The same problem occurs when a modifying phrase rather than a modifying word either precedes or follows a word in a series:

> No pupil shall, on the ground of religious belief, be excluded from or placed in an inferior position in any school, college or hostel *provided by the council.*[19]

Do the italicized words modify only *hostel*, or do the words modify *school* and *college* as well?

A statute from an actual case illustrates the same problem when using multiple conjunctions rather than just a simple conjunction:

> No person shall engage in or institute a local telephone call, conversation, or conference of any anonymous nature and therein use obscene, profane, vulgar, lewd, lascivious or indecent language, suggestions or proposals of an obscene nature and threats of any kind whatsoever.[20]

This problem will make you dizzy if you try to identify which words relate to what other words. To begin, consider just one question: Must the call, conversation, or conference contain *both* a "threat" *and* "obscene, profane, vulgar, lewd, lascivious or indecent language, suggestions or proposals''? Whenever you have a conjunction with a modifying word, you must be sensitive to this type of problem.

## TERMINAL ''BECAUSE'' CLAUSE

Consider this example:

> The developer may not delay construction during the preliminary phase because of financing.

There are two plausible interpretations: First, the developer might claim the right to delay construction on the ground that the developer is experiencing financing problems. Second, the developer cannot delay construction because the delay would endanger financing or a financing commitment.

The double meaning in this example results from the terminal *because* clause. The problems are not always easily spotted by the inexperienced drafter. Look for problems whenever you use the *because* clause.

## THE VAGUE PARTICIPLE

A participle is a verb converted to an adjective. It can modify a noun or pronoun. The present participle usually ends in -ing: shipping, running, examining. A past participle ends in -d, -ed, -t, -n, or changes to a vowel: seen, rung.

Problems with a present participle usually arise when the participle can be interpreted as either describing a duty (or a state of condition) or describing when the action is to be performed. In the sentence ''A contestant racing a car in the Pinewood Derby shall not be near the track,'' the question is whether this means that a contestant cannot be near the track *during* the race or that a contestant must never be near the track.

In fact, one writer says that the ''use of the participle as a modifier is a major cause of vagueness and inadequacy in documents.''[21] Consider the following example and explanation:

> ''The license requirements of this ordinance do not apply, until three years have expired, to a person transporting garbage upon a public way before (at the time of) the effective date of this ordinance.'' Presumably ''person transporting'' could be used as ''person who transported'' or ''person who was transporting'' before the effective date. . .'' Would a person who transported garbage once prior to the effective date qualify? Is this provision limited to persons who are engaged in the business of transporting garbage?

Equivocation can also arise with the past participle.

> In the description
>
> Every person who was imprisoned on the 1st day of January, 1970
>
> there is doubt whether the verb is the passive of *to imprison* or the active *to be* plus an adjective as subjective complement. Does the description refer to persons upon whom a sentence of imprisonment was pronounced on the named day, or to a person who on that day was in a state of imprisonment?[22]

The solution in many of these cases is to recast the sentence using another structure, such as a subordinate clause.

## THE IMPORTANCE OF SPOTTING DISEASED WRITING

Paralegals must be able to recognize that certain sentence structures lead to certain predictable equivocation problems. By recognizing recurrent problem grammatical constructions, the drafter can spot problems before the client sees the document. As a rule, when a writing precept has been violated, problems will surface.

## ENDNOTES

1 E. Allen Farnsworth, "Some Considerations in the Drafting of Agreements: Problems in Interpretation and Gap-Filling," 39 *Okla. B.A.J.* (1968) 917, 918–19.

2 *Id.* at 918.

3 *Id.* at 919.

4 *Udell v. Cohen*, 282 A.D. 685, 122 N.Y.S.2d 552 (1953).

5 *United States v. Brawner*, 471 F.2d 969 (D.C. Cir. 1972).

6 *Hastens v. Hightower*, 119 Ind. App. 144, 81 N.E.2d 207 (1948).

7 Elliott L. Biskind, *Simplify Legal Writing* (New York: Arco, 1975) pp. 100–101.

8 Maurice B. Kirk, "Legal Drafting: Some Elements of Technique," 4 *Texas Tech. L. Rev.* (1973) 297, 302.

9 *Id.* at 303.

10 F. Reed Dickerson, *Materials on Legal Drafting* (St. Paul: West, 1981) p. 182.

11 E. L. Piesse, *The Elements of Drafting*, 5th Ed. (Sydney: The Law Book Company Limited, 1976) pp. 108–109.

12 J. B. Thomas, "Problems in Drafting Legal Instruments," *Ill. State Bar J.*, vol. 39 (September, 1950) p. 55.

13 Maurice B. Kirk, "Legal Drafting: Some Elements of Technique," 4 *Texas Tech. L. Rev.* (1973) 297, 315.

14 *Id.* at 42–43.

15 F. Reed Dickerson, *Materials on Legal Drafting* (St. Paul: West, 1981) p. 231.

16 *Id.* at 234.

17 622 F.2d 1279 (7th Cir. 1980).

18 622 F.2d at 1291.

19 E. L. Piesse, *The Elements of Drafting*, p. 26–27.

20 *State v. Hill*, 245 La. 119, 157 So.2d 462 (1963).

21 Maurice B. Kirk, "Legal Drafting: Curing Unexpressive Language," 3 *Texas Tech. L. Rev.* (1971) 23, 45.

22 Id. at 45–46.

23 Elmer A. Driedger, *The Composition of Legislation; Legislative Forms and Precedents*, 2d ed. (Canada: The Department of Justice, 1976) p. 23.

# 11 STYLE: POLISHING YOUR WRITING

The legal profession has long suffered the reputation that it says and does odd things with words. (M. B. Kirk, "Legal Drafting: Some Elements of Technique," 4 *Texas Tech. Law Rev,* 1973.)

"No writer long remains incognito," asserts coauthor E. B. White in the third edition of *The Elements of Style.*[1] When you write, you reveal something about yourself—your disposition, your personality, your outlook. Of course, when you prepare a transaction document or a pleading, you do not intentionally reveal any of yourself to the reader. However, if ten legal professionals were to write the same paragraph of a contract, each version would be different. That difference is attributable to **style**.

In the past, writing style has not been a focus for the legal professional. Yet that lack of concern has earned legal professionals a reputation for generating obscure, cluttered documents and is probably why Will Rogers quipped that lawyers make a living out of trying to figure out what other lawyers have written. Awareness of the principles of style is no less important to a legal writer drafting a will than to a novelist writing a best-seller. Style aids precision and readability. Style is the mark of a good writer. In this chapter we will explore some ways to polish your writing style.

## BUILD SENTENCES AROUND VERBS

As you write a sentence, consider the verb first. The verb expresses the action in the sentence. You can write

The court held that the lawyer's conduct was unethical.

Or you can write

> The court disbarred the lawyer for her unethical conduct.

Although the first sentence is technically accurate, the verb "held" does not capture the action of the court. Consider the following:

> There was a collision of a car with a truck.
>
> The truck rammed the car.

The second sentence uses a descriptive verb. Always select a verb that describes the action of the sentence.

### Avoid Overuse of Inert Verbs

When you fail to use words describing the action, you are likely to use an inert verb—that is, a verb that shows no action. The verb *to be* is an example of an inert verb. Overuse of inert verbs leads to awkward sentences.

> A rambling, unwieldy sentence generally hangs from an inert verb—the verb *to be* (*am, are, is, was, were, being, been*), some other vague, actionless verb like have or exist, or a passive form (the verb *to be* plus a past participle; e.g., *is believed, was seen*). Pay attention to the verbs you use, and when you find a weak one, try substituting something more vigorous.[2]

The verb *to be* does not indicate action. Always ask what is the action in the sentence. Then recast the sentence with a verb that describes that action.

### Avoid Superfluous Verbs

Another problem is the use of superfluous verbs. Consider these examples:

| | | |
|---|---|---|
| make an attempt | *change to* | try |
| make a study of | *change to* | study |
| provide a summary | *change to* | summarize |
| do an investigation | *change to* | investigate |
| give consideration to | *change to* | consider |
| have a tendency to | *change to* | tend to |
| reach a decision | *change to* | decide |

The cure in these cases is to convert the noun to a verb and eliminate the superfluous verb.

## CHOOSE ACTIVE RATHER THAN PASSIVE VOICE

Almost every writing manual recommends active voice over passive voice. Active voice is when the subject is doing the action described by the verb. Passive voice is when the subject expresses the object of an action:

> Rick hit the ball. (active voice)
>
> The ball was hit by Rick. (passive voice)

Overuse of passive voice is a symptom of a writing problem. Many legal professionals tend to overuse passive voice, perhaps because students are taught to depersonalize their writing or to hide their opinions. Surprisingly, the more educated the writer, the more the writer tends to use passive voice.

### Active Voice Identifies the Person Responsible for an Action

In preparing transaction documents, style is only a secondary reason for choosing active voice. Consider the following provision:

> A dog must be kept on a leash.

Because this sentence is written in passive voice, the person whose duty it is to keep the dog on the leash is not identified. If the dog is not kept on the leash, who pays the fine—the owner or the person walking the dog? Using active voice, you might provide the following:

> Owner must keep dog on a leash.

In using active voice, you will confront the question of *who does what to whom* when you select a subject for the sentence. Active voice aids the process of identifying the person who is being granted a privilege or given a duty.

A contract might provide the following:

> Insurance shall be maintained on the premises.

The fallacy of passive voice in this context is that the party who must pay the insurance is not defined. Context sometimes supplies an answer. In many situations, however, the reader does not have any other reference for discerning who the actor is. Consider another example:

> A car parked in such a zone may be ticketed.

Here we cannot ascertain who must pay the fine: the owner of the vehicle or the driver. If this sentence were written in the active voice, the writer would recognize the problem.

As the complexity of a document increases, active voice helps the writer check the proper delegation of duties and responsibilities. Conscious concern with voice helps double-check how duties and responsibilities are to be apportioned.

### Active Voice Aids Readability

Active voice also aids readability. With active voice, you start with an actor who performs an action and follow this development as you read the sentence.

### When to Use the Passive Voice

Passive voice is sometimes appropriate. If the object is important, there is no reason not to use passive construction. For example, "The weapon was found by the child." In active voice, the sentence would read "The child found the weapon." Since the object (weapon) is more important than the actor, use the passive voice to emphasize "weapon" by making it the subject of the sentence. Passive voice is also appropriate when the actor performing the action is unimportant. For example, "This lease was terminated by a default." In this sentence, who defaults is unimportant. As a legal writer you may use passive voice to focus emphasis away from the actor if, for instance, your client has committed a less than exemplary act. For example, "The money was taken by my client." In this sentence, the passive construction deemphasizes the wrongdoing. As a general rule, less than one-third of your sentences should be passive.

## DO NOT OVERUSE PREPOSITIONAL PHRASES

A problem related to the use of passive voice is the overuse of prepositional phrases. In fact, passive voice leads to overuse of prepositions. Chapter 10 discussed how the use of successive prepositional phrases caused modification problems. In addition, strung out prepositional phrases make sentences unnecessarily wordy—a condition known as **prolixity**. If you want to add a person to a passive construction, you must add a prepositional phrase. Notice if you say: "The money was taken from the home on Monday," that if you want to say who took the money you must add another prepositional phrase: "by my client." Most works on technical writing caution against overuse of prepositions. One writer notes,

> A ratio of one preposition to every four words is a bad prognostic sign. The overuse of prepositions is a severe and extremely common fault. Indeed, if I wanted to offer a single rule for improving the quality of writing, I would unhesitatingly say, reduce the number of prepositions.[3]

Addressing how many is too many, he continues,

> Long sentences that are not easy to understand and that have only one or two verbs, either active or passive, should make you aware that the entire sentence has too many prepositions.[4]

Be aware of the placement and number of prepositional phrases. Changing passive voice to active voice usually imposes an automatic limit on prepositional phrases.

## AVOID FAT NOUNS

It is too bad that there is no scale to weigh sentences. Then you could easily avoid the overweight sentence burdened with inactive verbs and fat nouns. A fat noun is usually a **nominalization**—a verb or an adjective changed to a noun—or a superfluous noun.

### The Nominalized Noun

A nominalization converts a verb or adjective into a noun by adding a suffix such as *-tion*, *-ment,* or *-ence* to a verb or *-ity* or *-ance* to an adjective. Look at these nominalized words common to legal documents:

appurten*ances*
amortiza*tion*
acquitt*ances*
assign*ments*
posse*ssion*

enforce*ment*
applicabil*ity*
enforceabil*ity*
specific*ity*
determina*tion*

The problem with a nominalized word is that it is inefficient at doing the work of a verb. In most instances the solution is to rebuild the sentence by converting the nominalized word back to its original form as a verb or an adjective.

**Before** The *applicability* of that statute to this case is arguable.

**After** The parties can argue whether that statute *applies* to this case.

Usually nominalization results from using passive voice. Writing in active voice usually prevents the problem.

### The Superfluous Noun

Legal writers seem to share a fondness for inserting nouns that do nothing to enhance their sentences. Look at this list.

- **The case of** *Smith v. Jones* is directly on point.
- **The concept of** reasonable doubt is a significant focus of the criminal trial.
- **The extent of** the damages in this case is not controverted.

*Case, concept, extent*—these nouns add nothing but length to the sentences. Delete superfluous nouns.

## BE POSITIVE, NOT NEGATIVE

Always write in positive terms unless you have a good reason for using the negative. The positive makes a statement; the negative can only deny the positive.

### Negatives Convey Imprecision

Negative terms are often imprecise. A negative pregnant is a negative statement that does not actually deny an accusation. Consider the following negative pregnant examples:

The deceased was not dishonest.

I deny I owe you $10.00.

In the first sentence, you are not saying that the deceased was honest. In the second sentence, you are not claiming that nothing is owed: you could owe $1.00 or $100.00.

At times you want some imprecision:

My client's actions were not unlawful.

My client is not unwilling to accept the offer.

The negative is usually more difficult to understand than a positive statement, especially the double negative. However, the negative is appropriate to emphasize a command:

Do not play in the street.

No smoking.

According to Maurice Kirk, switching to the negative

> permits a more specific identification of the supposed duty and of the consequences that can flow from the breach of it.[5]

Sometimes the negative is more accurate:

I am not unhappy.

The defendant did not commit perjury.

### Negatives Emphasize Important Points

Sometimes you will deliberately select the negative for emphasis. For example, in a brief you might write the following:

The bank's argument is not logical.

The defendant's facts are not stated accurately.

However, in most cases we recommend using the positive rather than the negative. The rule is to use the positive unless you have a good reason to be negative.

## USE CORRECT TENSE

There are certain conventions to follow for using present and past tense in legal writing.

### Briefs and Memoranda

1. Use past tense to describe the facts of a case, unless the actions are ongoing.
   The accident happened at 4:00 a.m.
   The bank refused to honor the check.
   The defendant was questioned at police headquarters about the robbery.
2. Use past tense to describe the procedural posture of the case.
   The jury deliberated for four hours.
   The complaint was filed on January 2, 1991.
   The trial court denied the motion to dismiss.
3. When writing about a statute, court rule, regulation, or ordinance still in effect, use the present tense.
   The town ordinance prohibits public drinking of alcoholic beverages.
   The mail fraud statute contains criminal penalties.
4. When writing about a court decision, use the past tense.
   In *Smith v. Lewis*, the court analyzed the issue of legal malpractice and held that . . .
   Judge Douglas sentenced Pamela Smart to life imprisonment.

### Transaction Documents

A transaction document should be written in the present tense. Although the parties may not consult the document until a future time, the provisions should speak as of the time they are read. In other words, you use present tense in a contract or lease because you assume that it is being read when it is applied, not when it is written. It is simpler to say "if the tenant fails to pay" than "if the tenant shall fail to pay." However, an exception to the use of present tense in transaction documents occurs if the event is a past event when the problem arises—for example, when you impose a condition or a duty to act. Thus, you might write in a lease: "if the damage was *caused* by a third party, then the landlord shall make any repairs."

## THINK SINGULAR (EVEN WHEN YOU USE PLURAL)

Especially when preparing transaction documents, you should draft in the singular rather than the plural. When you use the plural, you tend to overlook problems that might arise in particular situations. By rethinking the problem in the singular, you will often spot problems you might not think about in using the singular:

> So far as substantive meaning permits, it is desirable to use the singular rather than the plural. This will avoid the question whether the predicate applies separately to each member of the subject class or jointly to the subject class taken as a whole.[6]

Consider this example:

> The plaintiff must give the parties a notice of the filing of a motion.

Does each party get a notice, or is one notice sufficient? Consider another example:

> My beneficiaries will be paid a monthly allowance of $1,000.

Does each beneficiary get $1,000 a month or do the beneficiaries divide the $1,000? Think in the singular even if you use the plural.

## USE THIRD PERSON EXCEPT FOR CORRESPONDENCE

When you write a pleading, a motion, a transaction document, or a memorandum, do not use the first person. Avoid saying, "I think," "I submit," "I suggest" or "we think," "we submit," or "we suggest." Instead of the first person, use the third person: "the Smiths contend that . . ." or "the Bank submits . . ." Remember that in most instances you are writing for the client and should not refer to yourself even in the third person (e.g., "this writer feels . . ."). In most cases you can simply delete the inappropriate reference:

**Before** My opinion is that the bank would have no claim.
**After** Thus the bank has no claim.

### Transaction Documents

Some readability experts advocate using "I" and "you" in transaction documents, and this is a considerable improvement over the awkward designations "party of the first part" and "party of the second part." However, the objection to using personal pronouns in transaction documents is that one never thinks of oneself as the "you." A better practice is to use the parties' last names ("Smith agrees to deliver 500 completed units to Jones") or some other abbreviated terms ("Southern Bank," "Acme Store").

### Correspondence

In correspondence you will often use first person because there is less formality and less reason to write yourself out of the discussion. Use of the first person is appropriate in most correspondence. Your client would consider you strange if you wrote "The writer needs these documents by Friday" rather than "I need these documents by Friday." You can use first person in informal memorandum as well.

## USE NONSEXIST LANGUAGE

Language reflects trends of society. Years ago, few women were involved in business. Therefore many terms evolved with a male bias: chairman, draftsman, draftsmanship, businessman, salesman, foreman, mankind, manpower. You see the same vestige in letters addressed "Dear Sir" or in references to *he* or *him* when meaning either sex.

Today women assume equal responsibility for supporting themselves and their families. Sex-biased words offend the concept of equality. If you are sensitive to your audience, you will change sexist words to neutral terms: draftsman to drafter, chairman to chairperson, foreman to supervisor, and so on.

### Avoid Standard "Gender Definition" Paragraphs

In the past, contracts and leases commonly use the words *he* and *his*. At the end of those documents a standard clause said that reference to a male included a female where appropriate. This clause would be offensive today.

### Replace Gender Pronouns

In most cases you can rewrite a sentence without using gender pronouns. One method is to replace the pronoun with a noun.

**Before** A default occurs when he does not pay the rent.

**After** A default occurs when the party does not pay the rent.
or
A default occurs when the rent is not paid.
or
The nonpayment of rent constitutes a default.

Another method is to replace a possessive pronoun with an article.

**Before** The defendant must file his answer on time.

**After** The defendant must file an answer on time.

Remove personal pronouns completely from the sentence to avoid gender problems. Use *she or he* and *his or her* only when all other possibilities have been exhausted. Never use *she/he* or *his/her*. Avoiding sexist language is simply an offshoot of the general rule that the writer must respect the audience.

## AVOID INTRUSIVE WORDS

The basic sentence consists of subject-verb-object. As you build on this structure, you can remove the object or put words between the basic elements. Language experts study the most opportune placement of words in the sentence. Here are a few basic ideas on the most effective placement of words.

### Keep the Subject and Verb Together

When you insert words between the subject and the verb, you tend to interrupt the actor-action thought. You distract the reader. This problem occurs whether the subject-verb is a simple sentence or the main clause of a complex sentence. Consider this example:

> The argument *that the guest act does not apply because the guest had painted the drivers' home prior to the accident* is certainly consistent with the applicable case law.

This sentence is classic sprawl. The cure is simply to remove the intruding clause:

> The guest act does not apply because the guest painted the driver's house prior to the accident. This conclusion is consistent with the applicable case law.

Keep the subject and verb together.

### Keep Objects with Their Verbs and Prepositions

Do not separate a verb or a preposition from its object by placing words between them. The result is the same as when you separate the subject from the verb.

## PUT MODIFIERS IN THEIR PLACE

The general rule is that a modifier should be placed immediately next to the word it modifies. For instance, most adjectives appear immediately before the words they modify. In legal writing, however, some adjectives will follow the object of a verb that gives an opinion (e.g., *consider*, *think*, *find*). An example:

> I consider the evidence irrelevant and immaterial.

Here the adjective phrase *irrelevant and immaterial* follows the object, *evidence*. (An adjective phrase usually appears immediately after the word it modifies).

### Split Infinitives Only to Prevent Ambiguity

The most common problem with adverbs involves the infinitive verb (to belong, to be, to find). An old rule cautions against splitting an infinitive by placing an adverb after the *to*. The rule does not apply to a past participle—the *ed* form of a verb (''to have been poorly represented'').

Most legal experts advocate splitting an infinitive if the split prevents ambiguity. Consider this example:

> To understand the result in that case, you have to carefully weigh decided opinions versus public policy.

The adverb *carefully* is best placed between the words *to* and *weigh* rather than after weigh. If you place *carefully* after *weigh*, then it could modify *decided*.

The fundamental rule is to place modifiers where there can be no mistake as to reference. This rule is usually satisfied by placing the modifier next to the word it modifies.

### Use Familiar Words

Legal professionals deal with abstract subjects, with principles and analysis. Because they use abstract ideas, they tend to select abstract words. When you use concrete or familiar words, however, your writing will be much clearer. Why use a pretentious word when a simple word will suffice? Table 11-1 at the end of the chapter is a guide for replacing some commonly used legal terms with simpler words.

## OMIT NEEDLESS WORDS

Most writers could immediately improve their writing by heeding Strunk and White's famous admonition: "Omit needless words." Sadly, it seems that most legal professionals seek to add words rather than delete them. Rare indeed is the legal writer who errs by using too few words. You have already seen how to delete noun and verb strings, superfluous nouns and verbs, redundant pairs, and over specificity. Let's look at some examples of unnecessary words.

### Intensifiers

Avoid using the so-called intensifiers—very, extremely, intensely, overly—in legal documents. These words add nothing to a sentence and are characteristic of writers who are trying to bolster a weak point.

Legal professionals do use elastic words (e.g., reasonable, duly, necessary) to solve difficult questions. Do not use elastic terms unless you have a reason to do so, however.

### The Unnecessary Windup

A common mistake made by those who write briefs and memoranda is beginning sentences with an unnecessary wind up. Consider these examples:

> *We will set out to show that* a host in an automobile is not liable unless the host acted willfully and wantonly.
>
> *It is submitted that* the law is against the plaintiff in this case.

The italicized words can almost always be eliminated. This habit probably stems from poor writing instruction or insecurity. In either case, avoid the unnecessary windup. Your writing will almost certainly be more confident.

Other common windups include the following:

> It is important to note that . . .
>
> We intend to discuss . . .
>
> We would like to stress that . . .

### Words Between "The" and "Of"

Many nouns that appear between *the* and *of* can be eliminated (along with the *of* that goes with them). These words add no meaning to the sentence.

- the amount of
- the area of
- the case of
- the concept of
- the extent of
- the number of
- the purpose of
- the sum of

Try deleting the entire phrase and beginning the sentence from that point. Does it disturb the meaning? Make it a habit to determine what words are baggage and delete them. Only then will you begin to become a *good* writer.

## INCLUDE ALL NECESSARY WORDS

Converse to the rule to omit needless words is the rule to include all necessary words. Two examples make this point: *that* and the *whiz deletion.*

### "That"

When I started my legal career, I sometimes wrote briefs for a talented lawyer. He would edit the briefs that I had prepared and strike most of the *thats* I used. He said they were unnecessary. I disagreed. I argued that they aided readability. I continued to use *that*, and I forgot this debate until I started writing this text. Another talented lawyer read an early version of my manuscript and struck most of my *thats*. I did not reinsert them. However, my consulting editor, a lawyer and writer, put the *thats* back in. Although there is some debate on this issue, the general consensus of the writing experts is the word *that* can aid comprehension. *That* may not be an unnecessary word.

However, omit the *that* that begins a sentence in a complaint or other document just to make the sentence seem more legal sounding. That *that* is unnecessary.

### The Whiz Deletion

The whiz deletion says that when you have a relative pronoun (e.g., which, who, that) and when the verb is a form of "be," then both the verb form of "be" and the relative pronoun can be deleted.

**Before** The lawyer *who is* assigned the case. . .

**After** The lawyer assigned the case. . .

**Before** The court that is to decide. . .

**After** The court deciding . . .

**Before** The text that is in my locker. . .
**After** The text in my locker. . .

The whiz deletion results in shorter sentences, but language experts tell us the sentences may be harder to read after the deletions.

The point is, you must satisfy yourself that each word in a sentence is performing some function. If it is, keep the word; if not, delete the word. Remember that legal professionals tend to use too many words rather than too few.

## WRITE NATURALLY

The rule that seems to bother legal professionals most is the rule to write naturally. Many legal professionals believe that they must try to impress others. That belief clouds more writing than the breach of any other rule discussed in this book. The idea, not the words, should impress the reader.

Select words that mirror your ideas. Use familiar words rather than pretentious words. Use concrete words rather than abstract words. The objective of writing is to communicate. Anyone who criticizes you for writing clearly and concisely knows nothing about writing.

Writing naturally does not mean writing informally or colloquially. It means saying what you mean so that the reader understands it. The rule to write naturally applies to all writers—not just legal writers.

**TABLE 11-1 A GUIDE FOR REPLACING LEGAL JARGON WITH SIMPLER WORDS**

| Don't use this | if this will work as well | Don't use this | if this will work as well |
|---|---|---|---|
| accord | give | has the option of | may |
| adequate amount | enough | indicate | show |
| afford | give | in excess of | more than |
| allocate | give, divide | initiate | begin |
| applicable | that applies | in lieu of | instead of |
| as to | about, relating to | accorded | given |
| attain | reach | admit of | allow |
| attributable to | from, by | all of the | all the |
| by reason of | because of | attains the age of | becomes. . .years old |
| cease | stop | attempt (as verb) | try |
| commence | begin | calculate | compute |
| conceal | hide | cause it to be done | have it done |
| effectuate | carry out | institute | begin |
| exclusively | only | in the event that | if |
| expiration | end | maintain | keep, continue support |
| for the duration of | during | necessitate | require |
| for the purpose of | to, for | on or before | by |
| for the reason of | because | on the part of | by |
| furnish | give, provide | originate | start |

**TABLE 11-1 A GUIDE FOR REPLACING LEGAL JARGON WITH SIMPLER WORDS (Cont.)**

| Don't use this | if this will work as well |
|---|---|
| per annum | a year |
| prior to | before |
| procure | get |
| promulgate | issue |
| provided that | however, if |
| pursuant to | under |
| retain | keep |
| render | make, give |
| shall | must, may, will |
| solely | only, alone |
| sufficient | enough |
| submit | send, give, contend |
| subsequent to | after |
| said, same, such | the, this, that |
| terminate | end, finish |
| unto | to |
| utilize | use |
| without the United States | outside the United States |
| adequate number of | enough |
| afforded | given |
| approximately | about |
| at the time | when |
| by means of | by |
| category | kind, class, group |
| cease | stop |
| commence | begin, start |
| complete (as verb) | finish |
| contiguous to | next to |
| corporation organized and existing under the laws of Indiana | Indiana corporation |
| deem | consider |
| does not operate to | does not |
| during such times as | while |
| effectuate | carry out |
| enter into a contract with | contract with |
| excessive number of | too many |
| expend | spend |
| feasible | possible |
| for the purpose of holding (or other gerund) | to hold (or comparable infinitive) |
| forthwith | immediately |
| hereafter | after this . . . takes effect |
| in cases which | when, where |
| indicate | show |
| in order to | to |
| in sections 2023 to 2039, inclusive | in sections 2023–2039 |
| is able to | can |
| is binding upon | binds |
| is entitled (in the sense of "has the name") | is called |
| it is the duty | shall |
| law passed | law enacted |
| maximum | most, largest, greatest |
| modify | change |
| obtain | get |
| consequence | result |
| donate | give |
| during the course of | during |
| endeavor | try |
| evince | show |
| expedite | hasten, speed up |
| expiration | end |
| frequently | often |
| in case | if |
| inform | tell |
| in lieu of | instead of, in place of |
| inquire | ask |
| interrogate | question |
| in the interest of | for |
| is authorized | may |
| is empowered | may |
| is unable to | cannot |
| it is directed | shall |
| it shall be lawful | may |
| manner | way |
| minimum | least, smallest |
| necessitate | require |
| occasion (as a verb) | cause |
| no later than June 30, 1992 | before July 1, 1992 |
| on his own application | at his request |
| on the part of | by |

**TABLE 11-1 A GUIDE FOR REPLACING LEGAL JARGON WITH SIMPLER WORDS (Cont.)**

| Don't use this | if this will work as well | Don't use this | if this will work as well |
|---|---|---|---|
| paragraph (3) of subsection (a) of section 2000(e) | section 2000(e)(a)(3) | until such time as | until |
| party of the first part | (the party's name) | of a technical nature | technical |
| per annum, per day, per foot | a year, a day, a foot | on and after April 13, 1992 | after April 13, 1992 |
| per centum | percent | on or before April 13, 1992 | before April 13, 1992 |
| period of time | period, time | or, in the alternative, | or |
| portion | part | possess | have |
| proceed | go, go ahead | preserve | keep |
| prosecute its business | carry on its business | prior | earlier |
| purchase | buy | prior to | before |
| require | need | procure | obtain, get |
| retain | keep | provision of law | law |
| specified | named | remainder | rest |
| summon | send for, call | state of Indiana | Indiana |
| to the effect of | that | the manner in which | how |
| | | under the provisions of | under |

## ENDNOTES

1 William Strunk Jr. and E. B. White, *The Elements of Style,* 3d ed. (New York: MacMillan, 1972).

2 Claire Kehrwald Cook, ''The MLA's Line by Line: How to Edit Your Own Writing,'' p. 3.

3 Lester S. King, *Why Not Say It Clearly* (Boston: Houghton Mifflin, 1985) p. 34.

4 Id. at 34.

5 Maurice Kirk, ''Legal Drafting: Some Elements of Technique,'' 4 *Texas Tech. L. Rev.* (1973), 297, 307–308.

6 F. Reed Dickerson, ''Materials on Legal Drafting'' (St. Paul: West, 1981) p. 183.

# 12 EDITING

> If life had a second edition, how I would correct the proofs? (John Clare)

Perhaps the most difficult step in the drafting process is editing—especially editing your own work. The tendency in writing is to quit too soon or to read over the same mistake. Editing skills are different from writing skills. The best editors are not necessarily the best writers. In fact, in most professional writing a separate specialist performs the editing function. The legal professional does not have the luxury of these editing specialists. Paralegals may very well perform an editing function for the law firm. Certainly you will be responsible for editing your own writing.

Editing is an important stage of the writing process. Unfortunately, some legal professionals skip this stage altogether or give it only cursory attention. It is wise to remember that a legal professional is paid substantial fees for legal writing, and a client may long remember a misspelling or a grammatical mistake.

## THE DIFFERENCE BETWEEN MACRO AND MICRO EDITING

Legal writers commit a wide gamut of mistakes ranging from simple misspellings to critical errors of logic. The editor must catch all the mistakes. A legal editor must check the broad picture, a process that involves looking at the flow of an argument, for example, or considering whether a transaction will work. This is termed **macro editing**. A legal editor must also examine the myriad details of a legal document: spelling, grammar, punctuation, citations, word usage, capitalization, tabulation, and so on. This process is termed **micro editing**.

## MACRO EDITING

Paralegals must review legal documents to determine whether the main ideas have been expressed as clearly as possible.

POINTER: You will find that the most difficult editing is editing your own writing. If at all possible, the first step in the macro editing process should be to put your writing away for several days. What you were so proud of on Friday may seem like a sorry excuse on Monday. Time does dampen infatuation with your writing. Time also helps you see errors you might earlier have overlooked.

Before a paralegal submits any legal document for an attorney's review, a number of questions must be addressed.

### Is the Tone Appropriate?

Tone is the expression of your attitude through your writing. Almost everyone has heard a parent or other authority figure bark: "Don't use that tone of voice with me!" In writing, the word *tone* has the same connotation.

A letter can be too formal or too informal. A brief can be written with too much sarcasm. You can write a memorandum with too much levity. If you are angry when you write, that anger will usually filter through your writing. The same is true for most other emotions.

In some forms of legal writing, such as memoranda or transaction documents, your tone will be deliberately neutral. In other forms of writing, such as briefs, you will deliberately inject some emotion. However, the basic concern should always be the *appropriateness* of your tone. How will the sarcasm be interpreted by the judge who reads your brief? Does the humor detract from the argument? Remember that what you find clever might seem banal to the reader.

When intentionally inserting tone, read and reread the document from the standpoint of the reader. Do not assume the reader shares your bias on the issue you are presenting. Sometimes it is helpful to assume the reader will be reading your document when in a bad mood; then try to envision how the sarcasm, humor, or anger will be received. Read all final copy for tone.

### Is the Writing Coherent?

In a memorandum or legal opinion, the conclusion should follow from the proof. In a brief, your argument should be coherently developed. In a transaction document, the deal must be workable. At some point in the writing process you must read beyond the words to see if your ideas are coherent.

**Coherency in Expository and Argumentative Writing.** It is always difficult to spot your own errors of logic. However, a legal professional should be acutely sensitive to logic faults. Here are some common examples.

***Improper Cause and Effect.*** Suppose you have never seen a horse. Suppose also that you can peek into a barnyard only through a slit in a fence. A horse walks by the slit every day. First you see the horse's head, then you see the horse's tail. You might conclude that the horse's tail was caused by its head. This is an improper conclusion as to cause and effect. Consider a more realistic example. You sneeze every time you visit a friend's house. You might erroneously conclude that you are allergic to your friend, whereas perhaps your allergy is only to your friend's cat.

***Wrong Proof, Right Conclusion.*** A conclusion depends on your proof. If your assumption is wrong, if you use the wrong rule, or if you use wrong data or facts, then a seemingly valid conclusion may be false.

Consider this syllogism:

> A tells B, "I give you my ring." As A is saying this, A puts the ring back into his pocket. Now A will not give B the ring. B sues A.
>
> A student concludes the following:
>
> A made a gift to B. The rule is that a completed gift entitles the donee to the right to the ring as against the donor. Thus B should prevail.

The flaw here is the conclusion made in the student's first sentence, "A made a gift to B." A gift is made only when there has been a delivery of the gift to the donee. If there is no delivery, there is no gift. The conclusion is wrong because the premise is wrong. In legal writing, often the error of logic is in the basic assumptions made about the facts of the case or in selecting the wrong rule of law to apply to the case.

***Right Proof, Wrong Conclusion.*** Sometimes the conclusion is not warranted by the proof. Consider the following:

> $A$ plus $B = 2$
>
> $A \neq 1$ or $0$
>
> Conclusion: $A$ must equal 2 and $B$ must equal 0.

However, this conclusion is not necessarily true since $A$ could be a negative number.

***Absolute Right and Wrong.*** Some arguments assume that only one of two claims is correct. Abortion is either right or wrong. The argument is framed in terms of an absolute right or wrong. In fact, the argument may permit a middle judgment. The fault is to frame issues as absolutes when other options are possible.

***Insufficient Sampling.*** Suppose you flip a coin 1,000 times and it happens to come up heads 600 times and tails 400 times. You conclude that flipping that coin results in a 60 percent chance that it will come up heads on the next toss. This is a hasty generalization. Here the problem is that your sample is not sufficient. In law you see several courts rule favorably for a particular class of litigants. You conclude that the law favors that class. In fact, these results might be explained by other conditions.

***The Personal Attack.*** In the personal attack, the writer denigrates the other party without focusing on the real issues. The attack distracts the reader from the real issues. Such an attack is termed an ***ad hominem*** attack. The converse of this approach is when one tries to curry sympathy for a client. Law should be based on principles, not personal feelings.

In expository and argumentative writing, logic is critical to the writing. You must be able to spot logic flaws in your own writing just as you try to spot them in an opponent's writing. Edit for logic.

**Coherency in Transaction Documents.** Coherency is a concern in transaction documents also. A transaction document puts a deal together. Read every transaction document to see if the deal will work. A transaction document engineers a relationship. The relationship must be workable. You need to see the transaction as a series of events; make sure these events appear in a logical order. For instance, a purchaser will not usually complete a real estate closing before inspecting the house; nor will a seller usually transfer title to real property before the buyer pays for the house or makes acceptable arrangements for the payment. A landlord will usually provide for a security deposit to protect the landlord if the tenant leaves the premises in a damaged condition.

Paralegals must edit transaction documents looking for ways a transaction might be misinterpreted and for any loopholes that the opposing side may spot.

As you check for coherency in transaction documents, ensure that all the concepts are consistent. If there are related documents between the parties, check each against the others to be sure that all are consistent.

Many copy editors use a style sheet to ensure that style remains consistent throughout an article or text. Such an approach is beneficial in self-editing a transaction document, but instead of checking style, check first for consistency of words and phrases. If the document is complicated or lengthy, a style sheet can be helpful to make sure the same words, phrases, and clauses are used throughout. If several documents are used, ensure that the same words and expressions are used consistently in each of the documents.

## Is the Writing Complete?

Most legal professionals think a document is complete when all the fine details are added. However, there are other dimensions to deciding whether a writing is complete.

**The Background.** After you spend months researching a legal issue, you gain insights into the law that your readers lack. A judge may know nothing about the legal issue you are arguing. Read all documents to see if you have provided a thorough background to the reader. Lead the reader through the steps of your logic. The reader may not follow a logic leap. Do not assume that the reader knows everything you know on the subject.

**The Oversight.** Sometimes, in the hurry to put a document together, a writer leaves out a critical point. For example, in many contracts there are standard clauses to cover various eventualities. In editing, you must ensure that all critical provisions have been included. Remember that a court presumes that omissions are intentional. If you omit an important provision, make sure you did so intentionally.

### Does the Document Comply with all Laws?

The most artfully drawn deed will do a client little good if it has not been notarized. The most cogently drawn complaint will not be accepted by the clerk for filing if the complaint is typed on the wrong size paper. A detailed will will be of no effect if not properly witnessed. A brilliantly crafted brief will not be accepted for filing if you present it one day late. The editor must be familiar with all requirements affecting the legal document. A document is complete only if it satisfies all applicable legal requirements.

## MICRO EDITING

Publishing houses employ copy editors—professionals who edit each individual line of copy for style and substance. Most law firms employ no one who performs this function exclusively; hence you will often find yourself in the copy editor role. Tackling the detail work is not fun if you have already spent too much time drafting the document. There is a point in the drafting process when you cannot read your draft "one more time." The pointers that follow help at that point.

These editing techniques are not necessarily exclusive to legal documents or to the drafting process. They apply to most types of writing and should serve as tools for evaluating your own work objectively.

### Check Style

It is tough to look at your own copy to see if your style is clear. Here are several ways to diagnose your own writing faults.

**Circle all Prepositions.** Turn to a random page and circle all the prepositions. Then count the circles. If there is more than one preposition for every four words, you have probably overused passive voice. Reread the section in Chapter 11 on active voice.

**Underline Nominalized Words.** On the same page where you circled all the prepositions, underline all words ending in *-ance, -ity,* and *-ant.* These are nominalized words, which we discussed in Chapter 11. Convert these nouns back into their original verb and adjective forms. Rewrite the sentence without nominalized words.

**Circle all Sentences with the Verb *to be.*** In a different color pen, circle all sentences containing the verb *to be.* Then rewrite each sentence without that verb. Remember that *to be* is an inert verb. The fewer inert verbs you use, the better you will write.

**Strike all Unnecessary Words.** Try to strike all unnecessary words. Look for windups, superfluous nouns and verbs, and unnecessary modifiers. In editing your own work, deleting words will usually prove to be the most difficult task. Most writers find it easier to add than to delete, but deleting is how writing is fine-tuned.

**Count Words in Sentences and Paragraphs.** Count the words in a sentence. Did you use short sentences? Are the paragraphs too long? Experts disagree as to the optimal length of paragraphs. (Some advocate four to six sentences; some like seven. Others specify 75 to 125 words per paragraph.) While you may use longer sentences in a brief than you do for correspondence, you need to know the length of the sentences you use. Actually count the words in your sentences to see if the length is within reason.

## Check Spelling

Certain legal words are commonly misspelled. Here is a list of frequently misspelled words:

| | |
|---|---|
| **Admissible** | When writing about *admissible* evidence, the word ends in *-ible,* not *-able.* |
| **Allege** | There is no *d* in *allege.* |
| **Breach** | You *breach* a contract. (Your *breech* is behind you.) |
| **Causal** | If something is related to the cause, the word is *causal*—not *casual.* |
| **Decedent** | A person who is dead is a *decedent.* An offspring is a *descendant.* |
| **Defendant** | The person sued in a case is a *defendant.* The word ends in *-ant.* |
| **Exercise** | There is no *z* in *exercise.* |
| **Foresee-ability** | This words consists of the words *foresee* and *ability.* |
| **Judgment** | Judgment drops the *e* from the word *judge.* |
| **Merchant-ability** | This word consists of the words *merchant* and *ability.* |
| **Personalty** | This word refers to personal property. |
| **Plaintiff** | A party who files a lawsuit. |
| **Realty** | This word refers to real property. |
| **Rescission** | When you put an end to a contract, you *rescind* it. |
| **Separation** | As in *separation* agreement; resist the temptation to make the second vowel in *separation* an *e* instead of an *a.* |
| **Supersede** | There is no *c* in *supersede.* |
| **Tenant** | A person who leases property from a landlord. |
| **Therefore** | Unless you put an *e* at the end of *therefore,* the word will mean "for this or that." |
| **Waiver** | Put an *i* in *waiver* unless you are referring to a person who waves. |

POINTER: Almost all law offices now use word processing systems. Most word processors have spell-check features. Make sure this feature is used. The vocabulary on the computer may not be complete, but it will catch many mistakes you might have overlooked.

## Check Word Usage

Here are some words frequently confused by legal professionals:

| | |
|---|---|
| **Advice, advise** | *Advice* is a noun meaning an opinion. *Advise* is a verb meaning to give advice. |
| **Affect, effect** | To *affect* is to influence; to *effect* is to bring about or to cause: "The argument visibly *affected* the jury and it ultimately *effected* a settlement of the case." *Effect* as a noun can mean either influence or result. For instance, "The *effect* of the argument was apparent." "The discussions led to the desired *effect*." The noun *affect* is a psychological term: "The patient had a flat *affect*." |
| **Appellant, appellee** | The person taking an appeal is an *appellant*. The person who defends the appeal is an *appellee.* |
| **Assure, Insure, Ensure** | *Assure* means to make sure, as in "I assure you that I am honest." It also means to promise, as in "I *assure* you that the news is true." To *insure* means to guarantee against loss. *Ensure* means to make certain of, as in "I will *ensure* the shipment gets to you." |
| **By law, bylaw** | When something is required or permitted under a law, it is *by law*. A *bylaw* is an organizational principle for a corporation or a local unit of government. |
| **Can, may** | *Can* refers to the ability to accomplish something. *May* refers to permission. |
| **Compare to, compare with** | You use *compare to* when making an analogy between unlike items. You use *compare with* when you compare like items. |
| **Connote, denote** | *Connote* is what a word suggests. *Denote* is what a word means. |
| **Counsel, council** | *Counsel* means to advise. A *council* is a group of people serving in an administrative, legislative, or advisory capacity. |
| **Disinterested uninterested** | If you are impartial or have no bias or gain, then you are a *disinterested* person. If you are not interested in a subject, then the correct word is *uninterested*. |
| **Guilty, liable** | *Guilty* refers to a conviction of a crime. *Liable* refers to the responsibility to pay civil damages. The distinction depends on whether the matter is criminal or noncriminal. |
| **Imply, infer** | To *imply* means to hint. To *infer* means to interpret from something known or assumed. |
| **Lessor, lessee** | The landlord is the *lessor*, and the tenant is the *lessee*. |
| **Libel, liable** | *Libel* is written or printed defamation. *Liable* refers to the responsibility to pay civil damages. |
| **Mortgagor, mortgagee** | The person who gives a mortgage is the *mortgagor*. The person to whom the property is mortgaged is the *mortgagee*. The mortgagee is usually a banking institution. |

| | |
|---|---|
| **Oral, Verbal** | *Oral* means spoken, not written. Oral literally means "from the mouth." *Verbal* means "in words" whether the words are spoken or written. Hence, a contract not in writing should be an *oral* contract. |
| **Principal, principle** | *Principal* is a noun meaning the main thing or the head person, as in the *principal* of a school. *Principle* is a noun meaning a rule. |

When you first use any word with a legal connotation, look up the word in a legal dictionary. A professional needs to learn the words of the trade.

## Check Grammar

It is beyond the scope of this text to review the basic principles of grammar. But after grading thousands of pages of paralegal student papers, I have focused on several areas that deserve particular attention.

**Sentence Fragments.** A sentence fragment is an incomplete sentence. The most frequent cause of a sentence fragment is the substitution of a participle for the finite verb.

| | |
|---|---|
| **Sentence fragment** | The court resolving the issue. |
| **Complete sentence** | The court resolved the issue. |

Sentence fragments sometimes occur in legal writing when sentences begin with *whereas*, *because*, *although*, *if*, *where*, *when*, and *since*:

> Because the reasoning of the court led to that result.

Check final copy for sentence fragments.

**Run-on Sentences.** A run-on sentence is two or more sentences improperly joined together:

> This paralegal text discusses run-on sentences, editors must control these errors.

The remedy for a run-on sentence is either to remove the comma and insert a period or to link the sentences together where appropriate with a semicolon.

**Dangling Modifiers.** When a sentence contains a dependent clause and a main clause, the subject in the main clause has to agree with the implied subject of the dependent clause. For example:

> Having worked as a paralegal, I had the experience to prepare my own will.

The subject of the dependent clause, "Having worked as a paralegal," is an implied "I," as in "I have worked as a paralegal." Hence the subject of the dependent clause is the same as the subject in the main clause. Now look at these incorrect examples:

> Being free on bond, the victim was shot by the felon.
>
> Hitting the brakes, the car went out of control.

In these sentences the subjects do not agree. In the first sentence the implied subject of the dependent clause is "the felon," while the subject in the main clause is "the victim." In the second sentence the implied subject in the dependent clause is "the driver," but in the main clause the subject is "the car."

Dangling modifiers have clumsy meanings and interfere with comprehension.

**Subject-Verb Disagreement.** In most sentences you automatically make the subject and verb agree without much thought. In English, except for the verb *to be*, the third person singular (*he, she,* or *it*) is the only verb that changes form. In other words, we say:

| | **Singular** | **Plural** |
|---|---|---|
| **First person** | I talk | We talk |
| **Second person** | You talk | You talk |
| **Third person** | She talks | They talk |

Only she *talks* (*he talks, it talks*) changes form. As you know, the third person changes form by adding an *s* or *es* to the verb. Here are some problem situations.

***Compound Subjects.*** When a sentence contains two or more subjects, it needs a plural verb. Consider this:

You and I are both legal professionals.

In this example, *You and I* requires a plural *are* as opposed to a singular *is*. The problem usually occurs when the subject is not at the beginning of the sentence.

| | |
|---|---|
| **Wrong** | Enclosed is the letter and the check I referenced. |
| **Right** | Enclosed are the letter and the check I referenced. |

However, if the compound subject refers to the same person or thing, then use a singular verb:

The *sum and substance* of the report was that the corporation was experiencing serious financial problems.

*Sum and substance* has a singular meaning; hence it requires a singular verb.

***Subject Complements.*** At times you will have a subject that does not take the same number as the complement:

The critical concern of the parents was the speed limit on that road.

Here the subject, *concern,* is singular although the complement, *parents,* is plural. Remember that the subject, not the complement, determines number.

***Alternative Subjects.*** When subjects are linked by *or* or *nor*, the rules are simple. First, if both subjects are singular ("a dog or pony is in the show"), then use a singular verb. Second, if both subjects are plural ("the dogs or the ponies are in the show"), then use a plural verb. Finally, if one subject is plural and another subject is singular ("neither the paralegal nor the attorneys agree on this subject''), then the verb should agree with the nearer subject. In this last situation, however, some experts disagree, and some suggest using separate verbs or rewriting the sentence.

## Check Pronoun Reference

An interesting problem of pronoun reference occurred in the U.S.-Soviet missile treaty:

> ''Both sides would agree to confine itself [*sic*] to research, development and testing which is permitted by the ABM treaty for a period of five years. . .'' went the language of the first proposal on this subject submitted to the Russians, according to the text provided later by the State Department.
>
> Wrong. *Itself* does not agree with *both sides*. To fix it, the framers could have tried ''both sides would agree to confine *themselves*,'' which is correct, but the plural construction ill fits a singular ''side.'' Another way, ''Each side would agree to confine itself,'' matches up the pronoun with the antecedent, but makes it appear that the side is agreeing with itself.
>
> I would like to think that we created this grammatical bind to confuse the Russians, but it is more likely that it was the result of last-minute drafting by negotiators under great stress.[1]

This problem could have been solved by drafting in the singular. In editing your writing, pay attention to pronoun reference. Personal and relative pronouns require special concerns.

**Personal Pronouns.** Subjective case pronouns are *I*, *he*, *she*, and *they*. Objective case pronouns are *me*, *him*, *her*, and *them*. The subjective case is used when the pronoun is the subject of a sentence or clause:

> The paralegal and I will be going to the seminar.

The objective case is used when the pronoun is the object of a sentence or clause or the object of a preposition. For instance,

> My professor will take my roommate and me to the seminar.

To make the correct choice between the objective and the subjective personal pronoun, mentally recite the pronoun and verb together.

**Relative Pronouns.** Many legal professionals have difficulty with deciding whether to use *who* or *whom*. The rules here are simple: If the relative pronoun is the subject of a sentence or clause, use *who,* and if the relative pronoun is the object of a sentence or clause or the object of a prepositional phrase, use *whom*. A good test is to substitute a personal pronoun for the *who* or *whom*. If the substitution requires an objective case pronoun, use *who*. If the substitution requires a subjective case pronoun, use *whom*.

> The boy (who/whom) is sitting on the porch is very quiet.
>
> The boy (who/whom) the parent reprimanded was subdued.

Using the substitution rule, you would change the first sentence to read: ''The boy (he) is sitting on the porch. . . .'' Using this rule in the second sentence, you would change it to read: The boy (the parent reprimanded him) was subdued.

Another decision is whether to use *that*, *which*, or *who* (*whom*). *That* is used in a restrictive clause when the preceding noun is nonhuman.

> The stolen truck that struck the plaintiff's vehicle was unregistered.

*Which*, preceded by a comma, is used in a nonrestrictive clause when the reference is nonhuman.

> The plaintiff's vehicle, which was totaled, was hauled to a junkyard.

*Who* is used in both a restrictive and a nonrestrictive clause when the preceding noun is human.

> The youth who drove the stolen truck fled the scene.
>
> The plaintiff, who is still hospitalized, was unable to appear in court.

## Check Punctuation

Punctuation breaks up material for the reader. Without punctuation, reading is difficult. A period concludes a thought. It tells the reader that one thought is complete and a new thought will begin in the next sentence. A comma tells the reader to pause briefly before completing the thought. Punctuation errors can cause equivocation problems:

> Sometimes such ambiguity is the result of inadequate punctuation, as in an unpunctuated telegram, or as in the sentence, "Woman, without her man would be a savage." Do you add a second comma after "her," as the ladies are inclined to do or after "man," as the gentlemen prefer?[2]

Here are some punctuation rules to heed.

**Restrictive and Nonrestrictive Elements.** A restrictive modifier limits the meaning of the word or words it modifies. Restrictive modifiers are not set off with commas or other punctuation marks. A nonrestrictive modifier provides additional information about the word or words it modifies. Commas are used to set off nonrestrictive elements.

**Restrictive** The federal statute that deals with mail theft can be applied when mail is taken from an apartment floor.

**Nonrestrictive** The mail theft statute, which has been discussed in Chapter 2 of this text, applies to situations where a credit card has been taken from an apartment floor after it has been dropped through a mail slot.

The test here is whether deleting the modifier changes the meaning of the sentence. If it does not change the meaning, use commas.

**Parentheses, Dashes, Colons, and Semicolons.** Inexperienced writers tend to use only periods and commas. Don't be afraid to use parentheses, dashes, colons, and semicolons for special effects. In math, you use a parenthesis for precision. Assume you see the following:

$$a \times b + c$$

At this point you do not know whether to add *b* and *c* or multiply *a* by *b*. In either case, parentheses solve the problem:

$$(a \times b) + c$$

or

$$a \times (b + c)$$

Occasionally parentheses are used in the same way in legal writing:

> . . . in the phrase "active duty (other than for training) performed before July 1, 1964," it is clear that the phrase "before July 1, 1964," refers to "active duty (other than for training)" and not "training."[3]

A dash can be used for emphasis, as in the following sentence:

> The defendant's position is contrary to the decision of *Smith v. Jones*—not to mention that it is contrary to logic and common sense.

A colon can be used to signal that a list or explanation follows, as in this example:

> Hence the defendant's position is simple: first, the statute is unconstitutional; second, the statute does not apply to this situation; and third, the defendant did not commit the offense charged.

A semicolon can bind together two sentences that contain linking ideas.

> My paralegal and I make a good team; working together we have won all our cases.

Use a variety of punctuation marks.

## Check Capitalization

In legal documents, there are some unique practices as to capitalization. Here are some rules.

**Capitalize Titles and Headings of Court Documents.** Titles of court documents are usually capitalized, as are headings, and subheadings within them. Often headings will appear in all capitals. Look at the way headings were done in the briefs filed by the appellants and appellee in *Griswold v. Connecticut*, which is in the Resource Manual Appendix.

**Capitalize Introductory Words and Phrases in Legal Documents.** As a matter of practice, some beginning words of legal documents appear in all capital letters. For example:

> IT IS HEREBY ORDERED . . .
>
> RESOLVED, THAT . . .
>
> FOR VALUE RECEIVED . . .
>
> IN WITNESS WHEREOF . . .

These words are capitalized more for show than for substance. Nonetheless, your firm may follow such a practice.

**Capitalize Trade Names.** When you use a trade name (Kleenex, Kodak, Vaseline), use a capital letter. If the word is a generic term, use lowercase.

**Capitalize Names of Corporate and Governmental Entities.** Official government names are capitalized.

> Equal Employment Opportunity Commission (EEOC)
>
> Social Security Administration (SSA)
>
> Environmental Protection Agency (EPA)

Names of companies are also capitalized. However, do not capitalize words such as federal, government, and company unless they are part of a title or name.

**Do Not Capitalize Words to Make Them More Important.** Although some firms do capitalize words to highlight them, the general rule is that you should not capitalize words merely to make them more important or to show respect. Legal professionals tend to capitalize the word *court* in pleadings or briefs when referring to the court in which the pleading or brief is filed. However, even in that situation, court should not be capitalized.

## Check Enumeration

It has become customary in legal drafting to use enumeration as a means to express coordinate ideas. One writer explains:

> A drafter will find it convenient to be systematic in the use of numbers and letters for sub-clauses and paragraphs: (1), (2), (3), etc., for sub-clauses each ranking equally in arrangement, without introductory words; (a), (b), (c), etc., for the paragraphs in a sub-clause, or in a clause with introductory words; (i), (ii), (iii), etc., for sub-paragraphs in a paragraph; small Roman capitals, (I), (II), (III), etc., or capitals (A), (B), (C), etc. for further subdivision. The same pattern of numbering or lettering should be used throughout the document.[4]

Related paragraphs can also be grouped by a numbering system such as 1.1, 1.2, 1.3; 2.1, 2.2, 2.3; and so on. Careful enumeration eliminates equivocation problems and serves as a useful drafting tool. Here are some enumeration rules:

> (1) All items in the tabulated enumeration must belong to the same class. (The enumeration must have a common theme or thread.)
>
> (2) Each item in the tabulated enumeration must be responsive, in substance and in form, to the introductory language of the enumeration (the material immediately before the colon).
>
> (3) If the sentence of which a tabulated enumeration is a part continues beyond the end of the enumeration, the part of the sentence that follows it must be appropriate to each item.
>
> (4) All of each item in the enumeration must be indented.
>
> (5) Material immediately preceding or following the enumeration must not be indented, unless it marks the beginning of a paragraph.

(6) If the tabulated material takes the form of a sentence in which the enumeration is an integral part, each item should begin with a small letter and end with a semicolon, except that (1) the penultimate item should end with a semicolon followed by an "and" or an "or" and (2) if the last item ends the sentence, it should end with a period.

(7) If the tabulated material takes the form of a simple list following a sentence that is otherwise complete, each item should begin with a capital letter and end with a period. No "and" or "or" follows the penultimate item.[5]

When you use enumeration, always maintain parallelism. Do not vary the enumeration system.

Overuse of enumeration can inhibit readability, so limit enumeration to places where it enhances understanding.

*Tabulating* simply means setting materials in an indented format such as columns or rows. When you make a list, you use a tabular format. Here are some rules to follow in tabulating items:

- Indent the tabulated items.
- Use parallel structure for each item.
- Use numbers or letters for each particular item.
- Use a comma or semicolon after each item except the last item.
- Put an *and* or *or* after the next-to-last item.

Tabulating provides visual variety for the reader and often makes material more readable.

## Check Dates, Ages, and Weights

Some dates leave the reader wondering whether the date you refer to is included.

- This act is effective until April 13. (Is it effective *on* April 13?)
- The act is effective from April 13 to December 30. (Is it effective *on* April 13? *On* December 30?)
- This option to purchase must be exercised by April 13, 1992. (Can it be exercised *on* April 13, 1992?)

Correct this problem by being specific:

- This act is effective beginning on April 13 and ending on December 30.
- This option to purchase must be exercised on or before April 13, 1992.

The same problem arises when age ranges are given:

- A trust shall be imposed for any beneficiary between the ages of 21 and 30. (Does it include a 21-year-old and a 30-year-old person?)

Again, be specific:

- A trust shall be imposed for any beneficiary 21 years of age or older and under 31 years of age.

When you are giving weights, make sure you designate the appropriate unit of weight. Again, determine whether there is any ambiguity as to the inclusion or exclusion of a certain weight. Edit with these problems in mind.

## Check Definitions

Most drafting books will reserve a separate chapter for the use of definitions. However, definitions are too often abused as a drafting device. The rules relating to when and how to use definitions are not that complicated.

**Use Definitions for Shorthand References.** The simplest use of definitions in a legal document is the abbreviated word or phrase indicating what the topic or subject will subsequently be called. Just place the word or phrase parenthetically after the referent:

> The Northern Sand & Gravel Company, Inc. (Northern Sand)

The method is commonly used to refer to parties or to real property after the legal description has been given.

**Use Definitions Consistently.** A frequent problem with definitions arises when the drafter uses another word in substitution for the defined term. A drafter may give a legal description and refer to the property as the ''leased premises.'' Later the drafter may refer to ''the premises'' or ''the property.'' Adherence to the consistency doctrine would obviate this problem.

**Omit Unnecessary Definitions.** Students sometimes define a word that is used only once in a document. This definition can almost always be worked into the sentence where the word appears.

Use a definition only if the definition can assist understanding and only if the word or phrase is used in a common or natural sense. As Abraham Lincoln said, ''If you call a tail a leg, how many legs has a dog? Five? No; calling a tail a leg won't make it a leg.'' In other words, when you decide to use a definition, make sure the definition fits the idea. For example, you would not say:

> The term *fixture* as used in this contract includes the land and all personal property owned by seller.

A fixture is neither real estate nor personal property. This is an unnatural definition.

## Check Citations

*A Uniform System of Citation*, popularly known as the Blue Book, tells us most of what we need to know about citations. It is published and distributed by the Harvard Law Review Association, Cambridge, Massachusetts. A paralegal needs to learn to cite law as other legal professionals do. You should check each citation with the original to make sure that the citation reference is accurate. As a citation is copied and typed and retyped, many mistakes may be made.

**References to Specific Points.** Legal authority is used in the body of briefs and memoranda rather than in footnotes. As you edit legal writing, make sure that if the writer refers to a specific point, a specific page reference is given for that point. When you use a quotation from a particular source, give the exact page for the quotation. This rule aids the reader. In looking at the final copy, check the accuracy of the information. Make sure pages have been accurately cited. Make sure that any quotations are on the page cited. A misspelling of a case name can raise questions as to the accuracy of your ideas. A typographical error in the numbers can send a judge on a wild goose chase through the law library—a chase you would prefer did not take place.

**Repeating Citations.** Assume you have just referenced the case of *Griswold v. Connecticut*, 381 U.S. 479 (1965). The next time you reference this case in your writing, you can use a shortened version:

> *Griswold*, 381 U.S. at 485.

or

> *Griswold v. Connecticut*, 381 U.S. at 485.

If *Griswold* was the immediately preceding citation, then you can use the abbreviation *Id.* For example, if your next citation is page 487 of the *Griswold* decision, the citation will be *Id.* at 487. However, after you have given a citation for a particular point, you do not have to repeat the citation for the same point.

## Check Quotations

Legal professionals frequently use quotations from cases or statutes. On the final copy, proofread the quotations just as you proofread the rest of the text. Like citations, quotations can fall prey to typographical errors. Here are a few other rules to follow in editing quotations:

**Use Quotations Sparingly.** When paralegals are told to use quotations sparingly, they tend to use none at all. Try to strike a reasonable balance. Too many quotations cause the reader to lose interest in the text material, but too few quotations in legal writing raise doubt as to the authenticity of your analysis.

The guiding rule is to use quotations to state a precise rule (e.g., language from a case or statute), to state a precise point, or to state something more succinctly or eloquently than you could have said it. This does *not* mean you can use a quote when you fail to understand the material. In that situation, take extra time to understand what you are writing about.

**Use Short Quotations.** Just as too many quotations cause a reader to lose interest, so do quotations that are too long. Edit quotations for the main point or points. Paraphrase or summarize quotations. Use key words from a quotation and delete the remainder.

**Fit Quotations to the Text.** The sentence preceding the quotation should lead directly into the quotation. The sentence following the quotation should pick up the idea of the quotation. Integrate quotes into the textual materials.

## SOME FINAL EDITING TIPS

Often you will have little time to edit your copy because of deadline pressures. The easiest solution is to anticipate deadlines by beginning to write as early as possible. The more time you have, the better job you can do editing copy.

### Edit and Reedit

The longer you have worked on a project, the harder it is to edit the final copy. To change the routine, you might try to read the document aloud. The best approach is to put it away and read it another day if possible.

### Shorten the Document

I once prepared a brief for the Seventh Circuit, which had a fifty-page limit for printed briefs. I called the printer to see how many typewritten pages constituted fifty printed pages to make sure I observed the limit. Unfortunately, the printer was wrong and my brief ran twenty pages too long—a brief that I thought was letter perfect. Yet, with only hours until my deadline, I sliced twenty pages from that brief. Most of the verbiage and surplusage was eliminated. What I could not change earlier proved reducible by twenty pages without harm to content. That experience forced me to approach the editing process more earnestly. Most documents can be shortened and in the process made more readable by simply excising the surplusage.

### Proofreading Symbols

Figure 12-1 is a list of common proofreading symbols. Teach your support staff to read these proofreading symbols so you can use them to edit text materials efficiently with minimal directions.

## CONCLUSION: THE IMPORTANCE OF THE REDRAFT

H. G. Wells wrote: "No passion in the world, no love or hate, is equal to the passion to alter someone else's draft." Whenever you complete a substantial writing project, you tend to become maternalistic toward it, eschewing anything but a cosmetic change to what you have drafted.

Drafters must learn to deal objectively with their work product. Always view your document as if it were someone else's work. From that perspective it is easier to make changes. If you reuse your document, try to make some improvement on your previous effort. Each improved redraft leads toward a more litigation-proof document.

## ENDNOTES

1 William Safire, "The Erroneous Eagle and the Cross-Eyed Bear," *New York Times Magazine*, Nov. 2, 1986, p. 10.

2 E. Allen Farnsworth, "Some Considerations in the Drafting of Agreements: Problems in Interpretation and Gap-Filling," *39 Okla. B.A.J.* (1968) at 918.

**FIGURE 12-1 COMMON PROOFREADING SYMBOLS**

| Symbol | Meaning |
|---|---|
| ^ | Insert item here. |
| # | Insert space here. |
|  | Transpose these items. |
|  | Delete this item. |
| stet | Let the original stand; disregard changes already made. |
| ¶ | Begin a paragraph here. |
| no ¶ | Do not begin a paragraph here. |
|  | Move left. |
|  | Move right. |
|  | Move up. |
|  | Move down. |
|  | Separate; move apart. |
|  | Close up; move together. |
|  | Move copy as indicated. |
| SS | Single-space. |
| DS | Double-space. |
| TS | Triple-space. |
| caps or ≡ | Capitalize this item. |
| lc | Use lowercase letters; not capitals. |
| ital or ___ | Italicize this item. |
|  | Insert period. |
|  | Insert comma. |
|  | Insert colon. |
|  | Insert semicolon. |
|  | Insert hyphen. |
| ? | Insert question mark. |
| ! | Insert exclamation point. |
|  | Open a quotation. |
|  | Close a quotation. |
| SP | Spell out. |

3 F. Reed Dickerson. *The Fundamentals of Legal Drafting* (Boston: Little, Brown, 1965), p. 74–75.

4 E. L. Piesse, *The Elements of Drafting*, 5th Ed. (Sydney: The Law Book Company, 1976), p. 35.

5 F. Reed Dickerson, *The Fundamentals of Legal Drafting* (Boston: Little, Brown, 1965), p. 85–86.

# APPENDIX

**Monte MAULLER and Carol Mauller, Appellants-Plaintiffs,**
**v.**
**CITY OF COLUMBUS, Board of Commissioners of Bartholomew County, Appellees-Defendants.**
**No. 73A01-8910-CV-418.**

Court of Appeals of Indiana,
First District.
April 4, 1990.
Transfer Denied July 6, 1990.
RATLIFF, Chief Judge.

## STATEMENT OF THE CASE

Carol and Monte Mauller appeal a summary judgment entered against them in their action against the City of Columbus, Indiana (City), and the Board of Commissioners of Bartholomew County, Indiana (County Board). We affirm.

## FACTS

On August 12, 1986, Carol Mauller (Carol) was playing left field in an organized softball game at the Bartholomew County Stadium, where she had previously played more than two dozen games. Prior to the game, Carol observed that dirt was removed from the area surrounding home plate and into the batter's box areas and that as a result there was a depression around home plate.

During the course of the game, after Carol had batted, she attempted to score from second base when one of her teammates hit the ball to the outfield. When she rounded third base, her coach instructed her to slide into home plate. When she slid into home plate, the rubber cleats on Carol's softball shoes caught under the edge of home plate and she suffered a double fracture and dislocation of her right lower leg and ankle.

Carol and her husband, Monte Mauller, sued the City and the County Board for negligence in failing to properly maintain the playing field in a safe condition. Bartholomew County was the owner of the property and had contracted with the City for the City's services in properly maintaining the playing field at the Bartholomew County Stadium.

The City and the County Board filed motions for summary judgment, contending there was no issue as to any material fact regarding liability and Carol had incurred the risk of injury. The trial court examined pleadings, briefs, and depositions and held the City and the County Board should be granted judgment as a matter of law because there was no genuine issue of material fact.[1] Further facts will be provided as necessary.

## ISSUE

Whether the trial court erred in entering summary judgment against Carol and Monte when Carol's deposition established she was aware of the specific conditions of the home plate area, and the potential for injury, yet she intentionally slid into home plate?

## DISCUSSION AND DECISION

Carol contends the trial court erred in granting summary judgment to the City and to the County Board because there was a genuine issue of material fact as to whether Carol incurred the

1. The City's and County Board's motions for summary judgment contained several afffirmative defenses, but their supporting memorandums, and Carol's response argued only about the defense of incurred risk. The Record before us does not contain the oral argument made to the trial court on the motions for summary judgment and the judgment contains no indication on what theory the grant of summary judgment was based. However, all parties on appeal assume the trial court granted the motions because it determined Carol had incurred the risk of injury.

risk of injury. When reviewing a grant of summary judgment, we use the same standard of review as the trial court: summary judgment is proper only when there is no issue of material fact and the moving party is entitled to judgment as a matter of law. Ind. Trial Rule 56(c); *Seiler v. Grow* (1987), Ind.App., 507 N.E.2d 628, 630, *trans. denied.* In determining whether a genuine issue of material fact exists, we consider all matters in a light most favorable to the nonmovant. *Watson Rural Water Co. v. Indiana Cities Water Corp.* (1989), Ind.App., 540 N.E.2d 131, 132, *trans. denied; Jackson v. Warrum* (1989), Ind.App., 535 N.E.2d 1207, 1210. Generally, incurred risk is a question of fact for the jury. *Kroger Co. v. Haun* (1978), 177 Ind.App. 403, 407, 379 N.E.2d 1004, 1007. "Incurred risk can be found as a matter of law *only* if the evidence is without conflict and the sole inference to be drawn is that the plaintiff (a) had actual knowledge of the specific risk, and (b) understood and appreciated the risk." *Stainko v. Tri-State Coach Lines, Inc.* (1987), Ind.App., 508 N.E.2d 1362, 1364, *trans. denied.*

The incurred risk defense requires not "merely a general awareness of a potential for mishap, but . . . demands a subjective analysis focusing on the plaintiff's actual knowledge and appreciation of the specific risk involved and voluntary acceptance of that risk." *Get-N-Go, Inc. v. Markins* (1989), Ind., 544 N.E.2d 484, 486 (citing *Beckett v. Clinton Prairie School Corp.* (1987), Ind., 504 N.E.2d 552, 554). "By definition . . . the very essence of incurred risk is the conscious, deliberate and intentional embarkation upon a course of conduct with knowledge of the circumstances." *Power v. Brodie* (1984), Ind.App., 460 N.E.2d 1241, 1243, *trans. denied* (quoting *Gerrish v. Brewer* (1979), Ind.App., 398 N.E.2d 1298, 1301).[2] Thus, we may affirm summary judgment only if the evidence, viewed in a light most favorable to Carol and Monte, supports the sole inference that she had actual knowledge of, and voluntarily intended to expose herself to, the risk of sliding into home plate when dirt was displaced creating a depression near the plate.[3]

Carol's deposition testimony establishes her team prohibited softball players from wearing metal cleats, shoes designed and recommended for playing softball are rubber soled and contain rubber cleats, and she wore such softball shoes. Carol's deposition testimony also establishes she was aware of the general risk of sliding in a softball game, she had been provided training by her coach on the proper way to slide in order to avoid an injury, and she knew a woman softball player who had injured herself sliding into a base during a previous summer. Carol's deposition also establishes she was aware, before the game of August 12, 1988, that dirt was dug out around home plate and the batter's box areas on both sides of home plate. Carol also saw during her first time at bat on August 12, 1988, that the holes around home plate had not been filled in. She had encountered similar conditions at the playing field on about five out of the thirteen occasions when she had played softball that summer. Carol stated she did not consider not playing the game due to the condition

2. Carol and Monte argue Carol must have had actual knowledge of the condition of the ground around home plate at the time she was rounding third base and attempting to score. Carol and Monte argue Carol had forgotten about the ground conditions around home plate and they cite *Gerrish* for the proposition that Carol could not intentionally incur a risk she had forgotten about. We note *Gerrish* held that, by definition, the doctrine of momentary forgetfulness is not a part of the doctrine of incurred risk. *Id.* at 1301.

3. Carol and Monte contend the specific risk of which Carol must have had actual knowledge in order to have voluntarily exposed herself to it was the risk that she could catch her rubber cleats under home plate because the dirt surrounding home plate was removed. We disagree. Knowledge of specific risk does not "connote that the victim had prescience that the particular accident and injury which in fact occurred was going to occur." *Tavernier v. Maes* (1966), 242 Cal.App.2d 532, 543, 51 Cal. Rptr. 575, 582 (action by participant in softball game for injuries sustained when sliding).

of the field around home plate. Carol's deposition establishes she knew home plate was implanted solidly in the ground and would not "give" as first, second, and third bases would when she slid into them. Finally, Carol's deposition establishes she decided to slide into home as soon as her coach instructed her when she was rounding third base. She stated she never considered not sliding when he instructed her to do so that day.

Carol's deposition thus shows that she had actual knowledge and appreciation of the specific conditions around home plate and of the general danger of sliding into home plate, and that she consciously, deliberately and intentionally slid into home plate with knowledge of those circumstances. Therefore, her deposition establishes she voluntarily accepted the risk of injury when sliding into home plate under those conditions.[4]

4. We agree with well-established law that "[a] person who voluntarily participates in a lawful sport, game, or contest assumes the ordinary risks of such activity." 57A Am.Jr.2d *Negligence* § 835 (1989). *See also* 4 Am.Jur.2d *Amusements and Exhibitions* § 98 (1962); and Annotation, *Liability for Injury to or Death of Participant in Game or Contest.* 7 A.L.R.2d 704(II)(a) (§ 3) (1949).

The only evidence before the trial court was Carol's deposition and the affidavit she presented with her response to the City's and County Board's motions for summary judgment. There was no conflict in the evidence. Conflict existed only upon the parties' interpretation of the evidence. Therefore, the trial court did not err in stating that as a matter of law Carol had incurred the specific risk of injury and that summary judgment against her was appropriate as a matter of law.[5] We affirm the trial court's grant of summary judgment in favor of the City and the County Board as against Carol and Monte.

Affirmed.

SHIELDS, P.J., and ROBERTSON, J., concur.

5. As the County Board notes, incurred risk is a complete defense in a negligence action involving a governmental entity because Indiana's Comparative Fault law does not apply to tort claims against governmental entities. *See* IND. CODE § 34-4-33-8.

TITLE: Right of Privacy – Griswold
REQUESTED BY: Sara Supervisor
SUBMITTED BY: Clark Robinson
DATE SUBMITTED: December 5, 1961

## Memorandum

### Statement of Facts:

On November 1, 1961, the Planned Parenthood League of New Haven opened a center to provide advice to married couples as to the means to prevent conception. Estelle T. Griswold was the executive director of the league. Her husband, Lee Buxton, was a physician licensed to practice medicine in the State of Connecticut and a professor at the Yale Medical School. The defendants gave information, instruction and medical advice to married couples as to the means of preventing conception. Buxton made all medical decisions as to the type of contraceptive advice that should be given. He also examined several patients. Estelle Griswold interviewed patients, took case histories, conducted group orientation sessions and described to patients the various methods of contraception.

On November 10, 1961, a warrant was issued charging C. Lee Buxton and Estelle T. Griswold with violating Sections 53-32 and 54-196 of the General Statutes of Connecticut. This indictment charged the Griswolds with "assist(ing), abet(ting), counsel(ing), cause(ing) and command(ing) certain named women to use a drug, medicinal article and instrument, for the purpose of preventing conception."

### Statutes Involved

Section 53-32 provides:

> "Any person who causes any drug, medicinal article or instrument for the purpose of preventing conception shall be fined not less than fifty dollars or imprisoned not less than sixty days nor more than one year or be fined and imprisoned."

Section 54-196 provides:

> "Any person who assists, abets, counsels, causes, hires or commands another to commit any offense may be prosecuted and punished as if he were the principal offender."

Issues Presented

I. Whether Sections 52-32 and 54-196 of the General Statutes of Connecticut constitute an unwarranted invasion of privacy in contravention of the Third, Fourth, Fifth, Ninth, and Fourteenth Amendments to the U.S. Constitution.

II. Whether Sections 52-32 and 54-196 of the General Statutes of Connecticut deprive married couples of their ''liberty'' without due process of law as defined by the Fourteenth Amendment.

Discussion

Issue I: There is no express right of privacy in the Constitution nor have the courts yet recognized an implicit right of privacy sufficiently broad to shelter our clients' activities.

Nowhere in the Constitution -- and in particular the Bill of Rights -- is there mention of ''privacy.'' Nor is any one of the protections set forth in the Bill of Rights or elsewhere sufficiently broad to shelter, by itself, the activities of Buxton and Griswold from government interference. Nevertheless, several provisions of the Bill of Rights, read together, imply the existence of a right of privacy, at least in the views of certain constitutional commentators. Justice Brandeis, dissenting in a prohibition-era search-and-seizure case, used the phrase ''the right to be let alone'' to describe a fundamental right implicit in many provisions of the Constitution. Olmstead v. United States, 277 U.S. 438, 478 (1928). Dean Erwin Griswold of the Harvard Law School recently stated that '''[t]he right to be let alone' is the underlying theme of the Bill of Rights.'' The Right to Let Alone, 55 Nw. U. L. Rev. 216, 217 (1960).

The Bill of Rights Manifests a Concern for Privacy

A review of various provisions of the Bill of Rights supports the view that protection of personal privacy was foremost in the minds of the drafters. The First Amendment, protecting as it does religion and free expression, marks out a man's faith and thought -- the private workings of the mind -- as an area into which the state shall not intrude. The Third Amendment recognizes the sanctity of the home; no soldier may be quartered in a house without the consent of the owner or process of law.

The most resounding guarantee of privacy is that of the Fourth Amendment: there is a ''right of the people to be secure in their persons, houses, papers and effects." The Supreme Court has considered the intent and breadth of this provision in the area of police searches, and has been willing at times to read it broadly. Discussing the reach of the Fourth Amendment in 1886, the Court stated: "It is not the breaking of [the citizen's] doors, and the rummaging of his drawers, that constitutes the essence of the offense; but it is the invasion of his indefeasible right of personal security, personal liberty and private property . . ." Boyd v. United States, 116 U.S. 616, 630. And more recently, the Court has described a "right to privacy, no less important than any other right carefully and particularly reserved to the people." Mapp v. Ohio, 367 U. S. 643, 656 (1961). See also: Weeks v. United States, 232 U.S. 383 (1914); Ex Parte Jackson, 727 (1878). But see: Frank v. Maryland, 359 U.S. 360 (1959) (claim of privacy outweighed by need to protect public health); Marron v. United States, 275 U.S. 192 (1927). See generally: Beaney, The Constitutional Right to Privacy, 1962 Sup. Ct. Rev. 212. The Fifth Amendment privilege against self-incrimination likewise illustrates the concern of the drafters of the Bill of Rights for the sanctity of the individual, implicitly recognizing a private sphere that the state shall not invade.

In addition to these enumerated protections, the Bill of Rights contains a general provision that "the enumeration in the Constitution, of certain rights, shall not be construed to deny or disparage others retained by the people." U.S. Const. Amend. 9. In a recent article on the Ninth and Tenth Amendments, Professor Redlich states: "The language and history of the two amendments indicate that the rights reserved were to be of a nature comparable to the rights enumerated." Are There "Certain Rights . . . Retained by the People"?, 37 N.Y.U. L. Rev. 787, 810 (1962). Thus, the specific provisions of the Third, Fourth and Fifth Amendments, which appear to contemplate invasion, search and coercion by military and law enforcement officials were not intended to be an exclusive list of personal liberties protected by the Bill of Rights.

The U. S. Supreme Court has given little recognition to a right of privacy outside of Fourth Amendment search and seizure cases.

In fact, review of Supreme Courts cases dealing with these protections shows only an occasional willingness of that body to extend the realm of protection beyond specific situations described in the Third and Fourth Amendments. In 1886 the Court struck down a law requiring the production of private papers, failing which the government's allegations were deemed valid. No search or seizure was actually involved, but the Court found the Fourth Amendment broad enough to cover this invasion of privacy. Boyd v. United States, 116 U.S. 616. In Siverman v. United States the Court found that driving a "spike microphone" into the wall of a suspect's house violated the Fourth Amendment, even though the actual invasion of the home was only a few inches. 365 U.S. 505 (1961). Justice Douglas, concurring, emphasized that the real evil was the invasion of privacy, not the technical trespass. Id. at 512-513.

There are also Supreme Court decisions refusing to take an expansive view of the Fourth Amendment. In a prohibition-era case, Carroll v. United States, the Court held that the warrant requirement of the Fourth Amendment did not extend to a search of an automobile, where there was probable cause, even though a search of a house based on the same information would require a warrant. 267 U.S. 132 (1925). In a 1928 wiretapping case the scope of the Fourth Amendment was fully explored by the Court. The majority opinion, authored by Chief Justice Taft, concluded that the searches referred to in the Fourth Amendment must be of physical things: papers, houses, people or property. Olmstead v. United States, 277 U.S. 438, 464. Justice Brandeis, dissenting, emphasized that constitutional provisions protecting individuals against specific government abuses must be capable of adaptation as the world changes. The Fourth and Fifth Amendments, according to Brandeis, apply to "every unjustifiable intrusion by the government upon the privacy of the individual." Id. at 478-79.

There is no precedent that would protect the activities of our clients, but these activities fall within a "right of privacy" that some students of the Constitution have urged the courts to recognize.

The Supreme Court has not recognized a broad right of privacy implicit in the Bill of Rights, despite learned commentary and thoughtful dissenting opinions to the effect that such a right exists. Although the Connecticut statues at issue intrude into what have been traditionally the most private areas of personal life -- intimate decisions of married couples affecting procreation -- they do not offend any specific provision of the Constitution. However, because Buxton and Griswold provided contraceptive information and devices only to married couples, the facts of this case raise strong privacy concerns, more so than had counseling been provided to the public in general. Thus, if we are to urge on the courts the view that there is implicit in the Constitution a right of privacy, Buxton's and Griswold's claims would appear to fall within the zone of protection described by the constitutional scholars and dissenting Justices who believe in a constitutional "right of privacy."

Issue II: The due process clause of the Fourteenth Amendment provides protection of "personal liberties."

The due process clause of the Fourteenth Amendment provides that no State shall "deprive any person of life, liberty or property without due process of law . . ." The Supreme Court has held that the Fourteenth Amendment extends the protections of the First, Fourth and Fifth Amendments to the States, not merely the Federal government. Gitlow v. New York, 268 U.S.652 (1925); Mapp v. Ohio, 367 U.S. 643 (1961). Moreover, the "liberty" interests so protected go beyond those specifically set out in the First, Fourth and Fifth Amendments. In 1952 the Court considered a case in which police entered a dwelling, seized a suspect in his bedroom and forcibly pumped his stomach to retrieve contraband he had swallowed. This bodily invasion was found by the Court to violate the due process clause -- rather than the Fourth or Fifth Amendment -- because it offended "personal immunities . . . rooted in the tradition and conscience of our people." Rochin v. California, 342 U.S. 165, 169. The rule that emerges from Rochin appears to be that some invasions of personal privacy are too shocking to be permitted under a process of law.

There is also a well-established line of cases holding that infringements of personal "liberty" by the states must meet certain requirements to be upheld under the due process clause: state laws must not be arbitrary and capricious, and must have a reasonable relationship to a legitimate legislative purpose. In 1923 the Court struck down a Nebraska law forbidding the teaching of German to pupils below the eighth grade level. The Court held that the statute impinged upon choices of parents, students and teachers so fundamental that the state could not justify this limitation. Thus, the "liberty" interest identified in the due process clause was implicated. Meyer v. Nebraska, 262 U.S. 390. In contrast, in 1934 the Court upheld a New York law setting milk prices -- arbitrarily, it was complained -- on the grounds that economic regulation is a proper legislative concern of the state. Nebbia v. New York, 291 U.S. 502. The rule that emerges from Meyer and Nebbia is that laws infringing on personal liberties require a higher degree of justification under the due process clause than laws pertaining to traditional state functions such as economic regulations.

The state statutes restricting the activities of our clients will not meet the tests applied by the U.S. Supreme Court to laws infringing personal liberties under the "due process" clause.

The Connecticut statutes used to restrict the activities of Buxton and Griswold have serious implications for personal liberty: Buxton, a physician, is restricted in practicing his profession; his patients are deprived of information and services affecting their marital well-being and even health; Griswold, a public health counselor, is prevented from counseling her clients according to her conscience and her perception of their needs; her clients -- married couples -- are foreclosed from certain procreative decisions by action of the state. The facts in this case would require the courts to subject it to a due process analysis of the type applied in Meyer. Regulation of the sexual and procreative decisions of married couples must be neither arbitrary nor capricious and must have a demonstrable relation to a proper legislative objective.

## Conclusions

The courts have not recognized a broad right of privacy, but it is possible that they may do so.

The courts have never recognized a constitutional right to privacy broad enough to protect the activities of our clients, Buxton and Griswold. There is, however, scholarly commentary to the effect that such a right exists. More importantly, there have been and continue to be justices on the highest court who believe that such a right is implicit in the Bill of Rights. These justices have always been a minority.

Fundamental personal liberties are protected under the due process clause.

The meaning and scope of the due process clause of the Fourteenth Amendment has been considered by the Supreme Court and the contours of due process law are well established. It would appear that the Connecticut statutes in question cannot meet the tests applied under the due process clause to laws restricting fundamental personal liberties.

<u>Litigation strategy: we should advocate (1) due process protection of our clients' activities and (2) recognition of a right of privacy implicit in the U.S. Constitution.</u>

We should urge, as the primary theory of our case, that the statutes in question deprive married couples of fundamental personal liberties without due process of law, as defined in the Fourteenth Amendment and the cases construing it. As a secondary matter, we should urge the court to recognize a constitutional right of privacy protecting the activities of married couples and those who assist them in intimate decisions. Success on this latter theory is not likely, however.

UNITED STATES DISTRICT COURT
SOUTHERN DISTRICT OF INDIANA
EVANSVILLE DIVISION

BARBARA F. EVANS, Personal )
Representative of the Estate of )
Roy Evans, Deceased )
) CAUSE No. EV 64-C-85
vs. )
)
GENERAL MOTORS CORP. )

## FIRST AMENDED COMPLAINT

### Count I.

Plaintiff complains of the defendant and for her cause of action, alleges and says:

1. The plaintiff is a citizen and resident of the State of Indiana residing on Wortman Road in Vanderburgh County, Indiana.

2. The defendant is a corporation duly organized under and by virtue of the laws of the State of Delaware and is therefore a citizen of said state. The defendant maintains its principal place of business in Detroit, Michigan, and is therefore also a citizen of said state.

3. This controversy, exclusive of interest and costs, exceeds the sum of Ten-thousand Dollars ($10,000.00). By reason of the above and foregoing facts this court has jurisdiction of the within controversy.

4. The plaintiff is the duly appointed and acting Personal Representative of the Estate of Roy Evans, deceased, having been duly appointed and qualified by the Probate Court of Vanderburgh County, Indiana.

5. The defendant is a corporation engaged in the design, manufacture, sale, and distribution of many products including automobiles, and trucks designated and identified by the trade name "Chevrolet."

6. On the 25th day of January, 1964, Roy Evans was the owner of a certain 1961 Chevrolet Station Wagon automobile which had been designed, constructed, manufactured and assembled by the defendant, General Motors Corp.

The defendant had negligently and carelessly designed, constructed, manufactured, and assembled this automobile by incorporating in the automobile a frame known as an "X frame" which frame was weak in the middle and did not have side rails to protect drivers involved in side impact collisions. Because of this design, construction, manufacture and assembly of the "X frame" Roy Evans, as the driver of the automobile, was seated outside of the "X frame" and had no outer frame protection from side impact collisions.

7. On the 25th day of January, 1964, while Roy Evans was driving this 1961 Chevrolet Sation Wagon automobile, and as a direct and proximate result of the negligence of the defendant in designing, constructing, manufacturing and assembling of this automobile in such a manner as to render its use dangerous to life and limb, Roy Evans received fatal injuries when the left

side of said automobile collapsed into and against his person inflicting upon his body and person fatal injuries. The collapse occurred when an automobile was struck from the left side by another automobile at the intersection of St. Joseph Avenue and Schenk Roads in Vanderburgh County, Indiana, and there was no outer frame protecting him from such a side impact collision.

8. Roy Evans's automobile by reason of the "X frame" and the absence of any side guard-rail type frame, perimeter type frame or any other type of outer frame protection failed to afford him protecton from side impact collision. The "X frame" did permit the collapse of the body of the Chevrolet automobile against the body and person of Roy Evans.

9. In the design, construction, manufacture, assembly and inspection of said Chevrolet automobile the defendant, General Motors Corp., knew or in the exercise of reasonable care and caution should have known that it was reasonably foreseeable that persons driving the automobile could be involved in side impact collisions such as described above and that drivers in the automobiles would be seriously injured or killed because of the absence of outer frame protection.

10. In the design, construction, manufacture, assembly, and inspection of the Chevrolet Station Wagon automobile the defendant knew or in the exercise of reasonable care and caution should have known that it was creating an unreasonable risk of causing substantial bodily harm and/or death to persons driving the automobile, including plaintiff's decedent, by not having reasonable and adequate side guardrail protection from side impact collisions.

11. This occurrence and Roy Evans's death occurred directly and proximately by reason of each one of the following negligent and careless acts or omissions to act upon the part of the defendant, General Motors Corp.:

(a) The defendant negligently made the automobile under a design which made it dangerous for persons seated in the driver's seat of the automobile, including plaintiff's decedent, when involved in side impact collisions, such as described above, because of the absence of a side guardrail type frame, perimeter type frame, or *any* other type of outer frame protection.

(b) The defendant negligently failed to exercise reasonable care in the manufacture of the automobile when it knew that its manufacture was creating an unreasonable risk of bodily harm to persons seated in the driver's seat of the automobile, including plaintiff's decedent, when involved in side impact collisions such as above described, because of the absence of a side guardrail type frame, perimeter type frame, or any other type of outer frame protection.

(c) The defendant negligently assembled the automobile with an "X frame" when it knew or in the exercise of reasonable care and caution should have known that it was assembling an unsafe automobile and was creating an unreasonable risk of bodily harm to persons seated in the driver's seat of the automobile, including plaintiff's decedent, when involved in side impact collisions because of the absence of a side guardrail type frame, perimeter type frame, or any other type of outer frame protection.

(d) The defendant negligently and carelessly failed to test and subject the design of the automobile to the effect of side impact collisions on drivers seated in the front seat of its 1961 Chevrolet Station Wagons.

(e) The defendant failed to make a test or safety check of models on the 1961 Chevrolet Station Wagon automobiles when subjected to side impact collisions, when the defendant knew or in the exercise of reasonable care and caution should have known that such tests and safety checks would have revealed the weakness of said "X frame" from side impact collisions.

(f) The defendant negligently failed to warn drivers of 1961 Chevrolet Station Wagon automobiles, including Roy Evans, that said automobile did not have a side guardrail type frame, perimeter type frame, or any other type of outer frame protection, and was weak in the middle and had no strong side frame protection to protect drivers when involved in side impact collisions.

(g) The defendant negligently and carelessly failed to install adequate safety devices in the automobile to protect drivers of the automobiles, including plaintiff's decedent, from side impact collisions.

(h) The defendant failed in the design of the automobile to plan for safety frame protection for drivers of the automobile seated in the front seat when said defendant knew or in the exercise of reasonable care and caution should have known that the automobiles could and would be subjected to side impact collisions.

(i) The defendant in the manufacture of said automobile failed to measure up to the automobile idustry's standards and to keep abreast of current scientific knowledge by using the "X frame," when the defendant knew or in the exercise of reasonable care, and caution should have known, that the auto industry was affording protection to drivers of automobiles from side impact collisions by the use of a side guardrail type frame, perimeter type frame, or any other type of outer frame protection.

12. At the time of his death, Roy Evans left surviving his wife, Barbara F. Evans, and four (4) minor children, namely, Kerry, Jeffery, Linda, and Lisa, all of whom were completely dependent upon him.

13. By reason of the above and foregoing, the plaintiff has been damaged in the sum of Four-hundred-eighty thousand Dollars ($480,000.00).

Wherefore, plaintiff demands judgment of and from the defendant in the sum of Four-hundred-eighty thousand Dollars ($480,000.00), for her costs herein, and for all further just and proper relief in the premises.

**Count II.**

Plaintiff for Count II of her amended complaint against the defendant states the following facts:

1. Plaintiff restates and repeats the allegations contained in Rhetorical paragraphs numbered 1, 2, 3, 4, and 5, inclusive of her Count I of her amended complaint, as is fully set forth herein.

2. Prior to the 25th day of January 1964, plaintiff purchased a 1961 Chevrolet Station Wagon automobile. That at said time said automobile was purchased there was implied warranties from the defendant, General Motors Corp., that the automobile was of merchantable quality and was reasonably fit for use as an automobile.

3. These implied warranties were breached in that the automobile was not reasonably fit for use as an automobile nor was it of merchantable quality for the following reasons:

(a) The automobile was unsafe because it had an "X frame."

(b) The automobile did not have reasonable and adequate side guardrail type frame, perimeter type frame, or any other type of outer frame protection.

4. On the 25th day of January, 1964, while Roy Evans was driving the automobile, he received fatal injuries when the left side of his said automobile collapsed into and against his body and person inflicting upon his body and person fatal injuries. The collapse occurred when said automobile was struck from the left side by another automobile at the intersection of St. Joseph Avenue and Schenk Roads in Vanderburgh County, Indiana. That his death resulted from said automobile not being reasonably fit for use as an automobile nor of merchantable quality for the reasons set forth above.

5. At the time of his death, Roy Evans left surviving his wife, Barbara F. Evans, and four (4) minor children, namely, Kerry, Jeffery, Linda, and Lisa, all of whom were completely dependent upon him.

6. By reason of the above and foregoing, the plaintiff has been damaged in the sum of Four-hundred-eighty thousand Dollars ($480,000.00).

Wherefore, plaintiff demands judgment of and from the defendant in the sum of Four-hundred-eighty thousand Dollars ($480,000.00), for her costs herein, and for all further just and proper relief in the premises.

## Count III.

Plaintiff further complains of the defendant and for her Third Count of complaint herein alleges and says:

1. Plaintiff restates and repeats the allegations contained in rhetorical paragraphs 1, 2, 3, 4, and 5 inclusive of Count 1 of her Amended Complaint, as if fully set forth herein.

2. Prior to the 25th day of January, 1964, defendant had engaged in the business of manufacturing and selling a certain 1961 Chevrolet Station Wagon automobile, which automobile was then and there in a defective condition, unreasonably dangerous to the users thereof. At the time of defendant's manufacture and sale of this automobile it was expected that such automobile would reach the users thereof without substantial change from the condition in which it was sold.

3. This automobile was dangerous to users thereof in that it was then and there equipped with an "X frame" which did not have any side frame protection located outside the drivers and passengers. That the automobile reached the plaintiff's decedent, Roy Evans, the user thereof, without substantial change in the condition in which it was originally sold by the defendant with the "X frame" still incorporated in the automobile and there still being no side frame protection located outside the driver.

4. On the 25th day of January, 1964, while Roy Evans was driving the automobile, he received fatal injuries when the left side of the automobile collapsed into and against his body and person inflicting upon his body and person fatal injuries. This collapse occurred when the automobile was struck from the left side by another automobile at the intersection of St. Joseph Avenue and Schenk Road in Vanderburgh County, Indiana, and there was no frame outside his left side.

5. The defendant's placing of the automobile into the stream of commerce without frame protection located outside the driver was the reason for the same to collapse and proximately causing the injuries and death of plaintiff's decedent. By reason thereof, defendant is strictly liable to plaintiff.

6. At the time the defendant manufactured this automobile the defendant General Motors knew that it was reasonably foreseeable that users of the automobile could be involved in side impact collisions, and would be subject to more serious injuries and/or death because of the absence of outer frame protection.

Wherefore, plaintiff prays judgment of and from the defendant in the sum of $480,000.00.

(Signed)______________________

Attorney for the Plaintiff
[Address]
[Telephone Number]

STATE OF INDIANA )
) SS:
COUNT OF VANDERBURGH )

IN THE VANDERBURGH SUPERIOR COURT

XYZ CORP., an Indiana corporation,
Plaintiff,

v.

CAUSE No. 82CO2-9001-CP-0123

JOHN C. WASHINGTON,
Defendant and Counterclaimant,

v.

XYZ CORP., an Indiana corporation,
Counterclaim Defendant.

COUNTERCLAIM

Counterclaimant, for his cause of relief against the counterclaim defendant, states:

1. Counterclaimant and counterclaim defendant are residents of ____________ County, Indiana [or incorporate allegations from plaintiff's complaint].

2. At the commencement of this suit, the counterclaim defendant was and still is indebted to counterclaimant upon a promissory note which was executed by counterclaim defendant on [date] in the sum of $__________. A true and accurate copy of the note is attached hereto as Exhibit A.

3. Counterclaimant is willing and entitled to set off against any sum found to be due and owing to the counterclaim defendant by counterclaimant in this action.

WHEREFORE, counterclaimant requests judgment against the counterclaim defendant in the sum of $__________, for setoff of this amount against counterclaim defendant's claim if he prevails, for the costs of this action, and for all other appropriate relief.

(Signed)____________________
Attorney for Counterclaimant
[Address]
[Telephone Number]

UNITED STATES DISTRICT COURT
SOUTHERN DISTRICT OF INDIANA
EVANSVILLE DIVISION

| | | |
|---|---|---|
| BARBARA F. EVANS, Personal<br>Representative of the Estate of<br>Roy Evans, Deceased<br><br>vs.<br><br>GENERAL MOTORS CORP. | )<br>)<br>)<br>)<br>)<br>)<br>) | CAUSE No. EV 64-C-85 |

**Defendant's Answer to First Amended Complaint.**

In response to the allegations of Count I of Plaintiff's Amended Complaint, defendant states:

1. Defendant admits the allegations contained in rhetorical paragraph 1 of Plaintiff's Amended Complaint.

2. Defendant admits the allegations contained in rhetorical paragraph 2 of Plaintiff's Amended Complaint.

3. Defendant admits plaintiff is demanding defendant pay to her an amount in excess of $10,000, exclusive of interest and costs, which defendant denies, and by reason of these facts this Count has jurisdiction of this case.

4. Defendant is without information sufficient to form a belief as to the truth of the allegations contained in rhetorical paragraph 4 of Plaintiff's Amended Complaint.

5. Defendant admits the allegations contained in rhetorical paragraph 5 of Plaintiff's Amended Complaint.

6. Defendant admits that on January 25, 1964, Roy L. Evans was the owner of a 1961 Chevrolet Station Wagon automobile that had been designed, constructed, manufactured and assembled by defendant, and that the automobile had an ''X frame,'' but denies allegations of rhetorical paragraph 6 not specifically admitted.

7. Defendant denies the allegations contained in rhetorical paragraph 7 of Plaintiff's Amended Complaint.

8. Defendant denies the allegations contained in rhetorical paragraph 8 of Plaintiff's Amended Complaint.

9. Defendant denies the allegations contained in rhetorical paragraph 9 of Plaintiff's Amended Complaint.

10. Defendant denies the allegations contained in rhetorical paragraph 10 of Plaintiff's Amended Complaint.

11. Defendant denies the allegations contained in rhetorical paragraph 11 of Plaintiff's Amended Complaint.

12. Defendant is without information sufficient to form a belief as to the truth of the allegations contained in rhetorical paragraph 12 of Plaintiff's Amended Complaint.

In response to the allegations of Count II of Plaintiff's Amended Complaint, defendant states:

1. Defendant incorporates by reference its answers to rhetorical paragraphs 1, 2, 3, 4 and 5 of its answer to Count I of Plaintiff's Amended Complaint.

2. Defendant admits that prior to the 25th day of January, 1964, plaintiff or plaintiff's husband, Roy L. Evans, purchased a 1961 Chevrolet Station Wagon automobile, but not from the defendant or any authorized dealer of defendant, and denies that there was any implied warranty from defendant to plaintiff of any character.

3. Defendant denies the allegations contained in rhetorical paragraph 3 of Plaintiff's Amended Complaint.

4. Defendant denies the allegations contained in rhetorical paragraph 4 of Plaintiff's Amended Complaint.

5. Defendant is without information sufficient to form a belief as to the truth of the allegations contained in rhetorical paragraph 5 of Plaintiff's Amended Complaint.

6. Defendant denies the allegations contained in rhetorical paragraph 6 of Plaintiff's Amended Complaint.

**First Affirmative Defense.**

Defendant, for its first affirmative defense to Plaintiff's Amended Complaint, and to each Count thereof, states that neither Count of Plaintiff's Amended Complaint states a claim against defendant on which relief can be granted.

**Second Affirmative Defense.**

1. Within Vanderburgh County, Indiana, there is a wide, paved, public highway of the county running in a general direction of north and south, which is commonly known and designated as St. Joseph Avenue. St. Joseph Avenue is intersected at right angles by a county road, which is commonly known and designated as Schenk Road. Schenk Road forms a "T" intersection with St. Joseph Avenue.

2. On the 25th day of January, 1964, at approximately 4:15 p.m., Roy L. Evans was driving his 1961 Chevrolet Station Wagon in a southwesterly direction on St. Joseph Avenue and was in the process of making a left-hand turn off Schenk Road toward the south on St. Joseph Avenue, at which time Alan Ray Tolley, a 17-year-old youth, was driving a 1957 Ford Tudor Sedan automobile in a northerly direction on St. Joseph Avenue at a high rate of speed.

3. At that time and place Roy L. Evans was negligent in the operation of his 1961 Chevrolet Station Wagon, as a result of which negligence, or combined with the negligence of Alan Ray Tolley, while such 1961 Chevrolet Station Wagon was in the process of entering St. Joseph Avenue and in the process of turning to the south it was struck in the left side by the 1957 Ford with such force that the 1961 Chevrolet Station Wagon was driven fifty (50) feet in a northwesterly direction from the point of the collision and the 1957 Ford Tudor was driven one hundred (100) feet in a northerly direction from the point of impact.

4. The death of Roy L. Evans was the direct result of:
   a. His negligent failure to look for other vehicles using St. Joseph Avenue as he approached and drove onto that through highway;
   b. His negligent entering onto St. Joseph Avenue at a time when in the exercise of reasonable care it would have been obvious that it was unsafe to have done so, and his negligent failure to take any steps to avoid being struck by the automobile of Alan Ray Tolley;
   c. His negligent failure to yield the right of way to the automobile driven by Alan Ray Tolley;
   d. His negligent failure to stop and exercise reasonable care before and on entering St. Joseph Avenue as required by law.

5. The death of Roy L. Evans was the direct result of the negligence of Alan Ray Tolley, to wit:
   a. That Alan Ray Tolley at said time and place negligently drove the Ford automobile, which he was then and there driving at a high and dangerous rate of speed of seventy (70) to seventy-five (75) miles per hour, which rate of speed was greater than was reasonable and prudent at the time and place.

b. That Alan Ray Tolley negligently and carelessly failed to keep a proper lookout for traffic at the intersection and on St. Joseph Avenue including the automobile in which plaintiff's decedent was driving.

c. That Alan Ray Tolley negligently and carelessly failed and neglected to keep the Ford automobile under his reasonable and proper control at the time and place so as to have avoided the collision.

6. The only proximate cause of the collision and death of Roy L. Evans was such negligence on the part of Roy L. Evans or Alan Ray Tolley or both of them.

**Third Affirmative Defense.**

1. On February 21, 1964 the plaintiff, Barbara F. Evans, as the personal representative of the estate of Roy L. Evans, deceased, filed a complaint for the same damages sued for here in the amount of $600,000 against such Alan Ray Tolley and Wilburn D. Tolley, the father of Alan Ray Tolley, in the Vanderburgh Circuit Court, alleging that the collision in question and the death of Roy L. Evans was the direct and proximate result of negligence on the part of Alan Ray Tolley, a certified copy of which "Complaint for Damages" is attached hereto marked Exhibit A.

2. Some time after February 21, 1964, the exact date being unknown to defendant, a complete settlement of the claim of this plaintiff for the alleged wrongful death of Roy L. Evans against Alan Ray Tolley and Wilburn D. Tolley was finally and completely settled by the payment of $20,000 by Alan Ray Tolley and Wilburn D. Tolley to the plaintiff, and plaintiff Barbara F. Evans executed at such time, in consideration for such $20,000, settlement papers constituting a complete release of Alan Ray Tolley and Wilburn D. Tolley. Barbara F. Evans, having already recovered for the wrongful death of her husband Roy L. Evans, is now barred from seeking a second recovery or additional recovery from this defendant.

Wherefore, defendant prays for judgment and for all other proper relief.

**Fourth Affirmative Defense.**
(To All Paragraphs of Complaint.)

1. For a long number of years prior to January 25, 1964, thousands of drivers and passengers in automobiles of all kinds, makes and models, with all kinds of frames and body constructions, have been injured or killed each year in automobile accidents in the State of Indiana and throughout the United States.

2. Such accidents, injuries, and deaths have been well publicized in newspapers, on the radio and television and elsewhere, and the fact of their occurrence has been common knowledge. Plaintiff's husband, therefore, had knowledge that drivers and passengers were being so injured and killed in such accidents involving all kinds of automobiles.

3. In operating his 1961 Chevrolet Station Wagon on the public streets and highways, plaintiff's husband necessarily assumed the risks of being involved in such accidents including the risk of being struck by another automobile, such as the Ford that actually struck him, traveling at a high rate of speed and with force sufficient to cause death.

UNITED STATES DISTRICT COURT
SOUTHERN DISTRICT OF INDIANA
EVANSVILLE DIVISION

BARBARA F. EVANS, Personal )
Representative of the Estate of )
Roy Evans, Deceased )
) NO. EV 64-C-85
vs. )
)
GENERAL MOTORS CORP. )

**Written Interrogatories to be Answered by the Defendant, General Motors Corp.**

You are hereby notified to answer under oath the next numbered interrogatories from 1 to 99, inclusive, as set out below, within fifteen days from the time service is made upon you, in accordance with Rule 33 of the Federal Rules of Civil Procedure:

**Interrogatory No. 1.**

Do you maintain production records that indicate the date that a 1961 Chevrolet Station Wagon Model No. 1835 bearing Manufacturer's Identification Number 11835F138206 was manufactured and distributed? If so, state:

(a) The date that you began manufacturing models of this type.
(b) The location of the plants where models of this type were produced.
(c) The location of the plant where this particular automobile was manufactured.
(d) The date that this particular automobile was manufactured.
(e) The date it was shipped to a retail distributor.
(f) The name and address of the retail distributor to whom it was shipped.
(g) The name and address of the purchaser of said automobile from the retailer.
(h) The names and addresses of those persons who have the care, custody and control of production records of this automobile.
(i) The records and how they are described which the defendant has as to this particular automobile.

**Interrogatory No. 2.**

Did the 1961 Chevrolet Station Wagon Model No. 1836 bearing Identification Number 11835F138206 include in its assembly what is commonly known as an "X frame"? If not, state the kind and type of frame this vehicle contained. (If the answer to this interrogatory is in the negative, all interrogatories subsequent hereto are amended to change said interrogatories from "X frame" to the kind of frame given in defendant's answer thereto).

**Interrogatory No. 3.**

How many models of this type of automobile did the defendant manufacture?

**Interrogatory No. 4.**

Did all of the defendant's 1961 Chevrolet Station Wagons have an "X frame"? If not, state:

(a) The kind of frame used.
(b) The number which did not use the "X frame."
(c) The reason for using a different type of frame.
(d) The kind of frame used in place of the "X frame."
(e) The reason for using a different type of frame.

**Interrogatory No. 5.**

What are the names and addresses of each person who participated in the original design of the "X frame" used in the 1961 Chevrolet Station Wagon?

Signed______________________
Attorney for Plaintiff
[Address]
[Telephone Number]

LAW OFFICES OF
SMART & WHITE
One Schoolhouse Square
Suite 23
P.O. Box 1119
Evansville, IN 47708-1234

January 8, 1991

Grant and Pawlyk
Post Office Box 502
Evansville, IN 47708-1234

RE: Our Client: Alex Martin
Insured: Juanita White
D/Incident: 4/1/90

Gentlemen

Mr. Smart and I are interested in pursuing settlement discussions concerning the claim of our client, Alex Martin. I have taken the liberty of supplying you with medical information, medical bills, and photographic information concerning Mr. Martin's injuries. We would like to give you and XYZ Insurance Company an opportunity to compromise and settle this claim prior to the incurrence of defense costs, and settle this claim for the policy limits.

Facts of the Collision: On April 1, 1990, Alex Martin was the owner and operator of a 1985 Buick Regal sedan. He was traveling in a southerly direction on Pennsylvania Avenue. As he approached the parking lot of Bailey's Tavern in Evansville, Indiana, Juanita White, pulled directly into the path of his vehicle, intending to execute a left turn. She completely blocked Mr. Martin's lane of travel, and he had nowhere to go to avoid the collision.

Immediately after the collision, your insured stated that she looked both ways but did not see Mr. Martin. She acknowledged that she pulled directly into his path and that the accident was her fault. Sometime later someone told her that Mr. Martin may have been drinking, and this was the first time she attributed any fault to Alex Martin.

As your client's vehicle exited into his lane of travel, Mr. Martin instinctively veered to the left. There was not sufficient time to do anything else. The right front of your client's vehicle struck the right passenger side of the Martin vehicle, causing it to go out of control. I have enclosed two of the official police photographs depicting this damage.

I have also spoken with Justin Williams, the passenger who was riding with

Mr. Martin. He verified that your client pulled directly into the path of the Martin vehicle. He stated that Mr. Martin's only options were to strike the truck in the driver's side in a "T-bone" configuration, or to try to avoid the collision by trying to steer to the left of the truck. He informed me that no matter what course of action Mr. Martin took, the collision was inevitable because of the actions of Ms. White.

Injuries Sustained by Alex Martin: I have enclosed copies of the medical records that detail Mr. Martin's very severe injuries. As you can see from the enclosed records, he had a gaping laceration on his forehead and a fractured jaw. His most severe injury was a "burst fracture" of one of the vertebrae in his lower back, L1. The fracture of the vertebra caused portions of the bone fragments to be driven in to the spinal canal and damage the area of the spinal cord known as the cauda equina.

Mr. Martin was taken by ambulance to the Ames Community Hospital. He was seen and treated by Dr. Banpote Saw. Records show that he had a deep laceration on his forehead and a fracture of his left mandible as well as the fracture of the L1 vertebral body. Dr. Saw repaired the severe laceration over the forehead. Fixation devices were placed on his teeth and his jaw was wired shut. He continued to have difficulty with his lower extremities, i.e., weakness of both legs and numbness of his legs below the knee area. He was also complaining of severe pain.

Dr. Saw contacted Dr. Watson Lane, who maintains offices in Evansville, Indiana. Dr. Lane's consultation notes are enclosed. The consultation notes show that Mr. Martin had numbness below the knees and he was unable to urinate. The doctor felt that a CT Scan should be performed. Sensory tests showed numbness over the foot areas and very poor ability to distinguish sensations in the legs. The x-rays showed a fracture of L1 with a large bone protrusion into the spinal canal. The doctor felt it was quite probable that Mr. Martin would require surgery on his back.

Dr. Lane had Mr. Martin transferred to Black Hospital for surgery. Copies of those records are also enclosed. Suffice it to say the automobile collision crushed his vertebra and caused damage to his spinal cord, Dr. Mary Lamb, an orthopedic surgeon, was also contacted, and she and Dr. Lane performed surgery on Mr. Martin. Those operative notes are enclosed. As you can see from the records, a very lengthy surgery, over five hours, was performed. The fracture was so severe that metal bars known as Harrington Rods were placed in his spine. I have enclosed a page from a medical encyclopedia that describes and depicts Harrington Rods.

The bone spurs and chips caused a compression at the bottom of the spinal cord. This is the area known as the cauda equina. I have also enclosed a diagram depicting the location of the cauda equina. As you can see, the cauda equina divides into many nerves that extend into the pelvis and the lower extremities.

After the surgery, Mr. Martin was a paraplegic. He was unable to walk and had numbness throughout his entire body below the level of the fracture. He was unable to urinate. The surgery was quite lengthy and complicated, causing him much pain during his rehabilitation process.

As with all spinal cord injuries, the physicians did not know the extent of Mr. Martin's paralysis nor the extent of his recovery. After surgery, he was referred to physical therapy. When he was released from the hospital, he was unable to walk without using a back brace (depicted in two photographs) and a walker.

After he healed from his surgery, Mr. Martin continued follow-up treatment with Dr. Lane. Dr. Lane referred him to Community Hospital for in-depth physical therapy. I invite you to review the physical therapy notes. They show that he began his therapy in July of 1990 and continued until the end of November 1990. The physical therapist noted some improvement in certain muscle groups.

I know that it is quite difficult to review medical records and obtain an accurate description of the injuries suffered by a person. Because of that difficulty, I have taken the liberty of enclosing with this letter approximately five minutes of videotape that depicts Alex Martin as he is today. When Mr. Martin was released from physical therapy, he was instructed to perform exercises a minimum of three times per day in order to strengthen his legs and to learn how to walk. He does perform those exercises, sometimes five to six times per day. Mr. Martin has noticed absolutely no improvement in his walking, his standing, or his leg strength in the past two months. He has continued to visit with Dr. Lane on a regular basis. Dr. Lane, as of Mr. Martin's last visit in September 1990, feels that there has been little or no improvement.

You will note from the videotape that Mr. Martin is unable to walk on his toes. The doctor has felt that the weakness in his feet has remained unchanged for the past several months. He has difficulty standing still. He has a tendency to lose his balance and needs external support. You will note from the tape that he stands in a very rigid manner. This is because of the Harrington Rods. I have also enclosed several still photographs that depict the surgical sites, and you can see that the scars are quite extensive.

Mr. Martin is unable to run. I have asked him to do so and invite you to review the tape. It is a very sad sight to see. Mr. Martin is thankful that he is able to walk, but from a review of the tape, it is obvious that he is basically unemployable in many types of jobs, is unable to run, is unable to walk fast, and has much difficulty.

The tape does not show his additional difficulties. He still has severe pain in his back. He becomes physically exhausted after twenty minutes of exercises. After he does his physical therapy for approximately twenty minutes, he must lie down for forty to sixty minutes. Once he regains his strength, he is able to continue his physical therapy exercises for another twenty minutes. It totally and completely exhausts him to do his exercises three to five times per day.

Mr. Martin is unable to urinate. He has to utilize a catheter, which as you know is a long plastic tube. It is boiled in order to sterilize it, coated with medicated oil, inserted in his penis through his ureters and into his bladder. He must then tap himself in the side until the urine flow starts. After his bladder is empty, he must take the catheter out, boil it in water to kill all of the germs, and wait until he needs to urinate again. This is quite a degrading experience for this young man. Mr. Martin also has problems with his bowels. If he is unable to reach a bathroom immediately upon feeling his bowels move, he soils himself. This has happened to him on several occasions while riding in automobiles with friends, while sleeping, and while walking near his home for exercise.

Another unfortunate incident of his injuries is the fact that he is now having sexual problems. He is able to attain an erection, but since the injuries he has been unable to have an orgasm. I have enclosed information from a medical encyclopedia that discusses this unfortunate but common occurrence in people with spinal cord injuries.

Medical Specials of Alex Martin: I have enclosed the medical bills of Alex Martin. They are as follows:

| | | |
|---|---|---|
| Dr. Banpote Saw | 4/1/90 - 5/1/90 | $ 665.00 |
| Evansville EAS | 4/1/90 | 1,902.30 |
| Ames Community Hosp. | 4/1/90 - 4/3/90 | 3,681.54 |
| Dr. Watson Lane | 4/2/90 - 9/15/90 | 3,163.00 |
| Ames Ambulance | 4/3/90 | 175.00 |
| Black Hospital | 4/3/90 - 4/20/90 | 16,869.85 |
| Dr. Mary Lamb | 4/4/90 - 4/6/90 | 5,056.00 |
| Ames Med. Radio | 4/4/90 - 4/6/90 | 336.00 |
| Ames Physical Therapy | 7/15/90 - 11/8/90 | 700.85 |
| Ames Physical Therapy | 11/23/90 | 36.00 |

TOTAL MEDICAL SPECIALS..................................$ 30,785.54

You will note from the office notes of Dr. Watson Lane that he has recommended foot orthotics with a platarflexion spring. These are basically braces that fit onto specially made shoes. The specially made shoes will then bend forward because of springs. Mr. Martin has lost all use of the muscles that allow the foot to go up and down. Consequently, Dr. Lane feels these shoes are needed. Mr. Martin has been informed that the shoes cost approximately $4,000.

From a review of the medical bills, medical records, photographs and videotape, it is quite obvious that this gentleman has sustained severe, excruciating, and permanent injuries. He is left with multiple scarring on his face, his back, and his hip area. He has constant pain in his back and has little or no use of his legs. He cannot function sexually and cannot urinate. He has noticed no change in his walking ability for at least two months. It physically exhausts him to do his exercises.

Settlement Demand: We have been authorized by Mr. Martin to compromise and settle his claim for bodily injuries for the sum of $500,000 or the single limits of the policies of insurance that were in full force and effect covering Juanita White and the vehicle she was operating. It is my understanding that you have informed Mr. Smart that the applicable coverage in this case is $25,000 on Ms. White and $25,000 on the vehicle she was driving for total insurance benefits of $50,000.

Mr. Martin has sustained devastating injuries. There is insufficient insurance to compensate him for his injuries in this case. Please be advised that the offer to compromise and settle the claim for the applicable policy limits will remain open for a period of thirty (30) days from the date of this letter. In order to compromise and settle the claim on those terms, we will need not only your drafts but also certified copies of the policies of insurance including the declaration sheets. We will also need affidavits executed by your insured stating that there are not additional insurance policies that cover this accident, the vehicle involved, or Ms. White.

Please be advised that the videotape and the photographs enclosed are being lent to you with the understanding that they remain my property and will be surrendered to me upon my request.

If there are any items that I have in my file that may aid you in the evaluation of this claim, do not hesitate to call and I will see that they are provided. Thank you for your consideration in this matter. I will look forward to hearing from you.

Very truly yours

Sam White
Attorney At Law

SW/jw

Enclosures

LAW OFFICES OF
SMITH, TOLENTINO & SHORT
402 Williamson Blvd.
Evansville, IN 47708-1234

November 7, 1990

UNIVERSAL INSURANCE SOCIETY
One Bank Plaza
Suite 1187
P.O. Box 7007
Hartford, Connecticut 46240-7007

Attn: Mr. James South

Re: Claim Number: 33456
Insured: Noland Sandefur
Claimants: Jessica and Donald Morely
Date of Loss: January 3, 1990

Dear James

On Thursday, November 6, 1990, I met with the insured, Noland Sandefur. Based on my meeting with the insured, and a review of the investigation file, I submit the following preliminary report concerning this case. Please note the comments and suggestions contained at the end of the report for your consideration.

**FACTS**

On January 3, 1990 at 2:55 p.m. Noland Sandefur completed his school day at Harrison High School on the east side of Newburgh, Indiana. Noland went to his 1980 Olds Cutlass and left school to go home. In the car with him was Sean Clark, son of Frederick Clark, who resides at 203 South Garfield Avenue, telephone 555-1678. Noland took some of the back roads to the west of the high school to arrive at the intersection of Tyler and South Lake Road. Tyler is a two (2) way, two (2) lane residential street that runs east-west and dead ends to the east into another north-south road of homes and to the west into South Lake Road. South Lake Road is the main north-south artery on the east side of Newburgh, which provides access to several fast food restaurants and shopping malls/stores. South Lake is actually five (5) lanes, two (2) north, two (2) south, and one (1) center turn lane for traffic going both north and south. Traffic is light on Tyler, but is almost always heavy on South Lake Road; and, if the traffic is not heavy on South Lake Road, there are always several cars and trucks turning off and onto this Road.

As Noland arrived at the intersection of Tyler and South Lake Road he stopped at the stop sign that controls the traffic coming onto South Lake. He had the front of his car partially sticking into the east lane of the

UNIVERSAL INSURANCE SOCIETY
Mr. James South
November 7, 1990
Page 2

north lanes of South Lake, as his view to the north was blocked by cars parked on a car lot on the northeast corner of Tyler and South Lake. Also, his view to the south was partially blocked by a ceiling fan and lighting retailer located on the southeast corner of Tyler and South Lake. Noland watched for oncoming traffic from the south, while his passenger, Sean Clark, was watching the traffic coming from the north. As Noland and Sean waited for the traffic to clear, a white delivery van or truck in the east lane of the north bound lane of South Lake, approached the intersection with its turn signal on indicating its intention to turn right or east onto Tyler. Sean then informed Noland that there was no traffic coming from the north, and Noland saw no traffic coming from the south other than the slowing truck with its turn signal on, so he glanced north and then proceeded to pull across the north bound lanes of South Lake and into the center turn lane to go south. As his vehicle was almost all the way into the center lane going south, the driver's side rear of his car was struck behind the wheel well opening by the driver's side front of a car driven by Louise Johnson and occupied by her mother-in-law, Jessica Morely.

It seems that the 1972 Olds Cutlass driven by Mrs. Johnson was directly behind the delivery truck and was not visible to Noland as he pulled from the intersection. Further, Noland describes the impact as being rather mild and not doing much damage to either car (i.e., each car was able to be driven from the accident scene; the impact did not really move Noland's car). As soon as Noland's car came to a rest, he got out of his car and went to the Johnson car a few feet away. Louise Johnson was having difficulty opening her driver's side door, and it was at this time Noland noticed Ms. Johnson had a passenger in the front seat (Jessica Morely). Also present in the car were an infant in a car seat in the rear seat of the car and a child seated on Ms. Morely's lap in the front seat. The child seated on Ms. Morely's lap was crying, and it was apparent to Noland that Ms. Morely was trying to comfort the child. Noland did notice that Ms. Morely was not wearing a shoulder harness while seated in the car, but that she could have had a lap belt on as he could not see her lap since the child was sitting on it.

When Louise Johnson got out of her car, Noland told her that he ''couldn't see her'' when he pulled out. The only comment Noland recalls Ms. Johnson made was ''thanks a lot.'' They then went to call the Newburgh Police Department. About twenty (20) minutes later, the police arrived, had them move their cars, and then talked to Louise Johnson and Noland in the police cruiser. Responding to the officer's question, Louise stated that everyone in her car was okay. The officer then filled out a short form police report. He told Noland the accident was Noland's fault, but he did not issue a ticket to Noland, and he let the parties go. During the entire time, Ms. Morely stayed in the vehicle of Louise Johnson.

UNIVERSAL INSURANCE SOCIETY
Mr. James South
November 7, 1990
Page 3

After the accident, Noland and Sean Clark were contacted by an investigator employed by plaintiff's counsel and each of them did give a recorded statement to the investigator. Neither Noland nor Sean has a copy of his statement.

**MEDICAL EXPENSES AND INJURIES**

The medical expenses incurred by Ms. Morely relating to the accident are primarily for diagnostic purposes and noninvasive treatment. Ms. Morely has not been admitted to the hospital and has not had any surgery as a result of the accident.

**A. Protestant Hospital Emergency Room:**

Ms. Morely first sought medical care on the same day as the accident (January 3, 1990) at the Protestant Hospital Emergency Room. She was at the Emergency Room from 10:24 p.m. to 11:27 p.m. Her chief complaints were of neck pain, right knee pain, and headache. X-rays of the right knee and cervical spine were taken. She was also noted to have multiple contusions. The history she gave as contained in the nurses' notes was of being in a motor vehicle accident at 2:30 p.m. where she was a "restrained" passenger in a vehicle that was hit by another car in the side. She said she had been "thrown around in" the car but did not lose consciousness, and also gave a "Hst cervical spine surg" or history of cervical spine surgery. Her neurological examination was normal and she had "no obvious --------" (I am assuming this means no obvious injury). The x-ray findings were normal except for some "reversal of the usual cervical lordotic curve" the significance of which was listed as "uncertain." The doctor discharged her with prescriptions for Flexeril and Naprosyn (muscle relaxant and antiinflammatory), and told her to apply heat to her neck, rest the weekend, and be rechecked at Protestant or with her family doctor, Ronald Hawk, if needed after three (3) days.

Her primary care has been provided by Family Practitioner Ronald Hawk, M.D. However, she has also been seen since the accident by Anthony Jacoby, M.D., an internist who holds himself out to be a pain specialist, and a neurologist, Steven Saint, M.D.

**B. Ronald Hawk, M.D.:**

**1. Treatment before the accident:**

Ms. Morely has apparently been a patient of Doctor Hawk's for some time. The most complete copy of Hawk's office notes that we have show he has seen her at least since November 23, 1988. Before this accident, on January 23, 1989 she complained of "constant frontal HA (headache) under stress -- husband

UNIVERSAL INSURANCE SOCIETY
Mr. James South
November 7, 1990
Page 4

in hospital, doesn't sleep well. Plan -- Elavil 25 mg - 50 - (?)." On January 19, 1989, she was also prescribed the painkiller Darvocet; and on February 3, 1989 she reported that her "HA's (headaches) not as bad no (?)," but she was still taking the antidepressant Elavil at this time.

**2. Treatment since the accident:**

Hawk's office notes establish he treated Ms. Morely with ultrasound, heat, injections and medication following the accident from January 24, 1990, at least until June 27, 1990. During this time, the patient was seen by Dr. Jacoby on February 9, 1990 (it is unclear whether this was of her own doing or a referral by Dr. Hawk), was scheduled to see Dr. Jacoby again on April 11 to have a thermogram performed on April 27, 1990, and to be seen by Dr. Saint on April 18, 1990. Two (2) MRIs have been performed at Protestant Hospital, one on May 19, 1990, at 2:30 p.m. for her lower back (i.e., L4-5, L5-S1 vertebrae) and one on May 20, 1990 at 1:00 p.m. for her neck (i.e., C4-C7 vertebrae). The office notes of Hawk for May 14, 1990 say that Dr. Jacoby concluded the thermogram was "abnormal" and an MMPI was "abnormal" showing "depression" and "somatic form pain disorder." The MRI results were both negative for ruptured discs according to a May 23, 1990, office note. Her symptoms during the time Hawk has treated her ranged from acute pain to being pain free. She experienced tremendous relief from pain after obtaining and using her TENS unit in May of this year.

A letter from Hawk dated July 20, 1990, says that he started treating Ms. Morely on January 16, 1990. However, the earliest office note we have is January 24, 1990. This letter chronicles the changing nature of the patient's symptoms during the time he has seen her (headache and neck pain; sacroiliac back pain; back pain and headaches; dysesthesia of the right thumb).

**C. Anthony Jacoby, M.D.:**

Doctor Jacoby's February 9, 1990, letter says there was no sign of injury according to the lumbosacral spine and left hip x-rays; but that he believed as a result of the accident she was having back, neck, hip and headache pain that could be treated with medicine, injections, exercise, education, and "psychophysiologic reactivation." A later letter, dated May 2, 1990, refers to thermography having been performed on Ms. Morely which "objectify the patient's subjective complaints." An MRI, EMG and nerve conduction study of the right and possibly left arm were then recommended by Jacoby. Jacoby's last letter was dated August 29, 1990, and based on her history and "psychological testing" he gives her a nineteen percent (19%) whole body partial permanent impairment based on problems "involving neck myofascial pain, headaches associated with trauma, occipital and/or radicular neuralgia as well as significant psychological factors affecting her physical condition."

UNIVERSAL INSURANCE SOCIETY
Mr. James South
November 7, 1990
Page 5

**D. Steven Saint, M.D.:**

Steven Saint's consultation letter reviews the objective testing done on Ms. Morely, which was found to be normal, and then concludes:

> She does have tenderness of the occipital nerve on the right side, causing severe pain over the suboccipital and occipital area on the right side.
>
> Impression: This patient does have an occipital neuralgia as manifested by the tender right occipital nerve. Secondly, she has a sensory loss which does not conform to any dermatome pattern; but it is more in keeping with a psychophysiologic reaction or conversion reaction, which could also account for the heavy feeling in the right arm and difficulty using it also.
>
> My recommendation at this time is strictly conservative treatment. I have no objections to heat or some ultrasound; as far as subjective treatment, I do not feel that she is a candidate for multiple injections at trigger points. She also just picked up a TENS unit and I have no objection if this gives her some relief. I think more important, however, that she remain on some type of a muscle relaxer, perhaps an antidepressant or nerve type pill; and I think that as soon as she gets back to her normal activities the better off she will be. I think this is more of an emotional type problem rather than a true physical injury.

**E. Medical Expenses:**

The documented out-of-pocket medical expenses appear to be, according to plaintiffs' counsel's most recent calculation, $9,245.70, itemized as follows: Anthony Jacoby, M.D. $565.00; Ronald Hawk, M.D. $5,465.00; Ambulance (City of Newburgh) $161.75; Meny's Pharmacy $155.90; Paul's Pharmacy $111.83; Tri-State Radiology $40.00; Newburgh Medical Radiological Services $375.00; Protestant Hospital, Inc. $2,285.07 [$1,826.00 of which was for the two (2) MRIs]; Neurological Consultants (Steven Saint, M.D.) $86.00.

**PROPERTY DAMAGE AND SUBROGATION INTERESTS**

Plaintiffs' insurer, Farm Bureau Insurance, has paid its medical limits of $1,000. The file reflects that a draft in the amount of $1,719.88 was sent

UNIVERSAL INSURANCE SOCIETY
Mr. James South
November 7, 1990
Page 6

to the plaintiffs' attorney on or about November 6, 1990. According to the file, this settlement amount attributed to $1,000 for personal injury and $719.88 for property damage. There also was a letter that accompanied this draft explaining it was for settlement of ''your Property Damage & Bodily Injury claims.'' Please confirm whether this draft was sent and cashed. If it was, then we may be able to argue plaintiffs have released the insured from any further liability.

SETTLEMENT NEGOTIATIONS

Plaintiffs' attorney offered to settle their claims for $75,000 by letter dated September 20, 1990. A counteroffer was made by UNIVERSAL Insurance on October 31, 1990 of $11,750. This offer was rejected by letter dated November 9, 1990.

**PLEADINGS**

A two (2) Count Complaint was filed in the Vanderburgh Circuit Court in Newburgh on October 9, 1990. Count I of the Complaint seeks damages for Jessica Morely for the negligence of Noland Sandefur; while Count II is a claim for loss of services and consortium for the spouse of Jessica Morely, Donald Morely. Plaintiffs requested trial by jury. Served with the Complaint were Interrogatories and a Request for Production of Documents which I have discussed in previous correspondence to you. Our Answer to the Complaint is presently due December 7, 1990.

**LAW OF THE CASE**

**A. Liability:**

As you know, this case will be decided under Indiana's statutory form of modified comparative fault. Under this system, a plaintiff can be prevented from recovering if her fault for the accident was more than 50%. If plaintiff's fault is less than 50%, she may still recover, but her recovery will be reduced by an amount equal to her fault for the accident.

The liability issues in this case are: whether Mr. Sandefur acted as a reasonable man under all the circumstances; whether Jessica Morely was negligent; and whether Louise Johnson was negligent, and if so, may this negligence be imputed to Jessica Morely? There are sufficient facts for the plaintiffs to argue Mr. Sandefur was negligent even though we have an argument that he acted reasonably.

**1. Negligence of Jessica Morely:**

It will be very difficult to prove that Jessica Morely was negligent:

> . . . a passenger is required to exercise reasonable care for his own safety and will be barred from recovery if he voluntarily rides with

UNIVERSAL INSURANCE SOCIETY
Mr. James South
November 7, 1990
Page 7

> a driver he knows to be intoxicated, reckless, or incompetent, or unreasonably fails to warn the driver of danger which he discovers, or, in the exercise of reasonable care, should discover. A passenger is required to use that degree of care for his own safety that an ordinary prudent person in like circumstances would use. An occupant may have a duty to warn the driver of a danger of which the occupant is aware. However, an occupant may ordinarily rely on the assumption that the driver will exercise ordinary care and caution and need not generally keep a lookout for approaching danger.

Goodhart v. Board of Commissioners of County of Parke, Ind. App., 533 N.E.2d 605, 610, (1989), transfer denied.

**2. Ability to impute any negligence of Louise Johnson to Jessica Morely:**

It will likewise be difficult to argue that any negligence of Louise Johnson should be imputed to Jessica Morely under Indiana law. As the **Goodhart** case cited above explains,

> It was settled law in Indiana at the time of this accident (i.e., 1989) that the negligence of a driver will not be imputed to the passenger absent facts which would make the passenger vicariously liable as a defendant, such as ability to control or joint enterprise.

**Id**. In other words, for us to impute the fault of the driver to the passenger, we will have to discover some facts to establish they were on a trip where they each had an equal opportunity to decide or control where they were going, when they would leave, what route they would take, etc.

**B. Damages:**

**1. Lost wages:**

Our best arguments will be with respect to the issue of damages. From the Complaint it appears Ms. Morely was not employed at the time of the accident. Therefore she should have no lost wage claim.

**2. Impairment of earning capacity:**

She will still have, however, a claim for impairment of earning capacity. Impairment of earning capacity is distinguished from the concept of lost earnings, since the term ''impairment of earning capacity'' means the impairment of the ability to engage in a vocation rather than past and future earnings lost as a result of the injury. **Dunn v. Cadiente**, Ind. App., 503 N.E. 2d 915, 918-919 (1987). The measure of damages for the impairment of

UNIVERSAL INSURANCE SOCIETY
Mr. James South
November 7, 1990
Page 8

earning capacity is the difference between the amount which the injured person is capable of earning before the injury, and the amount which he is capable of earning thereafter. **Id.** In short, the Indiana substantive law recognizes that an injured claimant may not only have been deprived of lost past and future earnings, but of the ''enjoyment of employment and earning capacity he once held.'' **Id.**

However, this does not mean that a jury may consider the injury's effect upon loss of enjoyment of life as an independent basis of recovery. **Id.** In fact, it is error to include in a jury instruction that the jury may consider the effect of the plaintiff's injuries upon the quality and enjoyment of plaintiff's life as a separate element of damages when the jury is also instructed they may award damages for pain and suffering or for permanent injury as this constitutes an ''impermissible duplication of damages'' and therefore makes for an erroneous instruction. **Canfield v. Sandock**, Ind. App., 546 N.E.2d 337, 338-340 (1989), **Seifert v. Bland**, Ind. App., 546 N.E.2d 342 (1989), **Marks v. Gaskill**, Ind. App., 546 N.E.2d 1245 (1989).

I am hopeful, given Ms. Morely's age of 64, that we will be able to argue that these damages are *de minimis*.

**3. Pre-existing injury:**

From what little records we have, it also appears that we may be able to argue that we only aggravated a pre-existing injury. The office notes of Hawk show she had problem headaches before the accident, and the nurse's notes from Protestant also say she had had previous neck surgery. The law in Indiana concerning liability for pre-existing injuries or conditions is as stated in **Skaggs v. Davis**, Ind. App., 424 N.E.2d 137, 140-141 (1981), and **Louisville, N.A.&C. Ry. v. Jones**, 108 Ind. 551, 9 N.E. 476 (1886) (cited in **Skaggs** at 424 N.E.2d 140-141). This law is as follows:

> If you find that Plaintiff had a pre-existing condition or disease . . . and that the accident in question did in fact aggravate such pre-existing condition, you should assess only those damages directly and proximately resulting from such aggravation and not from the disease or pre-existing condition itself.
>
> If, however, you find that the Plaintiff had a pre-existing condition or disease . . . and that the accident in question did not aggravate such pre-existing condition, then you should find for the Defendant and against the Plaintiff on that issue. **Id.**

**4. Continuing damages, pain and suffering:**

However, our best argument for limited damages has been supplied by Steven Saint's report letter wherein he states,

UNIVERSAL INSURANCE SOCIETY
Mr. James South
November 7. 1990
Page 9

Impression: . . . Secondly, she has a sensory loss which does not conform to any dermatome pattern; but it is more in keeping with a psychophysiologic reaction or conversion reaction, which could also account for the heavy feeling in the right arm and difficulty using it also.

> . . ., I think more importantly, however, that she remain on some type of a muscle relaxers, perhaps an antidepressant or nerve type pill; and I think that as soon as she gets back to her normal activities the better off she will be. I think this is more of an emotional type problem than a true physical injury. (emphasis added)

This information gives us the opportunity to argue that the principal cause for her continuing complaints is her over-reaction to the limited physical injuries she suffered in the accident.

Finally, she has not undergone any surgery, has not been told she needs future surgery, and has not been admitted to the hospital.

**5. Right to Request a Change of Judge or Venue:**

Under Indiana law we have the right to take an automatic change of venue of the case or a change of judge. My experience with the judge handling the case is limited as he has been on the bench a little over a year. However, as this matter will be tried to a jury, my experience with Vanderburgh County juries is that they are conservative. Given these reasons, I do not recommend taking either a change of judge or venue and will assume this recommendation meets with your approval unless instructed otherwise.

**SETTLEMENT EVALUATION**

Given the information currently in our possession, and based upon the relatively conservative jurors in Vanderburgh county, the settlement value on this case would be between $15,350 and $19,500; while the possible jury verdict ranges would be $23,250 to $32,500. These opinions may vary as the case progresses.

**COMMENTS AND SUGGESTIONS**

A Request for Production of Documents needs to be served upon the plaintiffs' attorney so we can obtain a copy of our client's transcribed statement. We also need to contact Mr. Sean Clark to see if he will agree to obtain a copy of his statement as well and then furnish us with a copy.

Interrogatories need to be served upon plaintiff, Jessica Morely, in an effort to find out the names of her health care providers for the last several

UNIVERSAL INSURANCE SOCIETY
Mr. James South
November 7, 1990
Page 10

years. Given what we have already discovered, I am hopeful we will discover additional beneficial information.

We need to seek to obtain a medical authorization from the plaintiff, Jessica Morely, so we can obtain a complete copy of her medical records from Doctor Hawk (i.e., missing office notes for January 16 to January 24, 1990, and office notes previous to 1988, if any); and from Doctor Jacoby (i.e., all his office records, and especially the test results from the MMPI).

A deposition of Jessica Morely should also be scheduled to determine if she did have a child on her lap when the accident occurred and if the child was injured. If the child was not injured, this would imply that Ms. Morely was not injured; or if Ms. Morely says she was injured because she was trying to hold onto the child, then we would have an argument that Ms. Morely did engage in contributory fault; or if the child was injured, then we may have an argument that the child suffered most of the impact and injuries.

Also, as noted above, we need to confirm whether the settlement draft sent for payment of all claims of bodily injury and property damage was cashed.

I will assume the above recommendations meet with your approval and will proceed accordingly. I would also appreciate the benefit of your thoughts as to my analysis of this case and as to its further handling.

Very truly yours

SMITH, TOLENTINO & SHORT

By: Marcia E. Short

MES/rer

GARP LAW OFFICES
STEVEN P. GARP — DRUCILLA W. GARP
16 Lakeside Park
Piedmont, IN 47709-1234

February 21, 1991

Mr. John Doe
17 XYZ Street
Evansville, IN 47708-1234

Re: Tomorrow Corporation, Account No. 62-156-7, $376.25

Dear Mr. Doe

This office has been retained to liquidate the above claim. Your creditor requests that you direct full payment to this office without delay.

You must make payment or contact us either by telephone or by mail within seven days. This will avoid increasing your indebtedness by the addition of the costs involved in litigation.

If we do not hear from you within seven days, we will assume that you do not wish to resolve this matter amicably and will proceed accordingly.

Very truly yours

GARP LAW OFFICES

Steven P. Garp

SG/jw

LAW OFFICE OF RALPH L. DOWNER
111 N.W. Hudson Street
Evansville, Indiana 47708-1234
Telephone 812/422-0000

January 4, 1991

Mr. and Mrs. John C. Chang
123 4th Street
Evansville, IN 47708-2345

Description: The following described real estate located in Vanderburgh County, Indiana:

Lot One (1) in Block Two (2) in Walkway Subdivision, an Addition to the City of Evansville, as per plat thereof, recorded in Plat Book D, page 111, in the office of the Recorder of Vanderburgh County, Indiana.

Tax Code: 11-111-11-111 City Center Township

Fee Title: Joseph P. Quarrels andd Ida Quarrels, husband and wife, as tenants by the entirety

Abstract: No. 91,111 under cover of Indiana Abstract and Title Company Inc. finally dated and certifying to December 31, 1990 at 8:00 A.M.

Dear Mr. and Mrs. Chang

I have examined the abstract of title to the above described real estate and based on the abstract, I find that title is as above stated, subject to the attached Schedules I and II and Exhibit A.

This opinion is for your use and benefit exclusively.

Yours very truly

Ralph L. Downer

Abstract No. 91,111
Page 2

**SCHEDULE I**

**LIENS, ENCUMBRANCES AND CERTAIN OTHER MATTERS AFFECTING TITLE**

1. Entry 20, page 40, shows that the real estate taxes for the year 1989, payable in 1990, are unpaid, as follows:

May Installment $278.50
Delinquent, Subject to Penalty
November Installment $278.50
Delinquent, Subject to Penalty

Real estate taxes for the year 1990, payable in 1991, are now a lien. Real estate taxes for the year 1991, payable in 1992, will become a lien on March 1, 1991.

2. Entry 5, page 25, shows a mortgage executed to Indiana State Bank dated March 15, 1980 and recorded in Mortgage Drawer 2, card 55555, securing an original indebtedness of $45,000.00 You must have this mortgage released of record.

3. Entry 2, page 3, shows the plat of Walkway Subdivision with building and use restrictions. In addition, the plat shows a building setback line along Main Street.

4. There are easements affecting the captioned lot as follows:

a. The plat shows an easement for public utilities along the rear of the captioned lot.

b. Entry 10, page 30, shows an easement in favor of Southern Indiana Gas and Electric Company recorded in Deed Drawer 1, card 11111, to construct, inspect, maintain, operate, enlarge, rebuild, and repair a pole and wire line. It is impossible to determine from the language of this easement whether this easement actually affects the captioned lot. Southern Indiana Gas and Electric Company has complete maps showing the location of all their easements. By contacting Southern Indiana Gas and Electric Company, you will be able to determine whether this easement directly affects the captioned lot.

5. Entry 15, page 35, shows a coal lease titled "underground coal lease" recorded in Lease Drawer 1, card 321. Although it is titled as an underground coal lease, a review of the lease discloses that in certain circumstances the lessee has the right to use the surface of the captioned lot, including to discharge water and to core drill. You may wish to consider requesting that the lessee release the lessee's surface rights under this lease. Otherwise, you must recognize that these are continuing rights that may affect your use and enjoyment of the surface.

Abstract No. 91,111
Page 3

6. Entry 18, page 44, shows an oil and gas lease dated October 15, 1961 and recorded in Lease Drawer 1, card 543. In the event there is still production under this lease, title to the captioned lot is made subject to the rights under this lease. You should reach an understanding with the present owners as to whether they intend to sell to you any of the current royalty interests they may be receiving under this lease. However, in the event this lease is no longer in effect, under the current status of law, you should either obtain a release of this lease or an affidavit confirming that this lease has expired by its terms. Pursuant to such an affidavit, a request to the Recorder of Vanderburgh County, Indiana, to release this lease should be made.

Abstract No. 91,111
Page 4

**SCHEDULE II**

**OBJECTIONS AND OTHER QUESTIONS CONCERNING TITLE**

1. There are various defects in the early chain of title to the captioned lot, all of which because of passage of time can be safely waived.

Requirement: None.

2. The captioned lot was formerly owned by Sam L. Jones. The abstracter discloses a judgment against a Sam Jones, which is unreleased of record. There is nothing to confirm whether the former owner, Sam L. Jones, is the same person as the judgment defendant, Sam Jones.

Requirement: Either information must be placed of record to establish that the former owner of the captioned lot, Sam L. Jones, is not the same person as Sam Jones against whom there is an unreleased judgment or said judgment must be released of record.

3. One of the present owners, Ida Quarrels, has filed an action against Joseph P. Quarrels to dissolve their marriage as Cause No. 82D04-9009-DR-1234 of the Vanderburgh Superior Court. As of the final continuation date of the abstract, no court order prohibiting the sale of the captioned lot has been entered nor has a decree relative to said action been entered.

Requirement: Before completing the purchase of the captioned lot, you must again review the current proceedings in this dissolution of marriage action to determine that no orders of any kind have been entered that would in any way limit or prohibit the sale of the captioned lot by the present owners.

**EXHIBIT A**

**GENERAL EXCEPTIONS AND COMMENTS**

This title opinion is based on the examination of an abstract. As a consequence, the information and conclusions set forth herein are based solely on the matters certified to by the abstracter, which matters primarily include records in the offices of the County Recorder, Auditor, Assessor, Treasurer and Clerk. Some abstracters also certify bankruptcy court records. There are other matters that may affect, either directly or indirectly, the captioned real estate, but no coverage or protection is furnished for such either by this title opinion or said abstract. As a consequence, you may wish to obtain additional information, instruments, or other protection. These matters include, but are not limited to, the following:

1. Survey: This title opinion is subject to such information that would be disclosed by a current and complete survey. Although the information included in a survey varies, information that should be set forth in such a survey includes, but is not limited to: (a) the existence and location of improvements, visible easements, rights-of-way, drains, and ditches; (b) evidence of encroachments, overlaps, and shortages in area; and (c) whether the captioned real estate abuts and lies adjacent to a street, roadway, or other easement providing access.

2. Parties in Possession. In the event there are occupants or users of the captioned real estate other than the record owners, then you must determine to what extent they may have any interest in and to the captioned real estate.

3. Mechanic's Lien. In the event any material, machinery, work, or labor has been furnished within the last 60 days for the captioned real estate, then the title is subject to the possibility of a mechanic's lien being filed and becoming a lien on the captioned real estate. This lien must be filed within 60 days from the time the material, machinery, work, or labor was last furnished. No lien for such material, machinery, work, or labor shall attach to real estate purchased by an innocent purchaser for value without notice, provided said purchase is of a single or double family dwelling for occupancy by the purchaser, unless notice of intention to hold such lien shall be recorded as provided under the Indiana Mechanic's Lien Law prior to the recording of the deed by which such purchaser takes title. However, this applies only to new construction.

4. Real Estate Taxes. The current status of real estate taxes for the captioned real estate is set forth under Schedule I. However, pursuant to I.C. 6-1.1-9, if the captioned real estate has been undervalued in the assessment or omitted from an assessment, there is the possibility of an increase in assessed value or an assessment of the captioned real estate.

5. Restrictions and Covenants. Recorded restrictions or covenants affecting the captioned real estate that have been included in the abstract

Exhibit A (cont'd)

are referred to under Schedule I. However, I do not certify whether the captioned real estate and the use thereof are in conformity with any such restrictions and covenants.

6. Zoning and Thoroughfare Ordinances. The abstract does not certify as to the present zoning of the captioned real estate nor to what extent any thoroughfare ordinances may affect the captioned real estate. You should determine through the Area Plan Commission whether the intended use of the captioned real estate is in compliance with said zoning and thoroughfare ordinances.

7. Availability of Utilities. An independent investigation is necessary to determine the availability of water, electricity, gas, sewer, and other utility services to the captioned real estate.

8. Sewer. The abstract may disclose that there are agreements for the construction of sanitary sewers that directly or indirectly affect the captioned real estate and a general reference to such agreements may be included under Schedule I. However, the abstract does not certify as to: (a) the availability of a sewer line to the captioned real estate; (b) if any tap-in and connection charge for the use of any sanitary sewer line has been paid; or (c) if such sanitary sewer line has been accepted for maintenance by appropriate governmental authorities. This information may be obtained from appropriate governmental authorities unless the sewer line is a part of a private sewer system, in which event the owner of the captioned real estate must be contacted. The abstract does not certify as to whether any improvements located on the captioned real estate are actually connected to and using any such sanitary sewer line. A plumber would be able to advise you of this. If a sanitary sewer line is available to the captioned real estate and a tap-in and connection charge has not been paid or if said charge has been paid and the line is not being used by the improvements upon the captioned real estate, there is a possibility that appropriate governmental authorities in enforcing applicable laws and regulations may eventually force the use of said sewer facilities and require the payment of any unpaid tap-in and connection charges.

9. Streets. The abstract does not disclose whether or not any streets adjacent to or which serve the captioned real estate have been accepted for maintenance by appropriate governmental authorities. Until the owners of the real estate adjacent to any such streets improve such to minimum standards, then the applicable governmental authorities will not accept such streets for maintenance. If access is from private streets that have not been dedicated to the public, then appropriate governmental authorities will not assume the maintenance of such streets.

10. Minerals. Irrespective of any information that may be referred to under Schedule I concerning minerals, this title opinion does not certify and assumes no responsibility whatsoever as to the ownership and title to minerals, including but not being limited to coal, oil, gas, and all other

Exhibit A (cont'd)

minerals of every kind and nature. Without limiting the generality of the foregoing, this title opinion does not cover and assumes no responsibility for: (a) the validity or existence of any oil or gas leases; (b) the validity or existence of any coal or mining leases; (c) any rights that may exist under any instruments affecting mineral rights, including for the development of the captioned real estate and the use of the surface in such development.

11. Uniform Commercial Code. Except to the extent pointed out under Schedule I, according to the abstracter, there are no financing statements filed in the Fixture Index covering any fixtures on the captioned real estate. However, the abstracter's certificate is limited by the possibility that there may not have been an adequate legal description filed in the Fixture Index and as a consequence, the abstracter may not have been able to determine the existence of a fixture filing for the captioned real estate. In addition, the search of the abstracter does not cover or include crops or other farm products.

12. Laws, Ordinances and Governmental Regulations. This title opinion affords no protection for whatever effect laws, ordinances, and governmental regulations may have upon the captioned real estate, including but not being limited to the following:

a. City or County: Building codes, subdivision control, flood and surface water drainage, health, sanitation, land planning, and development.

b. State: Usury, building codes, subdivision requirements, consumer protection, land planning, and development.

c. Federal: RESPA, truth-in-lending, consumer protection, interstate land sales, environmental protection, land planning, and development.

13. Period of Coverage. The coverage of the abstracter extends to a specific date. There will be elapsed time between the date of the abstract and the completion of your intended transaction. Title is obviously subject to such matters that occur subsequent to the date of the abstract and the completion of your intended transaction. Title is obviously subject to such matters that occur subsequent to the date of the abstract and prior to the proper recording of instruments relative to your transaction.

14. Title Insurance. This title opinion is merely an opinion and in no way represents a guarantee of title. It is not comparable to a title insurance policy and does not give the protection afforded by such a policy. For example, this title opinion affords no protection against any defects that may exist but that cannot be ascertained by the examination of an abstract, including such things as forgeries, alterations of instruments, incompetency of parties, improper execution of instruments, the failure to deliver

Exhibit A (cont'd)

instruments, fraud, duress, coercion, errors in public records in governmental offices, or inaccurate or misleading information from affidavits, deeds, and other instruments of record. A title insurance policy, however, would give protection against loss or damage by reason of such in addition to certain other protections and coverage.

The foregoing General Exceptions and Comments are not all-inclusive and other matters may also affect, either directly or indirectly, the captioned real estate.

MINUTES OF THE FIRST ANNUAL
MEETING OF THE SHAREHOLDERS OF
XYZ CORPORATION

The first annual meeting of the Shareholders of ______________________________ was held at _______________ Evansville, Indiana, on _____ 199_, at _____ P.M.

The meeting was called to order by _________________________ President of the Corporation, who presided and who also acted as Secretary of the meeting and recording the minutes thereof.

The Secretary submitted to the meeting the following:

a) A Waiver of Notice of this meeting, waiving the time, place, and purpose thereof signed by ____________________________________________

b) A complete list of the holders of the common shares of the Corporation as of the close of business _____________ 199_, the record date fixed by the Board of Directors for the Shareholders entitled to notice of and to vote at this meeting.

The Chairman directed that a copy of the waiver be annexed to the minutes of the meeting. Inasmuch as the list of holders of the common shares of the Corporation contains only the name of ________________ it is not appended to these minutes.

The inspector of elections examined the list of shareholders and made a poll of the shares represented at the meeting in person or by proxy. It was reported that 1,000 shares were entitled to vote at the meeting and that all shares were present in person. The Chairman announced that a quorum was present for all purposes, and that the meeting was lawfully and properly convened and competent to proceed to the transaction of the business for which it had been called.

A motion was duly made, seconded and carried waiving the reading of the annual report.

The Chairman called for nominations for directors to serve for one (1) year or until his successor or successors are elected and qualified. On behalf of management, ___________________________ was nominated to serve as the sole director of the Corporation.

The Chairman called for further nominations, but none were made. The inspector of elections was instructed to take a ballot and acted as teller.

After all ballots had an opportunity to vote, the Chairman declared the polls closed. Upon inspecting the report of the inspector of elections, the Chairman reported that the holder of 1,000 shares of the Corporation have voted in favor of ________ as the sole director of the Corporation, inasmuch as no other votes were cast in opposition. The Chairman declared that ______ ___________ had been elected to serve as the sole Director of the Corporation for one (1) year and until his successor was elected and qualified.

The Secretary then made the following motion:

''RESOLVED that the firm of ______________________________
continue to serve as auditors of the Corporation in 1983.''

On motion duly made and seconded, and since there was no objection, a voice vote was taken and the Chairman declared the motion was unanimously accepted.

The Secretary and Treasurer then presented for review the Interim Financial Report as well as the Minute Book of the Corporation. On motion duly made and seconded, a voice vote was taken and it was unanimously:

RESOLVED that all proceedings of the Board of Directors as set forth in the Minute Book of the Corporation and all actions pursuant thereto taken by the members of the Corporation or by officers of the Corporation are hereby ratified and approved in all respects.

Upon motions duly made and seconded and upon vote duly taken, the following resolutions were passed:

RESOLVED that the Resolution of the Board of Directors assuming the duties and responsibilities of the Employment Agreements with _________________ and _________________ are hereby ratified and approved.

RESOLVED that the Resolution of the Board of Directors regarding the salary of _________________ adopted at the meeting of _________________, 199_, be ratified and approved.

RESOLVED that the offices of this Corporation be changed from _____________ , Suite ______, Evansville, Indiana, to _________________, Evansville, Indiana.

RESOLVED that the Corporation be authorized to designate the initial 1,000 shares of the Corporation issued by the Corporation as 1244 stock.

There being no further business before the meeting, the meeting was adjourned.

______________________________, 199_____
Dated

APPROVED:

______________________________
Secretary

# GLOSSARY

**Achieving document** Document that records a transaction and provides a framework for a future relationship; e.g., a lease, option, or contract.

***Ad hominem* attack** Personal attack in which a writer denigrates the opposing party without focusing on real issues.

**Affiant** A person making an affidavit.

**Affidavit** A written statement of fact made under oath.

**Annotated code** Private publication of statutes that follows the official code format; provides additional information and summarizes key interpretations of each statute. Considered the most useful source for statutory research.

**Answer** The formal written response of a defendant, admitting, denying, or stating defenses to the matters raised in a complaint.

**Appellant** The party that files an appeal seeking to overturn the judgment of a lower court.

**Appellee** The party that defends an appeal and asserts that the judgment of the lower court should be affirmed.

**Articles of incorporation** A document prepared at the time a corporation is formed to serve as a record that the corporation is properly incorporated.

**Barrister** In the British legal system, a lawyer who presents oral arguments to the court.

**Bilateral agreement** An agreement containing reciprocal or mutual obligations.

**Binding precedent** A case decided by a higher court in the same jurisdiction on the same issue.

**Blue Book** Popular sobriquet for *A Uniform System of Citation*, now in its fifteenth edition (Cambridge, MA: The Harvard Law Review Association, 1991).

**Brief** A written argument of factual and legal reasons why a party's position should prevail.

**Certificate of service** A signed statement at the end of a pleading indicating that you have mailed or otherwise served all other parties with the pleading at the time it is filed.

**Classification** In a document, the arrangement of information under the appropriate grouping or subgrouping.

**Code pleading** A system predating the Federal Rules of Civil Procedure whereby claims had to be asserted by making the allegations fit within prescribed categories.

**Common law** Law established by previous court decisions.

**Complaint** A legal document filed in a civil proceeding stating the basis of a lawsuit and identifying the relief sought.

**Concurring opinion** A decision by a judge or justice who agrees with the majority result but disagrees with the logic used to reach that result.

**Consideration** An act, forbearance, or promise that has an economic value and is used to create an enforceable contract.

**Contract of adhesion** Standardized contract drafted by a party of superior bargaining strength and presented on a take-it-or-leave-it basis.

***Contra proferentem* rule** A court rule providing that ambiguity in a document be construed against the document's author.

**Corporate bylaws** Rules that establish a corporate board of directors, identify officers and their duties, and set forth requirements regarding voting or shareholder issues.

**Counterclaim** A pleading in which the defendant in a lawsuit asserts a claim against the plaintiff.

**Court order** See *Decree*.

**Cross-claim** A pleading in which one party states a claim against another party—e.g., defendant against codefendant.

**Decree** Formal statement of a court's ruling on a motion or on the merits of a case; also known as a *court order.*

**Deductive logic** A form of reasoning wherein specific conclusions are inferred from accepted general principles.

**Defendant** The party against whom a complaint is filed in a civil action or against whom charges are brought in a criminal action.

**Demand** The part (usually at the end) of a pleading that asks the court for a specific relief.

**Discovery process** Procedure through which both sides in a legal action obtain information about each other's case.

**Design** The format according to which ideas are organized within a document.

**Dissenting opinion** The opinion of a judge or justice who disagrees with the majority opinion.

**Diversity cases** Lawsuits filed in a federal district court involving parties who live in different states.

**Division** The main headings of an outline for a document.

***Ejusdem generis*** A rule stating that specific words limit the meaning of general words.

**Elegant variation** The use of more than one word (synonyms) to indicate a single meaning within a document; courts assume different words intend different meanings.

**Emotive language** Language meant to provide an emotional response; e.g., a sales pitch or an attorney's summation to a jury.

**Encircling the concept** Using a string of words to capture the concept of a provision.

***Expressio unius est exclusio alterius*** A rule providing that if a writing specifies an exception or condition, then other exceptions or conditions not mentioned were intentionally excluded.

**Fact synthesizing** Assessing whether the facts of a case are similar to or different from cases already decided.

**Federal administrative agency** An entity established by law to administer a congressional grant of power.

**Federal regulations** Rules passed by federal administrative agencies to define and clarify the scope of their discretion.

**Form book** See *Procedural form book, Substantive form book.*

**Freedom of contract** The wide latitude permitted by law to parties structuring transactions and relationships.

**Fulfilling document** Document that records an event; e.g., a deed.

**Guest acts** Laws passed in the early 1900s preventing guests (passengers) in an automobile from suing the driver for negligence.

**Headnotes** Case summaries that appear before decisions in unofficial reporters.

**Holding** The decision of a court.

**Inductive logic** A form of reasoning wherein general conclusions are drawn from particular situations.

**Interrogatories** Written questions exchanged by adversaries during the discovery process.

**IRAC** Acronym to guide the structure of a memorandum's discussion section: Issue, Rule of law, Application of rule to facts, and Conclusion.

**Lease** A bilateral agreement that sets forth terms for the rental of real estate.

**Legal drafting** The preparation of transaction documents.

**Local rules** Individual court rules that supplement federal or state rules; e.g., a district court may have rules that supplement the Federal Rules of Civil Procedure.

**Loose sentence** Sentence that contains its main idea at the beginning.

**Macro editing** Checking the broad content of a drafted document for order, sense, and coherence; e.g., examining the flow of an argument or considering whether a transaction will work.

**Material facts** Facts that have an impact on the outcome of a case.

**Memorandum** An intraoffice or attorney-client document describing the law as it relates to a particular situation; also called a *statement of points and authorities.* (Note: Some lawyers may refer to a brief as a memorandum, but in this text the two are treated as discrete entities.)

**Micro editing** Checking the details of a drafted document: spelling, grammar, punctuation, consistency, citations, word usage, capitalization, and tabulation.

**Motion** A formal request to the court to take some sort of action.

**Motion in limine** A motion made before trial to prevent a party from introducing prejudicial evidence at trial.

**Nominalization** A verb or an adjective changed into a noun.

**Nonemotive language** Language that lacks emotional content.

***Noscitur a sociis*** A rule suggesting that the meaning of a word or phrase be interpreted by surrounding words; "general and specific words are associated with and take color from each other" (*Black's Law Dictionary*).

**Notice pleading** Pleading under the modern rules, which provide that the primary purpose of a pleading is not to frame issues but to notify another party of a claim.

***Obiter dictum*** A judge's extraneous comment in a case; something said "by the way" and not binding on other courts.

**Official reporter** Set of books designated by a court as the place where slip opinions of its cases must be published.

**Overreaching conduct** Outwitting a party through trickery or deceit.

**Parallel citation** A citation to both an official and an unofficial reporter.

**Parol evidence rules** Rules that provide that no party can by means of oral testimony contradict or vary the terms of a written document.

**Periodic sentence** Sentence that contains its main idea at the end.

**Persuasive precedent** Case decided on the same issue by a court in another jurisdiction or by a lower court in the same jurisdiction.

**Plain English movement** A movement away from so-called legalese; e.g., Plain English activists promoted the passage of laws calling for consumer documents to be written in understandable language.

**Plaintiff** The party who files a complaint in a lawsuit.

**Pleadings** The formal documents through which parties in a legal action allege claims against one another or assert their defenses.

**Pocket part** Supplement published periodically to update a law book; so named because it is designed to fit into a pocket at the back of a book.

**Pragmatics** The effect of words on those who hear or see them.

**Prayer** The part of a motion that asks the court for a specific order: e.g., dismissal of the case or production of a document.

**Preamble** Introductory part of a legal document, which identifies the parties and the type of document.

**Primary authority** Rules of law contained in constitutions, cases, statutes, court rules, regulations, and ordinances.

**Procedural form book** Book that provides forms for court-related documents: e.g., complaints, answers, motions, interrogatories, and jury instructions.

**Procedural posture** Section of a case brief that tells at what stage of a case the dispute was decided.

**Prolixity** The state of being unnecessarily wordy, often the result of strung out prepositional phrases.

***Ratio decidendi*** A holding or principle of law decided by a court.

**Recitals** Statements that follow the preamble in a transaction document, outlining the purpose of the agreement and providing a brief background for the reader.

**Regulating document** Document that provides for a means to resolve future problems: e.g., a collective bargaining agreement or corporate bylaws.

**Relevant facts** Facts that relate to the issue to be decided in a case.

**Remand** Send (a case) back to the trial court for a new trial.

**Reporter** See *Official reporter, Unofficial reporter.*

**Request for admission** A method of discovery in which one party submits a written request that another party admit to the truth of facts, the genuineness of documents, or the application of law to fact.

**Request for examination** A written request that the opposing party in a legal action be examined by an impartial physician; part of the discovery process.

**Request for production of documents** A written request to examine documents held by the opposing party in a legal action, part of the discovery process.

***Restatements of the Law*** Set of books written by a panel of experts—lawyers, judges, and professors—who have developed principles of how the law should be decided.

**Rhetorical paragraphs** Within a pleading, numbered paragraphs reciting the supporting facts and the basis for the pleading.

**Secondary authority** Something written about the law (e.g., an encyclopedia, an article, or a book).

**Semantics** The meaning of words.

**Semiotics** The study of the rules of our speech community.

**Sequencing** The order of the outline for a document; which items precede other items.

**Shepardize** To research a case, statute, constitutional provision, or administrative regulation in the appropriate volume of *Shepard's*; the coined verb "shepardize" commonly begins with a lowercase *s*.

***Shepard's*** One of a series of books published by Shepard's Citations, a division of McGraw-Hill, exclusively to update case law and other legal authority.

**Signals** Abbreviated ways of telling the reader how legal authority supports an argument.

**Slip opinion** The typewritten decision in a case, sent by the court to the parties and to the official and unofficial reporters.

**Solicitor** In the British legal system, a lawyer who advises clients and prepares written memoranda to assist barristers with their arguments.

**Squinting modifier** A modifier placed ambiguously between two possible referents.

***Stare decisis*** Doctrine that says legal precedents must be followed.

**Statement of points and authorities** See *Memorandum.*

**Statutes of frauds** Laws that govern transactions; among their provisions is the requirement that certain transactions be documented in writing. Statutes of frauds vary from state to state.

***Statutes at Large*** The official federal sessions record, which presents laws in chronological order as they are passed by Congress.

**Style** The individualized way someone writes.

**Subpoena** A written order by a court advising a witness to appear at a particular place at a designated time.

**Subpoena *duces tecum*** A subpoena directing a witness to bring certain documents or items to a particular place at a designated time.

**Substantive form book** Book that provides forms for transaction-related documents: e.g., wills, trusts, leases, and contracts.

**Summary judgment** A motion requesting the court to rule in a party's favor on the basis that there are no genuine issues of material fact and the moving party is entitled to judgment as a matter of law.

**Summons** The document advising a defendant that some action must be taken within a specified period.

**Syntactics** The relationship of words to one another.

**Table of authority** An alphabetical list of every case cited in a brief.

**TAPP rule** Acronym for Things, Actions, Persons, and Places, a recommended method for penetrating a legal index; enables researcher to categorize facts into ways a publisher may have indexed a legal problem.

**Transaction documents** Documents that memorialize events: e.g., deeds, wills, trusts, contracts, bills of sale, and corporate minutes.

**Treatise** Book written by an expert on a particular area of law; treatises contain the classic explanations of certain areas of law.

**Ultraquistic subterfuge** The use of a word with multiple meanings to express different ideas within a single document.

**Unconscionability doctrine** Doctrine prohibiting provisions so one-sided as to be oppressive and unfair.

***United States Code* (U.S.C.)** A congressional compilation of *The Statutes at Large* that groups laws according to subject matter.

**Unofficial reporter** A private publication containing court decisions (slip opinions) and case summaries.

# INDEX

## d



## e



## f